THE GERMAN
OFFENSIVES
OF 1918

Battles & Campaigns

A series of illustrated battlefield accounts covering the classical period through to the end of the twentieth century, drawing on the latest research and integrating the experience of combat with intelligence, logistics and strategy.

Series Editor

Hew Strachan, Chichele Professor of the History of War
at the University of Oxford

Published

Ross Anderson, *The Battle of Tanga 1914*
'An excellent book' *Peter Hart*, author of *Jutland 1916*

Ross Anderson, *The Forgotten Front: The East African Campaign 1914-1918*
'Excellent... fills a yawning gap in the historical record' *Gary Sheffield, Times Literary Supplement*

William Buckingham, *Arnhem 1944*
'Startling... reveals the real reason why the daring attack failed' *The Daily Express*

Brian Farrell, *The Defence and Fall of Singapore 1940-1942*
'An original and provocative new history of the battle that marked the end of the British
Empire' *Professor Hew Strachan*

David M. Glantz, *Before Stalingrad*
'Another fine addition to Hew Strachan's excellent Battles and Campaigns series'
BBC History Magazine

Michael K. Jones, *Bosworth 1485*
'Insightful and rich study of the battle... no longer need Richard play the villain'
Times Literary Supplement

Martin Kitchen, *The German Offensives of 1918*
'Comprehensive and authoritative... first class' *Professor Holger H. Herwig, War in History*

M.K. Lawson, *The Battle of Hastings 1066*
A *BBC History Magazine* Book of the Year 2003

Marc Milner, *Battle of the Atlantic*
'The most comprehensive short survey of the U-boat battles' *Sir John Keegan*

A.J. Smithers, *The Tangier Campaign*
'The fullest account of the British Army's first major expedition abroad'
Professor Hew Strachan

Tim Travers, *Gallipoli 1915*
'A book of the highest importance... masterly' *John Lee, The Journal of Military History*

Matthew C. Ward, *The Battle for Quebec 1759: Britain's Conquest of Canada*

Commissioned

Stephen Conway, *The Battle of Bunker Hill 1775*
Martin Kitchen, *El Alamein 1942–1943*
John Andreas Olsen, *Operation Desert Storm*
Michael Penman, *Bannockburn 1314*

THE GERMAN OFFENSIVES 1 OF 1918

MARTIN KITCHEN

TEMPUS

This edition first published 2005

Tempus Publishing Limited
The Mill, Brimscombe Port,
Stroud, Gloucestershire, GL5 2QG
www.tempus-publishing.com

British Library Cataloguing in Publication Data.
A catalogue record for this book is available from the British Library.

ISBN 0 7524 3527 2

Typesetting and origination by Tempus Publishing Limited
Printed and bound in Great Britain

Contents

About the Author

Martin Kitchen is one of the world's leading experts on twentieth-century German history. He was Professor of History at the Simon Fraser University in Canada until his recent retirement. He is the author of *The Cambridge Illustrated History of Germany*, *A Military History of Germany*, *Nazi Germany at War*, and *Nazi Germany: A Critical Introduction*, also published by Tempus.

Praise for Martin Kitchen:

The German Officer Corps 1890-1914

'An excellent, lucid, well-documented book'
Correlli Barnett, *The Sunday Telegraph*

'A valuable summary of the nature and political significance of that overweening and, to the modern eye, antediluvian body, composed of thousands of German gentlemen who believed it to be their divine right to domineeer over their neighbours at home and massacre their neighbours abroad.' M.R.D. Foot, *English Historical Review*

'He is gifted with lucidity in the exposition of an unusually complex subject and with an acute judgement of men and affairs'
Times Literary Supplement

The Silent Dictatorship: The Politics of the German High Command under Hindenburg and Ludendorff 1916-1918

'Deeply researched and vigorously written... the fullest and best account' Brian Bond

Acknowledgements

First and foremost I would like to thank the Deutsche Akademische Austauschdienst (DAAD) for their generous support. This is particularly appreciated at a time when most granting agencies are loath to support what at first sight appear to be merely stories of white men killing one another.

I would like also to thank the staff of the Bundesarchiv (Militärarchiv), Freiburg, the Hauptstaatsarchiv: Militärarchiv, Stuttgart, the Bibliothek für Zeitgeschichte, also in Stuttgart, the Bayerisches Hauptstaatsarchiv, Kriegsarchiv, Munich, the Sächsisches Hauptstaatsarchiv: Sächsisches Kriegsarchiv, Dresden, the Service Historique de l'Armée de Terre, Vincennes, and the Public Record Office, Kew. Their help and assistance in tracking down a vast amount of out of the way material was invaluable.

In Dresden, Gert Schirok was most kind and helpful. I am especially grateful to Gerhard Hirchfeld, Prudence Lawday and Irena Renz at the Bibliothek für Zeitgeschichte for their expertise and enthusiasm.

Lastly I would like to thank the series editor Hew Strachan for his lively interest in this project, and Jonathan Reeve, Tom Cairns and Richard Bray at Tempus for their support and encouragement.

List of Abbreviations

AWOL	Absent without leave
BEF	British Expeditionary Force
CIGS	Chief of Imperial General Staff
DAN	Northern Army Detachment
DDP	German Democratic Party
EMA	Foch's headquarters
GAE	Eastern Army Group
GAN	Northern Army Group
GAR	Reserve Army Group
GHQ	Haig's headquarters
GQG	Pétain's headquarters
OHL	German supreme command
OHLA	Foreign bureau of the OHL
SPD	German Social Democratic Party
USPD	German Independent Social Democratic Party

1

The Western Front:
February 1917–February 1918

When Hindenburg and Ludendorff were appointed to the High Command (OHL) in August 1916 they were soon convinced by the admiralty that once the situation on land was stabilized unrestricted submarine warfare would bring victory.[1] The submarine offensive began in February 1917 and initial results were most encouraging. Hindenburg and Ludendorff remained optimistic that Britain would soon be forced to sue for peace, but by October it was clear that Germany's third great *va banque* play after the Schlieffen Plan in 1914 and the Verdun offensive in 1916 was a failure.

The disappointing results of the submarine campaign, heavy losses in the army as a result of the Allied offensives on the Western Front, frustration that the war continued in the East in spite of the collapse of the Tsarist regime, severe shortages of food and galloping inflation resulted in a serious decline in morale both at home and at the front. On 6 July 1917 the Centre Party leader, Matthias Erzberger, gave a sensational speech in the Reichstag in which he stressed the failure of the submarine campaign, the gravity of the military situation and the collapse of Germany's allies. He concluded that Germany should disavow any territorial claims and begin immediate negotiations for peace.

On 19 July 1917 the Reichstag passed an ambiguously worded peace resolution. Shortly afterwards members voted to stop the prosecution of those among them who had been involved in a mutiny in the fleet.[2] In October the minister of war, von Stein, who had been hand picked for the job by Hindenburg and Ludendorff after they had secured the dismissal of his predecessor, was howled down in the Reichstag. The OHL countered these alarming developments by a programme of 'Patriotic Instruction' in the army and by active support for a new extremist right-wing party, the *Vaterlandspartei*, founded by Admiral Tirpitz, the architect of the German high seas fleet, and Wolfgang Kapp, who was later to lead a putsch against the Weimar republic.[3]

None of this had much effect, and morale continued to decline. The Bolshevik revolution with its call for an immediate peace had a startling effect on the home front in Germany. Few were attracted by Communism, but many endorsed their appeal for a peace without annexations, reparations or indemnities. It had proved impossible to escape from the stranglehold of the Allied blockade, and food shortages, although not as serious as in the previous year, still caused widespread discontent. In January 1918 there was a wave of strikes in Germany and Austria-Hungary during which – amidst other demands – there were calls for an immediate end to the war. The OHL's wish that strikes should be made a treasonable offence was not met.

On 15 February 1918 the *Bureau für Sozialpolitik* sent a report on the January strikes, which were concentrated in Berlin and Leipzig, to the war ministry in Berlin; it was forwarded with comments by the ministry to all Army Corps two days later.[4] The Bureau pointed out with some satisfaction that the wave of strikes had lasted only a week, had ended with the total capitulation of the strikers and, in spite of many rumours to the contrary, were unlikely to be repeated. The authorities had acted with the utmost severity. Special Courts Martial handed out lengthy prison sentences. The Social Democrat Wilhelm Dittmann was given a five-year prison sentence for addressing the strikers. Many strikers in Berlin were drafted: a course of action that did much to undermine the morale of the army by filling the ranks with the disaffected.[5]

The report suggested that the strikes were motivated by economic and political considerations. The principal economic cause was the shortage of food, which the bureau felt was the direct result of the British naval blockade and which resulted in a flourishing black market. This the war ministry vigorously denied, insisting that the black market was the cause and not the effect. The Bureau also blamed the strikes on the Auxiliary Labour Law, which restricted workers' freedom of movement, but once more the Ministry claimed that this was rubbish. It pointed out that the unions were well aware of the many advantages of the Auxiliary Labour Law, and that opposition to it was based on the misleading propaganda of radical socialists.

Enormous profits, which could clearly be seen in the annual reports of public companies, were also the cause of considerable discontent, and the arrogant behaviour of senior management as they crowed over these excellent results was sharply criticized. Complaints were also widespread about the Employers' Association's brusque rejection of any demands for a greater say for workers in management. The growing disparity in wages between skilled and unskilled workers, as well as between different industries was seen as grossly unjust. Unions bitterly complained that there were a growing number of workers who were not union members and who transferred from one branch of industry to another without the proper qualifications. Food shortages had led to widespread demoralization throughout the population, and the resulting discontent could all too easily be manipulated for political ends.

The length of a war which had no end in sight was the main political motive behind the strike. It was compounded by the political crisis in the second half of 1917 when the Chancellor, Bethmann Hollweg, was dismissed at the instigation of Hindenburg and Ludendorff and his successor Michaelis proved to be weak and indecisive. The snail's pace of domestic political reform, the protracted peace negotiations with Russia, the aggressive utterances of the extreme annexationists, the excessive influence of the OHL over certain political parties, squabbles within the Social Democratic Party over both domestic and foreign policy, the anti-war propaganda of the Independent Social Democrats (USPD), the virulent attacks on the Majority Socialists (SPD) in the right-wing press, the wishy-washy stance of the SPD's party newspaper and its editor Stampfer and the influence of the Bolshevik revolution, all contributed to a general feeling of disillusionment and war-weariness. The Army authorities in the East were concerned about the spread of Bolshevik propaganda. The High Command reported that soldiers returning from Russian prisoner of war camps were using the normal postal service, rather than the army's, in order to smuggle subversive material back to Germany. Army Group Linsingen was alarmed at the number of pamphlets in circulation among the troops with 'rabble-rousing and unpatriotic content'.[6] General Linsingen was outraged when he heard that a poster had been found in the men's latrine, which ended with the words: 'Down with the War! Down with the Government! Long Live Socialism and Peace!' and demanded that the culprit should be hunted down and severely punished.[7] Subsequent investigation suggested that these were isolated instances and that the Bolsheviks had minimal influence on the Army.

Radical elements within the working class were greatly encouraged by the apparent victory of the strikers in Austria-Hungary. In early January there had been a wave of brief strikes in Hungary, Transylvania and Poland, but they seemed to be of little consequence. Closer examination showed that many of these strikes had been inspired by radical sympathizers of the Bolsheviks so that calls for an end to the war and the overthrow of the capitalist system were mixed with immediate and short-term economic demands.[8] At the same time the national minorities, particularly the Czechs, voiced their opposition to the way in which the delegates of the Central Powers at Brest-Litovsk disregarded the principal of the self-determination of peoples.

On 14 January the workers at the Daimler factory in Wiener Neustadt led a march to the town hall in protest against the reduction of the daily flour ration from 200 to 165 grams. Workers from other factories joined in and the strike movement spread throughout the empire from Silesia to Trieste, and from Transylvania to Tyrol. The strikers had four main demands: that the negotiations at Brest-Litovsk should not be allowed to fail because of excessive territorial demands; that there should be a radical reform of the system of food distribution in order to render it more equitable; that universal suffrage should be introduced for local elections; and lastly that the control over certain industrial plant by the military should be ended.

As the strike continued the overriding demand that the war should end and that the workers should seize power pushed all other points into the background. This terrified the Social Democratic Party who feared that they were losing control. The army was also helpless, for the strike was soon so widespread that it could not possibly be suppressed by force. Regardless of this fact a shadow military government was formed under General Prince Aloys Schönburg-Hartenstein, but the Emperor was still undecided and there was powerful opponents to the idea of a military dictatorship, among them General Arz, the chief of general staff and the War Minister, Stäger-Steiner. Nevertheless preparations for this drastic action went ahead.

On 19 January the Austrian Minister President, Baron Ernst Seidler von Feuchtenegg who promised that he would respect all four of the strikers' original demands, received a deputation of prominent Social Democrats, including Viktor Adler, Karl Seitz and Karl Renner. The Hungarian Minister President, Sándor Wekerle, gave a similar guarantee. On 21 January the Social Democrats called for an end to the strikes. It soon proved to be a hollow victory. Neither Seidler nor Wekerle were in any position to give such undertakings. There simply was not enough food available to make any improvements. The electoral districts had yet to be decided upon. Nothing was done to end the military control of certain key industries. Foreign Minister Czernin's declaration that he would make no territorial demands on the Russians overlooked the fact that it was the German delegation that was calling the shots. It was small wonder that the strikers felt they had been cheated. Enraged workers in Wiener Neustadt briefly held Karl Renner prisoner, but fear that the military would intervene resulted in relative industrial peace for the next few months. The establishment reassured itself by claiming that the strikes had been the work of agitators from Germany who had been unable to force their government to begin negotiations for a compromise peace, and had thus begun to work on their ally.

Among the causes of political discontent in Germany were the slowness of the progress towards electoral reform in Prussia, the protracted negotiations at Brest-Litovsk, the attitude of the Fatherland Party towards the war-wounded, and the effect of a large number of leaflets calling for an immediate end to the war. Whereas the Bureau felt that these pamphlets were of secondary importance since most of them were very primitive and articulated ideas that had been around for some time past, the war ministry thought they were the principal cause of the strikes. The Bureau argued persuasively that they merely listed grievances that already existed, while the Ministry considered that they were the prime cause of those complaints. Once again the war ministry refused to see that there were genuine grievances and mistook the effect for the cause.

The report insisted that the manner in which the strikes had been suppressed had been most impressive, but that if the government did not pursue an energetic and enlightened social policy Germany would soon fall prey to a fresh wave of strikes. Once again the war ministry protested that this argument was absurd and said that it created the false impression that the government's social policies during the war had not been both energetic and enlightened. The Bureau's report suggested that an enlightened social policy would help to undermine the Social Democrats at a time when the left was weakened by the divisions between the SPD and the USPD, and when the Trades Unions were sharply critical of the radical course of the Independent Social Democrats who had torpedoed the negotiations between the Unions and the government, and had thus caused the strike movement to fail miserably.

The Bureau considered that the SPD and the Unions had done nothing to encourage the strikes, but that given the widespread support for industrial action they had found themselves unable to take a firm stand against them. The strikers felt that the Unions had let them down, and had failed to give them any support, and the Bureau felt that this was a justified complaint from their perspective. In many areas the unorganized workers were far more radical than the union members whom they mocked for paying union dues that simply paid for 'brake-shoes that slow down the movement'. Similarly many workers felt that the SPD was partially responsible for the Auxiliary Labour Law which had done so much to undermine their freedom of employment. The Christian and Hirsch-Duncker union leaders had condemned the strikes, but since they had such a miniscule membership their condemnations fell on deaf ears. In March the trade union boss Karl Legien, who headed of the General Commission of German Trades Unions, asked the military authorities for permission to publish a leaflet in which he denounced the recent wave of strikes. He argued that they were 'purely political' and were designed to provoke a general strike. The unions were in no way involved. Permission to publish was unhesitatingly granted.[9]

The USPD's propaganda against the Auxiliary Labour Law had proven most effective and forced the Trades Unions to go on the defensive.

They now felt obliged to uncover the slightest infraction of the law. A particular problem was to determine precisely what the Arbitration Committees, in which the workers were represented, could and could not do; and in what cases their decisions were binding on employers. Frequent injustices strengthened the case of the USPD against a law, which had passed in the Reichstag with the support of the SPD. That a number of questions were asked in the Reichstag about abuses of the law provided further arguments for the USPD.

Although the strikes caused great concern they did not serious disrupt the production of war materials and the numbers involved were comparatively small. Throughout 1918 there were 391,000 strikers in Germany, causing the loss of 1,452,000 days of work. In Britain the labour movement was far more radical with 923,000 strikers causing the loss of 6,000,000 working days.[10]

In spite of the strikes and many bitter disappointments Germany's overall situation in 1917 had improved greatly. The Western Front was stable. In the East, Romania, which had entered the war in the summer of 1916, was defeated and in Russia the Bolsheviks had signed an armistice. Although there was concern in some quarters that peace negotiations might become unnecessarily protracted because of excessive demands there was reason to believe that troops could soon be released from the Eastern Front and moved to the West.[11] This would help offset the shortage of recruits from home. There were only 400,000 men in the class of 1900, and they would not be called up until the autumn of 1918. There were now grounds for hope that a massive offensive in the West in the following spring would bring a final victory.

In early 1918 the Germans had 239 divisions and five independent brigades of infantry, eight divisions and three independent brigades of cavalry. Given the shortages of raw materials, recruits and horses it was unlikely that this situation could be significantly improved.[12]

An infantry regiment consisted of three battalions each consisting of four rifle companies equipped with five light machine-guns and two mortars, a machine-gun company with twelve heavy guns, and a mortar platoon with four light mortars. In most regiments the three mortar platoons were joined together and acted as one unit. Each battalion had a signals platoon.[13]

Most of the cavalry regiments had long been serving as infantry owing to the need for replacements in the infantry and the desperate shortage of horses. In March 1918 five of the remaining divisions were converted into mounted rifle regiments (*Kavallerie-Schützen-Regimenter*). Each infantry division was allotted a squadron of cavalry, and apart from a few regiments in the East all that remained of the cavalry were three divisions, and three independent brigades. In spite of these changes the German army was still seriously short of horses. There were just about enough for a defensive campaign but a chronic shortage for an offensive. Two days before the offensive was due to begin a number of units reported that they were unable to move because of the dearth of horses.[14] Lack of industrial capacity and the shortage of fuel made it impossible to make up this deficiency with motor vehicles. By 1918 the Germans had only one-sixth of the number of motor vehicles that the Allies had on the Western Front. The lack of transportation was one of the major concerns of the OHL as they began planning for the forthcoming offensive.[15]

The Germans were relatively slow in developing tanks and in December of 1916 the OHL had turned down a suggestion that tanks should be given the highest priority rating. They were not impressed by the performance of British tanks, and they were of little value as long as the Germans maintained a defensive stance. It was only after the French counter-attack at Villers-Cotterêts in July 1918 and the British offensive in the following month at Amiens that tanks began to present a serious problem for the thin and increasingly demoralized German line of defence.[16] Given the scarcity of horses, top priority was given to building trucks, thus leaving precious little additional capacity for the development and construction of tanks.

In October 1916 the OHL first suggested to the war ministry that the tank was a potentially useful weapon and that work should begin to develop a German version which could be mass-produced. In the following month the war ministry issued instructions to its technical staff and to industry to begin work.

The first German tank, the A7V named after the department of the War ministry responsible for its development, was not completed until the end of October 1917 and had obvious shortcomings. The bow was too low, ground clearance insufficient, the running gear was highly unreliable, it had maximum range of only twenty-five kilometres and the thirty-ton vehicle with two 100hp Daimler engines was woefully underpowered.[17] Initially it had been decided to build thirty-eight tanks but the OHL decided that only twenty were needed. There were three Assault Tank Units (*Sturm-Panzer-Kraftwagen-Abteilungen*) and further units were in the process of being set up, equipped largely by captured British vehicles. The A7V had its baptism of fire south of Saint Quentin on 21 March 1918. Plans for a light tank were abandoned as the armour was too thin. A better-protected light tank was planned by the Krupp works, but would not have been ready until the spring of 1919. A mammoth 150-ton tank never got beyond the drawing board as it was felt that should this leviathan eventually be built it would present a very tempting target to enemy artillery. In the course of the final year of the war the Germans were only able to use seventy-five captured tanks and fifteen of their own. The British and French had several thousand.

The German army was more than adequately supplied with rifles and the number of machine-guns had far outstripped the target figures of the Hindenburg Programme, which was designed greatly to increase armaments production. The artillery, pioneers and supply troops could now be provided with machine-guns, which were particularly useful for defence against attack from the air.

The supply of mortars was also adequate, the only serious problem with this weapon being its short range of under 1,300 metres. The field artillery was also well provided for, the difficulty here being that the new guns – the field gun (*Feldkanone 16*) and howitzer (*leichter Feldhaubitze 16*) – had greatly improved ranges but were also extremely heavy. Given the shortage of draught animals this presented a serious problem were the army to go on the offensive. The heavy artillery was somewhat short of guns and the new 18cm howitzer, which was designed to combine the characteristics of a howitzer and a heavy mortar, did not prove a success. There were ample supplies of ammunition thanks to the relatively quiet winter months on the western front, and to a remarkable increase in production, in spite of the January strikes in the armaments industry.

In July 1917 the 'America Programme' was announced. It was an ambitious attempt to outstrip Allied aircraft production by building 2,000 airplanes per month and 2,500 engines. The War ministry soon had to admit that this figure was unrealistic and reduced the figures to 1,600 airplanes and 1,800 engines. The Germans made some impressive technical advances including the building of the Junkers all metal monoplane which was far safer than the highly flammable wooden aircraft. In spite of these efforts the Germans were never able to match the Allies in aircraft production and Allied command of the skies was a vital component of their final success.

Between 1 November 1917 and 21 March 1918 the OHL moved thirty-three divisions from other fronts to the Western Front, bringing the total up to 200 divisions of infantry, two divisions of cavalry and three independent brigades.[18] This amounted to an increase of almost a million men. The Germans now had more than 4 million men on the Western Front. One and a half million remained in the East. The peace negotiations with the Bolsheviks at Brest Litovsk dragged on until 3 March, and the extremely delicate peace talks in Bucharest were not completed until 7 May. The Germans could not afford to move any more troops to the Western Front given the unstable situation in the East and the outrageous conditions imposed on both Russia and Romania. German troops also occupied the Baltic states, intervened in the civil war in Finland, and mounted a major campaign in the Ukraine to ensure grain supplies.

The eastern army was officered by older men who were not suitable for the rigours of a major offensive, and equipment was reduced to a bare minimum. Nevertheless the German victory in the East acted as a great encouragement to troops on the Western Front, and strengthened their conviction that the offensive would be a complete success and would bring peace in 1918.[19] It also gave further encouragement to those who were demanding excessive annexations after a crushing defeat of Germany's enemies and the imposition of a 'Hindenburg Peace'. Almost the entire nation, including many Social Democrats, was temporarily swept away by the intoxicating vision of an annexationist peace. In such an atmosphere Ludendorff was able to dismiss the arguments of those who urged caution and who suggested that given Germany's limited resources a flexible defensive strategy would be the more prudent choice. Hindenburg succinctly summed up the attitude of the German leadership when he told the Kaiser in early January 1918: 'We have to defeat the Western Powers in order to secure the political and economic position in the world that we need.'[20] The Kaiser was in full agreement. When it was suggested that it might be possible to reach an agreement with England he roared: 'Impossible! Someone has to cop it – and that one's England!'[21] In the same month he scribbled a characteristic marginal note:

> Germany's victory over Russia was the precondition for the revolution which led to Lenin, and Brest! The same will happen in the West. First a victory in the West and the collapse of the Entente, then we set the conditions which they will have to accept! They will be absolutely according to our interests.[22]

Since a compromise peace was unthinkable, and in any case probably unobtainable, there was no viable alternative to an offensive.

The arguments against a defensive strategy were far more compelling than those for an offensive. Germany's reserves of men and material were fast dwindling. Her allies were falling apart and were unlikely to be able to continue the struggle for another year. By the summer of 1918 they would be facing a large, fresh and excellently equipped American army.

There were limits to the number of men that could be moved from the East. Romanian oil and grain was indispensable for the German war effort and thus an army of occupation had to remain to ensure that the terms of the peace treaty were enforced. The Romanian army had not been fully demobilized so that it could be used to counter the Bolshevik threat. The Germans had eleven territorial battalions and eight cavalry regiments in Romania, the Austro-Hungarians ten territorial battalions. With a few additional companies and squadrons this was the barest minimum and the Military Government in Romania complained that they were desperately short-handed.[23]

The situation of near anarchy in the Ukraine was most worrisome to the Central Powers. In the winter of 1917/18 food shortages in

Austria-Hungary were so acute that there were widespread riots. Deliveries of grain from the Ukraine were deemed to be essential to halt a further deterioration of civilian morale. Furthermore, a poorly equipped Ukrainian army of about 40,000 men faced more than 100,000 armed Bolsheviks. As in the rest of the Russian empire the transport network had broken down, and there was no longer even a semblance of law and order. It was calculated that if the Central Powers were to secure the 300 truckloads of grain per day promised in the peace treaty with the Ukraine of 9 February, in return for a guarantee of the Ukraine's independence from Russia, they would have to station at least 500,000 men in the country.[24]

The urban middle class, who were predominantly Russians, welcomed the Germans who protected their property and whom they regarded as a guarantee against the nationalist and socialist policies of the Ukrainian government, the Rada, which had returned to Kiev on 7 March 1918, but which had little authority outside the city walls. A German Army report of 3 April 1918 summed up the situation: 'The Ukrainian government's authority extends as far as the tips of our bayonets.'[25] On 23 April the Rada government was overthrown and General Paul Skoropadski, a great landowner with fervent anti-socialist convictions, established a dictatorship and gave himself the title of Hetman. He accepted the peace treaty and agreed to co-operate with the Central Powers. The peasantry, who formed the vast majority of the Ukrainian population, understandably loathed the Germans who seized their crops, the Rada's agents having proved incapable of collecting them. The peasants resisted, so that the German Army found itself fighting a guerilla war at a time when the excellent crops of 1918 rendered grain shipments from the Ukraine superfluous.

Austria-Hungary's need for food imports was far greater than Germany's and they were even more heavy-handed in the Ukraine than their allies. They also took more than their fair share of the proceeds, which led to bitter exchanges between Berlin and Vienna, to the point that the alliance became seriously strained.

In fact the argument that German troops had to remain in the Ukraine in order the guarantee grain supplies does not bear close examination. A total of 9,132 railway cars full of grain where sent from the Ukraine. Of these seven out of seventeen, a total of 3,760, went to Germany. Each car contained 10,000 kilograms of grain so that the total amount was 37,600,000 kilograms. The population of Germany was 67 million; therefore Ukrainian grain provided approximately an additional pound per person. Even given that the Germans got 56,000 horses and 50,000 head of cattle from the Ukraine this was a very high cost to pay for tying down seventeen infantry and three cavalry divisions in the Ukraine when they would have been more usefully employed on the Western

Front. Even if they were not first-rate combat troops they could have made up for the chronic lack of labour in the rear echelons where they could have improved the defences that could well have held up the Allied advance during the 'Hundred Days' from August 1918. It is furthermore highly probable that the Germans could have got as much, and possibly even more, food and livestock from the Ukraine by normal trading practices. The bayonet is never the most effective agricultural implement.[26]

German troops were also involved in training anti-Bolshevik Finns to fight in the Finnish civil war, and a Baltic Division under General von der Goltz landed at Hango with the intention of occupying the Åland Islands. The Baltic Division co-operated with Marshal Mannerheim's forces and helped clear southern Finland of Bolsheviks. They advanced to Vyborg whence they kept a watchful eye on Petrograd. They continued to fight Bolsheviks in the Baltic States after the armistice.[27]

German troops were also fighting in Turkey, Macedonia and the Caucasus, but on a very modest scale. The 'Asia Corps' was formed to support the abortive Turkish offensive against Baghdad in the autumn of 1917, and fought with distinction against the British Army in Palestine. Fifteen of the eighteen infantry battalions on the Bulgarian front in Macedonia were withdrawn to fight on the Western Front in the spring of 1918 along with most of the cavalry and artillery. The Bulgarians protested vigorously against this move and in September 1918 the Germans were obliged to send four divisions in a desperate attempt to save Bulgaria from collapse. Two brigades were sent to the Caucasus in September 1918 to support two Bavarian regiments and a handful of support troops in an attempt to secure the oil resources of Baku, which were desperately needed to provide fuel for the German airforce.

Given Germany's exotic war aims in the East and their belief that the resources of the Ukraine and the Caucasus were essential, especially for Austria-Hungary, it is difficult to imagine how it could have been possible to move more troops to the Western Front. The forces in other theatres were minimal and would have made little difference. The OHL insisted that abandoning the Ukraine would have made the spring offensive an even greater gamble. If it failed it would have been well nigh impossible to continue the war into 1919 and Austria-Hungary would have almost certainly collapsed. The troops that remained in the East were of very poor quality, those that were moved to the west in the summer of 1918 went AWOL in large numbers and did all they could to avoid service at the front.

The OHL was determined that the Austro-Hungarian army should provide as many men and as much heavy artillery as possible to assist in the offensive. The request was first made to General Baron von Waldstätten, the Austrian representative to the joint army command, in November 1917. The request was repeated on 15 and 23 December, and on 26 December the Austrian emperor finally agreed in principle.[28] Count Czernin, the Austrian foreign minister, had serious reservations about the forthcoming German offensive. He argued that were it to be successful and the Germans were to take Paris, the war aims of Austria-Hungary's ally would become even more excessive. General Baron Arthur Arz von Straußenburg, Austria-Hungary's chief of general staff, felt that a spring offensive had every chance of success provided that peace was achieved in the east, and agreed that heavy artillery should be sent to support the Germans in this endeavour. He was less keen to send single divisions to the western front that would be subordinated to individual German armies.

General August von Cramon, the German representative at the Austro-Hungarian High Command, reported that the Empress Zita was violently opposed to the idea that Austrian soldiers should fight in France. He suggested that the OHL should insist that the Austrians should send three divisions, as previously agreed. The OHL concurred and ordered Cramon to stand firm on this issue. It was all to no avail. General Arz told him that: 'it was not agreeable at the highest level' that Austrian troops should fight on the Western Front.[29] It would seem that the Empress' veto was the decisive factor and that the army would have been willing to send a few divisions to fight alongside their German ally. The OHL was not particularly upset by this refusal as they had a low opinion of Austrian troops. They felt that the best help the Austrians could give would be to mount another offensive in Italy to relieve some of the pressure on the Western Front. It was not until the summer of 1918, when the German offensive had got stuck, that the OHL began to make urgent requests of the Austrians to send troops to the Western Front. The Austrians dragged their feet, divisions were sent in dribs and drabs, and most arrived too late to have any effect on the outcome of the campaign.

A total of forty-four divisions were initially allocated to the offensive. These 'Mobile Divisions' were brought up to full strength and were admirably armed and equipped. Each 'Mob' division was allotted a machine-gun sniper unit, air support, a communications unit and a full compliment of logistical and medical support. The desperate shortage of horses and fodder remained a major problem.[30]

Shortly after Christmas 1917 units designated as 'Mob' divisions were withdrawn from the front to begin intensive training in offensive tactics based on Ludendorff's pamphlet 'The Offensive in Trench Warfare'.[31] Since the Germans had been on the defensive on the Western Front for eighteen months, with the exception of the counter-attack at Cambrai in November 1917 this was a major undertaking. In addition to the training camps at Valenciennes and Sedan a further camp was established in Wörth in Alsace where officers and NCOs were schooled in the new tactics.

Particular attention was paid to the rapid penetration of the enemy positions, to taking out machine-gun nests and to co-ordination between the infantry and artillery so that the rolling barrage kept pace with the infantry's advance. Infantrymen were equipped with light machine-guns and mortars and were given intensive training with these weapons. Ludendorff stressed the importance of training in the use of the rifle grenade, which he considered an excellent weapon against machine-gun nests. Mortars firing in a low trajectory were also to be used in this role.[32]

Morale was high and the troops looked forward to the offensive with confidence. One German soldier's diary entry for New Year's Eve 1917 read: 'People now talk of Calais, Amiens and Paris as they did in the first months of the war, and at the same time they speak of peace as of a fact which will happen as surely as the beginning of spring or the solstice.'[33]

In addition to the forty 'Mob' divisions that were fully equipped, thirty divisions were given extensive training in offensive tactics, but they could not be as well equipped as the elite divisions, which had taken much of the best matériel. They in turn stripped the divisions that were still in the trenches of much needed resources. Those troops that remained on the defensive were rendered almost immobile as they lost the bulk of their draught animals to the seventy divisions now designated for the offensive. This was a particular problem for the field artillery which lacked teams of horses to move their guns. The selection of the divisions that were to take part in the offensive was kept absolutely secret. As late as two weeks before the offensive was due to begin only the divisional commanders had access to this information.[34]

In spite of tremendous efforts by all concerned the German army could not match the resources of the Entente. Their only hope was that superior leadership, thorough training and highly motivated troops would bring them victory at last. At the end of February, Army Group German Crown Prince made a number of conclusions from recent divisional exercises. It was felt that the key to success was to silence the enemy's artillery. Once this was achieved the rest would be easy. In accordance with Ludendorff's instructions the Crown Prince emphasized that local commanders should be given the highest possible amount of discretion. Higher commanders should resist the temptation to get the operation back onto its original track, and reserves should only be sent in where troops were already advancing, and not be sent to units that were calling for help. Particular attention was to be paid to the flanks during an advance so that a close watch could be kept on the enemy, but also on neighbouring units. In the past too many excellent chances had been lost by failing to provide flanking fire.[35]

The OHL knew that one of the keys to success lay in surprise. This was exceedingly difficult to achieve given the enormous numbers of men involved, and the vast piles of supplies that had to been brought up to the front in preparation for an offensive on such a huge scale. The task was so awesome that Army Group German Crown Prince felt obliged to appoint a Quartermaster General who had overall responsibility for building roads and railways, and controlling the stockpiling of supplies.[36] It was virtually impossible to conceal all this activity from aerial reconnaisance. In preparation for the offensive 3rd Army's pioneers had 5,000,000 sandbags, 4,100 tons of barbed wire, 62,000 square metres of corrugated iron, 160,000 square metres of planking and 13,200 tons of cement.[37] Stockpiling such vast amounts of material could not pass unnoticed. There were, however, certain countermeasures that could be taken. All major movements of men and supplies were done at night. Extensive use was made of camouflage and dummies.[38] Details of the objectives of the offensive were kept secret until the very last moment. Mail was rigorously censored, and telephone conversations overheard. Minimal changes were made in the front line. Diversionary attacks were launched in an attempt to conceal the main thrust of the offensive.

The OHL made a careful study of British and French offensives and analyzed the reasons for their failure. They concluded that the principle reason was the lack of surprise. The Entente had an overwhelming superiority in artillery, but massive bombardments could not make up for the inability to take the enemy by surprise. This had been achieved at Cambrai in November 1917 with the skilful use of tanks, but the initial breakthrough had not been consolidated and further objectives had not been attained. The success of the German counter-offensive was also attributed to surprise, even though they had no tanks and had to rely on a short preliminary barrage. Nevertheless the Germans penetrated the British positions up to eight kilometres, and the results would have been more impressive had they had sufficient time for preparation.

Ludendorff argued that with careful preparation a breakthrough was relatively easy to attain. The problem was to maintain momentum and to keep the enemy off balance. Hindenburg insisted that the break-through would succeed, but some officers, among them Crown Prince Rupprecht, were dubious. The Germans had failed at Ypres, the British at Arras, on the Somme, in Flanders and at Cambrai. Some feared that the British might withdraw as the Germans had done in 1916 and thus upset the planning for the offensive. All realized that the war could not be allowed to continue much longer, but there was disagreement about the chances for success of this final bid for victory. If it failed the consequences would be dire.[39]

Ludendorff entertained no such doubts and continued to insist that surprise was the key to success. To ensure surprise the preliminary artillery barrage should only last a few hours, for smaller operations only a few minutes. The artillery's main objectives were to silence the enemies guns, keep the enemies' heads down in the front-line trenches, shell the reserves and supply lines, and support the infantry's advance by a rolling barrage (*Feuerwalze*).[40]

The infantry was to push forward as fast as possible, searching out weak spots in the enemy's defensive to exploit, and bypassing strong points which would be taken out by succeeding waves of troops. When the front line troops were exhausted, the supporting troops should push ahead, thus giving the enemy no respite.

The final plans for the offensive were drawn up after lengthy debates and numerous preparatory studies. Ludendorff began to think about the possibility of a major offensive on the western front as early as April 1917. In the course of a meeting with General Max Hoffmann, the chief of staff of the eastern army, he announced that were Russia to collapse he could move troops from the eastern to the western fronts and mount an offensive, which could well decide the outcome of the war. He emphasized that it would be far more difficult to mount an offensive in the west than in the east, and he intended to prod the Entente's front in order to find a weak point where a breakthrough might be possible.[41]

The OHL began to examine the question of an offensive on the western front in earnest in October 1917. They were expecting another massive offensive by the Entente in the spring, and decided to deal the enemy a preemptive strike. Major Wetzell, who had been carefully chosen by Ludendorff to be chief of the operations division of the general staff (Section I), presented a study on 23 October, the day before the battle of Caporetto began, for an attack on the right flank of the British front in Flanders with the main thrust by the right wing of the 6th Army towards Armentières and Lens with the 4th Army support-ing the attack to the right. Wetzell earmarked thirty divisions for this offensive, which was to be launched at the end of February, by which time the Americans would not have been able to bring many troops up to the front. Ludendorff's laconic comment on this plan was: 'Good, everything depends on Italy.'[42] The Italians suffered a crushing defeat at Caporetto, but it was far from being a decisive victory for the Germans. The Italians were now in a stronger position on the Piave and Allied co-operation greatly improved after the conference at Rapallo which led to the creation of a Supreme War Council.

Meanwhile, at the headquarters of Prince Rupprecht of Bavaria's army group, plans were also being made for a spring offensive. These offi-cers were less optimistic than Wetzell's staff. Crown Prince Rupprecht's chief of staff, General von Kuhl, in particular had a low opinion of Wetzell's tactical skills, and held him responsible to for 7th Army's heavy losses of men and material on the Aisne.[43] He argued that since the Entente was now being strengthened with American troops their numerical superiority was such that a major offensive had little chance of success. For the same reason Germany could not afford to adopt a purely defensive stance for in a war of attrition the Entente was vastly superior in manpower and material. He therefore suggested that the army should retire rather than fight a costly defensive battle, and then make a series of powerful counter-attacks. Kuhl argued that since the submarine campaign had obviously failed it would be possible to retire in Flanders, even if the submarine bases were thereby placed in danger. A number of sorties should also be made against sections of the front that had not yet been attacked, for example on the Lys front between Armentières and Bailleul.[44]

Ludendorff remained more optimistic and argued that provided the general situation was favourable there was a real possibility of smashing the British army in Flanders, as long as enough troops could be released for the offensive without seriously weakening the front elsewhere, and provided that the attack could be launched early in the year. Haig, with his back to the Channel, would not be able to trade space for time.

By November Ludendorff's optimism seemed justified. The Bolshevik revolution plunged Russia into a bloody chaos and the end of the war in the east was in sight. The Entente was beginning to flag in Flanders and the offensive in Italy was a success. On 9 November Major Wetzell produced another memorandum which addressed the question of a 'decisive offensive' in the spring of 1918. He insisted that only a large-scale offensive with an ambitious goal could have any real effect on the overall situation. He had serious reservations about an offensive against the British. He first analyzed a proposed attack against the British army in Flanders by the 6th Army in the direction of Hazebrouk. He felt that such an offensive would have an initial success, but given the water-logged terrain in Flanders at that time of year and the substantial British reserves, he doubted that it would be possible to exploit the situation and deal a decisive blow. He therefore agreed with Prince Rupprecht's staff that a series of sorties designed to disrupt preparations for a British offensive was the most that could be achieved.

Wetzell insisted that an offensive against the French had far better chances of success. In his view the only point on the Western Front which offered a real opportunity for a major victory was the huge salient around Verdun. This could be attacked from the north from the Argonne, and from the south from Saint Mihiel and over the Maas. Were Verdun to fall the effect on the French would be so devastating that it could be decisive in bringing the war to an end. The French would then be in no position to mount an offensive along with their American allies, and the Germans could concentrate on the knockout blow against the British.[45]

Colonel Count von der Schulenburg, the chief of staff to the German Crown Prince's army group had reached a similar conclusion. He did not believe that a partial victory over the British army would be enough to convince the British to end the war. On the other hand he hoped that the Verdun salient could be nipped off and that the fall of Verdun would shatter French morale and force them to seek peace.[46]

Whereas Wetzell and Schulenburg, both of them highly gifted staff officers, were convinced that the answer lay in an attack on the Verdun salient, Crown Prince Rupprecht's staff concentrated on the Lys front and following the OHL's request they concentrated on planning a number of limited attacks on the British positions. The more they studied the situation the more they became convinced that it would be possible to strike a decisive blow against the British in Flanders.

On the fatal date of 11 November Ludendorff met with the chiefs of staff of the army groups Crown Prince Rupprecht and German Crown Prince, along with the chiefs of staff of the 6th and 2nd armies at Crown Prince Rupprecht's headquarters in Mons. General von Kuhl, Crown Prince Rupprecht's chief of staff, presented a proposal code-named 'Saint George' for an offensive starting from the line Frélinghien-Festubert in the direction of Bailleul and Hazebrouk, the left flank protected by the La Bassée canal, in order to cut off the British forces in north-eastern France. This plan was similar to that which Wetzell had rejected, but he argued that it had every chance of success. He pointed out that the British were in an extremely awkward position with the sea to their north and west. If the Germans were to push westwards resolutely and not swing north too soon, the bulk of the British army could be trapped in an operation broadly similar to von Manstein's 'Plan Yellow' in 1940. Owing to the Lys flooding its banks in winter it would not be possible to launch the offensive before the beginning of April. Kuhl concluded that the operation would require thirty-five divisions and 400 batteries of heavy artillery.[47]

Schulenburg, supported by Wetzell, presented the familiar arguments in favour of an offensive against Verdun. Ludendorff was not impressed by this scheme and argued that the British would be unlikely to send troops to help out the French and would attack in Flanders, thus placing the Germans in a precarious situation. He preferred an offensive near Arras or Saint Quentin. Kuhl objected vigorously to this suggestion. He argued that the further south the offensive the less it would be possible to exploit the awkward position of the British in Flanders. The British could easily move troops south, and the French would threaten the left flank of Ludendorff's proposed offensive.

After three hours of intense discussion Ludendorff concluded that the situation in Russia and in Italy was such that it should be possible to launch a major offensive in the west with thirty-five divisions and 1,000 pieces of heavy artillery. He insisted that the offensive would have to begin at the end of February or the beginning of March before the Americans were able to bring significant numbers of troops up to the front. Taking heed of von Kuhl's warnings about the condition of the land in Flanders so early in the year, he proposed a diversionary attack on Verdun, along the lines suggested by von Schulenburg, to be followed by the attack on the flank and rear of the British army in Flanders. The words were hardly out of his mouth before he added that Germany lacked the forces to carry out such a massive operation. He therefore suggested moving the spearhead of the attack further south to Saint Quentin. Having established a position along the Somme from Péronne to Ham, the attack would move north-west and begin to roll up the British front. Critical to the success of this operation would be the bombardment of the enemy's railway stations and the concentration points of their reserves.

Reflecting after the war on his decision to seek a decisive victory over the British rather than the French, Ludendorff wrote that he felt that the British were far more likely to agree to an armistice than would the French, given that they were not fighting on their home turf. Furthermore he considered the French army to be operationally more skilful and flexible than their British allies.[48]

It is significant that Ludendorff's nominal superior, Hindenburg, was not present at this important conference. It is typical of the state of affairs in Germany that the Kaiser was not invited, and it is also remarkable that the Crown Prince was also not in attendance. Crown Prince Rupprecht spoke to Ludendorff beforehand, but he appears also not to have been present at the conference. Even if he was there he did not speak.[49]

Both Wetzell, recently promoted to the rank of Lieutenant-Colonel, and von Schulenburg felt that Ludendorff's proposal for an offensive at Saint Quentin was overly ambitious. On the day after the meeting at Mons von Schulenburg sent Ludendorff a copy of the memorandum he had prepared for the Crown Prince in which he reaffirmed his belief that an attack on the Verdun salient was preferable to an offensive at Saint Quentin. He remained convinced that a breakthrough on the British front would soon get stuck and end in a slogging match against greatly superior forces which would place the Germans in a very precarious position. Wetzell also still favoured an offensive against the French.[50] Ludendorff's objections to this strategy, which he had already voiced at Mons, was that the British were unlikely to send help to the French at Verdun and would go ahead with their offensive in Flanders, thus placing the Germans in a most precarious position.

Responsibility for planning any offensive against the British lay with the Army Group Crown Prince Rupprecht. Von Kuhl and his staff ignored Ludendorff's insistence that the offensive should be near Saint Quentin and stuck to their original 'Saint George' plan for an attack further north in Flanders. It was now intended as a powerful counter-attack in the event of a renewed British offensive in Flanders. They forwarded their report to the OHL on 20 November 1917.[51] It analyzed two possibilities: the Army Group would either seek a decisive breakthrough, or it would mount a limited offensive to take the pressure off an attack against the French around Verdun. They remained convinced that von Kuhl's 'Saint George' plan for an offensive in the direction of Hazebrouk against the flank and rear of the Ypres salient had every chance of success, provided that the weather was favourable. It was felt that the British army lacked the operational skill and ability to improvise to counter a determined attack. It should not prove too much of a difficulty to break through the Portuguese lines on the Lys and since the British would clearly not be expecting an attack at a point where they had posted their weakest units it would be relatively easy, with careful preparation, to catch them by surprise. The main danger was that the French would bring troops north by rail and counter-attack on the left flank of the German advance. This eventuality would be countered by bringing in substantial reserves. It was estimated that at least forty divisions were needed for this offensive, supported by 500 heavy batteries and fifteen regiments of field artillery – in other words a far larger force, particularly in artillery, than that envisioned by Ludendorff on 11 November.[52]

It was admitted that the offensive might have to be postponed because of weather conditions, and it was felt possible that the British might be the first to go on the offensive. Should that occur the Army Group should withdraw and prepare the counter-stroke.

The memorandum also discussed Ludendorff's proposal for an attack at Saint Quentin by 2nd Army. The left flank of this attack would be protected by the Somme, the thrust would be north-west towards the Channel coast. The precise course of the operation would depend on the enemy's reactions. There were a number of serious difficulties with this plan. The offensive would require much stronger forces than were foreseen for 'Saint George'. A minimum of fifty-five divisions would be required for the initial blow, supported by 600 heavy batteries and eighteen regiments of field artillery. Furthermore, once the breakthrough had been achieved the Germans would have to advance through the wasteland they had left behind them when they withdrew to the 'Alberich' line in 1917, and they would have also to fight across the cratered landscape of the Somme battlefield of 1916. Taking a leaf from the British Tank Corps it was suggested that batteries should be equipped with fascines and heavy planking in order to help bring the artillery forward, but this presented the additional problem of how such large amounts of equipment could be moved under such extreme conditions, or whether the fascines would be available in time. It was also pointed out that the two-horse wagons used by mortar units were utterly useless in cratered areas, whereas the one-horse version did very well.[53] It was felt that Ludendorff's belief that the enemy's railway network could be seriously damaged by artillery and aerial bombardment was overly optimistic, given poor weather conditions and the disappointing results of previous attempts in Flanders. Lastly, the offensive would have to begin in a south-westerly direction towards the Somme from a line from Quéant to Bellicourt and from Vendhuille to the Oise, and then move in a north-westerly direction towards Saint Pol and the Pas de Calais thus necessitating a ninety degree change in the direction of the main thrust. On the other hand the timing of the offensive was not so dependent on weather conditions, the British defensive positions were weaker, and they had fewer reserves on that section of the front. Crown Prince Rupprecht's staff concluded that 'Saint George' was a superior plan with good chances of success.

A further memorandum from Major Stapff, chief of general staff to 2nd Army, and an officer whose reputation was soon to be enhanced by his handling of the Cambrai crisis, was also forwarded to the OHL. He argued in favour of a series of co-ordinated attacks across a broad front on either side of the Somme with the main force of the attack in the direction of Ham. The offensive was to push on towards Amiens and then begin to swing north towards the Channel coast. The left flank of this operation was to be protected against the French by the Oise. This operation was codenamed 'Saint Michael'.

The situation was radically altered when the British launched their offensive at Cambrai on 20 November 1917 in which tanks were first used on a large scale and to great effect. The Germans were caught completely by surprise, but they soon launched a successful counter-attack and cancelled all the British gains. The British then began to spread their reserves more evenly across their front, thus plugging some of the weaker points which the Germans had hoped to exploit. In the East negotiations began with Russia which made it seem likely that peace was imminent and that the Germans would therefore be able to move substantial number of men from east to west. Crown Prince Rupprecht's staff now assumed that after the setback at Cambrai the Entente was unlikely to launch an offensive in the spring of 1918, but would wait for the Americans and attack in the summer.

These changes meant that the arguments in favour of 'Saint George' were no longer compelling. The British were now not concentrated in the Ypres salient, and there was no immediate need to relieve the pressure on the German positions in Flanders, given the movement of British troops from Flanders to the Somme, and the strengthening of German defences with the release of men and material from the east.

Nevertheless, the staff of Army Group Crown Prince Rupprecht continued to work on 'Saint George'. There was complete agreement that the initial British success at Cambrai once again showed that surprise was the key to success, and von Kuhl repeatedly warned of the dangers of getting stuck in a battle of attrition.[54] He pointed out that the worst mistake the British had made was to keep hammering away at the same point in the hope that the Germans would eventually break. If the 'Saint George' offensive were to get stuck at any one point then they should prod elsewhere until a point was found where a breakthrough was possible. These ideas were forcefully presented in a memorandum dated 15 December, which was forwarded to the OHL.[55] It was still intended that the offensive should be along the Lys front from Armentières and the La Bassée canal with the aim of reaching the Channel coast near Dunkirk, thus threatening Calais. It was now proposed that a diversionary thrust should also be mounted in the area around Cambrai where the British were expecting to be attacked. This would divert reserves from Armentières and the situation was to be rendered even more confusing by delivering blows north of Lens and near Saint Quentin.

After further consideration of the problem, it was agreed that if the 'Saint George' offensive were to get stuck the offensive would have to be continued at another point on the front. This would either be around Ypres or preferably the 'Michael' offensive could be launched. If the 'Saint George' offensive were to be successful then it could be supported by 'Michael' and the whole British front north of the Somme could be rolled up.[56]

2

Plans for the
Spring Offensive:
December 1917–March 1918

The British were given some hint of German intentions when the southern section of the greatly over-extended 2nd Army of General von der Marwitz, positioned around Saint Quentin from the Omignon to the Oise, was reorganized to form the 18th Army under General von Hutier, an expert in surprise attacks who had been moved from the Russian front. The new army's headquarters were to be in Avesnes.[1] Von Hutier received the news of his appointment while addressing a meeting of his subordinates in the castle at Riga on the evening of 12 December. He was overjoyed to be thrown once again into the thick of the fray.[2]

He was given a warm farewell by his staff and after Christmas, with his wife and children in Berlin, he arrived at his new headquarters on 26 December. His first striking impression of the Western Front was the sharp contrast between the industrial wealth of the west and the poverty of the east, and the frightful destruction meted out on the towns and villages where he had been stationed three years previously. Although every inch a soldier, crowned with the glory of his remarkable victory at Riga, von Hutier was painfully aware of the horrors of war. He hoped and prayed that 1918 would at last bring an end to this terrible conflict.[3]

On 12 December Colonel Wetzell presented a new memorandum in which he agreed with Ludendorff that the French army was superior in every way to the British. He argued that the French leadership, both military and civilian, was far more determined, the army more experienced and skilful both in defence and attack. It was supported by an increasing number of Americans. Wetzell found the British operationally clumsy and tactically unimaginative. Their only military virtue was their toughness. He therefore argued that the best chances for success were to be found in Flanders. Hindenburg also had a low opinion of the British Army. He described it as clumsy, unable to adjust quickly to changing situations, and set in its ways. On the other hand he too admired its steadfastness and toughness, and felt that although they were unimpressive in attack they were likely to put up a dogged defence. He felt that the French were less resolute in defence. Their artillery was superb, but the infantry lacked the grim determination of the British.[4]

Since the British had ample reserves and a dense network of railways they would be able quickly to bring in support against any German attack. Wetzell therefore proposed that the Germans should attack at several points along the British front, but he disagreed strongly with Ludendorff that an offensive against the British section of the front could bring a decisive victory. He remained convinced that only a decisive victory over the French Army would end the war. He nevertheless suggested that it might be possible to close the British salient towards Cambrai and force a wide gap in the British front from Bapaume to Péronne and on to La Fère. Two weeks after this object had been achieved he proposed a second offensive to the north and south of Armentières in the direction of Hazebrouk which might make it possible to roll up the British flank northwards. Forty divisions would be needed for the first phase, thirty for the second. He insisted that an offensive by Hazebrouk, as foreseen in Army Group Crown Prince Rupprecht's 'Saint George' plan, might be successful, but that it would have to be postponed too long because of the weather, and would need more men than an attack on the Verdun salient. The offensive by Saint Quentin had the distinct disadvantage that it was to take place on a quiet section of the front and it would therefore be extremely difficult to disguise the preparations for the offensive. It would thus be virtually impossible to achieve any degree of surprise. The battle would also be fought over the pockmarked terrain of the old Somme battlefields, which would greatly benefit the defenders. In Wetzell's opinion the only chance of decisively beating the British Army was to launch a series of attacks against them with a final blow in the direction of Hazebrouk. He therefore suggested an offensive at Saint Quentin followed two weeks later by an attack at Hazebrouk.

General von Kuhl's insistence on the importance of surprise, and on the Pulkowski method of dispensing with a lengthy preliminary barrage, was opposed by those who argued that careful preparation was even more important. In the course of a series of heated debates between von Kuhl and Ludendorff it became apparent that Ludendorff was increasingly sympathetic to the opposition.[5] Kuhl's argument that it was possible to combine careful preparation with surprise left few convinced. Wetzell continued to raise objections to both 'Saint George' and 'Michael', and was convinced that the war could only be won by a major operation against the French in the Verdun salient, which could begin as early as February.

After visiting all the armies in Army Groups German Crown Prince and Crown Prince Rupprecht, Ludendorff finally decided on 21 December that the 'Michael' offensive both sides of Saint Quentin should go ahead. He argued that 'Saint George' would have to be postponed until too late, and that the 'Mars' offensive at Arras would be too difficult. On the same day Crown Prince Rupprecht's staff again addressed the problems facing the 'Michael' offensive. The British had greatly strengthened their positions on the Somme, and the French had built up reserves on their left flank. Nevertheless they argued that 'Michael' should go ahead if weather conditions in Flanders made it impossible to mount 'Saint George'.

It was proposed that 'Michael' should be carried out by 2nd and 18th Armies, each having about twenty divisions, on a broad front from Villers-Guislan to the Oise by la Fère. Some distance away on the right flank of 2nd Army a separate group of six to eight divisions should attack the northern part of the bulge in the British lines in the direction of Cambrai. They would start from the line from Riencourt to Inchy and advance in the direction of Bapaume. 2nd Army would thus advance west towards the line Péronne-Bapaume and then swing northwest supported by between twelve and fifteen divisions of reserves. Von Hutier's 18th Army was responsible for the section south of Péronne thus securing the left flank of the advance. It was hoped that von Hutier would soon be able to release some of his divisions to support 2nd Army's advance. Attached to the Army Group's paper was a proposal by 2nd Army in which Major Stapff repeated his suggestion that the 'Michael' offensive should be made up of a series of attacks, and that it should straddle the Somme, the left flank now being on the Oise.

On 25 December the Army Group decided that the decision whether to go for 'Michael' or 'Saint George' would have to be postponed until not less than four weeks before the offensive was due to start.

Army Group German Crown Prince assumed that they would be on the defensive in the spring and concentrated on discussing where the French were likely to attack and what measures could best be taken to counter them. Ludendorff sent General Krafft von Dellmensingen to the Army Group Duke Albrecht in the south to examine the possibility of launching an offensive in Alsace about one week before the main offensive. Krafft was a highly regarded staff officer who had just returned from the Italian front to take up the post of chief of staff to General von Below's 17th Army. The aim of this offensive was to draw in French reserves, free the only part of Germany occupied by the

French, and improve Germany's bargaining position for territorial gains after the war.[6]

On 25 December Colonel Wetzell wrote another memorandum in preparation for a conference with Ludendorff to be held two days later. He remained convinced that the offensive should be directed against the French. He pointed out that the British had sixty-seven divisions in the trenches on a front of 180 kilometres. The French had 105 divisions on a front of 510 kilometres. The British had twenty divisions in reserve behind their front, the French only thirty-five of which three were American. Wetzell argued that the British were expecting a German attack and that they could be encouraged in this belief by moving troops up to Crown Prince Rupprecht's Front. The French might then move troops to their left flank near Saint Quentin. An offensive against the Verdun salient would then catch them by surprise. Wetzell insisted that decisive victory could not be scored over the British, whereas the fall of Verdun would bring down the French government and the war might well then be over.[7]

On 27 December Ludendorff ordered the chiefs of general staff to the three army groups to attend a conference at Bad Kreuznach to discuss the spring offensive.[8] At this meeting he stressed that the offensive would have to begin as early as possible before the Americans were able to bring a significant number of troops up to the front. In spite of Colonel Wetzell's forceful arguments, he remained convinced that the offensive should be directed against the British, but he had not yet decided the exact point on the British front where the blow should be delivered. Thus the three army groups were ordered to prepare for all eventualities.

Army Group Crown Prince Rupprecht was ordered to plan a break-through near Armentières ('Saint George I'), an offensive against the Ypres salient ('Saint George II') and an attack from the Loretto heights near Lens to Arras ('Mars'). The 'Michael' offensive on the fronts of the 2nd and 18th Armies was now divided into three: 'Michael I' in the direction of the line Bullecourt to Bapaume, 'Michael II' from north of Saint Quentin to north of Péronne and 'Michael III' from south of Saint Quentin to La Fère.

In the event of a French offensive in the Champagne early in 1918 the 3rd Army in Army Group German Crown Prince was to give way in the Argonne ('Hector') and counter-attack with the 1st Army in the Champagne ('Achilles'). Army Group Duke Albrecht was to prepare an attack on the Breusch valley ('Strasburg') and go on the defensive in the Sundgau ('Belfort'). Lastly Army Groups German Crown Prince and Duke Albrecht were to make preliminary plans for a joint offensive from the north and east of the Verdun salient ('Castor' and 'Pollux').

Ludendorff told General von Kuhl that Army Group Crown Prince Rupprecht would deliver the decisive blow and for this reason had been strengthened by General von Hutier's 18th Army with General von

Sauberzweig as his chief of general staff. It would soon be joined by General Otto von Below's 14th Army, which was being moved from the Italian front. Hindenburg solemnly warned von Kuhl that his offensive had to succeed. Kuhl confided in his diary that that was 'easier said than done'.[9]

On New Year's day 1918 Ludendorff telephoned von Kuhl and repeated that full responsibility for the success of the spring offensive lay with him, and that Army Groups German Crown Prince and Duke Albrecht would merely play a supporting role.[10] On the same day von Hutier reported to Crown Prince Rupprecht's headquarters and was impressed by his new commanding officer's pleasing manner. He was also tremendously impressed by General von Kuhl, whom he had always held in the highest regard.[11] On 4 January von Hutier at last received the directives for 'Michael' from Army Group headquarters.[12]

Planning as ordered by Ludendorff on 27 December was made exceptionally difficult because peace had still not been signed with Russia, so staff officers did not know how many men and how much artillery would be available to them. Nevertheless, Colonel von Klewitz, general staff chief of 3rd Army, felt that the attack on the Verdun salient from the Argonne ('Castor') had every chance of success. Staff officers at Army Group German Crown Prince did not share his optimism. They pointed out that the success of 'Castor' depended very much on 'Pollux' which was a much more difficult operation. The difficulties of crossing the Meuse alone were enormous. The chief of staff to Army Group Duke Albert, Colonel Heye, shared these serious reservations about 'Pollux' and felt that it was questionable even as a feint. In mid-January Ludendorff, who had never shared Wetzell's enthusiasm for an offensive against the Verdun salient, ordered that planning for 'Castor' and 'Pollux' should be abandoned.

General von Krafft had similar reservations about the proposed offensive in Alsace. He argued that only an offensive along the entire length of the front had any chance of success, and he doubted whether the thirty-two divisions needed for this operation would be available. Krafft's concerns were shared by the staff at Army Group Duke Albert who pointed out that weather conditions in Alsace in March were extremely dubious.

Ludendorff took note of these objections and on 16 January ordered planning to go ahead for 'Strasburg' on a broader front, but he added that whether the offensive would be launched, and on how wide a front, would depend on the overall situation. Colonel Baron von Oldershausen, the chief of the military railways, then pointed out that the railways in Alsace were ill suited for an offensive. On 29 January Ludendorff therefore added that 'Strasburg' would be launched on a relatively narrow front only if the German offensive elsewhere were successful and the French were unable to strengthen their front in Alsace.

On closer examination it was estimated that 'Hector' and 'Achilles' would need forty-eight divisions and 1,000 batteries of heavy artillery to stand a chance of success. The staff of Army Group German Crown Prince therefore argued that 1st and 3rd Armies should adopt a defensive stance and should only go on the offensive if conditions looked favourable. Ludendorff visited the Army Group on 24 January and agreed with this assessment. All hopes for diversionary attacks by Army Groups German Crown Prince and Duke Albrecht had to be abandoned for lack of men, artillery and equipment.[13]

In order to maintain the highest degree of secrecy each of the armies in Army Group Prince Rupprecht believed that their offensives would be carried out. 'Michael I' and 'Michael II' were allotted to 2nd Army. 18th Army's 'Michael III' was designed to protect the left flank of the offensive by moving up to the Somme and the Crozat Canal. The question of whether it could be supported to the south by an offensive by La Fère was left open. Army Group German Crown Prince was asked whether General von Boehn's 7th Army would be able to support the left flank of the 'Michael' offensive.

Although Ludendorff hinted that 'Michael' was his plan of choice, Army Group Crown Prince Rupprecht argued in favour of 'Saint George I'.[14] Here the Germans faced the Portuguese, notoriously poor troops, but were the enemy to have strong forces behind the Lys the offensive would have little chance of success. Much also depended on the weather. Crown Prince Rupprecht's staff estimated that the 'Michael' offensive would only succeed if the Germans could mount diversionary attacks on the Ypres and Verdun salients. The problem here was that the offensive would have to be postponed until weather conditions in Flanders were favourable, and thus it would be unlikely that 'Michael' could be launched in March as Ludendorff had ordered. Crown Prince Rupprecht felt that the Ypres salient was a serious liability for the British and that it was held simply for reasons of prestige. There were signs that they were considering abandoning it.[15] If they were to do so it would make 'Saint George' pointless and 'Michael' the only viable alternative.

Ludendorff was unable to make up his mind whether von Below's 14th Army should be placed to the right for 'Saint George', or to the left for 'Mars'. Von Kuhl still wanted to concentrate on 'Saint George', even though placing Below's army to the right would give the British a strong sense of his intentions. Ludendorff argued that he should treat 'Mars' as equally important. The situation was becoming extremely confused, and Ludendorff was so preoccupied with a wide range of political questions that planning for the spring offensive lacked any sense of purpose and direction. Repeated request for clarification went unanswered.[16] Colonel Bauer, Ludendorff's right-hand man at the OHL and an inveterate political intriguer, created further confusion by suggesting that there was a plot afoot, involving the secretary of state for foreign affairs, Richard von Kühlmann, and the chief of staff in the East, General Max Hoffmann, to remove Ludendorff. Hindenburg had announced that were Ludendorff to be dismissed he would resign. Both the German Crown Prince and Crown Prince Rupprecht used all their influence to support Ludendorff, who in turn became increasingly intransigent over the peace terms with Russia. Ludendorff complained that political squabbles took up far too much of his time, telling von Kuhl that he was regarded in Berlin as a 'naughty boy' and was uncertain whether he would be able to stay at his post. Such uncertainty about the future created an atmosphere of nervous intensity among the senior commanders.[17]

On 13 January Ludendorff discussed the forthcoming offensive with General Krafft von Dellmensingen in Bad Kreuznach. Both men agreed that the 'Saint George' offensive was fraught with problems and would not bring a decisive victory. Krafft argued in favour of a 'Michael' offensive on a broad front to be supported by 'Mars'. Ludendorff said that he would see whether Germany had the necessary manpower and matériel for an offensive along 95 kilometres of front.[18]

General Lossberg, chief of staff in 4th Army, then replied to Ludendorff's request for a proposal for an offensive. He suggested an attack north of Lens designed to destroy the British forces to the north by attacking from the rear of Arras and then pushing on in the direction of Amiens. He warned against a frontal attack on the heavily defended Arras front and insisted it was essential to avoid the cratered landscape of the Somme battlefields which would slow down the German advance.[19]

Between 18 and 21 January Ludendorff visited the headquarters of the armies in Army Group Crown Prince Rupprecht and of General von Boehn's 7th Army in Army Group German Crown Prince. He had a series of detailed discussions with staff officers in order that he might make a final decision on the spring offensive. On 18 January he visited 4th Army, on the following day he went to the headquarters of 6th Army, on 20 January he continued with visits to 2nd and 18th Armies. Finally, on the next day, he discussed the situation facing 7th Army. He concentrated on tactical questions such as the importance of close artillery support for the infantry and problems of logistics. Some officers felt that he greatly underestimated the difficulties involved in following up an initial attack. He had gained his experience on the Eastern Front where geographical conditions were very different and the enemy inferior. The British and French armies were every bit as tough as the Germans, they would subject the attacking armies to intense artillery fire and would promptly throw in their reserves. It was also felt that Ludendorff underestimated the heavy losses that would be suffered in any offensive on the Western Front.[20]

At the meeting on 18 January it seemed that Ludendorff favoured 'Mars'. General von Krafft also spoke strongly in favour of 'Mars', possibly in combination with 'George I'. Crown Prince Rupprecht disagreed, arguing that an offensive against Vimy Ridge and the Loretto Heights would be far too difficult. He shared the concerns of those officers who felt that German war aims in the east were excessive and were holding up the peace process, which in turn meant that troops could not be moved from the Eastern to the Western Front. All were impressed by the strength of Ludendorff's willpower, but many doubted whether that was enough. It seemed that he failed to understand that if the offensive failed the war would be lost, and that success was very far from assured.[21]

In the afternoon of 21 January he shared his thoughts with two highly respected staff officers: Crown Prince Rupprecht's chief of staff General von Kuhl and Colonel Schulenburg, the chief of staff to the German Crown Prince's Army Group.[22] Ludendorff had reached the conclusion that 'Saint George' would have to be postponed too long, possibly until May, because of uncertainties about the weather. At the same time, he rejected the 'Mars' offensive near Arras as presenting too many tactical difficulties. Therefore he decided to go ahead with 'Michael' on a slightly broader front by moving the right flank up to the Scarpe. Here the Germans would be attacking the Entente at the weakest part of their front, the terrain presented no serious obstacles and the attack could be launched at any time of year. Ludendorff hoped that if the main blow (*Schwerpunkt*) were delivered between Arras and Péronne it would be possible to push on to the Channel coast and score a major operational success.

Ludendorff told the chiefs of staff of these two army groups that he intended to form a new army in Army Group Crown Prince Rupprecht. This 17th Army, commanded by General Otto von Below with General Krafft von Dellmensingen as chief of staff, would be made up of men taken from the former 14th Army, and from the 6th and 2nd Armies. It was to be placed between the 2nd and 6th Armies and take part in 'Michael 1'. Von Hutier's 18th Army would then be moved to Army Group German Crown Prince in order to protect the left flank of the offensive by advancing to the Somme at Péronne.

A new Army Group was to be formed under General von Gallwitz made up of 5th Army from Army Group German Crown Prince and Army Section C of Army Group Duke Albrecht, so that the front around Verdun would be under a single command. A new 19th Army under General Count von Bothmer, who had previously commanded the southern army on the eastern front, was to be formed in Army Group Duke Albrecht.

At that moment the OHL had sixty-three divisions on the Western Front. It was hoped to bring twenty-four more divisions from Italy and

Russia by late March, but that depended on how the peace negotiations with Russia progressed. In all Ludendorff hoped to have between
eighty-five and ninety divisions ready for the offensive.

Ludendorff's motive for moving von Hutier's army to the Army
Group German Crown Prince was to avoid leaving the 'Michael' offensive entirely in the hands of one Army Group. Were this the case he
feared that he would be less able to direct operations personally, and
General von Kuhl would be in too powerful a position. After the war
Ludendorff denied that 'dynastic considerations' played any role in this
decision, but von Kuhl noted in his diary that it was not possible to
exclude the Crown Prince from the great offensive.[23]

Ludendorff continually stressed that the first essential step was to
achieve a breakthrough. It was a question of tactics to decide at which
point on the front this was most likely to succeed. Once the breakthrough was achieved the operational objectives could be set. It was
hoped that a breakthrough would be possible between Péronne and
Arras. The 17th and 2nd Armies would then press on to the Channel
coast, the left flank being protected by 18th Army on the Somme. The
British and French Armies would thus be separated, and the British
Army forced back to the sea.

Here lay the fundamental weak of Ludendorff's plan. In his memoirs
he wrote that tactics were to be placed above strategy.[24] This was an
admission that the German Army was too weak to break through at
the point which offered the best opportunities for operational success, and would simply choose the point on the enemy front where it
was easiest to advance. Ludendorff claimed that this was to be a battle
which would annihilate the British Army, but he was prepared to settle
for a mere tactical victory since he admitted that it was unlikely that
a breakthrough was possible at the only spot that could be exploited
operationally. He told Crown Prince Rupprecht that he hoped that a
series of tactical defeats could possibly lead to a revolution in Paris or
London as had happened in Russia, but this was mere wishful thinking.
To base a vast military operation on such a distant hope was the height
of folly. Hindenburg also said that a series of blows might 'perhaps'
cause the enemy to collapse.[25] These were hardly the words of a master
strategist.

General von Kuhl clearly saw that 'Michael' had no operational goal,
and he was appalled at the prospect of fighting across the old 'Alberich'
positions which had been destroyed in 1917, and then on across the
battlefields of the Somme. He was also resentful that Crown Prince
Rupprecht had readily agreed to place von Hutier's army under the
command of the German Crown Prince. It was cold comfort that
the Bavarian Crown Prince soon realized that his chief of staff had
been quite right in warning of the unfortunate consequences of this

move. A further problem was General von Below. Although a forceful commander who had fought with distinction at Tannenberg and in Macedonia, had replaced Falkenhausen after the defeat at Vimy ridge and was the architect of the victory over the Italians at Caporetto, he was brusque, arrogant, unco-operative and exceedingly rude to Crown Prince Rupprecht.

The most difficult part of the operation was to be carried out by von Below's 17th Army. It was to attack in a south-westerly direction in order to nip off the Cambrai salient in conjunction with 2nd Army to the south and then change the direction of its advance to the north-west, in the direction of Arras and Albert. Speaking on behalf of Army Group Crown Prince Rupprecht, von Kuhl asked Ludendorff to strengthen 17th Army with troops from 18th Army, which was only playing a defensive role while 17th Army had an exceedingly difficult task ahead of it. Ludendorff refused on the grounds that he wanted 18th Army to ensure freedom of movement.[26] 'Mars' (17th Army's attack on Arras) would have to be postponed until 'Michael' had achieved its aims and the artillery could be brought up in support.

Given that the British position at Arras was exceptionally strong, that reserves would certainly be brought in and that it would be impossible to achieve any degree of surprise 'Mars' was a daunting prospect and 17th Army clearly needed some additional support if it were to have a reasonable chance of success.

Orders for 18th Army were somewhat vague. They were to guard the flank of the 'Michael' offensive by securing the bridgeheads across the Somme. It was suggested that it might be possible for it to advance in a south-westerly direction. The army was unnecessarily strong for a purely defensive role, and it would thus seem likely that Ludendorff was already considering a push to the south-west which would seriously compromise 'Michael's' chances of achieving its operational goals.

Due principally to the lack of artillery it would not be possible to launch any diversionary attacks. This was a serious weakness as an attack in Flanders would have made it exceedingly difficult for the British to release troops to strengthen the 'Michael' front. General von Kuhl was appalled when he heard that the attacks planned by 4th and 6th Armies would not take place. For him they were the essential precondition for 'Michael', since it was vitally important to pin down the British Army at Ypres and Armentières. Lack of artillery also meant that 'Michael I' would also be weakened and would not go as far as the Scarpe, where it was designed to provide protection to the flank near Arras. General von Kuhl once again urged Ludendorff to move troops from von Hutier's 18th Army to strengthen 'Michael I'. This proposal was rejected out of hand on the familiar grounds that von Hutier had to establish freedom of movement on the left flank of the offensive. Ludendorff then hinted that the offensive might be stopped and an attack made elsewhere. Such were Colonel Wetzell's 'hammer blow' tactics: attack, quickly regroup, and attack elsewhere. The major problem was that in operations on such a vast scale, and with limited resources, it was hardly possible to regroup quickly enough to catch the enemy by surprise.

Since surprise was essential to the success of the operation great care was taken to conceal the movements of men and material and the troops were kept in the dark as to the OHL's intentions. Special Security Officers were appointed at the divisional level who were responsible for watching the movement of troops and checking on camouflage. They also monitored telephone conversations and wireless transmissions to make sure that the correct code-words were used. The military police reported directly to the Security Officers on rumours circulating among the troops and on relations between the German Army and the French civilians, to make sure that no details of the forthcoming offensive had become common knowledge.

On 23 January Ludendorff reported to the Kaiser and on the next day orders were issued of the disposition of forces for the forthcoming offensive. Crown Prince Rupprecht's 17th Army was to undertake the left wing of a modified 'Mars' which, unlike von Kuhl's recommendation on 22 January, was now to straddle the Scarpe. 'Michael I' to the north-east of Bapaume was also entrusted to von Below. 'Michael II' was the responsibility of 2nd Army. 'Michael III' to the north and south of Saint Quentin was left to von Hutier's 18th Army under the German Crown Prince's Army Group. Von Boehn's 7th Army task was to attack south of the Oise in operation 'Archangel'.

The three 'Michael' offensives were to begin on 20 March, the flanking operations 'Mars' and 'Archangel' would start a few days later. The intent was to drive a broad wedge through the Allied lines from La Fère on the left wing to Péronne and then link up with 'Mars' so that the right flank would be at Arras. 'Archangel' was primarily designed as a diversionary attack to secure the high ground to the east of the Oise-Aisne canal. Should the 'Michael' offensive get stuck General von Einem's 3rd Army was to attack in the Champagne in operation 'Roland'. Planning for 'Saint George I' and 'Saint George II' went ahead and was completed by the beginning of April.

Crown Prince Rupprecht discussed 'Michael' with the staff of 18th Army at Avesnes on 20 January as a result of which he came to the conclusion that it would not be a decisive campaign. This was a matter of great concern as it was clear that the war could not be allowed to continue much longer. Furthermore Ludendorff's remarks to the effect that he was setting limited tactical goals for the offensive and would wait and see how the offensive developed before deciding how to proceed, were most disturbing. It was felt that this approach might have been appropriate against the Russian army, but that it was most unwise against the British and particularly against the operationally adept French.[27]

Crown Prince Rupprecht now realized that he should have listened to his chief of staff. He was now very upset that he had lost command of 18th Army, which was transferred to Army Group German Crown Prince. Not only would this mean that the OHL would be constantly interfering with operations if command over the attacking forces were thus divided, but the Crown Prince correctly assumed that this move implied an offensive south of the Somme. Crown Prince Rupprecht realized that such an offensive would be bound to fail, and would run counter to 'Michael'. It was an absurdity for the Germans to attack simultaneously in a north-westerly and a south-westerly direction. Somewhat late in the day he ordered von Kuhl to express these concerns to the OHL. The disingenuous reply was that 18th Army was to play a purely defensive role guarding the right flank of 'Michael' by only advancing as far as the Crozat Canal. This did not impress the Bavarian Crown Prince who was convinced that the German Crown Prince was being given an opportunity to mount an offensive that would enable him to restore his reputation which had been so badly tarnished at Verdun.[28] The appointment of von Hutier, an acknowledged expert in offensive warfare, to command 18th Army can only have confirmed Rupprecht's suspicions. He seriously doubted that the offensive would succeed and preferred an offensive against the Italians, which would put them out of the war. It might then be possible to concentrate on a final battle on the Western Front.

General von Kuhl did not share the OHL's reservations about 'Saint George' and continued to insist that 'Michael' had little chance of success unless British reserves were tied up by a diversionary action in Flanders. On 3 February Ludendorff met von Kuhl at Mons and told him that he could not spare the men and artillery needed for 'Saint George'. At best von Kuhl would only be able to mount limited 'demonstrations' against the British at Ypres and Armentières. Only if 'Michael' got stuck would it be possible to launch the 'Saint George' offensives, because the bulk of the British forces would be heavily engaged to the south.[29]

General von Kuhl concluded that the likelihood of 'Michael' succeeding was meagre owing to the serious lack of manpower. The OHL left 'Michael I' further deprived of manpower, leaving the right flank dangerously vulnerable. This in turn was due to the inability to conclude a peace in the east because of the excessive war aims of the OHL. Crown Prince Rupprecht was in full agreement with his chief of staff. The most that was likely to be achieved was that the Germans would create a salient, be forced to restored the Alberich defences which they had destroyed in the previous year, and they would then have to face the Americans.[30] Both Crown Prince Rupprecht and his chief of staff were thus very dubious indeed about the chances of success, and felt that only a stroke of luck would save the day. When they were told that if 'Michael' got stuck they should go ahead with 'Mars' they were convinced that Ludendorff had been listening to Wetzell, and that they would be called upon to deliver blow after pointless blow along the full length of the Western Front.[31]

The OHL was well aware of the manpower shortage facing the German army. Those born in 1898 were mobilized in 1917 and the 1899 recruits were already being trained. Hindenburg and Ludendorff made repeated efforts, beginning in 1916, to extend the age of service to sixty but this was refused by successive chancellors and the War Ministry. In the three months of fighting from May to July 1918 the German Army on the Western Front faced a deficit of 300,000 men.[32] This had been predicted and thus came as no surprise. The readiness of German soldiers to surrender and the increasing number of deserters and scrimshankers was an additional problem which was caused in large part by the realization by all ranks by the summer of 1918 that the war could not possibly be won and therefore had to be ended as soon as possible.

A major problem was the bitter struggle between the army and industry, which was continued, in the post-war literature. The army needed men and it needed armaments and munitions. Industry needed skilled workers to meet the army's demands. The army accused industry of holding back men that should have been fighting at the front. Industry accused the army of making unreasonable demands and insisted that they needed the workers.[33]

The shortage of manpower was used as an argument for rather than against an offensive. Storm-troop tactics meant that losses tended to be less in attack than in defence. Given that the Americans were arriving in ever increasing numbers Germany had no hope of fighting a protracted defensive war. The war had to be ended as soon as possible and thus an offensive was the only feasible course of action.

It was not until 9 February that the OHL decided precisely what form the offensive should take. They ordered that 'Michael' was to be the main thrust, to be followed by a modified form of 'Saint George'.[34] It was now suggested that if the British moved a sufficient number of men south to meet 'Michael' that 'George I' and '*Hasenjagd*' (hare hunt), either side of Armentières, might go ahead supported by '*Waldfest*' (forest festival) which would attack the Ypres salient from the north-west. This was seen as an acceptance of Colonel Wetzell's 'hammer blow' strategy of attacking first in one place and then in another.[35] General von Kuhl argued that if large numbers of British reserves were removed from Flanders to meet the threat from 'Michael' it would not be possible to disengage and move men and equipment quickly to Flanders for 'George'. The movement of artillery from 'Michael' to 'George' would also be a major problem. He continued to insist that a diversionary attack in Flanders in support of 'Michael' was much more likely to be successful.[36]

The planners in Army Crown Prince Rupprecht were very concerned that the right flank of the 'Michael' offensive was dangerously exposed to a counter-attack. They therefore begged Ludendorff to move the right wing of the offensive up to the river Scarpe which would provide excellent protection from the British troops to the north. Once again Ludendorff replied that the lack of men and artillery made this impossible. A successful advance on the right could however be supported by 'Mars – Left Wing' to secure the Scarpe. Requests by the Army Group Rupprecht to have the full control over the forces allotted to 'Mars' to be used at their discretion were denied by the OHL. General von Below's 17th Army would have to protect its right flank by Arras to the best of its ability. General Krafft von Dellmensingen, von Below's chief of staff, protested bitterly against this decision. General Sixt von Arnim, who commanded 4th Army, begged Crown Prince Rupprecht to complain to the OHL that he was being swamped with contradictory orders, which were far too detailed and made no allowances for local difficulties.[37]

In a series of further discussions Ludendorff stressed the importance of tactical co-operation between the left wing of 17th Army and the right of General von der Marwitz's 2nd Army in order to destroy the British forces in the Cambrai salient. In his view the success of the 'Michael' offensive depended on the success of this operation, and he continued to stress its importance. Von Kuhl's somewhat exasperated staff pointed out that this operation had already been studied in detail and orders given to both armies.

Von Hutier's chief of staff, General von Sauberzweig, pointed out in mid-January that the 18th Army would be able to reach the Somme and the Crozat Canal within two to three days. They were then to take up a defensive position while all reserves would support a north-westerly thrust towards Péronne. At the beginning of February this clear plan was changed. The new version had no obvious *Schwerpunkt*. On the left flank the attack at La Fère was designed to draw Allied reserves away from the main thrust of 'Michael'. Troops would Cross the Crozat Canal and advance south-west to the Oise. Ludendorff endorsed this proposal and offered 18th Army some additional battalions of light infantry (*Jäger*) to increase the chances of a successful advance at La Fère.[38]

By this time Crown Prince Rupprecht believed that peace had to be made with England. He was convinced that this was both necessary and possible. The German economy was in dire straits and the manpower shortage was acute. On the other hand there was some indication that the British were concerned that the longer the war lasted the more they would lose ground to the Americans. Furthermore they were concerned that Bolshevism would spread across Europe if the war continued. He felt that all that was needed was for Germany to make a clear and unambiguous statement that Belgium would be restored to its former frontiers and that this would then remove the *casus belli* with Britain. A visit to Munich in late February to attend his parents' golden wedding confirmed his fears, and he was appalled at the starry-eyed confidence of many civilians that the forthcoming offensive would be a resounding success.[39]

While in Munich Crown Prince Rupprecht talked to the Kaiser and expressed his serious reservations about the offensive. When he stated that he doubted whether it would be possible to achieve a decisive breakthrough the Kaiser blandly replied that this was not Ludendorff's intention. The idea was to deliver the enemy a series of blows that would weaken him seriously. Rupprecht doubted whether the German Army had the manpower to deliver a series of attacks, and in any case this strategy could not result in a decisive victory.

The Kaiser laboured under the curious illusion that the Flemish-speaking Belgians would like to be incorporated into the German Reich, and that their French speaking compatriots could be handed over to the French. Although there had been a number of desertions by Flemings from the Belgian Army, Rupprecht knew that the Kaiser was living in a fantasy world and nothing short of the full restoration of Belgium would be acceptable to the Entente.[40]

The Kaiser was accompanied in Munich by General von Plessen, the hot-headed chief of his *maison militaire*, and by General von Lyncker, the subservient head of his military cabinet. Rupprecht told both men that he feared that all the spring offensive would achieve would be to make a dent in the enemy's front, and that at an appalling cost.[41] This warning made no impression on these two stalwart armchair warriors.

On 11 February Ludendorff received a lengthy memorandum from Friedrich Naumann, chairman of the German Democratic Party (DDP), along with his colleagues Professor Jäckh and the industrialist Dr Robert Bosch.[42] They argued that if Germany were to make an unambiguous declaration that Belgium should be fully restored to its pre-war frontiers Lloyd George would have to announce that he was continuing the war for the sake of Alsace-Lorraine. This would undermine the fighting spirit of the British Army. Peace now would save the reputation of the army, but if it were felt that the OHL was insisting on the continuation of the war for annexationist aims the country could well fall apart.

On 7 March General von Sauberzweig discussed the question of the left flank of the 'Michael' offensive with Ludendorff at a meeting in Mons. He requested permission to cross the Somme, arguing that this would draw further French troops away from the *Schwerpunkt* of the offensive and serve to divide the French and British armies. Ludendorff enthusiastically endorsed this suggestion and said that 18th Army could cross the Crozat Canal and the Somme at places where they would not meet with serious resistance.[43]

Thus by the beginning of March plans for the 'Michael' offensive had some serious weaknesses. The right wing was dangerously exposed and was vulnerable to counter-attack. On the left it was proposed to push in a south-westerly direction, thus running the risk of weakening the *Schwerpunkt* of the attack which was in a north-westerly direction towards the Channel.[44]

Hindenburg issued final orders in 10 March.[45] The offensive was to begin on 21 March. The first tactical objective was for Army Group Crown Prince Rupprecht to trap the British in the Cambrai salient. They were then to push on so that the left wing would be on the Somme at Péronne. The 4th and 6th Armies would back up the right wing. 18th Army was to secure bridgeheads over the Crozat Canal and the Somme. The right flank was to push forward to Péronne. The left wing of 18th Army was likely to be strengthened by units from 7th, 1st and 3rd Armies. Planning was to proceed for 'Mars' and 'Archangel', but it would depend on the progress of operations whether these attacks were to go ahead. Army Group Crown Prince Rupprecht was responsible for protecting the right flank of the offensive. Army Group German Crown Prince would withdraw in the face of a massive French attack on 7th Army, except on the 'Archangel' front. The remaining Armies would undertake the feints outlined in the OHL's orders of 4 March 1918. These included attacks on the 'Saint George' front between Reims and Varennes by 1st and 3rd Armies, by Army Group Gallwitz around Verdun and by Army Group Duke Albrecht in Alsace and Lorraine. Massive artillery bombardments on the 'Saint George' and 'Archangel' fronts immediately before the 'Michael' offensive were designed to further confuse the enemy. Paris was to be shelled by long-distance artillery in order to impress the civilian population and undermine morale, and the Luftwaffe was to bomb the French Channel ports. To maintain the highest level of secrecy all troops should be led to believe that they were taking part in the decisive push. Further measures with regard to Army Groups Gallwitz and Duke Albrecht would be taken by the OHL according to the given situation. The OHL also retained direct control over the 2nd Guards Light Infantry, the 26th Württemberg Light Infantry and the 12th Light Infantry Divisions.

The Austro-Hungarian army had released some heavy artillery but felt unable to send any men to take part in the offensive. Therefore on 15 March the OHL begged the Austrians to mount yet another offensive against the Italians in order to take some of the pressure off the Western Front. Wetzell urged Ludendorff to release between six and eight divisions to support the Austrian offensive. Ludendorff refused to grant this request on the grounds that it was imperative not to weaken the German position on the Western Front.[46]

In spite of all this detailed planning Ludendorff stressed that the actual course of the campaign could not be determined until the enemy was engaged. 17th Army was impatient with this vague approach and requested that the three divisions under the direct command of the OHL should be placed under its command on the first day of the offensive. Army Group Crown Prince Rupprecht seconded this request. Ludendorff did not want to lose control over these divisions, but after some heated discussions it was agreed that they should stationed around Douai and be ready to support 'Mars' should the right flank of 'Michael' make satisfactory progress.

Ludendorff now began to consider moving the right flank further north so that it would straddle the Scarpe, take Vimy Ridge and encircle the British forces in Arras. The Staff of Army Group Crown Prince Rupprecht agreed in principle but argued that the right flank of 'Michael' south of the Scarpe would first have to reach the high ground to the south-east of Arras and thus tie down the British before it would be possible to push forward north of the river. They repeated the request that the three OHL divisions should support this initial thrust south of the Scarpe. Ludendorff somewhat surprisingly agreed and in doing so emphasized the fact that the *Schwerpunkt* of 'Michael' would be the right wing.

Reports from von der Marwitz's 2nd Army that the British had strengthened their positions on this section of the front and appeared to be expecting an attack persuaded Ludendorff to set less ambitious goals for this army. He urged von Hutier's 18th Army to press forward on von der Marwitz's left flank and to swing north-west in the direction of Beauvais, Tertry and Péronne. The direction of the offensive was thus clearly in a north-westerly direction towards Arras. Ludendorff complained bitterly that von der Marwitz had not brought sufficient bridging equipment forward to cross the Somme. The unfortunate general pointed out that his previous orders did not require him to cross the river, and hence he had no need for bridging equipment. The Army Group then ordered 4th and 17th Armies to send the missing equipment to 2nd Army.[47]

Von Hutier was far from delighted to be given the task of protecting von der Marwitz's flank while von Below's 17th Army reaped much of the glory. He therefore proposed crossing the Crozat Canal and the Somme and mounting a series of offensives against the French, who were likely to move up to support their British allies and then establish a defensive position on the Oise and the high ground to the west of Noyon. He estimated that in spite of the diversionary attacks on their section of the front large numbers of French troops would be sent by rail from Amiens to the Oise and that these could easily be defeated while they were being deployed.

Army Group German Crown Prince was impressed by von Hutier's arguments but correctly left the final decision to Ludendorff. He was now in a serious quandary on the eve of the offensive. In the conference at Mons on 7 March and in the orders of 10 March 18th Army had been given the task of protecting the left flank of 'Michael'. Bridgeheads were to be established over the Crozat Canal and the Somme in order to threaten French troops that were moving up to support the British. Now he was presented with plausible arguments that threats were not enough and that an offensive stance that was clearly designed to protect the flank was a far more satisfactory solution. But the risk was very great that the original role would be forgotten, that a battle would develop between the Somme and the Oise that would divert effort away from the essential task of defeating the British. The Germans would then be dividing their efforts in an attempt to score victories over both the British and the French. This could not be done with the forces available to them.

The most serious weakness of Ludendorff's strategy was that he forgot the fundamental Clausewitzian principle that behind every strategy there must be a clear political aim. Given that a decisive victory over the Entente was highly improbable Ludendorff assumed that the best that could be achieved was to deliver a series of blows that would a make the enemy prepared to negotiate a peace. But his minimal peace terms were so hopelessly unrealistic that neither Britain nor France would ever accept them. Ludendorff still dreamt of a victory that would achieve his exotic war aims when only a compromise peace offer had the remotest chance of being acceptable.

In February the Democratic Reichstag member Conrad Haussmann gained permission from the Chancellor to spend a few days in Switzerland to sound out neutral and Entente opinion. In the course of this trip he met the distinguished military historian Hermann Stegemann, who handed him a memorandum in which he argued that the most a German offensive could possibly achieve would be to seize Amiens and Reims. This would make the Entente even more determined to resist, and thus a negotiated peace would be impossible. Stegemann insisted that the Germans should use the threat of an offensive to begin peace talks and that Germany would have to agree to the complete restoration of Belgium. Haussmann was in complete agreement and forwarded Stegemann's memorandum to the Secretary of State for Foreign Afffairs, Richard von Kühlmann, with a covering note arguing that a successful offensive would make peace even less likely than the threat of an attack at a time when German superiority was generally acknowledged.[48]

Haussmann's views were echoed in a remarkably frank and forceful article in the liberal *Frankfurter Zeitung* in mid-February. It blamed the OHL and its supporters in the ultra-conservative *Vaterlandspartei* for the alarming decline in morale which had culminated in the wave of strikes in January and February. The newspaper argued that the vast majority were willing to fight on to defend Germany, but they were not prepared to continue to sacrifice their lives for the annexation of the Baltic States, Belgium or the coal fields of Briey. Confidence could only be restored by an unambiguous declaration that Germany was fighting a purely defensive war and had no territorial demands. The sacrifices required for the success of the widely rumoured forthcoming offensive on the Western Front would only be willingly made if it was clear that its political aim was to achieve a peace based on the *status quo ante bellum*. Subsequent events were to show how wise these words were.

The OHL held a diametrically opposite view. They believed that only if the Entente were to suffer a crushing defeat could they be persuaded to begin peace talks on terms which Hindenburg and Ludendorff would set. But there were precious few who believed that this was remotely possible.

On the eve of the offensive Ludendorff expressed the hope that if the initial breakthrough was successful the 17th Army should press on to Saint Pol, the 2nd Army reach the line from Doullens to Amiens and 18th Army head for the Oise at Noyon. [49] If von Hutier met stiff resistance from the French troops, 2nd Army could be sent to his assistance. Ludendorff was now taking a very serious gamble. For months he had been arguing that his forces were barely sufficient for a successful offensive against the British and that all efforts had to be directed to the 'Michael' front. Now he was throwing strategic caution to the winds and was thinking of delivering decisive blows against both the British and the French. It was a hazardous *va banque* play which many experienced staff officers felt had precious little chance of success. [50] The troops had been very well trained and looked forward to the fight. Rudolf Binding wrote on the eve of the offensive: 'The preparations are quite inconceivable in detail, and can only be described as the last word.'[51] Trooper Hans Spiess of 5th Reserve Light Cavalry Regiment told his sister that he had never seen such elaborate preparations for an offensive, and he felt that with a bit of luck the success in Russia would be followed a victory on the Western Front. But he complained about the lack of decent food, and only hoped that he would survive the offensive, remarking that his life was more important to him than an Iron Cross. [52] The great historian Gerhard Ritter, who was then a young officer in 18th Army on the front near Saint Quentin, was far less sanguine. He noted the general optimism, but he also was deeply concerned about the inadequate logistics, the lack of transport, the half-starved horses, and the poorly trained, exhausted troops under his command. How could such an army possibly destroy the enemy and achieve a total victory?[53] Hindenburg and Ludendorff, far away from the front, remained fully confident that the offensive would be successful. Their optimism was infectious and when the attack began on 21 March the German army moved forward in the belief that victory would soon be theirs.

3

The Allies:
January-March 1918

Major-General F.B. Maurice, the Director of Military Operations, reported at the beginning of January that the Germans had moved eleven new divisions to the Western Front since October, bringing the total to 157, which was double the number of the year before. There were regular reports of further troop movements so that by 22 January it was estimated that there were now between 170 and 175 divisions. CIGS, General Sir W.R.Robertson, felt that the Germans were adopting an offensive stance. The Director of Military Intelligence, Major-General Sir G.M.W. MacDonogh reported that some sixty-three divisions along with the artillery were undergoing special training. The French military attaché in Spain reported that the King had heard that the Germans were planning a major offensive. And yet the British Army watched the steady increase in the number of German divisions on the Western Front in January 1918 with a certain degree of equanimity.[1]

There were two principal reasons for this lack of any sense of urgency. In the first place, given the internal situation in Germany with a wave of strikes in the munitions industry, along with the usual bad weather in Flanders, where the attack was expected, it was estimated that nothing would happen for several months.[2] Haig was convinced that the Germans would stick to limited attacks on the Western Front during 1918.[3] Military Intelligence also claimed that the estimates of a massive build-up of German forces on the Western Front were greatly exaggerated. It was pointed out that their divisions had been reorganized and battalions reduced from 1,000 to 750 men, and that the total number of divisions had probably been over-estimated. The Director of Military Intelligence also did not anticipate an imminent attack. He also expected an offensive east of Reims, and thus on the French sector. The other possibility he entertained was an attack between Arras and the Argonne. In either case the British Army in Flanders would not be put to the test. The CIGS was not quite so confident. He estimated that German battalions were now 850 men, and pointed out that the French had reduced their battalions to 750 men.[4] The Minister of War, Lord Derby and Rawlinson, who was temporarily in command of the Second Army in Flanders during Plumer's secondment to the Italian front, warned Haig that if he continued to make reassuring remarks about the German threat it would be all the more difficult to get the government to authorize a sufficient number of recruits. Haig promptly changed his tune, but it was too late. The civilians now felt that he was simply crying wolf.

The British were also very slow in learning any lessons from the Cambrai counter-attack in which the Germans had used their infiltration tactics to great effect. The Cambrai Court of Enquiry did not examine the reasons for German success which was the result of a combination of an intense initial barrage, surprise, the weight of the attack and the skilful use of storm-troop tactics. A document entitled 'Lessons of Cambrai Counter Attack' began to circulate in mid-January at Rawlinson's insistence. As early as 3 January General Smuts had warned the War Cabinet that the Germans were very likely to use the same tactics on a much larger scale, but this admonition was largely ignored in the BEF.[5]

On 24 January at the insistence of General Robertson, Pétain, Foch and Haig met at the French headquarters in Compiègne to discuss the situation on the Western Front.[6] Both men agreed that their armies should stay on the defensive, whereupon Foch chipped in that planning should begin for a series of counter-attacks to meet all possible eventualities, and their eyes should be set on the 'final battle'. Pétain was sceptical, and Haig remained silent. Pétain then said that his front was weak ('*sensible*') in Alsace, around Nancy, in the Champagne and from the Aisne to Reims. Haig, who in December had been arguing for an offensive in Flanders as early as February, even if the Germans transferred as many as thirty divisions from the Eastern Front, remarked that his entire front was vulnerable and the only place he could retire was on his right flank near St Quentin.[7] Foch continued to plead for counter-offensives. Haig sourly interjected that only if he were able to bring British troops back from Salonika could Foch have his offensives. Foch immediately protested that he was talking about counter-attacks and not an offensive. The three men could agree on one thing: the Americans were being painfully slow in bringing their troops across to France. Pershing had promised that there would be eighteen Divisions in France by July, but would that be too little too late?

Haig's relationship with Lloyd George was even worse than it was with Foch or Pétain. Haig suspected that the Prime Minister wanted to get rid of him but lacked the courage to do so. This resulted in the most unfortunate and inexcusable situation in which Lloyd George pursued a devious and disingenuous middle way between sacking Haig and giving him all the support he needed. Haig too did not come clean. He did not provide the Prime Minister with a clear and unambiguous account of the situation facing the BEF, and did not put his job on the line when Lloyd George dug in his heels. Instead of a productive dialogue between the civilians and the military there was backbiting intrigue, distrust and downright antagonism.

Haig managed to convince himself that Lloyd George was hell-bent on turning Britain into a republic, and in order to do so had to discredit the army leadership and hand over control of the military to civilians. In early March 1918 he told his wife that if he 'reorganized' the House of Commons with the support of the Army and the press he would be immensely popular.[8]

Lloyd George for his part also saw Haig as a pocket Napoleon or mini Boulanger. He went as far as to suggest that Haig and Robertson hoped to overthrow the government and bring the new administration under the Army's control. He therefore decided to get rid of both of them. Robertson's days were numbered, and General Smuts was sent to the Western Front in January 1918 to scout around for a suitable replacement for Haig. Plumer, Rawlinson and Jacob came under consideration, but none of them were felt to be significantly better soldiers than Haig. The commander-in-chief still enjoyed the confidence of most senior commanders, and were he to be sacked there was likely to be a public uproar at home. Lloyd George therefore hoped that, with Wilson as CIGS and with a Supreme War Council at Versailles, Haig's wings would be sufficiently clipped.

On 25 January Pétain wrote to Haig asking him to co-operate in working out the details of joint action should the Germans attack.[9] Haig was very short of manpower, and was obliged to reduce the size of his divisions from twelve to nine battalions, a task rendered even more daunting by the impossibility of violating army tradition and abolishing regular battalions. Nevertheless 171 battalions were abolished and two of the five cavalry divisions were sent to Egypt. The British Army had sixty-two divisions on the Western Front in the summer of 1917, they now had only fifty-eight Divisions, and all of them were considerably smaller. As they braced themselves for the forthcoming battle they were painfully aware of an alarming shortage of reserves. Haig had manoeuvred himself into a difficult position. He tried to convince the Cabinet that he had seriously weakened the enemy as a result of his offensive in 1917, but at the same time he was clamouring for more men. He was determined not to surrender any of his freedom of action to the French, and yet he knew that he was likely to have to call upon them for support. News of the mounting threat to Third and Fifth Armies' front increased his uneasiness.

The question of manpower on the Western Front remains a matter of some controversy.[10] It would seem that the BEF had about 70,000 fewer fighting men on 1 January 1918 than on the same date in 1917. Since there were 1,077,343 fighting men in January 1917 this represents a reduction of less than seven per cent. This could well have been offset by increased firepower, as was the case in the German Army, and as Foch advocated. But this was resisted by the traditionalists at GHQ, who were also very sceptical of Churchill, who as minister of munitions proposed to rely more on technology than on manpower and concentrate on the production of aircraft, tanks, trench mortars and gas. GHQ resistance to the new technology prompted Lieutenant-Colonel J.F.C. Fuller, its most outspoken advocate, to refer to Douglas Haig as 'Dunder Headed' or a 'Military Trappist'. He christened his CGS, Major-General Sir Lancelot Kiggell, 'Ethelred the Unready'. General Wigram of the Operations Branch (OB) at GHQ became the 'Obsolete One'.[11]

Pétain gave General Humbert's III Army the task of working out the details of eventual support for the BEF on his left flank. Lieutenant-General Sir A. Hamilton Gordon was assigned to draw up plans for the relief of French forces. In the course of a series of meetings and numerous exchanges of memoranda the French concluded that their intervention in the British zone was highly probable, 'both intellectually and materially', but they concluded that GHQ remained sceptical about a counter-attack should the Germans break through. GQG was hardly more enthusiastic. Only Foch continued to insist that planning should go ahead for a combined counter-attack and for a 'joint offensive with clear goals'.

Details of co-operation between the British and the French Armies were completed by 15 March. Were the British to be attacked, the first echelon of Humbert's III Army, comprising six divisions, would be ready within four days to operate between Montdidier and Noyon, astride the Somme, or to the west of Arras. The second echelon would be sent as quickly as possible, depending on the state of the battle. GHQ assured the French that they could hold on for these vital four days.[12]

General Smuts, whose council was highly regarded in Whitehall, was very much concerned about the weakness of the Portuguese divisions on the Lys, and CIGS ordered an investigation into this weak spot on the front. Haig took the matter in hand, but acted in such a dilatory manner that the relief of the Portuguese was still not completed when the Germans attacked on the Lys in April.[13]

At a meeting of the Allied Supreme War Council at Versailles on 30 January 1918 there was general agreement that defensive and counter-offensive actions had to be carefully co-ordinated.[14] The British and

French commanders-in-chief agreed that they lacked the necessary manpower to mount any large-scale offensive. Pétain reiterated this point two days later when he told the Council that an offensive should not even be considered unless the effectives were forthcoming.[15] He preferred to wait for the Americans and for more tanks.[16]

Foch repeated the suggestions he had made at Compiègne during a meeting of the Supreme War Council held between 30 January and 2 February at Versailles with Clemenceau in the chair. Cadorna and Bliss expressed their approval. The CIGS, 'Wully' Robertson, the first ranker ever to have reached this exalted position and seen as an enthusiastic supporter of Haig's 'Western' strategy, also agreed, but suggested that the commanders-in-chief should first be heard. He was not to stay in office much longer. In February the champion of the Western Front was given command in Eastern England, having refused the post of British Permanent Military Representative at Versailles. Some felt that this was a deliberate joke at his expense. His place was taken by Sir Henry Wilson whom Lloyd George hoped would be more pliant. The Prime Minister was soon complaining that Wilson was also obsessed with the Western Front and was 'Wully *redivivus*', but at least he found the new CIGS a far more congenial colleague and enjoyed his sense of humour.[17] Haig was not particularly upset by Robertson's dismissal. He had come to the conclusion that Robertson was not sufficiently resolute in his support of the Western strategy, and had allowed valuable resources to be frittered away on distant theatres at the bidding of his political masters.[18] Milner, who was to become minister of war in April 1918, felt that Wilson's principal weakness was his determination to avoid any unpleasantness with his fellow soldiers.

Haig insisted that he was suffering from a serious lack of manpower after the bloodletting of Passchendaele which had left him with only thirty-five divisions. He also pointed out that it would not be possible to count on much help from the Americans in 1918. British divisions were trained for nine months at home, and then spent six further months in France on a quiet sector of the front. Thus the British and French armies would have to bear the full weight of any German offensive.

Pétain was in full agreement with the British commander-in chief. He pointed out that the French were as desperately short-handed as the British, whereupon Lloyd George expressed his surprise and demanded that exact figures be provided. These were made available the following day and the Prime Minister used them to argue that although the Allies were numerically inferior to the Germans on the Western Front, there was a sufficient number of divisions for the defensive. The Allies should therefore concentrate on knocking Turkey out of the war.

Clemenceau objected vigorously to Lloyd George's proposal. It would be hazardous, he growled, for the British to embark on 'distant expeditions' in search of 'a victory on the Euphrates', when the Germans were about to launch a massive offensive. Furthermore the campaign against the Turks was a purely British affair.

Clemenceau won the day and the conference concluded with a complete rejection of Lloyd George's proposal. The British government was obliged to promise not to send any more troops from the Western Front to the Middle East, and assured their ally that they would do everything in their power to secure the common front.[19]

In order to make the Entente's defences more effective the Council agreed on 3 February to the formation of a general reserve. This was a major set-back for Field Marshal Haig who felt that it was essential to go on the offensive in Flanders in 1918 in order the clear the coast, an objective which he had spectacularly failed to attain at Passchendaele the previous year.[20] Furthermore Haig wanted to have full control over his own reserves, and was thus determined to block any attempt to create a reserve army under a single command. Pétain also objected to the idea of leaving decisions as to how the reserves should be allotted to the representatives at Versailles

There were a number of problems involved with the formation of the General Reserve which strengthened Haig's belief that the scheme was unworkable. First and foremost there were very limited reserves to draw upon. Then there was the vexed problem of how it should be organized. Eventually the Council decided that an executive committee should be formed under General Foch, make up of the permanent military representatives of France, Britain, Italy and the United States.[21]

At the first meeting of the Executive Committee, which promptly accorded itself the rather more martial title of Executive War Board, it was agreed to form a general reserve of thirty divisions. This was too small a force to be effective, and too large to have any likelihood of ever being formed. Whereas armies normally allocated one third or one quarter of the total number of divisions to the reserve, thirty divisions was only one seventh of aggregate French, British and Italian divisions.[22] On the other side of the equation both Haig and Pétain resisted allocating any of their divisions to the General Reserve. They insisted that a German attack was imminent and that they could not withdraw any of their divisions without seriously compromising their defences. Pétain argued that a General Reserve was superfluous since should the British be attacked the French would immediately send reserves to their support, and he was fully confident that Haig would do the same should the Germans turn against the French. Although there was mounting evidence that the Germans were about to attack, the Supreme War Council caved in to the generals, and the general reserve was never formed.

The Supreme War Council had no sense of urgency because it was convinced, as was the French General Staff, that the Germans intended to attack in Flanders and would thus wait until May or June for the dry weather. Pétain's staff and the General Staff in London did not agree with this assessment. They felt that given the mounting unrest on the home front in both Germany and Austria-Hungary, and with the imminent arrival of large numbers of Americans in Europe, they would strike in March.[23]

The argument continued as to where the Germans would strike. The French were particularly concerned about Paris. The British pointed out that it was eighty miles from the German front to the French capital, whereas it was only fifty to the Channel ports which, were they to fall into the hands of the Germans, would be an unmitigated disaster. Haig's headquarters' staff therefore argued that the Germans would strike first between the Oise and the Scarpe against the British Third and Fifth Armies. They would set a limited objective such as capturing the Cambrai salient or Vimy Ridge, and then, when the British reserves were exhausted, they would strike in Flanders.[24]

Haig was therefore determined to concentrate on strengthening the Flanders front, thus protecting the Channel ports which were the essential lifeline of the BEF. General Gough, commanding Fifth Army, insisted that his forces were too thin on the ground and his defences too poor for him to be able to withstand the initial attack. He persistently called for more labour and more men to rectify this dangerous situation. Davidson, head of operations at GHQ, told Gough that such shortcomings could be overcome by the 'skilful handling of rearguards', to which Gough retorted: 'I do wish Davidson wouldn't always think it necessary to teach his grandmother to suck eggs.'[25] Haig's chief of staff, Lawrence, was even more patronizing to Gough and spoke of: 'Young Goughie, who seems to think that we have an inexhaustible source of soldiers.' When Gough complained to Haig that Byng's Third Army had far more troops relative to the length of its front Haig replied that Pétain had promised him to send in his reserves in the event of an attack, and that General Humbert had reassured him that his III Army would help out immediately.[26]

Gough came from a distinguished military family. His father, his uncle and his brother had all won the V.C., but he had enemies in high places because of his staunch opposition to Irish Home Rule, and his leading role in the Curragh Mutiny of 1914. He was widely unpopular with his arrogant manner, his slipshod methods, his lack of attention to detail, and above all his seemingly total disregard for the lives of his soldiers. Haig had chosen him to lead the attack at Passchendaele in 1917 because of his cavalryman's dash, but the result was a disaster. The War Minister, Lord Derby, wrote to Haig in early March pointing out quite correctly that Gough did not enjoy the confidence of the troops he commanded. The Prime Minister had received numerous complaints about him, and he was attacked from all sides, both civilian and military. Lloyd George informed Haig that he could fire Gough whenever he wished.[27]

Lord Derby and Wilson were among his strongest critics. Many soldiers remembered his disregard for their lives and referred to him as the 'Butcher' of the Somme and Passchendaele and dreaded a posting to Fifth Army. Whether original or not Haig said of him that he was a 'genial Judas' who 'like a cushion wears the imprint of the last arse that sat on him'.[28] But Haig and Robertson continued to support him, until Haig found him to be a useful scapegoat.

When Haig visited Fifth Army on 7 March Gough complained that the British Army was far stronger in the north than to the south. Haig replied that a defeat in the north would be far more damaging than in the south. He might lose the Channel ports of Dunkirk, Calais and Boulogne and that could mean the end of the war. In the south he had room to manœuvre.[29]

On 19 March, two days before the Germans attacked, Gough spoke to Herbert Lawrence on the telephone. He refused Gough's request to bring up the 50th (Northumbrian) Division and the 20th (Light) Division, and then launched into a condescending disquisition 'on the conduct of military operations in accordance with the teachings of the masters' purring the while 'like a damned cat'. Gough replied that he would 'fight the blighters in (his) battle zone as long as we can hold them there'.[30]

Pétain was far more concerned about the threat posed to Gough's army than was Haig, especially when von Hutier, a leading expert on offensive warfare, was placed in command of 18th Army to the south of the Cambrai salient. As early as 20 January 1918 the French commander-in-chief was considering sending up to forty divisions, almost half the effective strength of the BEF, to prop up his allies from the Oise to the North Sea within fifteen days of a German attack.[31] In the initial phase of the offensive he intended to send a number of divisions to help meet the immediate crisis, then if the Germans managed to break through the British front, or if they simply ran out of steam, he would launch a counter-attack with all available forces.

Foch was most concerned about the lack of reserves, particularly behind the British front where an attack seemed to be most likely. He therefore suggested to Robertson that British divisions should be brought back from Italy where Allied forces greatly outnumbered the enemy. Robertson agreed and two infantry divisions plus a squadron of aircraft were sent from Italy to France on 1 March.[32]

This proved to be only a partial victory for Foch. Neither Haig nor Pétain accepted the need for a General Reserve, and refused to entertain the idea of the Executive War Board having any say in how they were to fight their battles. Pétain was able to secure a significant reduction in the number of French divisions allotted to the general reserve. Haig announced that he had no intention whatsoever of modifying his plans in order to please the Executive War Board. He enjoyed the full support of public opinion which vociferously demanded that the British Army should remain independent and not place its fate in the hands of untrustworthy foreigners.

Two Anglo-French conferences at Nesle and Compiègne on 21 and 22 February resulted in an agreement whereby the French agreed initially to send six infantry divisions either to support Gough's Fifth Army, the most likely eventuality, or send them to some other point on the front. Further divisions would be released according to the development of the battle. The British reluctantly agreed to send a maximum of six divisions to help out the French VI Army on their immediate right. Should the French counter-attack the British agreed to send up to eight divisions to help out. The decisions of these two conferences were 'endorsed', in Clemenceau's words, at the London Conference on 14 and 15 March.[33]

By this time Lloyd George, having been violently attacked in the House of Commons over the decisions made by the Supreme War Council, had come to accept Haig's argument that the British Army could not spare any divisions for a General Reserve since it appeared that a major German offensive was imminent. Clemenceau announced that Pétain took precisely the same view, and that therefore mutual co-operation should take the place of forming a General Reserve. With some regrets Orlando and Bliss agreed that it would not be appropriate to form a general reserve at this critical juncture.

Foch was furious and complained bitterly that his Executive War Council was deprived of all authority. At a time when the Allies were expecting an attack at any moment, all attempts to co-ordinate efforts were being stifled. Lloyd George pointed out that the Supreme War Council in Versailles was kept in ignorance of the details of the plans of the French and British Armies. The question remained whether the enemy would grant the Allies enough time to rebuild a unified command, which had been abandoned almost as soon as it had been partially realized.

The French felt that these provisions were hopelessly inadequate, and took no account of the gravity of the situation. They felt that Pétain's Directive Number 4, which called for a defence in depth, based largely on the German model, combined with vigorous counter-attacks, was the recipe for success.[34] They were convinced that the British lacked the defensive skill, the moral determination and the offensive spirit adequately to meet the German threat.[35]

Clemenceau, the feisty seventy-six-year-old who in 360 days as wartime premier spent ninety with the troops and was thus hugely popular, hardly needed Foch's prompting to find Directive Number 4 unsatisfactory and ambiguous. He complained to Pétain that there were ambiguities in the plan that could well lead to a neglect of the first position, since it was implied that it was unlikely to offer much resistance. He insisted that all three lines should offer the maximum degree of resistance, and added that the British had virtually nothing behind their front line.[36] The French Premier thus betrayed his total ignorance of the basic principles of a flexible defence, and like Foch believed that not a centimetre of the sacred soil of France should be yielded to the Boche.

There was also a difference of opinion between GHQ and GQG as to where the German blow would fall. The British were convinced that it would be on their front, the French that the main offensive would be in the Champagne. French suspicions were strengthened when they shot down a German balloon on 20 March in which were found plans for an attack between Reims and Les Monts to begin on 26 March.[37] This confusion was an accurate reflection of the debates within the German leadership as to whether to attack in Flanders, on the Somme, or in the Champagne. The Deuxième Bureau, French military intelligence, calculated the point at which the Germans would attack the British Army with remarkable accuracy, but they were deeply concerned that the main thrust would be in the neighbourhood of Reims.[38]

By the end of February British Military Intelligence estimated that the Germans would attack at any time from the beginning of the next month, by which time the cadres would be full. Then it was felt that they would not be fully ready until the second week on March. They accurately calculated that the attack would come between Arras and Péronne, but a build-up of forces on the line from Soissons to Reims was also noted. Haig, with his obsession with Flanders and the Channel ports, estimated that the attack would be extended further north, and asked that General Plumer be returned from Italy to resume the command of Second Army in Flanders. The Cabinet granted this request: 'In view of the serious events anticipated on the Western Front, they could not refuse Sir Douglas Haig's request.' It proved to be a wise move.[39]

Haig finally accepted the arguments put forward by his intelligence staff and by the Supreme War Council in Versailles that the Germans were likely to attack in March on the Third and Fifth Army fronts, in an attempt to cut off the Cambrai salient.[40] He thus was provided with a highly accurate assessment of Ludendorff's intentions, and yet he allotted Rawlinson twice the number of men and artillery relative to the length of front than Gough. Gough's Fifth Army held forty-two miles of front with twelve infantry and three cavalry divisions, supported by 1,566 artillery pieces.[41]

He had first occupied these positions in January, when he took over from the French. After typically stubborn British tergiversation it was finally agreed at a surprisingly amicable meeting between Haig and Pétain on 17 December that the British Army should take over the French front as far as Barisis. Pétain fully realized that this was as far as Haig was prepared to go because the BEF had hardly any room to retreat without uncovering vital objectives such as the Channel ports and Amiens. He had precious little space to trade for time. The French thus began to withdraw General Humbert's III Army in mid-January and the process was completed by 3 February. Six infantry divisions and two cavalry divisions were thus added to French reserves, which included General Debeney's I Army which had been withdrawn from Flanders.[42] Here was another reason for Haig and Robertson's objections to extending the British front. More reserves came under French command, which in turn meant that the British were weakened both militarily and politically. As Robertson pointed out this gave main operational control to the French.[43] In the end the soldiers had to give way to massive political pressure, but they did so with ill grace.

In his memoirs Gough complained that the French sector had an inadequate trench system, and that French peasants were busy filling in trenches and removing the wire around Amiens in order to return the land to agricultural use.[44] The Germans were thus able to break through the British lines because they inherited such weak positions. Gough's army was particularly weak to the south. Between the Oise and the Omignon, particularly in the marshy area to the north of La Fère, the battle line was inadequately manned and was made up of isolated strong-points that were placed far too far apart. Gough's defences to the north of the Omignon were far stronger, but his third line of defence, the 'Green Line' was little more than a mark on the map. The number of labourers allocated to Fifth Army increased from 24,217 in February to 48,154 by 15 March, but never more than 8,830 men per week worked on the actual defences.[45] It would seem that Haig had adequate supplies of labour, the aggregate number having increased from 87,832 in 1917 to 354,577 in 1918.[46] Why, then, did Haig devote most of his resources to the Flanders front, where an attack was virtually impossible until April, rather than the Somme which he correctly felt was where the first blow would fall in March?

Haig's main defensive concern had always been for the Channel ports, which were to be defended at all costs. Just as the French thought that an offensive on the Somme would be designed to use up the Entente's reserves in preparation for a major offensive in the Champagne, Haig was convinced that it would be the preliminary move in a campaign in Flanders. He was therefore not prepared to give an inch in Flanders. If there were to be a retirement it would have to be on the Somme. On

4 February John Davidson, Director of Military Operations at GHQ, issued a memorandum entitled 'Principles of Defence on Fifth Army Front' which called for Gough to make detailed plans for a withdrawal to the line Crozat Canal-Somme-Tortille which, if skilfully executed, would cause the enemy 'to expend considerable force and generally dislocate his arrangements'.[47] In further exchanges between GHQ and Fifth Army it was proposed that Gough should launch counter-attacks from Péronne assisted by Third Army to the north, and possibly by the French from the south. Since Fifth Army was to retire and absorb the initial blow of the German offensive there was little point in preparing elaborate defences which were soon to be abandoned. Labour could best be expended on building a north-south railway, which would enable troops to be moved quickly to strengthen any point on the front that was in danger.

This was at best an extremely hazardous strategy. It was doubtful that the British Army had sufficient training and expertise to handle a rapid withdrawal in the face of a massive attack by highly skilled and motivated troops. As Gough pointed out, the defences around the Péronne bridge-head were seriously deficient and it was unlikely that Fifth Army would be able to counter-attack immediately after a hasty retirement. Gough accepted that Haig was correct in giving the priority to Flanders, but neither he nor Haig seemed to realize the risks involved. An attack on an over-extended and weakly defended Fifth Army threatened to sepa-rate the British from the French, Third Army's flank would be exposed and there was a serious danger that they would be unable to stop the Germans at Amiens, and thus lose a vital railhead.

Haig seems to have been blissfully unaware of these dangers and imagined that he had set a trap for the Germans. Fifth Army's retirement would lure them to their doom. The trap would be sprung, Ludendorff's masterly plan would be in ruins, and Haig would be free to mount a final push later in the year, by which time the Americans would have arrived and his army would be up to strength. Charles Bean, the bril-liant official Australian war correspondent, reported that he met John Buchan, the Director of Information, in Whitehall when the German offensive began. He was in high spirits and announced: 'The Germans have fallen into every trap we have laid'.[48] Clearly the top brass were blissfully unaware that the British army was about to suffer its worst defeat in the war.

Maurice's successor as Director of Military Operations at the War Office, Radcliffe, forwarded a report to CIGS on 27 May 1918 on the collapse of the Fifth Army in which he repeated the familiar excuses but pointed out that the BEF was trained down to the smallest detail in trench warfare and to attack, but had no idea how to fight in a retirement.[49] The divisions failed to co-ordinate their withdrawals so that the Germans had no difficulty in turning the line. Counter-attacks by exhausted troops with minimal artillery support were beaten back with heavy casualties.[50] John Buchan's optimistic enthusiasm was thus seriously misplaced.

There was a certain elegance in Haig's plan but it suffered from one serious flaw. He assumed that Ludendorff would disperse his efforts with a thrust towards Verdun, a prod at Reims and an attack on the scale of the Cambrai offensive on the Somme. Furthermore, although the British were fully aware of German offensive tactics, having got hold of von Hutier's plans for the attack on Riga, and had somewhat belatedly analyzed the German counter-attack at Cambrai, Haig was caught completely by surprise by the speed and ferocity of the 'Michael' offensive.[51] Right until the bitter end he was convinced that the Germans would fight a '*bataille d'usure*', and since they did not have an overwhelming numerical superiority GHQ was convinced that they would easily be defeated. Even when the Germans attacked in March it took several days before GHQ realized what had really happened.

In early January Smuts wrote a memorandum for the War Cabinet suggesting that the Germans were likely to mount a full-scale offensive using similar tactics to those used at Cambrai. Later in the month Rawlinson urged Haig to circulate the 'Lessons of Cambrai counter-attack' as he expected the Germans to use similar tactics in any future offensive. It is remarkable that Haig had to be reminded to pass on such an important document, which stressed that the Germans would strive to achieve surprise by a short but extremely intense barrage and launch a weighty attack using storm-troop tactics.[52] GHQ continued to insist that the Germans would stick to what the chief of staff, Herbert Lawrence, described as 'sound principles'. Haig agreed with Lawrence and believed as late as March that the Germans would fight in the manner of the BEF's costly slogging matches which were designed to weaken the enemy until a breakthrough could be achieved.[53]

The British Army's defences were not even adequate to meet an offensive based on 'sound principles' as they had not mastered the three-zone defence in depth which they attempted to copy from the Germans with its forward, battle and rear zones. There was considerable confusion as to whether the forward zone was designed merely to hold up the enemy advance or be held at all costs. Orders given to Fifth Army suggested that they wanted to do both. Gough insisted that the serious fighting would be in the battle zone, but orders were given that troops in the forward zone should not be allowed to retire. As a result the Germans swept through the forward zone and most of the troops surrendered. In subsequent attacks the forward zone retired when the barrage began and did not wait to be taken prisoner.

GHQ was satisfied that Fifth and Third Armies' forward zones were in good condition. The battle zone was felt to be in a fair state, but Fifth

Army lacked adequate dugouts. Third Army had two lines of trenches protected by belts of wire and numerous machine-gun nests, and had begun building a series of dugouts on the rear zone. Fifth Army's rear zone was a scratch in the dirt.[54]

A further problem was that Gough had placed the bulk of his army on the left and centre, whereas his right flank was lightly held by Lieutenant-General Butler's XVIII Corps.[55] Butler was hardly one of the BEF's finest generals, and was described by Lieutenant-Colonel J.F.C. Fuller as 'an intensely stupid man'.[56] Thus the British Army was particularly weak at the critical point from St Quentin to the Oise where they joined the French VI Army. Furthermore it was Butler's corps that protected the critically important Crozat Canal.

The British also were deeply suspicious of the German system of scattered machine-gun nests and preferred the familiar parallel lines of trenches. They either stuck to the trenches or placed their outposts so far apart that they were easily bypassed in the fog on 21 March. Furthermore Gough placed far too many of his machine-guns in the forward zone, all of which were lost in the early stages of the battle. Nor had they mastered the counter-attack, which was at the heart of German defensive tactics. The French, by contrast, had absorbed the lessons of the Cambrai counter-attack and von Hutier's brilliant coup at Riga, and had made a careful analysis of German defensive tactics. The key lesson was the importance of flexibility, a willingness to abandon space to gain time, and an emphasis on the need to have units at the ready for counter-attacks.

The crux of the problem was that GHQ assumed that the Germans were in no position to launch a really serious attack, and that there would be plenty of time to react. Thus, 88,000 troops were sent on leave on the eve of an offensive which most senior officers felt was imminent. These men were sent back to France as soon as the German offensive began, along with 106,000 mobile reserves and 18,000 trained recruits.[57] Haig was confident that the six French divisions that would be moved to Amiens within six days and ready to fight at Péronne within eleven were sufficient to defend the Somme bridgehead. Had he made a more careful study of the Cambrai report he would have realized that this was dangerously optimistic. The French divisions were urgently required within three days of the onset of 'Michael'.

In the early days of March there was a feeling that perhaps the Germans were not considering an offensive in the immediate future. CIGS reported that intensive aerial observation showed no indication of an imminent attack. Military intelligence came to the astonishing conclusion that the Germans had no less than 400 tanks, at a time when they had less than ten operational vehicles. Since there was no evidence of a massive tank build-up it was assumed that an offensive was not being contemplated.[58] Paul Cambon, the French ambassador in London, said that French military intelligence did not expect a major offensive. The Germans would launch a series of limited attacks, such as the recent operations on the Menin Road and at Houthulst Forest, which were designed to undermine Allied morale by constant threats of a full-scale offensive. Wilson concluded that all depended on how confident the Germans were that they could defeat the Allies in the field.[59]

At a conference with the French at Doullens on 2 March Haig announced that the British defences were so strong that the Germans were unlikely to attack. He added that he felt this would be a pity, as they would suffer a severe defeat should they do so. He gave a summary of intelligence reports that indicated that should the Germans decide to attack they would do so against the British Third and Fifth Armies.[60] There was considerable confusion over the timing of the attack. Brigadier General Cox, Haig's recently appointed chief intelligence officer, was not very helpful. He announced that the Germans 'might, or might not, attack in the near future'.[61] The ferocity and scale of the attack on Gough's Fifth Army came as a complete surprise to GHQ and the War Office, both of whom expected the main blow to fall further north. Under such circumstances it is hardly surprising that the War Cabinet was stunned by the news of the rapid German advance.

There were profound differences of opinion between the British and the French over German intentions. Pétain believed that there would be a massive attack against the British to the north of the Oise, followed by a second powerful attack against the French in the Champagne. He had argued for months that the Germans would aim a brutal blow against the front and exploit any breaks with speed and determination. Haig and his staff did not believe that they would be able to achieve a breakthrough in 1918 anymore than they had been able to do so in 1916 at Verdun or in 1914 and 1915 at Ypres. The British imagined that the Germans would seek a series of local successes so as to be in a strong position to begin diplomatic negotiations for a peace settlement. It would be yet another battle of attrition, and thus it was essential to strengthen the divisions in the lines, make sure that they were frequently relieved and ensure that they did not get side-tracked by Foch into launching counter-offensives.[62]

Haig's confident mood soon began to dissipate. He considered General Otto von Below, whom he frequently confused with General von Bülow, to be 'Germany's ablest commander' in the offensive. His 17th Army was poised to attack between Arras and Cambrai, the point where military intelligence thought an offensive was most likely.[63] The more he thought about the British defensive positions the less sanguine he became. There was a distressing tendency for divisions to put all their brigades in the front line and to have only battalions in reserve.

Haig preferred to have at least one division in reserve. Furthermore Fifth Army's defences were very poor, having been inherited from the French, Gough was short of the necessary labour and many doubted his competence.[64]

The British had forty-two divisions at the front and eighteen in reserve. Nine reserve divisions were placed behind Fourth and First Armies between Arras and Ypres. A further nine divisions were placed between the Scarpe and the Oise behind Fifth and Third Armies. Six of these were behind Fifth Army and three behind Third Army, which was also supported by the three remaining cavalry divisions.

Haig went back to England on 12 March, and conferred with Lloyd George and Bonar Law two days later. He claimed that the Germans were 'drunk with success' in Russia and would attack in force along a fifty-mile front. Lloyd George took this opportunity to once again press Haig to accept the idea of a general reserve, but to no avail.[65]

He returned to France on 16 March and began to wonder whether the Germans would indeed attack. Were they simply 'shaking their mailed fist at us from the other side of No Man's Land'? Could it be that they were considering making a peace offer? The German Army was fighting badly, their raids were remarkably poorly executed, and they ran away at the first sight of a British soldier.[66] On the eve of the 'Michael' offensive Haig would thus appear to have been in a confident mood.

When the Germans finally attacked on 21 March CIGS was still uncertain whether this was indeed the beginning of a major offensive, or just another diversionary attack designed to keep the British Army *in situ*.[67] Haig was not in the least perturbed and felt that the British Army was fighting very well.[68] Within twenty-four hours they realized that this, at last, was the real thing. The enemy had penetrated Fifth Army's battle zone and advanced twelve miles. The British had already lost 40,000 men and 600 guns.[69]

4

'Michael': The First Phase
21-23 March

The early months of 1918 were quiet along the whole length of the Western Front. The French and British raided the German lines in an attempt to discover where they intended to attack in the spring. The Germans replied in kind to seek out weak points on the Allied lines. At the end of February the Germans began a series of diversionary attacks in an attempt to conceal their real intentions from the enemy. Troops taking part in these operations were led to believe that they were indeed part of a major offensive so that were they to be taken prisoner they might further mislead the enemy. These attacks were concentrated on the French section of the front. None were undertaken on the 'Michael' front.

The British army was very active on the 'Michael' front. Their artillery was strengthened and persistently bombarded the German forward positions. British aircraft flew far behind the German front, but were hindered by poor visibility from making an accurate assessment of German intentions. The Germans did not move men and material up to the front in clear weather and German aircraft kept a careful watch on the effectiveness of camouflage.

Preparations for the offensive presented awesome problems. A network of roads and railways had to be built and preparations made to extend them over the British trenches and to link them with the roads and railways behind the front. The artillery needed solid platforms. Landing strips for aircraft and balloons were required closer to the front. Miles of telephone cable were laid. Light bridges and fascines were prepared so that enemy trenches could be crossed. Vast quantities of supplies had to be brought forward, hidden from the enemy and protected from the weather. Thirty-five divisions and 550 batteries had to be brought up to the front.

The movement of men to the front was done according to a strict timetable. Divisional headquarters, divisional artillery commanders and the staffs of the artillery regiments had to be in place by the end of February. From 1 to 5 March the first units of the attacking divisions were to be in place. These included artillery staff and munitions columns. From 8 to 10 March Luftwaffe units arrived along with the pioneers and supply columns. The divisions and Luftwaffe squadrons moved up to the front between 9 and 20 March. Finally, medical units and bridging specialists arrived between 17 and 20 March.[1]

On the whole these preparations went remarkably smoothly, though it was only possible to provide four days worth of ammunition rather than the five originally planned and reserves of food also fell short of target. There were frequent complaints about the shortages of food. Ensign Paul Knoch told his parents that: 'The rations for the offensive are bad. We have nothing to spread on our bread!!', and added as a postscript, 'There are takers here for any bacon or ham you might have that has gone mouldy.'[2] 17th Army faced the greatest problems because the 'Mars' offensive was being prepared simultaneously. In spite of these difficulties all preparations were completed on time. Even the weather co-operated. It rained on 19 and 20 March after several days of nice weather, but at midday on 20 March the meteorologists forecast good weather for the morning: the offensive could go ahead. Thirty-nine divisions stood at the ready in the first wave, twenty-two in the second and ten in the third with five in reserve – a total of divisions. They were supported by 6,608 guns, 3,534 heavy mortars and 1,070 aircraft.[3]

The assault troops were brought up to the front on 20 March without any serious difficulty. The British opened a barrage on the German frontline trenches that evening and the bombardment continued through the night.

Lieutenant-Colonel Bruchmüller, Germany's leading artillery specialist, acted as artillery advisor to 18th Army. He began the war as an obscure, middle-aged, retired officer who served in a *Landwehr* (Territorial) Division. He made his reputation on the Eastern Front orchestrating the artillery in von Mackensen's offensive in the Carpathians in 1915, and at Verdun in 1916. He then became the OHL's leading artillery specialist. He was one of a number of relatively low-ranking officers in the German Army who held highly responsible and influential positions. Bruchmüller was the master of the creeping barrage, which he had used to great effect against the Russians at Lake Narocz when he was von Hutier's artillery officer He made skilful use of aerial photographs to pinpoint targets, and centralized the firing command so as to keep a tight control over the details of his master plan.[4]

The key to Bruchmüller's approach was to use this careful planning to achieve surprise. This worked brilliantly on 21 March. Since there was no registration, only a few shots for range, General Sir Hubert Gough's Fifth Army was caught completely by surprise – the essential precondition for a German success. 'Michael I' began at 0440hrs on 21 March when the Germans bombarded the British batteries, trench mortars, command posts, billets and bivouacs, telephone exchanges and transportation network using mixed gas and high explosive. Phosgene was mixed with a lachrymatory gas against which British gas masks offered no protection, in the hope that the soldiers would remove their masks because of the intense irritation to the eyes, and thus inhale the phosgene. At 0530hrs the barrage was directed against the infantry's objectives for ten minutes. The British artillery response was feeble, suggesting that the gas attack had been successful, but a light wind blew the gas back towards the German lines which was taxing for the assault troops.

At 0640hrs German artillery checked the range on designated trenches. At 0710hrs counter-battery and long-range fire continued for seventy minutes while other batteries bombarded the infantry positions. After thirty minutes they swept the ground between the enemy trenches for fifteen minutes, other howitzers concentrated on designated centres of resistance and the field guns aimed at the strip between the second and third lines of trenches.

Firing continued at 0820hrs for seventy-five minutes with some changes in the long-range targets. At 0935hrs, five minutes before Zero, all howitzers fired as close to the front line trenches as possible, the light and medium trench mortars aimed deeper behind the British lines and the field guns, which only used high explosive, fired even further beyond them. Super-heavy guns and heavy trench mortars were trained at the second line of trenches while the remaining guns continued their counter-battery work. The creeping barrage moved forward with an initial bound of 300 metres, further bounds were 200 metres. After the initial bound the barrage paused for three minutes, subsequent bounds were followed by a pause of four minutes.[5]

On that first day the 6,608 German guns on the attacking front fired a total of 3.2 million rounds. A total of 4.3 million rounds were fired by the Germans along the length of the Western Front.[6]

At 0940hrs the infantry began their attack. They were in excellent spirits, well trained and confident that victory lay in their grasp, and that a war which they had grown to fear and to hate would soon be at an end. 17th Army which was positioned along the stretch of the front from east of Vimy Ridge to south-west of Cambrai had the most difficult role in the 'Michael' offensive. In accordance with the OHL's orders the *Schwerpunkt* of the attack was on the army's southern flank. Its objective was to nip off the Cambrai salient by pushing south towards Ytres while 2nd Army to the south of the bulge headed north towards Equancourt. Only when this salient had been taken could 17th Army head north-west towards Arras and Saint Pol. This was an extremely difficult proposition involving changing the direction of the offensive by ninety degrees against very tough opposition. 2nd Army had the somewhat easier task of heading west along the Somme to protect the left flank of the advance. The right flank of 2nd Army and the left flank of 17th Army were to head in the direction of Miraumont.

On the right flank of 17th Army 'Mars South' was to secure the flank south of the Scarpe. To the north of the river the I Bavarian Reserve Corps (Vimy Group) stood ready to exploit any opportunities afforded by the success of the main thrust. Further to the north 6th and 4th Armies were to engage the British to stop them moving troops to the 'Michael' front from the Ypres salient.

By 1000hrs 17th Army's infantry had crossed the 1,000 metres of no-man's-land and taken the front line of British trenches from Bullecourt to Boursies. Initial resistance had been feeble, but the Germans soon came under fire from skilfully placed machine-guns and the damp ground made it difficult to move up their artillery to within range in order to support the infantry's advance. The British gunners were able to adjust their sights with no such difficulty. British raiding parties had discovered gaps in the German wire and had taken prisoners during the night who had said that the offensive would begin in the morning. They had therefore strengthened their second line of defences and the German barrage confirmed their suspicions.

To the south of Bullecourt progress was somewhat slower and General Albrecht's XVIII Corps did not take the first line of British trenches until shortly after midday. Again the advance was hindered by the difficulty of moving up the supporting artillery. At some points it was nevertheless possible to reach the second line of British defences, although some British counter-attacks were successful in halting the advance.

VI and XIV Reserve Corps faced weak positions and at some points had no difficulty in penetrating the British lines and seizing some artillery. They soon met fierce resistance from the second line of British defences which had not been seriously damaged by the earlier barrage, but after some fierce hand-to-hand fighting they took these positions shortly after 1300hrs. At some points it was not until 1500hrs that the Germans were able to beat back British counter-attacks and finally secure their hold on the second line of defence.

General Kühne's XI Corps faced similar difficulties as it advanced towards Ytres. Operations were hindered by heavy fog, insufficient artillery support and fierce counter-attacks in which tanks were involved. It was not until the evening that Demicourt could be taken and reserves brought forward to continue the offensive in the morning. On the Corps' left wing it was not possible to advance beyond the first line of trenches.

General von Below knew that most of the British first line of defences had been taken by 1100hrs but then his communications broke down and he had little idea how the battle was progressing. His army had advanced about four kilometres on a front of fifteen kilometres, but the real fight had yet to begin. From intercepted British radio messages he knew that he would soon come up against fierce resistance. This was hardly the decisive breakthrough for which he had hoped. He was still seven kilometres from his objectives of Ytres and Bapaume, and only had 2,300 prisoners and a few guns to show for his efforts. Most of his reserves had already been thrown into action and determined British counter-attacks had forced his troops back at several points.

Von der Marwitz ordered the *Schwerpunkt* of his 2nd Army's attack to be directed towards Péronne and did not want to become too heavily involved in the Cambrai salient where the British forces were concentrated and where powerful counter-attacks could be expected. On the other hand he had received orders from the OHL to co-ordinate his offensive with von Below's 17th Army to the north and advance in the direction of Equancourt and Ytres to cut off the salient.

2nd Army's artillery barrage began at 0440hrs on 21 March marking the opening of 'Michael II'. At 0600hrs the XVI Reserve Division successfully gained the British front lines. The remainder of 2nd Army attacked at 0940hrs, heavy fog causing considerable confusion. Nevertheless, the attack was successful along most of the front. The advancing troops bypassed pockets of resistance and by midday had reached the second line of British defences.

Communications were also a serious problem for von der Marwitz. He was anxious to push his troops forward but his orders arrived too late and it was often impossible to carry them out. He had managed to advance about four and a half kilometres, but this left him six kilometres short of his immediate goal of Equancourt. He was not fully in possession on the second line of British defences, and in some places had not even been able to reach as far. The area behind the second line of trenches was securely in British hands. 2nd Army had taken 4,000 prisoners and fifty guns. Their own casualties had not been too severe. The Germans were greatly impressed by the British Army's equipment and marvelled at their leather jerkins, their puttees and their excellent boots. Soon they were smoking highly prized Virginia cigarettes, polishing their boots with shoe polish and riding around in cars with rubber tyres all captured from the British. Such luxuries were for the Germans 'unheard of things which belong to a fairyland of long ago'.[7]

In 'Michael III' von Hutier's 18th Army attacked the right wing of Gough's Fifth Army. The Germans estimated that Gough had seven divisions at the front and between one and four cavalry divisions in reserve. In fact Gough only had five and a half divisions at the front, but his two cavalry reserve divisions were so close to the front that they could be used on the first day. Von Hutier had twenty-six divisions – thirteen in the first wave, nine in the second and four in the third – at his disposition. One of the OHL's divisions was held in reserve. Gough was outnumbered eight to one, and could not count on GHQ for any support.

The attack was to the north and south of Saint Quentin and was designed to cross the Crozat Canal and the Somme and was to push forward as far as possible. No specific goals were set for the first day. General Baron von Gayl was given the special task of establishing a bridgehead over the Oise and the canal at La Fère for which he was allotted two divisions of special assault troops.[8] It was an exceedingly difficult task which could only be achieved if the enemy were caught by surprise.

18th Army's initial barrage began at 0400hrs on 21 March. The bulk of the infantry attacked at 0940hrs. The first detachment of von Gayl's troops emerged from the suburbs of La Fère at 0615hrs and crossed the bridges which the pioneers had set up during the night. The crossing was a success but at 0735hrs the advance was held up by British troops in defensive positions in the buildings along the road to Fargniers including a rolling mill. Heavy fog made further progress extremely difficult and von Gayl lost touch with his troops. Nevertheless the rolling mill was in German hands by midday and the second line of British defences was soon under attack. Progress was hampered by heavy artillery fire which made it almost impossible to bring up supplies to the front. In spite of these difficulties von Gayl's men succeeded in overrunning sections of the second line of British defences.

Elsewhere von Hutier's men took the first lines of the British defences with little difficulty, but they were held up by the second line, which had not been seriously damaged by the initial barrage. On many sections of the front they were held up by devastating machine-gun fire.

At the end on the day the right wing of von Hutier's army was positioned in front of the second line of British defences. This was in part because at this point on the front the distance between the two lines of defences was unusually large. On the left he met with greater success. He had overrun the second line of defences and advanced further than the other two armies. This left Gough in a perilous position. He only had one cavalry division in reserve south of the Somme and there was a gaping hole in his front caused by the German breakthrough at Hinancourt. On his own admission he was at a loss to know what to do. He could pull back to the emergency zone and make a stand, but there were virtually no defence works and no switch to Péronne. He could phone GHQ and ask for reserves to prop up his rear zone; but Haig had not phoned, he did not want to go begging, and above all wanted to avoid another pompous lecture from either Davidson or Lawrence. Lastly he could muddle through, and that is what he did to the limit of his very modest abilities. Muddling through soon involved a hasty retreat and Field Marshal Haig granted his request to withdraw to the line from Fontaine to Saint Simon and behind the Crozat Canal.[9]

Von Hutier had every reason to pleased with the day's work. He had taken 7,000 prisoners and eighty-eight guns, some of them heavy artillery. He had fourteen divisions in the front line and twelve divisions in reserve, so was in an excellent position to resume the attack in the morning.

The main difficulty for the Germans on this first day was the fog which persisted into the afternoon. This made it impossible to lay down a rolling barrage and the infantry was left without artillery support. Spotter planes were unable to fly and telephone communication was impossible in an advance. Many commanders in the field were loath to lose contact with higher commands and thus stayed at the end of a telephone and were often unaware of the situation at the front. Batteries could not be brought forward to support the infantry's advance because of the soft ground. Commanders lost control of their men in the fog and many units became hopelessly lost. It had been fairly easy to overrun the first line of defences, which were relatively lightly held, but they met fierce resistance from machine-gun fire in the second line and were without artillery support. Overall they had advanced four and a half kilometres and had only managed to go beyond the second line of British defences at two points: the 17th Army at Beaumetz and 18th Army at Hinancourt.

The British had suffered heavy losses on this first day, partly because of poor defences and partly because of the weather conditions which caused them as many if not more headaches than the Germans. The forward zone was disproportionately strong compared with the zones to the rear, which were inadequately prepared. They lacked machine-gun nests, pill boxes, deep dug-outs, tiers of wire and the maze of trenches and switches which would have rendered them effective. Fifth Army was to pay a heavy price for the lack of manpower and preparation, to say nothing of the British Army's inability to learn the art of defensive warfare from the Germans.

A further weakness was that Gough, lacking sufficient manpower, had placed his forward garrisons in strong points, rather than in lines. This only provided effective defence in depth when visibility was good, and when the artillery could bar the gaps between the strong-points. Where the Germans had launched frontal attacks against these strong-points they had usually failed, but they found it relatively easy to find ways around them and to press forward to the weakly defended rearward zones.

More than a quarter of the battalions attacked had been destroyed on the first day, and they had lost a large proportion of their machine-guns, which had been rendered almost worthless by the thick fog early in the day.[10] GHQ was unable to send Gough any divisions beyond the two reserve divisions he had already ordered forward. General Humbert visited Gough's headquarters in time for lunch, but disarmingly announced that he had no troops under his command adding: '*Je n'ai que mon fanion* (pennant)!' Furthermore Haig did not ask the French for support until after midnight and then, encouraged by Gough's overly optimistic situation report, he only asked for three infantry divisions – less than half the number that had previously been agreed upon in 'Hypothesis A'.[11] Pétain promptly sent these three divisions, and two reached the British front on 23 March, the third later that night. Pétain was thus quicker than Haig in sending support for the hard-pressed Fifth Army.

GQG were convinced that the attack on the British Fifth and Third Armies was a major operation, but there was indication that the Germans might also attack in the Champagne. The French V, VI and IV Armies, positioned between Soissons and the Argonne, were submitted to an exceptionally heavy bombardment in the night of 20 to 21 March. This continued during the day, and the Germans mounted a number of raids along the front. Although it was not clear whether this was preparation for a major offensive or a diversionary move at 4.45 p.m. Pétain ordered General Franchet d'Esperey to prepare to send units to help Gough's Fifth Army. On receipt of further information on the precarious situation between Saint Quentin and the Oise shortly before midnight Pétain ordered the 9th and 10th Infantry Divisions, the 1st Dismounted Cavalry Division along with three regiments of heavy artillery, a combat air group, anti-aircraft batteries, observation balloons and the headquarters of General Pellé's 5th Corps. Haig's request for assistance was dispatched three-quarters of an hour after Pétain had issued these orders.[12]

As further details of the fighting reached GHQ a most alarming situation was revealed. The 16th (Irish) Division had fought particularly badly, and several units had simply run away. By the end of the day the division ceased to exist, and its remnants were later transferred to XIX Corps of Third Army. Their positions, which had been inspected and approved by both Haig and Gough shortly before the Germans attacked, were hopelessly inadequate. Five of the six divisions were in the front zone, leaving only one in the battle zone. Furthermore they were placed in a salient with most of their forces at the tip. When Gough visited divisional HQ on 14 March Major-General Hull suggested that the battle zone should be strengthened, but Gough pooh-poohed the suggestion and complacently announced: 'The Germans are not going to break my line!'[13]

It was not only the Irish that cracked. General Sir Ivor Maxse's XVIII Corps lost nine battalions within hours, even though he was generally acknowledged as the finest troop trainer in the British Army. A Battalion Adjutant in Péronne was horrified to see infantrymen trudging back without their rifles. Gough was now ordered to retire to the Somme and to hang on to the Péronne Bridgehead, but this order came too late and merely precipitated a headlong rush to the rear in which what remained of the command structure crumbled.[14] Pétain remarked contemptuously that Fifth Army had 'run like the Italians at Caporetto.'[15]

The OHL was far from happy with the results of the first day of the battle. They had managed to penetrate deeper into the enemy lines than the French or the British had ever been able to do, but they had not achieved the goals they had set. Ludendorff had continually insisted that for 'Michael' to be successful the Cambrai salient had to be taken on the first day. This had not proved possible. Von Below's 17th Army had only managed to reach the forward positions of the second line of British defences and had covered just one-third of the distance to the Bapaume-Ytres line which had been set as its objective. All his reserves had been thrown into the battle and it seemed dubious whether he would be able to achieve his tactical goals in the foreseeable future.

Similarly von der Marwitz's 2nd Army had got stuck after its initial successes and was far from reaching its objective at Equancourt. Von Hutier was the most successful of the three army commanders but even his 18th Army had failed to reach its objectives on the first day, though he was confident that the task could be completed on the morrow. Crown Prince Rupprecht was furious that the Kaiser had sent a message to a provincial diet (*Landtag*) proclaiming a total victory.[16]

On the first day of the battle the OHL agreed to Army Group German Crown Prince's suggestion that reinforcements should be sent to back up 18th Army. One division was moved from von Below's 1st Army, two divisions from von Arnim's 3rd Army and one division from von Gallwitz's 5th Army. All of these armies were positioned to von Hutier's left.[17] Putting tactical above strategic considerations Ludendorff decided to add weight to von Hutier's army which had advanced the furthest of any army that day, rather than attempting to solve the problems facing 17th and 2nd Armies and push in a north-westerly direction according to the 'Michael' plan.

Ludendorff now ordered the left flank of 2nd Army to co-operate closely with the right flank of 18th Army. 2nd Army was ordered to push westwards south of the Omignon stream, supported by 18th Army and then continue in the north-westerly direction. The left flank of 18th Army was to be supported by General von Boehn's 7th Army. Thus by the second day although the objectives remained broadly the same, the weight of the offensive had shifted significantly from the right to the left.

On the evening of 21 March Crown Prince Rupprecht's staff told the two army commands in the Army Group that the Cambrai salient had to be taken and that 17th Army would therefore have to press on to Ytres and 2nd Army, which faced far greater difficulties, should achieve their strategic goal at Equancourt. The batteries which were designed for 'Mars' would be now used to support 'Michael'.

News from the OHL indicated that Colonel Wetzell wanted 'Saint George' to be the next operation, but this would not be possible until the end of April at the earliest. Crown Prince Rupprecht's staff was appalled and urged that 'Mars', or at least 'Mars South', should go ahead otherwise the offensive would lose its momentum and the British might mount a counter-attack.[18]

Their other main concern was that the British would retire from the Cambrai salient and thus avoid a serious defeat. Rupprecht's staff had hoped that the leadership of the British army would prove incompetent, but never in their wildest dreams had they expected them to fail so completely. It remained to be seen whether they could extricate themselves from the Cambrai salient and how well they would manage the difficult retirement over the old Somme battlefields and across the river south of Péronne.

Admiral von Müller, the chief of the naval cabinet, who was at headquarters, reported that the mood at breakfast on 22 March was low. There was a feeling that the offensive had come to a standstill, and the OHL was blamed for its undue optimism.[19] The fog persisted on 22 March and the artillery was still hampered by the soggy ground. In spite of these difficulties 17th Army made reasonable progress. XVIII Army Corps managed to seize the high ground to the north-west of Croisilles which caused a dangerous gap in the British lines and the British positions to the north were in danger of being overrun. The British XVII Corps therefore prudently withdrew. A series of British counter-attacks were beaten back. In the evening the British attacked near Morchies with twenty-five tanks. They were beaten back losing sixteen of their tanks.

General von der Marwitz ordered his 2nd Army to take Epéhy, a British strongpoint, which blocked the way to Equancourt. After fierce fighting from house to house the village was in German hands by 1400hrs. Prodded by the Army Group staff he pushed on towards Equancourt. Elsewhere on his front the British withdrew during the night and morning of 22 March he therefore ordered his artillery forward so as to provide cover in the event of a British counter-attack.

By the evening of 22 March the British were in full retreat on the northern flank of the 2nd Army and were forced back to their third line of defence. On the southern flank Lieutenant-General H.E. Watts' XIX Corps was pushed back even further and returned to the positions they had occupied in 1916-17. His heavy artillery was sent back behind the

Somme. 2nd Army had taken 10,000 prisoners and captured 200 guns but had also suffered some heavy losses. XIII Corps reported 4000 casualties in the fierce fighting near Fins against Lt-General Sir E.A.Fanshawe's V Corps. Von der Marwitz reported that his army's morale was high and he did not think that the third line of British defences were particularly strongly held. He looked forward to the next day with confidence.[20] Haig was appalled that Gough had retired behind the Somme and wrote: 'I cannot make out why the Fifth Army had gone back so far without making some kind of stand.' He promptly issued a special order of the day in an attempt to stiffen a demoralized army.[21]

The task allotted by the OHL to von Hutier's 18th Army on 22 March was to advance north of the Somme in order to put pressure on the flank and rear of the British forces facing 2nd Army. This task would be made easier by establishing bridgeheads across the Somme and the Crozat Canal thus relieving pressure on the troops to the north of the river.

On 18th Army's right flank General von Lüttwitz's III Army Corps made satisfactory progress against fierce opposition, but losses were high. One regiment lost 850 men. On the left the Germans established bridgeheads across the Somme and over the Crozat Canal by La Fère. Lieutenant-General Sir Richard Butler who was one of Haig's favourites whom he had wanted as Chief Staff Officer, but the War Office had turned down the request, managed to halt the Germans on the Crozat Canal north of La Fère with his III Corps. But he soon felt obliged to make preparations to withdraw from the canal to a line from Beaumont to Viry.

Thus on the second day of the 'Michael' offensive 17th Army had managed to advance a total of 6 kilometres. To the south of the Cambrai salient 2nd and 18th Armies had advanced an average of 15 Kilometres since the beginning of the offensive. General Sir Hubert Gough's Fifth Army was falling apart and it seemed highly doubtful that he would be able to stand fast on the Somme and the Crozat Canal.

Gough's orders to his corps commanders on 21 March caused further confusion. He told them that were the Germans to break though on a broad front they should fight a rearguard action back to the front line of the rear zone. Corps commanders were ordered to use their own discretion as to whether they should retire. Gough repeated this order on the morning of 22 March. It read: 'In the event of serious hostile attack corps will fight rear-guard actions back to the forward line of the rear zones, and if necessary to rear line of the rear zone.'[22] Unfortunately some corps commanders took this as an invitation to retire if the enemy deployed in strength. Command structure in the British Army was such that there was a 'top-down' corps line of command, but no adequate lines of communication between corps.[23] Further confusion was caused by Gough issuing orders directly to brigade commanders. Thus the precipitous retirement of Maxse's XVIII Corps left a gap between it and

XIX Corps which was unprepared for this move. The Germans were quick to exploit this situation. They pushed through the gap, crossed the Somme at Bethencourt and threatened Maxse's left flank.

The offensive had now reached a critical point. Whereas von Below's 17th Army on the right flank had got stuck von der Marwitz and von Hutier were on the brink of mobile warfare. It was thus imperative that Ludendorff should resist the temptation to push in a south-westerly direction against weak resistance and stick to his original concept of a north-westerly drive to the Channel coast.

At 1345hrs on 22 March Army Group German Crown Prince issued orders that the Crozat Canal should be crossed but there should be no further advance beyond the bridgeheads.[24] This order was fully in accordance with the orders issued on 10 March. But the weight of 2nd Army's advance was shifting away from the right flank so that von Below's 17th Army was not getting the support it needed, the British were not trapped in the Cambrai salient, and by warding off the attack were able to fight their way back. This situation was made worse when orders were issued at 2140hrs that 18th Army was to continue its advance. In the night further orders were issued that the Somme and the Crozat canals were to be crossed before the enemy brought in their reserves.

During the morning of 22 March Haig, who had only scant information on the situation at the front, considered that the Pellé Detachment would be sufficient to hold up the German advance. As the day passed he gradually became aware of the gravity of the situation. That afternoon he asked Pétain to send General Humbert's III Army north of the Oise to protect the seriously endangered right flank of Gough's Army, in accordance with the plans drawn up during the winter. Pétain promptly agreed. He ordered two infantry divisions (1st and 22nd), one regiment of 75's field artillery (41st), and three regiments of heavy artillery (283rd, 317th and 336th) to move into position. Four further infantry divisions, one heavy artillery regiment and a transport group with 240 trucks were to follow on 23 March.[25] General Humbert was also given command over all British forces between Saint Simon and the French VI Army.

At daybreak on 23 March III Corps on Fifth Army's far right had been driven from the Crozat Canal, and there was a dangerous gap about four miles wide between it and the French VI Army which French reinforcements were beginning to fill. XVIII Corps had retired to the line of the Crozat and Somme Canals from Ham to Bethencourt. Further to the left XIX Corps had its right flank on the Somme Canal and its left was in the air at Guizancourt. The corps had not yet been seriously attacked, but it had insufficient men to defend a wide front. VII Corps to XIX Corps' left had not had to retire quite so far, but V Corps to its left was in danger of being encircled, and the door through which it would have to retreat was being closed. Thus both flanks of Fifth Army were extremely vulnerable and in danger of imminent collapse.[26]

Clemenceau visited Pétain's headquarters at Compiègne that evening, accompanied by General Mordacq, the head of his Military Cabinet. The atmosphere was so deeply pessimistic that the premier felt that President Poincaré should leave Paris. Poincaré would not even entertain the idea, even though Pétain sent a senior officer to visit him later that evening to warn that the situation was extremely serious . He felt that Pétain had turned 'The Tiger' into a pussy cat, and yearned for a dose of Joffre's 'wonderful *sang-froid*'.[27] Back in London Hankey confided his concern to his diary that it might be unwise to send any more young men to France for the moment as the BEF could well collapse and England might then face an invasion.[28]

The tendency for the centre of gravity of the offensive to shift from the right to the left flank was emphasized on the following day. 17th Army continued to make only modest advances against stiff resistance. At 0750hrs on 23 March Ludendorff ordered the left flank of 17th Army to cross the Somme between Péronne and Saint Christ and head for the high ground to the south-west of Amiens. This movement was hindered by the British who destroyed the bridges over the Somme as they retreated, established strong defensive positions on the west bank of the river and laid down a heavy barrage. The Germans lacked bridging equipment as it was badly needed elsewhere. The French had also assumed, as early as 21 March, that the main German push would be towards Amiens.[29]

At 12.30 p.m. GHQ ordered Fifth and Third Armies back to positions conforming to the British and French lines prior to the ill-fated Battle of the Somme of 1916. At 5.00 p.m. a further order was issued that the line of the Somme had to be held at all costs, the bridgehead at Péronne was to form the pivot between Fifth and Third Armies which were to remain in close contact.[30] GHQ was hopelessly out of touch with the situation on the ground, and by the time the orders were dispatched the Somme had already been crossed, the Péronne bridgehead was being abandoned, and the Germans had driven a wedge between Third and Fifth Armies.

Part of the blame for this situation must lie with GHQ which failed to give General Sir Julian Byng, commanding Third Army, a definite order to abandon the Cambrai salient. There was also confusion at Third Army's headquarters. Byng was a cavalry officer who commanded the 10th Hussars, the 'Cherry Pickers', in the South African War. He had been at Gallipoli where he was a strong advocate for withdrawal. His reputation was further enhanced as the popular Commander of the Canadian Corps which under his effective leadership took Vimy Ridge. As successor to Allenby as head of Third Army, soon to be known as the 'Byng Boys', he planned and executed the Cambrai offensive and he was thus extremely reluctant to abandon the positions which he had won in 1917. He was given misleadingly optimistic reports of the situation facing Fifth Army, and Fanshawe who commanded V Corps which defended the salient was also out of touch with his divisions. His headquarters were too far to the rear, and he had little idea of what was going on at the front. As a result the Cambrai salient was in danger of being nipped off by the Germans. The withdrawal was left too late and was poorly executed.[31] The British withdrawal from the Cambrai salient was conducted in a state of confusion and near panic. It enabled the Germans to drive a wide gap between Byng's Third and Gough's Fifth Armies.

The Germans pressed forward into this gap until Third Army managed to extricate itself from the dangerous situation caused by their precipitous and disorderly retreat. Thanks to the grit and determination of IV Corps to the north of the salient and VII Corps to the south, the Germans were unable to close the jaws of the pincer, and Fanshawe was able to extricate his divisions at the very last moment.[32] Most important of all, although the risks were high, by hanging on tenaciously to the salient Byng's Army made Ludendorff change his tactics and go for an easy victory further south, thus abandoning the original plan for 'Michael'.

The situation was still confusing and highly dangerous. There was no continuous line on Third and Fifth Armies' fronts. Communications had broken down at all levels of command. Divisional commanders had no means of ascertaining where exactly their front line lay since their divisions were made up of men from different units, often interspersed with Germans. Pilots found it impossible to distinguish friend from foe, so that the air arm was useless. Tank squadrons had no experience of fighting rearguard actions and were plagued by mechanical trouble. The troops were pushed to the limits of endurance and were desperately short of ammunition and food. It was a chaotic scene reminiscent of Stendhal or Tolstoy, but unbeknownst to the British commanders, reeling under the weight of this massive assault, the situation was far from hopeless. Third Army had held up the German offensive at the decisive point, and Ludendorff, who refused to think above the tactical level, lost sight of his operational goals and turned his attention to the left flank where progress had been spectacular. In doing so the 'Great Battle in France' began to unravel.

Army Group German Crown Prince was full of praise for von Hutier's exploits and underlined the fact that unlike Crown Prince Rupprecht's armies he had achieved his initial tactical goals and was now pushing well beyond them.[33] Von Hutier's orders for 23 March were that the Somme and the Creuzat Canal were to be crossed and the enemy pushed back as far as possible. The crossings were successfully achieved, in spite of Pétain and Haig making every effort to stop them, and the strong British position across the Somme at Ham was taken by surprise. The strategically important town of Péronne was also in German hands. They were now confident that they could drive a wedge between the British and French armies and the way was open for von Hutier to drive in a south-westerly direction. His achievement was perhaps not quite so impressive when it is remembered that he had an overwhelming superiority in men and artillery. Von Hutier and his chief of staff, von Schulenburg, were eager to press on, regardless of the needs of 2nd and 17th Armies. Schulenburg exploited his friendship with Lt-Colonel Wetzell at the OHL to persuade Ludendorff to concentrate on consolidating 18th Army's successes at the expense of his overall strategic concept.

Ludendorff had always had the idea of a south-westerly push by 18th Army at the back of his mind. It was hinted at in his orders to Army Group German Crown Prince on 10 March. The idea was further developed by 18th Army's staff in a memorandum of 15 March. On 18 March Army Group German Crown Prince reported back to the OHL arguing that a powerful offensive by 18th Army was essential in order to tie down the French. This was preaching to the converted, and in the course of a telephone conversation on 20 March Ludendorff told von Schulenburg that 18th Army should be prepared to press on to Bray and Noyon.[34]

On 23 March Ludendorff faced a crucial choice. Whereas the left and centre of the offensive had made excellent headway, the right flank was held up at Arras. Should he cash in on the successes of 18th and 2nd Armies and push forward in a south-westerly and westerly direction, or should he reinforce 17th Army and stick to his original operational plan?

The Germans had now driven a gap eighty kilometres wide in the British front. On the right flank they had only advanced six kilometres – although this was an impressive distance when compared with other offensives in the war to date. Elsewhere they had overrun the British defences and penetrated up to twenty-two and a half kilometres. The Kaiser proclaimed: 'The battle is won, the English have been utterly defeated!' and toasted the Army and its great leaders with champagne.[35] In terms of distance this was an unparalleled victory, but in other respects the results were disappointing. The OHL had not achieved its primary aim of trapping Byng's Army in the Cambrai salient. Nor had they silenced the enemy's artillery. The British had been able to withdraw the bulk of their ordinance and had only lost 400 guns. The Germans had taken 40,000 prisoners but this was not an overwhelmingly impressive figure. They were also facing great difficulties in bringing supplies forward. Horses were undernourished and exhausted. Trucks mostly had no tyres and the roads were impassable. Only 2nd Army had managed to seize a number of British supply dumps which temporarily relieved the situation on the right flank. It is small wonder that Admiral Müller attributed the Kaiser's euphoria to 'a well-meaning lie by the Hindenburg-Ludendorff firm, which the German people will not believe for one moment.'

In spite of all these difficulties the tactical breakthrough had been achieved and the Germans had advanced further than either the British or the French had ever managed in any of their offensives. Ludendorff had only used fifty-nine divisions in these first three days and still had seventeen divisions in reserve. The battle had now reached the critical phase.

5

'Michael': The Second Phase 24-26 March

Not only the OHL but also the Army Group Commands were blinded by the early success of the 'Michael' offensive and grossly underestimated the fighting strength of the Allied armies. On 23 March Ludendorff managed to convince himself that it would be possible for the two Army Groups to defeat both the British and the French. Rivalries between the two Army Groups strengthened him in this illusion. Army Group German Crown Prince had always believed that the decisive blow should be struck against the French and that they would thus achieve the final victory. Army Group Crown Prince Rupprecht was equally convinced that the BEF was falling apart. Such differences between the army groups showed that it would have been wise to have created a unified command, for the German Army was plagued with every bit as much dissension as the British and French.

On the afternoon of 23 March Ludendorff gave a detailed report on the battle to the Kaiser and Hindenburg at a conference in the OHL's headquarters at Avesnes. It was attended by the chiefs of general staff of the two Army Groups. He announced that the British army had suffered a decisive defeat and that the French would be unable to mount an offensive since they would be obliged to go to the assistance of their allies. Ludendorff then stated that the operational objective was now to separate the British and French armies by advancing rapidly on both sides of the Somme. In place of the original 'Michael' plan for a swing in a north-westerly direction to the Channel coast Ludendorff now ordered an offensive due west along virtually the whole length of the British front north of the Somme. This would include the 'Mars' offensive and 'Ride of the Valkyries' (*Walkürenritt*): a drive between the Scarpe and Lens designed to take Vimy ridge. It was hoped that these attacks would 'destabilize the entire British front' and drive the British (who were always described as the English) into the sea.

The offensive against the French was to be in a south-westerly direction towards the line Amiens-Montdidier-Noyon. 18th Army would be supported by 2nd Army, which was to drive in a westerly direction south of the Somme towards Amiens.

The operational orders of 10 March had now been fundamentally altered. 17th Army continued to engage the British and push towards Saint Pol. It was supported by 6th and 4th Armies to the north, but it was now ordered to move in three directions simultaneously. The weight of its offensive was still to the north-west, but it was now also ordered to push west and to the south-west. 2nd Army no longer supported 17th Army's north-westerly thrust, but now lent its weight to the right flank of 18th Army's push to the south-west. If all went well Ludendorff hoped that von Boehn's 7th Army on von Hutier's left flank would be able to support this movement by crossing the Oise and advancing to the Aisne. The direction of the main thrust of the German offensive had now changed by ninety degrees.[1] Whereas 'Michael' was designed as an operation north of the Somme, and any activity to the south of the river was designed to be a diversionary effort, now the weight of the offensive had shifted to the south. The *Schwerpunkt* of a movement north-west had now been diffused, and offensive strength was seriously compromised by pushing in three directions at once.

The push towards the south-west made no strategic sense. There was no defined goal and available forces were insufficient. There was no need to change direction. There was nothing to stop 2nd Army's advance towards Doullens, which would have relieved the pressure on 17th Army, which could then advance in a north-westerly direction as in the original plan. Ludendorff could have backed up this thrust with the eleven fresh divisions, which he had allotted to 18th Army. Army Group German Crown Prince would still have had enough men to halt the French as they rushed to help their hard pressed allies.

The operation was fraught with difficulties. 2nd Army had now to push forward astride the Somme. This involved getting part of the army across the river's wide and swampy valley between Péronne and Saint Christ, a move that would only be possible if the British were in full retreat. The army lacked the equipment needed to bridge the river, and their only hope was that the British would fail to destroy all the bridges, as had happened at the Crozat Canal.[2]

It is difficult to see why Ludendorff made this totally unnecessary change of plan. He knew full well that his right flank would have difficulties because of the British stronghold at Arras, and that 2nd Army's advance would have ended this impasse. It would seem that he had thrown strategic considerations to the winds and simply taken the line of least resistance.

Ludendorff had certainly not lost his nerve. Such was his confidence that he sent a telegram to the High Seas Fleet requesting that they make plans to counter a British attempt to evacuate their troops from France via Dunkirk. The staff at Army Group Crown Prince Rupprecht was less sanguine. They felt that the idea that it would be possible to defeat both the British and the French was altogether too optimistic. 17th Army had suffered heavy losses and its combativeness was dwindling. Although they estimated that the British had lost between twelve and fourteen divisions the French army was virtually untouched, well rested and up to full strength.[3] The British still had fifty divisions to throw into the battle whereas von Below only had twenty-six divisions and 4th and 6th Armies had no mobile divisions, and were thus in no position to mount a major offensive in the immediate future.

On 24 March the exhausted troops of 17th Army made very little headway on the right flank. They were far more successful on the left flank and shortly after midnight they were in possession of Bapaume. 2nd Army made better progress against weaker opposition, but their efforts to help 17th Army were hampered by having to cross the old Somme battlefield: a landscape full of huge craters that was a serious obstacle even to the infantry, and virtually impassable for the artillery. Ensign Paul Knoch writing home to his parents was in high spirits, signing off as 'your offensive son', but complained bitterly that the shell holes made it very hard going.

> The area where the Battle of the Somme was fought, around Péronne etc., is a scene of terrible destruction. Crater after crater, some villages such as Bouchavesne have disappeared completely, only metre high stone walls remain. A few splintered stumps is all that remains of the trees. The roads are littered with dead horses, corpses of Germans, Englishmen and Frenchmen, strewn with equipment, weapons, ammunition, here and there damaged or abandoned English guns. One gets used to such sights, but one tries not to think about it.[4]

17th army could no longer concentrate on the push to the north-west and had to divert troops to operations in a westerly direction as well as south of the Somme. In spite of these difficulties von der Marwitz's men made some impressive gains including the town of Combles.

18th Army was further strengthened on 24 March so that operations south of the Somme were given still greater weight. On the afternoon of 23 March General von Sauberzweig reported that British resistance on the Somme was weakening. The OHL agreed with this assessment and stated that the enemy would not be able to bring in any reserves to strengthen their position on the river. At 2300hrs on 23 March Army Group German Crown Prince ordered 18th Army to advance to the line from Rosières to Noyon the next day. This was an exceedingly ambitious goal, but 18th Army was given three fresh divisions and von Hutier was confident that it could be achieved provided that his men moved quickly. Having reached this objective he promised that they would have a pause to rest, bring up supplies and secure the lines of communication.[5]

It was soon clear that the belief that they would encounter minimal resistance was false. The British XVIII Corps, which was commanded by Lieutenant-General Sir Ivor Maxse one of the finest generals in the war, was admittedly in a very awkward position, partly through his own fault for hanging on when Butler's left flank had been penetrated, thus exposing his right. But he was determined not to retreat any further without a stiff fight.[6] The French also put up a determined resistance. Von Hutier had hoped to advance twelve kilometres but he only just managed to cover one-third of the distance. His right flank was held up by the difficulty of crossing the Somme. On his left the French brought in fresh troops which slowed down his progress.

On 24 March the right flank of 17th Army was still stuck and was unable to overcome the resistance of Lieutenant-General Sir Aylmer Haldane's VI Corps and Lieutenant-General Sir Charles Fergusson's XVII Corps. The army made better progress on its left in the direction of Bapaume. 2nd Army had made significant progress and 18th Army was heading for Noyon and the Canal du Nord, its left flank moving along the Oise. Once again for no good reason Ludendorff changed the direction of the offensive. At 1630hrs on 24 March he ordered 17th Army to head west towards Doullens rather than north-west to Saint Pol. Ludendorff thus shifted the *Schwerpunkt* of the offensive from the right still further towards the left thus further altering his original strategic concept.[7] He now saw an opportunity opening up in the north where the British had withdrawn troops to prop up weak points further south, a situation that Haig described as 'serious'.[8] Ludendorff felt that it might be possible to launch 'Mars' and 'Ride of the Valkyries' with 17th Army co-operating closely with General von Quast's 6th Army who was to aim to capture Boulogne. He also proposed a scaled down version of 'Saint George' now modestly renamed 'Georgette'. He hoped that it would be possible to begin this last offensive in about eight days.[9] He now felt confident enough to telegraph his Army commanders that the battle had already been won.[10]

Colonel Wetzell then proposed that 'Saint George' should take the place of 'Mars' and 'Ride of the Valkyries' but Crown Prince Rupprecht objected strongly, repeating his argument that it would take far too long to change the plans and that it would give the British a breathing space.[11]

General von Kuhl was ordered to Avesnes on 25 March to discuss the problems of an offensive to the north. It was agreed that 'Mars' along both banks of the Scarpe should begin on 28 March, and 'Ride of the Valkyries' would begin on the following day. Preparations were to be made for 'Georgette' against the Portuguese to the north of the La Bassée Canal. The intention was to destabilize the entire British front.[12] In his orders issued on 25 March Ludendorff stressed the importance of Amiens as a railhead for the Allies and its strategic significance as the point where the British and French armies could be separated. Had he concentrated on the push towards Amiens he could have scored a major operational success, but he could not do so if 'Mars' were launched at the same time. Once again he made the serious blunder of trying to attack at too many points simultaneously with insufficient forces.

During the night from 22 to 23 March Haig begged Pétain to send as many divisions as possible to prop up Fifth Army. By this time the situation was so serious that it was obvious that the original number of French Divisions agreed upon by the two commanders-in-chief was insufficient. Pétain acted swiftly, even though he was still seriously concerned about the possibility of a German offensive in the Champagne. On the following day he formed a new Army Group, the Group of Reserve Armies (GAR), which was placed under the command of General Fayolle. It comprised General Humbert's III Army, General Debeney's I Army, and all British forces south of Péronne. The French now took over the battle between the Somme and the Oise and Fayolle was given the exceptionally difficult task of stabilizing the front to the south of Péronne. He had twelve infantry divisions, five cavalry divisions, and twelve regiments of heavy artillery under his command.

This soon proved to be inadequate. Haig met Pétain during the afternoon at Dury and promptly asked for twenty Divisions to prop up his Fifth Army. In fact Pétain had already alerted twenty-one Divisions, leaving him with only nineteen Divisions in reserve. Since it was estimated that the Germans still had fifty-five Divisions in reserve, and since the French still suspected that they might attack in the Champagne, any anxiety on Pétain's part was perfectly understandable.[13] The immediate question was whether Humbert's army could arrive before Gough's exhausted, demoralized and completely disorganized Fifth Army was totally destroyed.

The reorganization of the Entente's front took place during the night of 24/25 March. First all British troops north of the Somme were transferred to Third Army. Then command of Fifth Army was formally handed over to General Fayolle whose line now extended for about thirty-six miles, twenty-one and a half miles of which were held by the British, the remaining fourteen and a half miles by the French.[14]

Back in Whitehall the Director of Military Operations felt that 25 March was the critical day. The British Army had suffered 53,000 casualties since the beginning of the offensive, but the 88,000 men who were on leave at home were sent back to France, along with 106,000 fresh recruits. There were already 300,000 Americans in France, but it was not yet decided how best they could be used. Twelve French divisions had already arrived to support the British. General Maurice concluded that although the situation was 'undoubtedly serious, it was still far from desperate'.[15] In his estimation it would become desperate were the British Army to be pushed back across the Ancre. This was to happen within twenty-four hours.

There was inevitable delay in sending these divisions to the aid of the British, but Pétain was no slower than either Haig or Foch in getting his reserves up to the front. Thirteen of the twenty-one Divisions were relatively close to the action, the others were far away. The railway system was sorely taxed to move such large numbers of men, and many units were forced to march up to thirty kilometres. As the Germans pushed forward the two main roads running north-south were rendered useless, and the vital railhead at Amiens could no longer be used. The station at Beauvais that had to be used instead of Amiens was far to small to handle such significant traffic and could only manage two or three divisions per day. The roads were jammed with traffic, and there were not enough trucks available to move so many men with due dispatch.[16]

At the basis of the argument between Haig and Pétain was their different assessment of Ludendorff's intentions. Pétain rightly argued that Army Group German Crown Prince posed the greater threat. It had far more men, had advanced further, and posed a direct threat to Amiens and Beauvais. Haig still insisted that Crown Prince Rupprecht's Army Group north of the Somme was far more menacing. Foch also believed that the critical area was north of the Somme, between Péronne and Arras, and complained bitterly to Clemenceau that Pétain with his concentration south of the river seemed to be unaware of the danger.[17]

Haig wanted twenty French Divisions to straddle the Somme, and requested that all the cavalry divisions that were operating south of the Somme should be moved north. In the meantime he intended to withdraw and cover the Channel ports. No mention was made of the need to maintain contact with the French Army. Pétain was ordered by his government to ensure that Paris was covered, but he still kept a watchful eye on the Champagne and was deeply concerned about the breach between the British and French Armies. It should also be noted that at no time did Pétain express his intention of withdrawing to the defence of Paris.

At a conference at Pétain's headquarters at Compiègne on the afternoon of 25 March, attended by Clemenceau, Foch and Milner, the French commander-in-chief gave an account of the actions he had taken to date. When Milner was asked what the British Army intended to do to close the breach between the two armies, the secretary for war had to confess that he was not in a position to answer that question.

Foch, who had preached his 'parrot' strategy at the War College, was given to saying: 'The parrot, that sublime creature, when leaving his perch always makes sure that he has a new bar firmly in his grasp before leaving the old one.'[18] He was determined that Amiens should be defended, and that the gap between the British and French Armies should be closed. He therefore proposed that both armies should run the risk of moving troops from other fronts, the British from Flanders, the French from the Champagne. This proposal was obviously unacceptable both to Haig and to Pétain. It was therefore decided to invite both commanders-in-chief as well as Weygand, Foch's capable chief of staff who was rumoured to be the illegitimate son of the unfortunate Emperor Maximilian of Mexico, and Wilson to a conference at Doullens the following day in an attempt to find a solution. Although it was not mentioned at the time, it was clear that some form of unified command was the only possible solution to these fundamental differences.

There is still debate about the behaviour of Haig and Pétain during these first few days of the German offensive. The standard version, based on his diaries which were carefully re-written for publication, is that Haig was a tower of strength amid the collapse of Gough's Fifth Army and that Pétain bears the major share of the blame for the fiasco.[19] Haig describes the French commander-in-chief as panicking, refusing to help the British Army and solely concerned with defending Paris against an attack which he was convinced was imminent. According to this version on 25 March Haig requested that Wilson and Milner, the Secretary of State for War, should come to France and suggested that a resolute general like Foch should be appointed supreme commander in France so that Pétain would be stiffened. This was promptly resolved at a meeting at the town hall in Doullens on 26 March.

This account is a travesty of the truth and an insult to Pétain who, although something of a pessimist, was a valiant soldier, with a far greater understanding of flexible defence than Haig. Far from refusing to assist the BEF he immediately ordered three divisions to rush to its assistance once he heard that the Germans had broken through its lines. He did this before he received a request for help from Haig. When Pétain visited Haig on 23 March those present remarked on his calm and decisiveness.[20] At that meeting he emphasized the importance of Fifth Army maintaining contact with General Pellé's French V Corps. The suggestion that Foch be made supreme commander in France came not from Haig but from Clemenceau, not because he was worried about Pétain's failure of nerve, but because he was understandably concerned at the way Haig was handling the situation.

It would seem that it was Haig and not Pétain who was close to panic. On 24 March he wrote to CIGS and to Lord Milner that they should come to France immediately taking up Clemenceau's proposal that, unless Foch, or some similarly forceful general were given supreme command, there would be a disaster.[21] On the evening of 25 March he wrote to Foch's chief of staff repeating his request for twenty French divisions to be placed astride the Somme west of Amiens to assist the BEF as it retired to cover the Channel ports.[22] Having been turned down once he told Byng that little could be expected in the way of help from the French, that Gough's Fifth Army was finished and that his Third Army would have to protect the British Army's right flank as it withdrew to the north-west.[23] Haig's subsequent claim that Pétain panicked, refused to send any assistance and planned to retire in a south-westerly direction in order to cover Paris is thus the reverse of the truth. It was Haig who lost his nerve and withdrew to the north-west thus allowing the Germans to drive a massive wedge between the British and French armies. Indeed, GHQ was in a state of panic, Lawrence (Chief of General Staff), Davidson (Director of Operations) and Dawnay (Organization) having all lost their nerves.[24] This was certainly Pétain's view of the situation. He begged Clemenceau to do whatever he could to intervene with the British government and pointed out that Haig's withdrawal to the north-west and his refusal to do anything to bridge the gap between the French and British Armies had created an extremely dangerous situation.

It is true that Pétain was not unnaturally perturbed by the sudden collapse of Gough's Army, and initially suggested a withdrawal behind the Somme and the Avre and to the west of Amiens. When the situation north of the Somme stabilized somewhat, he then ordered a defence east of Amiens and that every effort should be made to reestablish contact with the British, as well as between the Fifth and Third British Armies.

Aerial observation revealed to the Germans that the British had withdrawn to their old Somme positions in front of 18th Army but that the French were moving troops up to Noyon. Ludendorff ordered that the town should be taken as quickly as possible, but once again he seriously underestimated the problems involved. He reinforced von Hutier's left flank in order to help him take the high ground to the north and east of Noyon from whence he hoped to be able to head south over the Oise. Originally he planned to defend the left flank of 'Michael' along the Somme. Then he moved the left flank down to the Oise. Now he was contemplating an advance south of the river. Thus by 24 March the offensive bore no resemblance to the original plan for 'Michael' and threatened to dissipate into a series of unco-ordinated attacks. Ludendorff now had about 40 per cent of his divisions in 18th Army, which had originally been designed to guard the left flank of 'Michael'.

On 25 March the right wing of 17th Army was rested in preparation for 'Mars'. The left flank, in co-operation with 2nd Army's right, was to push westwards and secure crossings over the Ancre. 2nd Army had made such excellent progress on the previous day that morale was very high. Spotter planes reported that the British were in full retreat from Bapaume to Albert and the Ancre. German fighter aircraft made this movement even more uncomfortable by constantly harassing the retiring troops. Von der Marwitz was now ordered to head for Albert. The town was soon in German hands, but the difficulties on his left flank were considerable. He had not yet been able to cross the old Somme battlefield where the British had established strong defences in the craters. The river Somme also presented a formidable obstacle.

The left wing of 18th Army was now ordered to push on over the Oise. The divisions allotted to this operation were placed under the command of von Boehn's 7th Army. Von Hutier's forces between the Somme and the Oise made excellent progress. They advanced towards Noyon and the Canal du Nord thus taking the pressure off 7th Army's right wing, but some of the attempts to cross the Oise failed because the British and French had withdrawn south of the river and were now in relatively strong defensive positions.

Although the Germans still faced some formidable obstacles the Kaiser was in an exultant mood. On 25 March he ordered the flags to be hoisted and a victory salute to be fired to celebrate the German triumphs at Monchy, Cambrai, Saint Quentin and La Fère. On the same day he awarded Hindenburg the iron cross with sun's rays which had been specially designed for Blücher after the victory at Belle Alliance and which had never been awarded since. Ludendorff received the grand cross of the iron cross. Neither of these decorations had ever been awarded before the end of a battle or a campaign and there were many officers who felt that the Kaiser was being overly optimistic, and some felt that he could have waited until Amiens fell before handing out such high honours.[25]

Notwithstanding the arrival of French divisions both the British Third and Fifth Armies were obliged to make substantial withdrawals along the entire line. The retirement was poorly synchronized, so that Third Army's right flank was more than four miles behind the left flank of the Fifth. Both Armies were hard pressed and the line had to be straightened to reduce the risk to Fifth Army's flank. Further withdrawals were necessary the following day, mainly by Fayolle's British and French troops south of the Somme who had to withstand the brunt of the German attack. By and large Third Army managed to hang on, and filled some of the gaps in the line[26] Haig persisted in his demand for French troops. In a urgent message to Weygand he argued that the Germans did not have enough troops to attack the French in the Champagne and that everything had to be done to stop the Germans from driving a wedge between the French and British Armies.[27]

On 26 March Wetzell suggested that if the British continued their withdrawal at Arras it might be better to cancel 'Mars' and go for a full-scale 'George'. Later that day 17th Army reported that the British had stopped their withdrawal south of Arras, but continued to pull back at Saint Léger. This enabled von Below to advance some five kilometres, but British resistance was stiffening and a number of counter-attacks had to be beaten off. Ludendorff was furious that von Below had not made better progress and ranted and raved on the telephone to Crown Prince Rupprecht at 7.30 in the evening of 26 March. He claimed that 17th Army had achieved nothing and threatened to fire its chief of staff, General Krafft von Dellmensingen, an officer whom he had previously held in the highest regard, along with the operations chief, Willisen. Crown Prince Rupprecht was appalled at Ludendorff's crude attempt to cover up his own mistakes by blaming his subordinates, and insisted that 17th Army had met with extremely stiff resistance and had done the best they could under the circumstances.[28]

Von Below was in an extremely awkward position. He was ordered by the OHL to attack the left flank of the French Army by Abbéville and at the same time combine with 'Mars North' and 'Ride of the Valkyries' to attack the British Army at Arras. He was thus ordered to push on in a northerly and north-westerly direction. These two objectives were far too wide apart and 17th Army lacked the manpower to undertake both.

The Kaiser and his entourage seemed oblivious to these problems. After a visit to the front he once again ordered champagne all round and announced that if a British delegation came to sue for peace they would have to kneel before the German flag, for this was a decisive victory of monarchy over democracy.[29]

Initially the OHL promised to send three reserve divisions to lend weight to 17th Army's advance in the direction of Doullens, but in the early afternoon of 27 March Crown Prince Rupprecht learnt that Ludendorff had changed his mind and had ordered them to move south of the Somme. In despair he cried out: 'Now we have lost the war!'[30] Ludendorff continued to blame Generals von Below and Krafft von Dellmensingen for 17th Army's slow progress, and Krafft's brusque and arrogant tone made the situation even worse. Even General von Kuhl felt that it was now time for Ludendorff to remove him.[31]

2nd Army met with little resistance to the east of the Ancre and von Kuhl hoped that it would be possible to break through the British front between Amiens and Doullens in close co-operation with the left wing of 17th Army. The Ancre proved to be a formidable obstacle. The river itself is of little consequence, but it runs through a swampy valley that is about 60 metres deep and which is covered in dense undergrowth. Von der Marwitz's men were unable to cross the Ancre at Thiepval, a village that had gained a certain notoriety in the battle of the Somme in 1916 and is now marked by Sir Edwin Lutyens magnificent memorial. Patrols crossed the river between Authuille and Aveluy, but without support on either side General von Watter, the commander of XIII Army Corps, felt it prudent to wait until the morning before attacking. The 3rd Marine Infantry Division was halted at Albert after some fierce house-to-house fighting. 13th Infantry Division crossed the river near Albert on the following day.

The British withdrew on 2nd Army's left wing between the Ancre at Albert and the Somme at Bray enabling 1st Infantry Division to advance in a westerly direction south of the Somme. On 2nd Army's far right 51 Corps pushed on in a south-westerly direction. There was considerable criticism of the conduct of the troops at Albert. Exhausted and undernourished troops pounced upon the ample supplies of food and drink left behind by the British. 3rd Marine Division and one of 2nd Army's crack units was accused of failing to pursue the British by getting drunk. Similar accusations were levied against the Silesian 9th Division, which had fought with great distinction since 21 March. Further investigation showed that although there were a number of instances of drunkenness, officers were in full command of their units and the principal reason why the Germans were unable to press on beyond Albert was not alcohol but the determined British defence.[32]

By this time many of the troops were utterly exhausted. 3rd Marine Division had been fighting for sixty hours without respite, and had not had any food for forty-eight hours. It is hardly surprising that after such exertions they were unable to fight their way across the Ancre, and that in the night of 27 March they tucked into British supplies with no little enthusiasm.

18th Army continued its advance in a south-westerly direction by heading for the line from Chaulnes to Roye and Noyon. Noyon was in German hands by the early morning of 26 March and von Hutier pushed forward between Montdidier and Noyon making rapid progress.

Thus in the first five days of the offensive the Germans had failed to trap the British troops in the Cambrai salient which, given that it did not extend very far, was hardly surprising. The advance was slow on the right wing where the Germans were held up by the strong British positions around Arras and at Bapaume, which had been reinforced to cover the withdrawal from the Cambrai salient. To the centre and left the Germans had made remarkable progress without suffering too many losses or expending too much ammunition. Between 21 and 26 March the British suffered 75,000 casualties, the Germans about 90,000. The Germans were already beginning to suffer from a noticeable shortage of officers and experienced NCOs.

General Dawson, an equerry to the King, had manned a machine-gun post until he was taken prisoner. In the best traditions of the soldier-eccentric he presented an 'extraordinary sight' to his captors, for he 'looked as if he had just stepped out of a Turkish bath in Jermyn Street'. When complimented by these seasoned warriors on the 'trouble' he had caused them he snorted: 'Trouble! Why, we have been running for five days and five nights!'[33]

The fact that the British Army had been on the run for so long caused concern and consternation in Whitehall. Lord Hankey could hardly believe that the Germans had driven the British so easily across the old Somme battlefields that were 'pitted all over with craters and is one vast military obstacle'. Sir John French, who commanded the Home Army, had no doubt at all who was to blame. He told Hankey that Haig 'surrounded himself with stupid people and bad commanders' and had completely ruined the British Army with his bungled offensive in 1917.[34]

The OHL was unable to change their troops often enough and they were getting very tired. They fought on for eight days unable to take off their clothes or their boots. The frequently had no water for washing, and even less for drinking. A quick wash in the cold water in a shell hole was the most they could hope for.[35] There was a chronic shortage of adequately trained and equipped divisions that could have been brought in from other sections of the front to give the front line troops a well-deserved respite. The OHL was also eager to maintain the momentum of the offensive and thus was unwilling to give the troops a breathing space. Under these circumstances it is remarkable that morale remained so high and that the troops were confident that victory was within their grasp. But as early as 27 March, when orders were given to dig trenches and go on the defensive, the first murmurs of discontent were heard. 'Trench warfare again!' was the bitter complaint.[36]

There is ample evidence that morale in the German Army was very high in March and it is only when the offensive ran into serious difficulties that it declined rapidly. There was widespread confidence that the offensive would be a resounding success and it would bring peace. Therefore every effort had to be made to ensure its success so that this terrible war would end. Many people commented that something of the euphoric spirit of August 1914 was recaptured in the weeks before the offensive. For this reason soldiers at the front had little sympathy for the strikers in January whom they denounced as 'rowdies' (*Radaubrüder*), 'idiots' (*Heimidioten*) and 'arseholes' (*Armlöcher*).[37] Once it was clear to most soldiers that the offensive had failed and that therefore the war could not be won, the army's confidence was lost and morale became a serious problem. The spring offensive did not fail because of low morale among the troops, but its failure led to a disastrous decline in fighting spirit.

The Germans were beginning to experience serious difficulties with supplies. As they advanced they moved further away from their railheads, which at some points were up 69 kilometres distant, and their supply lines lay across a battlefield pitted with craters. For the same reason they had great difficulty bringing their artillery forward and thus were unable to give the infantry adequate support. There was also an acute shortage of telephone lines to the front which caused serious delays in passing back information and issuing orders. It was not unusual for 24 hours to pass before an order issued by army headquarters reached the front.

These problems were partly offset when they reached the British back areas that appeared to the exhausted men as a land flowing with milk and honey. They dressed in British boots, jerkins and waterproofs. They gorged themselves with British rations and took to looting with considerable enthusiasm.[38]

Rudolf Binding could not understand why the advance was held up near Albert. As he approached the town he found a possible explanation:

> I began to see curious sights. Strange figures, which looked very little like soldiers, and certainly showed no signs of advancing, were making their way back out of the town. There were men driving cows before them on a line; others who carried a hen under one arm and box of note-paper under the other. Men carrying a bottle of wine under their arm and another one open in their hand. Men who had torn a silk drawing-room curtain from off its rod and were dragging it to the rear as a useful bit of loot. More men with writing-paper and coloured note-books. Evidently they had found it desirable to sack a stationer's shop. Men dressed up in comic disguise. Men with top-hats on their heads. Men staggering. Men who could hardly walk.

With a mixture of sympathy and disapproval, Binding noted that most of these men were from the Marine Division.

The Allies had overwhelming superiority in the air and their planes were doing a great deal of damage to the German infantry, particularly to 17th Army. The Luftwaffe was barely able to protect their own spotter planes and could do little to stop the Allies bombing and strafing the German troops. Although the Germans shot down 189 enemy aircraft on the Western Front between 21 and 26 March for a loss of sixty-five, Allied planes continued to harass the infantry.

Looking at the overall situation on the morning of 26 March Ludendorff saw the best opportunities south of the Somme. In a telephone conversation with von Kuhl he ordered the right wing of 2nd Army to advance south of the Somme towards Amiens and the left wing to move alongside the right flank of 18th Army in the direction of Miraumont. Ludendorff was confidant that the British southern wing had been defeated and that it would soon be possible to complete the separation of the British and the French Armies.

On the evening of 26 March Ludendorff ordered 18th Army to advance in a south-westerly direction towards Compiègne. 2nd Army was to move in the same direction south of the Somme towards the Avre. 17th Army was to proceed in a westerly direction towards Saint Pol and Abbeville. They would be supported by divisions that had been allotted to the 'Mars' offensive. 6th Army was to continue its preparations for 'Georgette', which had to be postponed for at least ten days because of a shortage of ammunition, and 4th Army was to prepare an attack against the Belgian Army, for which the OHL had a contemptuously low opinion.

By the time that the Allies met at Doullens it had become clear that Pétain's analysis of the situation on 24 March was broadly correct. German pressure north of the Somme had relaxed, but south of the river the French were confronted with the full weight of the German offensive. To the north the only real danger was that the British would retire too quickly, thus running the risk of a dangerous flanking attack. Fifth Army retired throughout the day on 26 March and by evening were only about ten kilometres from the final defence line east of Amiens. Even GHQ staff realized that the main weight of the attack was now in the south. In their overall assessment they wrote: 'The centre of gravity of the enemy's attack has shown a distinct southward tendency during the last twenty four hours.'[39]

By this time Pétain's staff realized that there was no immediate danger of an offensive in the Champagne, and therefore reserves were moved to the Somme from IV and V Armies. By the evening of 26 March a total of 40 French divisions had been committed to the battle, in other words about half the entire French Army.[40]

A partial solution to the struggles between Haig and Pétain was found at the Doullens conference that resulted in the appointment of Foch to co-ordinate the efforts of the British and French forces on the Western Front. Haig later claimed that it was he who pressed for Foch to be given the widest possible powers and his version is dutifully repeated by Edmonds in the official history, but there is scant evidence to support this claim.[41] Indeed Haig had throughout opposed Foch's appointment, insisting the while that he only took his orders from his King and his immediate superiors in the British Army. Foch, whom Clemenceau described as a 'right bugger', refused to stand on ceremony and had a directness and determination which Haig found disturbing.[42] Haig gave way to Foch with no little reluctance and reserved the right to appeal to the British Government against any orders he might give.

Under the terms of the agreement Foch was charged to 'coordinate the action of the Allied armies on the Western Front'.[43] It was not at all clear precisely what this meant, although Foch with his infectious energy and impetuosity imparted a certain sense of urgency and decisiveness amid the gloom. In the spirit of his 'parrot' strategy he announced: 'We must fight in front of Amiens, we must fight where we are now. As we have not been able to stop the Germans on the Somme, we must not now retire a single inch.'[44]

Foch was unable to do anything without the consent of Haig and Pétain, and for the moment the agreement only concerned the British and French Armies. The Americans, Belgians, Italians and Portuguese had to be consulted. Although it was widely felt that Foch was the most suitable man for the job, there were many who were alarmed at the prospect. Foch had been 'Stellenbosched', as one British officer put it, ever since the Somme and had been very much under a cloud ever since. He had suffered severe head injuries in a car crash, and his often violent, unpredictable and outspoken behaviour was sometimes attributed to his being off his head as a result of the accident.[45] Foch was also obsessed with the offensive and some felt that he was an unsuitable choice to co-ordinate a defensive campaign. He had fully mastered the principles of Ludendorff's '*grande tactique*' for the offensive, and was embued with '*l'esprit de Riga*', but unlike Pétain he failed to understand German defensive tactics. It would appear that it was Milner who pushed the strongest for his appointment, in the hope that he would be more willing than Pétain to move divisions up to Amiens. Furthermore Pétain would have had to have been promoted and given wider powers had he taken over the post. Otherwise this would be seen as a demotion. With Pétain as Generalissimo Haig would have been subordinated to a man whom he could not stand, and whom many felt lacked the drive, energy and flair to meet the current crisis.

There is considerable confusion on the British side as to what happened at the meeting in the first floor room of the modest little town hall in Doullens. The proceedings were mostly in rapidly spoken and agitated French. Most of the participants claim that they were the ones who proposed Foch. Lawrence later told Edmonds that Poincaré and Clemenceau wanted Foch to take over at Amiens, but Haig had insisted that this was too limited a task. Haig complained that the French had done nothing whatsoever to help. Lawrence agreed. All they did was send four divisions behind the Arras front 'where they did nothing but interfere with the lines of communication. Then they took over Kemmel and promptly lost it.'[46]

The French view of the British was equally unflattering. On his arrival at Doullens Clemenceau said that Haig wanted to uncover Amiens and fall back on the Channel ports. Haig assured Milner that this was not true, but added that it was imperative that he be covered by the French. Wilson proposed that Clemenceau should be appointed Generalissimo with Foch as his military advisor, but Foch felt that this would lead to an endless tug of war with Pétain. Milner claimed that he was the one who pushed for Foch, and that Clemenceau and Haig readily agreed.[47]

Haig argued that Foch's mandate should not be confined to operations around Amiens and to plugging the gap between the British and French Armies. He proposed that Foch should be given supreme command over the entire Western Front. His motives for making this suggestion are somewhat unclear. He later suggested it was to ensure that Foch would overrule Pétain, and that the gap between the French and British Armies was closed. But this was already covered in the earlier agreement. The most likely explanation is that Haig was still worried about his channel ports, and hoped that the appointment of Foch would open to way to French divisions being sent to Flanders in an emergency.[48]

Foch's first move after his appointment was to go on the same day along with his chief of staff, Weygand, to visit Gough at his headquarters in Dury. He behaved in a characteristically blunt, outspoken and insensitive manner. Gough was given a tremendous dressing down in French. Why, he roared, was he not at the front? Why had he retired? Why had he not stood his ground as at the first battle of Ypres in 1914? Foch then ordered the unfortunate Gough to hold the line at all costs. Having delivered this brief lecture on 'parrot' tactics he then stomped out of the room. He did not offer Gough any reinforcements, nor did he give him any further instructions. Gough was left smouldering, and reported to Haig that the French were retiring far faster than the British.[49]

Foch's orders to Gough that he should not retire under any circumstances were totally unrealistic, and would have led to further heavy losses to the remainder of Fifth Army. Gough continued to withdraw, roughly to the line proposed by Pétain on 24 March. Foch failed to offer him any relief, in part because he was now obliged to concentrate his reserves of the front from the Somme to the Oise, and began to regroup all available forces to form a strategic reserve ready for the next German blow.

Gough thus got nothing but an exhortation to stand and fight from Foch, but he was given rather more substantial support from BEF. An infantry division arrived from Italy and four Antipodean divisions, three Australian and one of New Zealanders, provided excellent support.[50] Foch's plans for the French troops were an ill-considered piece of 'parrot' tactics. He ordered General Debeney's I Army forward to join Gough's

Fifth Army so as to make a stand east of the Ancre. The army's right wing was very feeble, was hit hard by the Germans and was forced back. Montdidier had to be abandoned by the evening of 27 March, and contact was lost with General Humbert's III Army. By the end of the day the gap had widened to about fifteen kilometres. In spite of energetic leadership the army was pushed back between thirteen and fourteen kilometres. The right flank was somewhat more successful. It established contact with the British Army, but Gough's men were in such poor shape that the situation remained precarious.[51]

Pétain issued an order of the day urging the French Army to stand fast: 'This is The Battle! Soldiers of the Marne, of the Yser and of Verdun: the destiny of France is in your hands!' At the same time he ordered V Army, from the Champagne, and X Army, which was arriving from Italy, to be positioned south of Beauvais and to be placed in the GAR under the command of General Fayolle. There were ordered to prepare a counter-attack either in the direction of Péronne or towards Amiens.[52]

6

'Georgette':
The First Phase 9-14 April

The Germans had achieved remarkable results with the offensive to date. 2nd Army had advanced forty-five kilometres from its starting point, 18th Army up to sixty kilometres. They had taken 90,000 prisoners, of whom 75,000 were British, and 1,300 guns had been captured. But losses had been very heavy. The Germans suffered about 230,000 casualties in these two weeks; the Allies about 212,000. The Germans could not afford such losses whereas the Allies could make up their deficiencies with fresh American troops. More important still the Germans had failed to achieve their immediate goal of separating the British from the French forces which might have enabled them to begin the decisive campaign to end the war.

The British had suffered heavy losses and the Germans had made a huge dent in the Allied front, but the French had lost little of their fighting strength. The Germans had started from a front about ninety kilometres wide and now found themselves in a salient with about 150 kilometres of front with many weak spots which made them very vulnerable to counter-attack.

The further the Germans advanced across the waterlogged and cratered battlefields and across their own lines the greater the difficulty they had in bringing up supplies, artillery and fresh divisions. They could not build new railway lines nearly fast enough to meet the needs of the front-line troops. The Allies by contrast were able bring in reserves and supplies with relative ease on existing roads and railways, and they had an overwhelming superiority in draft animals and motor vehicles. When the 'Michael' offensive was called to a halt the Germans found themselves in defensive positions in the old trenches and craters of the Somme battlefield, up to their knees in mud, without shelter, incessantly bombarded by the overwhelming British artillery, bombed and strafed from the air.[1]

18th Army reported that transportation difficulties were by far the greatest problem.[2] Their lines of communication to the rear had not been completed when the offensive began, and, although they had adequate supplies of ammunition, a large amount of it had to be left behind as the army advanced. Lack of transportation also made it difficult to provide adequate medical treatment for the wounded. There were very few dressing stations in forward positions, and the wounded had to be sent to the rear unattended. This resulted in an unnecessary number of fatalities. Communications were also inadequate. Army Headquarters received information on requirements for ammunition and food several days late, and were slow to respond because of inadequate rail and road links beyond the starting line. Prisoners of war and local inhabitants were employed building lines of communication to the rear. Under such circumstances it was hardly surprising that the troops looted British food supplies, but the Army Group insisted that such serious breaches of military discipline could not be tolerated in future.

The appalling difficulties caused by mounting a large scale offensive across the old Somme battlefield inevitably raises the question whether it would have been better to strike elsewhere on the front. But Flanders was waterlogged in the early months of the year, and the British defensive positions between Béthune and Arras were particularly strong. An offensive in Flanders would have had to have been postponed until the end of April to ensure that the ground was dry, but the OHL could not risk waiting for so long for fear that by that time the Americans would have a large number of troops at the front. 'Georgette', which began on 9 April after a relatively dry spell, was to show that Flanders was not a suitable place for a major offensive.

It was possible to make a substantial advance south of the Somme, as the fighting in March showed, but this brought no operational gains. At least on the Somme the Allied position was relatively weak and a breakthrough would have brought a substantial and possibly even decisive victory. It was Ludendorff's fatal mistake that he lost sight of this essential aim, and was tempted by tactical gains into dissipating his efforts in looking for weak spots along the whole length of the Allied front. The gains that were made were all at the expense of the main thrust to the north-west, which alone made operational sense.

On 6 April the OHL made its assessment of the British front.[3] It was obvious that the strongest sector was around Arras. To the north the front was held by tired divisions that had been badly battered in the 'Michael' offensive. The Portuguese troops on the Lys were regarded as particularly weak, and the OHL had a similar poor opinion of the Belgians further north. The Belgian government was already thinking of evacuating the government and the remains of their army to England.

King George V kindly suggested that they might be accommodated in Tunbridge Wells.[4]

The French had taken over about 90 kilometres of the 'Michael' front and brought up at least twenty-seven reserve divisions to the front. These would soon be backed up by the Americans, by divisions taken from quiet sectors of the front and by territorials, totalling a further twenty-five divisions. From this the OHL concluded that the British were the weaker opponents. Thus 'Georgette' was ordered to go ahead, preceded by 'Archangel'.

'Archangel' had been designed as a diversionary action in support of the 'Michael' offensive, but as 18th Army had pushed far further south than was originally planned it was now intended to straighten the front, guard von Hutier's left flank and protect his supply lines. The object of the offensive was to seize the high ground to the east of the Oise-Aisne canal.

When the offensive between the Somme and the Oise came to a standstill Army Group German Crown Prince decided on the evening of 31 March to attack in the direction of the Oise-Aisne canal, but the operation had to be postponed for lack of troops and horses. 'Archangel' thus began on 6 April with the limited objective of taking the high ground at Amigny which the French were using as an artillery spotting point. At 0330hrs on 6 April the French artillery were shelled with gas. At 0425hrs 216 batteries shelled the French positions. The storm-troops attacked at 0530hrs and met with very little resistance. The attack was a complete success and General von Boehn ordered his men to continue the advance on the following day to establish bridgeheads across the canal.

While the French were struggling to hold on in the face of this determined attack Haig sent a handwritten note to Foch saying that there was clear indication that the Germans were about to attack the British positions between Béthune and Arras. He therefore asked Foch to launch a massive attack within five to six days to take the pressure off the British. Failing that he should either relieve the four British infantry divisions south of the Somme, or send four French divisions to support the British army in Flanders.[5]

Heavy rain during the night made the going very difficult on the following day and the French put up a more determined resistance. Nevertheless all the objectives were gained and von Boehn's men advanced further the next day. In the night of 8 April the French retreated from their positions east of the canal and dug in on the high ground on the west bank. The Germans therefore advanced to the canal without a fight.

The French complained that the British seemed to be unaware of the pressure that the Germans were putting on their army. It also seemed that the British did not have a clear idea of German intentions. On 7 April Wilson wrote to Foch saying that the enemy was preparing a major artillery barrage against Amiens in order to disrupt communications and supplies. This was clearly in anticipation of an offensive with between forty and fifty divisions between Albert and the La Bassée Canal. Wilson claimed that French help was essential, and he asked for strong French reserves to be placed either side of the Somme from Amiens to Abbeville.[6] On the other hand a colonel in the British General Staff argued that the Germans would attack the French who were 'war weary, and subject to panic; and there would be every chance of getting them out of the war'. By contrast the British north of the Somme were 'a hard nut to crack'.[7]

This impasse was typical of relations between the British and French Armies. In fact both agreed on the importance of Amiens, but the British wanted the French to defend the town, Foch wanted the British to launch a joint offensive to push the Germans back, and Pétain was loathe to commit any of his reserves to anything beyond a few limited operations.

'Archangel' had therefore achieved all its goals and all available troops were now placed at the disposition of the Army Group German Crown Prince. As a diversionary tactic limited attacks were made to establish bridgeheads on the other side of the canal. At a cost of 1,900 casualties von Boehn's 7th Army had shortened the German front by about seven kilometres, afforded the supply lines far better protection, and had taken some 2000 prisoners and captured one French battery.

After lengthy debates the OHL eventually decided that it was no longer possible to mount the 'Saint George' offensive. In its place they proposed a scaled-down version appropriately called 'Georgette', confined to the sector between Armentières and the La Bassée canal. This was to be launched when the British moved troops from this section of the front to strengthen their defences against the 'Michael' offensive, and when weather permitted.

The British finally moved their reserves at the end of the month when the 'Michael' offensive was already grinding to a standstill. On 29 March the OHL ordered General von Quast's 6th Army to go ahead with 'Georgette' and this was to be followed by an attack by General Sixt von Arnim's 4th Army against the Belgians at Dixmunde imaginatively code-named 'Flanders'.

On 1 April the OHL decided that 'Georgette' should begin on 8 April. At a conference with the chiefs of staff of Army Group Crown Prince Rupprecht and of 4th and 6th Armies held at Saint Armand on 3 April Ludendorff decided that all available troops should be thrown into the 'Georgette' offensive. Originally seven divisions had been allotted to the offensive, now Ludendorff called for seventeen assault divisions in addition to the troops already in the trenches. 4th Army was to give substantial support to 6th Army's right flank. A major problem was that most of these divisions had been engaged in heavy fighting in March and had lost many of their best officers and men. The veterans of 'Michael' were bitterly disillusioned that the offensive in which they had pinned such high hopes had failed to bring the expected results, and they now faced the prospect of a series of similar operations in which they had little confidence.[8]

Colonel Wetzell had argued in a memorandum dated 12 December 1917 that it would not be possible to make a decisive breakthrough at one point along the front. A number of 'hammer blows' would be needed before success could be achieved. He thus never believed that 'Michael' would achieve anything more than pull in British and possibly French reserves, thus hopefully weakening the front at another point. Furthermore, although he felt that an offensive against the French in the Verdun salient offered the best chances of scoring a decisive victory he, like Crown Prince Rupprecht and his staff, believed that an offensive in Flanders offered far better prospects than a major operation further south. He had hoped that 'Michael' would force the British to send reserves from the Flanders front and that it would be possible to attack near Hazebrouk against weakened British forces not more than two weeks after the beginning of 'Michael'. He thus saw 'Michael' as a diversionary offensive designed to prepare the way for a decisive blow in Flanders.[9]

Ludendorff did not agree with the chief of his operations staff. He felt that the German Army was simply not strong enough to mount two major offensives in such quick succession. He insisted that an offensive in Flanders should only be undertaken if 'Michael' did not achieve its objectives. In a memorandum dated 10 February the OHL had told Army Group Crown Prince Rupprecht that the 'Saint George' offensive should proceed if 'Michael' did not prove to be a complete success. It pointed out that there would be far less troops and artillery available for an offensive in Flanders than had been foreseen in the original plans of 4th and 6th Armies, but added that 'Michael' would lead to a serious depletion of the British forces in Flanders. The OHL was therefore confident that 'Saint George' was likely to be a resounding success.

The problem facing Army Group Crown Prince Rupprecht's staff was that for 'Saint George' to be successful it would have to follow immediately after 'Michael'. But forces from the 'Michael' front would have to be sent to Flanders, and it would take time to regroup, rest, bring the units up to strength after days of very heavy fighting, and stockpile huge quantities of essential supplies. The longer this problem was addressed the clearer it became that Colonel Wetzell's hope that 'Saint George' could be mounted immediately after 'Michael' was totally unrealistic.

The initial success of 'Michael' and the widening of the front to the north around Arras and Lens with 'Mars' and 'Ride of the Valkyries' left the British Army in disarray, and a full-scale 'Saint George' offensive was no longer deemed either possible or essential.

'Georgette' called for 6th Army to attack the Portuguese on the original 'Saint George' front between Armentières and the La Bassée canal, cross the Lys and push on to Hazebrouk and beyond. 4th Army was to attack the British on the flank and rear north of the Lys at Messines, the capture of which had been one of the very few Allied successes at Third Ypres in 1917.

Von Kuhl was understandably concerned that the operation was overly ambitious. 17th Army on the right wing of 'Michael' had got stuck. The 'Mars' offensive at Arras on 28 March had failed and consequently 'Ride of the Valkyries' had to be cancelled. The French managed to stop 18th Army's advance and on 4 April, when the attack on Amiens failed, he confided in his diary that this was Germany's last chance to score a decisive victory against the British. It would be impossible to mount any more offensives on this scale for lack of reserves, ammunition and horses.[10]

The 'Georgette' offensive would cross waterlogged country and had to tackle some strongly defended towns. These included Ypres which as 'Wipers' had become symbolic of the British army's determination and grit. Hazebrouk and Saint Omer were important railway junctions, which the British could not afford to lose, and would defend at all costs. The coalfields around Béthune were essential for France. Armentières was also a formidable obstacle. The Germans would have to cross a number of rivers and canals with their swampy banks that would not be reasonably dry until the middle of May.

The OHL decided to go ahead with the offensive because the British only had six and a half divisions on a front of twenty-six kilometres between Frélinghien, north-west of Armentières, and the La Bassée canal. Two of these were Portuguese divisions which the OHL did not consider as serious obstacles. Most of the rest were battle-weary Canadians and Australians who had been withdrawn from the 'Michael' front. Here was an opportunity, which was unlikely to recur.

The general staff at Army Group Crown Prince Rupprecht discussed Ludendorff's instructions on the evening of 3 April. They were in an optimistic mood and envisioned a massive breakthrough similar to 'Michael' followed by a thrust in a north-westerly direction that would drive the British back to the Channel coast. Orders were issued that evening and concluded with the words: 'If 'Georgette' is a great success all forces on the Army Group's front will be concentrated and as far as possible will immediately be put into action.'[11]

Army Group Crown Prince Rupprecht and 6th Army begged Ludendorff to postpone the offensive because rain made logistical problems virtually insurmountable. With great reluctance he granted one day's grace and ordered 'Georgette' to begin on 9 April. Ludendorff intended 4th and 6th Armies to attack simultaneously in order to protect von Quast's right flank, but General von Lossberg, 4th Army's chief of staff, protested that this was out of the question because he did not have sufficient artillery. Weather conditions were still poor, and it was therefore decided that 4th Army's attack should be further postponed until 10 April, and that some of 6th Army's artillery could be used for the preparatory barrage.

If the British were to abandon the Ypres salient, as seemed highly likely, 4th Army was to jettison the 'Flanders' offensive against the Belgian Army and pursue the British in operation 'Blücher'.[12] Ludendorff announced that his aim was now to destroy the British and Belgian forces north of the canal from Béthune to Saint Omer and then to push in a south-westerly direction. 17th and 2nd Armies were ordered to mount limited attacks in support of 'Georgette'.

General von Quast's 6th Army had seventeen divisions to throw into the attack, of which eleven had been specially allotted to it for the opera-tion. They were supported by 468 batteries. General Sixt von Arnim's 4th Army consisted of five divisions with 148 batteries. The Army Group and the OHL held six divisions in reserve.

The British, who had long been expecting an offensive in Flanders, were exceedingly nervous. They were unable to yield much ground, since the front line was only about fifty miles from the sea. A short push forward would put Calais and Boulogne within range of the German artillery. If the Germans managed to take Vimy Ridge they would be in a commanding position. If they broke into the coalfields of the Pas de Calais they would be in a position to cut off the British Second Army, along with their Belgian allies.[13]

British Army intelligence estimated that the Germans intended to attack Vimy Ridge, turning it on both flanks from Arras to the south and Lens to the north. It did not take great imagination to come to the conclusion that they would also hit the Portuguese front near Neuve Chapelle, and they knew full well that these demoralized troops would not be able to withstand a major attack. Haig had no confidence whatsoever in the French and his diary entry for 5 April reads: 'Personally I believe that the French Army, from the highest to the lowest, is thoroughly tired of the war, and they don't mean to attack to help the British.'[14] Nevertheless he sent Major-General Davidson, the head of the operations section at GHQ, to confer with Foch at his headquarters at Beauvais on 6 April in order to find out what the French could do to help. By now he was seri-ously concerned that the British Army would not be able to sustain another attack.

Davidson suggested three possible courses of action. The French could mount a major offensive, they could relieve the British Army all the way up to the Somme, or they could place reserves immediately behind Vimy Ridge. Foch gave no clear response, whereupon Haig repeated his request for a French offensive in a letter later that day.[15] Wilson also sent a message to Foch echoing Haig's concerns. Foch then suggested a meeting with Haig the following day at Aumale.

At that meeting Foch resolutely refused to send any reserves to support the British and repeated his call for a joint offensive by the British Third Army and the French I Army to block the German advance towards Amiens. Since he knew full well that Haig would never agree to such a proposal, the suggestion was purely for effect. Arguing that a German offensive against the GAR was every bit as likely as an attack in Flanders, the most he was prepared to do was to agree to place four infantry and three cavalry divisions west of Amiens, which could then be deployed either towards Amiens or Arras.[16] Haig complained in his diary about his tiresome allies: 'How difficult these "Latins" are to deal with! They mean to bleed the British to the utmost.'[17]

Foch also knew that Pétain would never agree to an offensive at Amiens, since it would require far too many divisions, thus leaving the remainder of the French front dangerously under-manned. Rawlinson also felt that the plan was unrealistic. His Fourth Army would need at least two more fresh divisions before even contemplating an offensive, and these were impossible to find.

Haig's worst assumptions about his French allies were now confirmed. He wrote: 'I found Foch most selfish and obstinate. I wonder if he is afraid to trust French divisions in the battle front?'[18] Convinced that they would do nothing he appealed to the Chief of Imperial General Staff, Sir Henry Wilson, who had already urged Foch to assist the British in forthright terms. Haig then begged Wilson to come to France in a final attempt to make Foch change his mind, but by the time he arrived on 9 April the Germans had already begun their offensive.

The Portuguese Corps had long been a matter of some concern.[19] When the ground began to dry in February and March it was thought prudent to relieve them, or at least shorten their front. Shortage of manpower made this difficult, and the movement of Portuguese troops away from the front had to stop when 'Michael' obliged First Army to send divisions south.

The relief of the Portuguese resumed on 5 April and the 1st Portuguese Division was withdrawn to a camp near Boulogne. Second Division remained in place, but was placed under XI Corps. It was short-handed, the men demoralized, the officers unreliable. It was therefore decided to relieve them on the night of 9/10 April, but this was too late.[20] The Portuguese thus felt the full impact of the German offensive and were overwhelmed.

While the British anxiously awaited an attack, and cursed the French for their apparent lack of concern, the Germans also had their problems. Immediately before 'Georgette' began both the French and the British launched threatening attacks. On 6 April the Bavarians beat back the French but losses were alarmingly high. On the following day the British attacked at Hangard and the French on the Trois Doms stream. Both attacks were stopped, but the cost was high. West of the Avre the Germans were suffering heavy losses from artillery fire.

Army Group Crown Prince Rupprecht realized from these attacks that their front from Castel to Montdidier was very vulnerable and that the situation had to be rectified. Various plans were considered. The left wing of 2nd Army and the right wing of 18th Army could press on and seize the high ground west of Castel and Villers-Bretonneux, or 18th Army could attack in a south-westerly direction. Another proposal was to improve their defensive positions by withdrawing behind the Avre and the Trois Doms stream.

General von Sauberzweig, 18th Army's hard-drinking, arrogant, but effective chief of staff, soon to be put out of action by a chronic heart condition, felt that these suggestions were far too modest, and pleaded for an offensive against Amiens which would separate the French from the British and open the way for a push to the south-west. The loss of Amiens would also have a shattering effect on Allied morale.

On 8 April Army Group Crown Prince Rupprecht proposed to the OHL that they should push simultaneously in three directions: towards Arras, Albert and south of the Somme. These attacks could begin at the earliest on 16 April. Ludendorff readily accepted this suggestion.

On the following day Crown Prince Rupprecht's staff changed their minds. They now argued that if the 'Georgette' offensive were to get stuck after an initial tactical success, a further offensive against the British would be needed. This would have to be a concentrated effort rather than three separate limited attacks designed to wear down the enemy. It would have to be on a broad front and aim for a breakthrough. The precise point at which the offensive would be aimed would depend on the outcome of 'Georgette'. The most promising spot seemed to be on the line from Saint Omer to Doullens. This would mean that operations south of the Somme would have to cease. Three weeks rest were needed for the troops and that was felt to be sufficient time to enable ammunition and supplies to be brought up to the front.

Ludendorff and Wetzell agreed with this suggestion and ordered that preparations should be made for what amounted to a continuation of 'Michael' on a broad front within two to three weeks. Meanwhile they awaited the outcome of 'Georgette'.[21]

The artillery barrage announcing the beginning of 'Georgette' started at 0415hrs on 9 April and since there was no wind the gas was very effective. As on 21 March a heavy mist covered the battlefield. The British response was feeble and the Germans were able to move their troops up to the front with little difficulty. The infantry attacked at 0845hrs in thick fog. Four German divisions made quick work of the Portuguese who hastily abandoned the battlefield without stopping to destroy the bridges as they fled. Two-thirds of the Portuguese division fled in panic, running headlong through the British rear zone. One-third remained in the trenches, but offered very little resistance. The officers failed completely, and morale was terribly low, in part because other ranks were never given home leave.[22] By 1000hrs the Germans were in possession of the third line of trenches in the first line of defence, and had moved up their artillery. By 1600hrs they had crossed the Lys and had established a bridgehead three kilometres wide east of Sailly. They had punched a hole almost nine kilometres deep and sixteen kilometres wide, and had thus scored a tactical success unparalleled on the Western Front. They took 6,000 prisoners and 100 guns but they still had failed to reach their goals. Once again mud made it impossible to bring the artillery forward and the British offered stiff resistance on the west banks of the Lys and Lawe and had some strong bridgeheads on the eastern banks. Nevertheless, the Germans hoped that 4th Army's offensive on the following day would enable the critical right flank to push forward. General von Hutier was delighted to hear that 6th Army had crossed the third line of British defences, but hinted that the offensive was likely to get stuck in spite of this remarkable initial success.[23]

XIX (Saxon) Army Corps, which attacked near Armentières on 9 April, reported that the offensive was 'theoretically' sound but 'practically' seriously flawed.[24] There were two major problems: staff work was seriously hampered by the OHL who constantly kept changing their minds, and there was a chronic shortage of transportation. Ludendorff had warned of the lack of careful preparation and the shortage of adequate transportation, but nevertheless the offensive had gone ahead. Rainy weather for several days before the attack had hampered air reconnaissance, made road building impossible, and had a disastrous effect on morale. Although the corps caught the enemy by surprise and advanced seven kilometres on the first day, taking 2,300 Portuguese and British prisoners and forty guns they soon got bogged down in the mud. The roads through no-man's land were beyond description. Fascines and planks sank into the mud, the one road forward that could be built was taken away from the division a few days later, and the infantry had to be supplied from the air.

Fourth Army's preliminary barrage began at 0245hrs on 10 April and three divisions of infantry attacked in twilight at 0515hrs on a twelve-kilometre front. Messines was encircled, but British resistance was strong on the high ground. The Germans also took Ploegsteert

– the 'Plugstreet' of Third Ypres – and drove the British out of most of the gaunt remains of Ploegsteert wood.

Sixth Army continued to fight on the Lys and Lawe during the night of 9/10 April and General von Quast ordered his men to continue the offensive at 0600hrs on the following day. They made very little progress since they had to ward off British counter-attacks without artillery support. Fighting was particularly fierce around the bridgehead at Sailly. Only when the artillery arrived in the afternoon could the Germans move forward on the right flank. The British Army now realized that Armentières would have to be abandoned, and they were pushed back across the Lys at various points, but their left flank remained stuck on the Lawe.

The achievements on this second day were remarkable given the poor weather conditions, the terrible terrain and lack of artillery support. Rudolf Binding wrote: 'There was a time when we laughed at Cadorna, the Italian Commander-in-Chief, because he reported that his offensive was held up by bad weather. Now it is the case with us, Machineguns which are buried in mud every time a shell bursts near them cannot shoot; men whose feet are clogged in it cannot charge.'[25] But the Germans had now taken 11,000 prisoners and 146 guns and it was clear that British resistance was weakening. XI and XV Corps had managed to meet the immediate crisis of the collapse of the Portuguese front, but the men were too tired and weak to hold the line for long.[26] The British had at first believed that the attack at La Bassé and Armentières was merely a 'demonstration'.[27] But now they had been pushed back across the Lys, and found themselves in two highly vulnerable salients at Armentières and Bethune, which would almost certainly have to be evacuated. Their troops were exhausted and the French were reluctant to send any more help.[28] Nevertheless, the Germans had not achieved their operational goals, and the vitally important line of hills was still between five and ten kilometres away.

The British desperately needed reinforcements from the French army, and Foch still refused Haig's calls for help. This prompted Lloyd George to send a telegram to Clemenceau on 9 April in which he agreed that Foch should be appointed Commander-in-Chief of the Allied Armies in France. The Americans enthusiastically supported this initiative, since the Doullens formula that gave Foch 'strategic direction' over military operations in France was altogether too vague.

The normally imperturbable Haig was once again in a panic. On 10 April he sent a hastily and shakily written note to Foch saying that the German offensive now extended all the way from the La Bassée Canal to Messines. He implied that while the British Army was under heavy attack the French stood idly by. Under these circumstances he felt obliged to point out that Foch's proposal to place four French divisions to the West of Amiens was an empty gesture and 'does not adequately meet the military situation of the British Army'. He insisted that it was 'vitally important' for the French Army to 'take immediate steps to relieve *some part* [underlined in original] of the British front, and to take an active share in the battle'.[29]

Foch told Haig that he had to stand firm and that voluntary withdrawal 'could only be interpreted by the enemy as a sign of weakness, and as an incitement to a further offensive'.[30] He refused to relieve the British forces in Flanders, but he shifted the weight of the French forces further north, thus leaving the front from the Oise to the Swiss border dangerously depleted. There were forty-nine divisions north on the river, and only sixty to the south. There were twenty-one reserve divisions between the Oise and Amiens, and only eleven from the Oise to the Swiss border. Nevertheless on 10 April he ordered General Maistre's X Army to the north of the Somme in order to relieve the British positions, and shortly afterwards ordered General Micheler's V Army to follow suit. He assured Haig that he would send French forces to Arras which would join in the battle if required.[31] Of necessity this took time, and the French troops did not begin to reach the British zone until 12 April, three days after the battle began.[32]

In the afternoon of 10 April the Germans added weight to their offensive against the British. 4th Army was ordered to slow down the 'Flanders' offensive against the Belgians and attack the northern flank of the Ypres salient in 'Tannenberg', a modified version of 'Blücher'. It was assumed that the British would soon abandon the salient.

The British withdrew from Armentières on 10 April so as to avoid encirclement, but the Germans captured 3,000 stragglers on the following day along with forty-six guns. Hazebrouck was now seriously threatened; were it to fall the British Army would lose an important communications centre and the Germans would be able to drive a wedge between First and Second Armies. Further gains were made on 11 April but they still had not reached the line of hills from Kemmel to Godewaervelde. The OHL still hoped that 'Georgette' would bring major results, and General von Quast urged his men to make one final effort.

Haig repeated his request to Foch for immediate help in another nervously written message on 11 April in which he requested not less than four French divisions to support his hard-pressed Second Army. Plumer had been forced to withdraw the right wing of his army, and had advised the Belgians to follow suit. He complained bitterly that the French reserve units that were sent to help him out were under strength and short of artillery. He urgently requested further help.[33] Foch sent a note to Davidson expressing his regrets that he was unable to offer any further assistance.[34]

Haig now felt that the coast from Calais to Boulogne was seriously threatened, and issued his Special Order of the Day exhorting his men to stand their ground and keep up the fight:

> Every position must be held to the last man: there must be no retirement. With our backs to the wall, and believing in the justice of our cause, each one of us must fight on to the end.

Reactions to this message were varied. To some it provided an inspiration, steeling them to do their best for King and Country; others found it merely insulting. One commanding officer refused to publish the order saying that if the morale of the higher command was low, his at least was not. Other ranks gave a hollow laugh and asked: 'What ruddy wall?'[35]

Wilson met Clemenceau in Paris on the morning of 10 April and warned the French Premier that the British Army was in grave danger of losing the Channel ports, the consequences of which would be disastrous for the Allied cause.[36] He then wrote to Foch stressing the extreme gravity of the situation in Flanders. He suggested that Foch should seriously consider flooding the country around Dunkirk, and from St Omer to the coast. Foch agreed with Wilson saying that the question of flooding was under serious consideration, and if absolutely necessary would be put into effect.[37] GHQ contacted Foch the following day asking for further details, and pointed out that it would help the British Army shorten its front. Answers were requested as to the circumstances under which flooding would take place, and who was to be made responsible. The suggestion was put forward that a joint Anglo-French Committee made up of engineers and other experts should be formed to study the problem. In the meanwhile some limited flooding could begin.[38]

Foch remained calm in the face of these setbacks. He was convinced that the main German offensive had been stopped at the end of March, and that the present situation was due almost entirely to the miserable performance of the Portuguese. He insisted that the best strategy was to stay put, not give an inch, never retire and plug any gaps as quickly as possible.[39] Clemenceau expressed his grave concerns to Haig about the threat to the Bruay coalfields, which were of critical importance since seventy per cent of the coal used in French munitions factories came from them. In response he was treated to another discourse on the precarious position of the British Army and the need for French reinforcements on his northern flank. Haig called for French and American reserves to be placed behind Second Army on a line from St Omer to Dunkirk, for French forces to be moved to Doullens, and for the inundation of the Dunkirk area.[40] Clemenceau avoided the issue by saying that

Haig should consult Foch. Getting no reply Haig told Foch that Plumer was obliged to withdraw his left to Pilkem Ridge.[41] General Grant, the British liaison officer at GQG, kept harping on the imminent danger to the Bruay coalfields, but Foch was unmoved. He was expecting attacks between Amiens and Arras and refused to send further reinforcements to Flanders.[42]

The French had a very poor opinion of the performance of the British Army in Flanders. They pointed to a disastrous failure of command at all levels. They had neglected to strengthen their second line of defence in anticipation of an attack. They were singularly inept at fighting in open ground. The infantry divisions that had been brought up from the Somme were tired after the recent fighting, mediocre, under-manned, and had been recently reorganized. The officers were mostly young and inexperienced. The poor performance of these divisions was a major reason for the setback suffered by the British Army in April. At the army and corps level no one seemed to have any idea what was going on. Small units retired without fighting, claiming that they had been given no orders. Reserves were thrown in willy-nilly, with no overall plan, and wasted in futile counter-attacks. GHQ was not on top of the situation, was unable to digest the information that flooded in from all quarters, and failed to organize a new line of defence behind the front to the north of the La Bassée Canal. The troops were excellent, morale was remarkably high even though they had lost 200,000 men since 21 March and had only received 150,000 replacements, but leadership was non-existent. An exception was made for Plumer who refused to give way to the prevailing mood of pessimism.

Colonel Desticker of the French General Staff indulged in a little pleasantry when he reported that Plumer's leadership had '*bien d'aplomb*'.[43] General Herbert Plumer looked exactly like Colonel Blimp and was detested by Haig, partly because he had been touted as a possible successor. Haig never lost an opportunity to put him down; but officers and men alike were devoted to 'Old Plum'. He was the only commander in Flanders who had an albeit partial grip on that increasingly chaotic situation which is often euphemistically described a 'soldiers' war'. Levelheaded, hard working, fair and every inch a gentleman, he was one of the finest generals in the British Army. He was not, however, a man of any great intelligence and partly for this reason Lloyd George did not give him Haig's job. Hankey was not far off the mark when he noted that Plumer was every bit as stupid as Haig.[44]

On 11 April, when 'Georgette' seemed to be making good progress, Army Group Crown Prince Rupprecht told the OHL that they were ready to attack south of the Somme in support of the offensive in Flanders. They proposed to improve their position in the awkward angle between the Ancre, the Somme and the Luce by attacking Villers-Bretonneux. This operation would help take the pressure off 'Georgette', provide better artillery emplacements for the bombardment of Amiens, and relieve the German salient west of the Avre. Ludendorff readily agreed. Crown Prince Rupprecht's Army Group had made remarkable progress, but now found themselves forced to take up a defensive stance in terrain that was totally unsuitable. The infantry was left with inadequate shelter and faced blistering artillery fire, particularly from the French 75s, along with an increasing number of bomber attacks, many of them by night. They suffered very high losses, even in the rear echelons. Their misery was compounded by cold and damp weather. Small wonder therefore that they longed for the offensive to continue that would enable them to abandon such vulnerable positions.[45]

Fourth Army made only minimal gains on 12 April and was held up by the strong British defences at Kemmel. Ludendorff therefore ordered that careful preparations should be made for an attack on Kemmel from the south and west. 6th Army made better progress on 12 April and advanced up to six kilometres. It had not been possible to bring the field kitchens forward across the muddy terrain and many undernourished units found it impossible to resist gorging themselves on the ample supplies of food in the captured British trenches, which held up their progress and caused some severe disciplinary problems.

The OHL brought in reserves, mainly from 17th Army in order to give more weight to the attack on the Ypres salient, but this meant that 17th Army's offensive had to be stopped. 2nd Army was ordered to keep attacking. Once again Ludendorff was diffusing the offensive by driving in three different directions. In addition to 2nd Army's push towards Albert he was attacking from the north-east in the direction of Bixchote, and from the south-east towards Mount Kemmel. Although these last two attacks were aimed to meet behind the Ypres salient, the immediate objectives lay 30 kilometres apart and were strongly defended.[46] The staffs of the armies involved raised no objections, and indeed this strategy had originated with von Kuhl at Army Group Crown Prince Rupprecht. At the OHL Colonel Wetzell argued in favour of keeping up continual pressure on the British until they broke, whereas Ludendorff wanted a large number of small-scale attacks. This led Crown Prince Rupprecht to have serious reservations about Ludendorff's ability as a strategist. He pointed out that small-scale attacks led to heavy losses, and used up a great deal of ammunition protecting the flanks.

Von Kuhl discussed the situation with Ludendorff at Avesnes in the course of which he objected strongly to Ludendorff's tactics of partial attacks and hammer-blows. Even Colonel Wetzell, who had first championed this approach, had come to realize that it simply wore down the troops, and resulted in no significant gains. The German Armies on the Western Front had lost more than 300,000 men, one-fifth of its effectives, since 21 March. General von Kuhl now argued that operations against the French south of the Somme should be halted, and every possible support should be given to 'Georgette'. If this operation got stuck they should call a halt and prepare for a major operation around Doullens. Small-scale attacks should be avoided at all costs. Ludendorff remained adamant, even though von Kuhl now got strong support from Wetzell. He insisted on a partial offensive by 2nd Army, and only if 'Georgette' could keep up the momentum would forces be taken from 2nd Army to give it more weight.[47] Kuhl gained the impression that Ludendorff was now thinking in terms of an offensive north of the Somme in the direction of Amiens. Reporting back to his Army Group commander he expressed his concern that Ludendorff would continue with a large-scale operation south of the river which would use up the fresh divisions needed for the push towards Amiens. Both men agreed that at this stage another major offensive north of the river was out of the question since there was a chronic shortage of manpower, artillery and labour.[48]

At a meeting of the general staff chiefs of the Army Groups at Avesnes on 12 April General von Kuhl repeated his opposition to any operations south of the Somme, and insisted that all efforts should be concentrated against the British. Full weight should be put behind 'Georgette', and there should be no hammer blows or partial attacks at other points on the front. Meanwhile preparations should be made for an attack by 17th Army in the direction of Doullens. Wetzell agreed with this assessment, but Ludendorff announced that there were not enough men available for such an operation.

Ludendorff having poured cold water on his proposal for an offensive against the British north of the Somme, Kuhl now returned on the following day to consideration of the proposed offensive at Villers-Bretonneux. Ludendorff gave the go-ahead, noting: 'Attack can begin on 20th or 30th but with thorough preparation'.[49]

13 April was an unlucky day for the Germans. They suffered heavy losses from the British artillery, which had been brought forward to well concealed positions with excellent observation posts. Reserves had also been brought in, and the Germans now faced very stiff resistance. As a gesture of respect the report on the day's fighting referred to the British (although they were still called 'English') as an 'opponent' (*Gegner*), rather than as the 'enemy' (*Feind*).[50] Nevertheless General Sixt von Arnim's X Reserve Corps was able to take Neuve Eglise, the high ground to the south of Mount Kemmel, but they were subjected to ferocious counter-attacks which forced them back almost to their starting positions. The British success at Neuve Eglise was a great boost to

morale, and there was clear indication that the German fighting spirit was beginning to slacken.[51]

The attack on Bailleul by six divisions of the Bavarian II Corps, of which two were fresh, was stopped by Major-General Nicholson's six brigades. The British were able to use observed artillery support from their high ground as the Germans attacked across the plain, and counter-battery fire was most effective. The Germans suffered heavy losses from machine-gun and rifle fire as the stumbled across the muddy fields, but they put up a tremendous fight. They were able to force Nicholson's right wing back up to 500 yards. When 200 men of 2/Worcestershire were brought in as reinforcements they fell almost to a man. The Bavarians were finally stopped by the Royal Newfoundland Regiment when they were within twenty-five yards of the trenches.[52]

The OHL sent in reserves to support the floundering attacks at Neuve Eglise and Bailleul, but to little effect. South of the Lys they were unable to make any progress at all against stiff resistance. Ludendorff was bitterly disappointed at the failure of his offensive and blamed the army commanders and their subordinates for failing to issue clear orders which had resulted in some unfortunate muddles at various points on the front. The II Bavarian Army Corps came under heavy criticism and was replaced by III Bavarian Army Corps. The crack Alpine Corps was removed from the front.

The Germans hardly made any progress on 14 April and at some points they lost ground. Ludendorff wanted to press on with the offensive regardless, but a number of corps commanders insisted that this was not possible. They were short of supplies and ammunition, the men were exhausted and they needed time for careful reconnaissance of the British defences. Some units were mutinous. Colonel von Lenz, chief of staff to 6th Army reported to Army Group headquarters that the men were refusing to fight even when ordered to do so and that the offensive had come to a standstill.[53] He insisted that it would be impossible to continue the offensive for at least three days. Troops would not attack without a massive creeping barrage, and it would take at least that long to bring up the ammunition. Since they were second-rate infantry units they relied on the artillery to take out the enemy's machine-gun nests. Ludendorff blamed Lenz for 6th Army's disappointing performance, and interfered with the Army's operations at every level. General von Kuhl told Ludendorff that if he no longer had any confidence in Lenz he should be removed, adding that Lenz was perfectly prepared to go, since he was extremely depressed as a result of Ludendorff's constant interference and unfounded accusations.

General von Kuhl was sympathetic towards Lenz because Ludendorff's increasing proclivity to issue orders directly to Army commanders, and even to their subordinates down to the divisional level, resulted in the

Army Group command being excluded from the decision making process. Crown Prince Rupprecht's staff had now always to ask the Army
commanders what Ludendorff had ordered before issuing their own
orders which otherwise might be contradictory. Frayed nerves at the
top and mutinous murmurings at the bottom did not bode well for the
German Army as the battle in Flanders ground to a halt.

7

'Georgette':
The Second Phase
15 April-15 May

Although the Germans had suffered a large number of casualties, most of them were lightly wounded. Once again it was the British artillery that had inflicted the most damage.[1] The large number of British machine-guns, placed in depth, also made it virtually impossible for the infantry to advance.[2] Haig, however, was still extremely nervous and at a meeting at Abbeville on 14 April attended by Milner he begged Foch to relieve some of his exhausted divisions, but the General-in-Chief replied that it was impossible to carry out relief operations in the course of a battle, since it immobilized the relieving troops as well as those being relieved. Once again he pointed out the threat the enemy posed to other sectors of the front. In his view it would thus be quite improper to move reserves to Flanders. Haig then asked Foch to move four divisions under General Maistre north to strengthen the line, either from the La Bassée Canal to Arras, or between Bethune and Hazebrouk. General Micheler's corps was designated to replace the British Army between Arras and the Somme.[3] This was further confirmation to the French that Haig was simply waiting for them to take over the battle.[4] Foch ended the conference by saying that not a single division should be removed from the front, and proclaimed with a dramatic flourish: '*La bataille d'Hazebrouk est finie!*' In Haig's opinion Foch 'spoke a lot of nonsense'.[5]

On the following day Haig sent a testy note to Foch demanding that the divisions which he had requested at the Abbeville meeting should be made available at once. He added the by now familiar warning that: 'I find it necessary to place on record my opinion that the arrangements made by you are insufficient to meet the present military situation'.[6] Haig continued to badger the unfortunate French Military Mission, constantly complaining that the French were not giving him enough support. The head of mission reported that Haig seemed to find it exceedingly difficult 'to appreciate the considerable support which the French army had already given him'.[7]

Haig's chief staff officer, General Sir Herbert Lawrence, now claimed that the Germans were about to attack the Arras salient, and Amiens from south of the Somme. In either case he needed considerable French support. He told the French Military Mission that he was going ahead with his flooding plans, and that he intended to withdraw to the west of Ypres. Preparations were being made for the evacuation of Dunkirk and for the destruction of the port facilities. The British Army had lost 220,000 men since 21 March. Of these 120,000 wounded had been returned to the United Kingdom, 20,000 were hospitalized in France, 60,000 had been taken prisoner and 20,000 were dead. He told the French that under these circumstances there could be no question of the Entente going on the offensive before 1919, by which time the Americans would have arrived in Europe in large numbers, and the new British conscription law would provide an additional 200-230,000 men.[8]

Wilson told Foch that the alternatives were to stand and fight, or retire to the flood line from Aire to St Omer and on to the Channel coast. Since Foch insisted on standing and fighting, the French would have to send between ten and thirty divisions to make this possible. Plumer had made it clear that he could not hope to hold the line with the existing number of troops if the Germans were to persist with their offensive, and Haig was in full agreement with this assessment.[9]

Plumer promptly requested six French divisions, adding that he would need more if the Germans continued to build up their reserves. Haig scaled this down to three divisions, but by this time the French were convinced that the British Army was out of danger. Morale was high after beating back the German attack, reinforcements had been well integrated, and commanders were confident about the future. Much of this was due to the massive intervention by the French high command. It was clear that Plumer's Second Army, which had born the brunt of the attack, was morally and physically exhausted; but Third and Fourth Armies were in good shape even though General Sir Henry Rawlinson, who commanded Fourth Army was charged with showing 'ill will' towards his allies, in spite of his ability to speak French. Senior staff officers were taken to task for their lassitude. Haig and GHQ continually complained about the drain on their forces, and the slowness of the French in sending reinforcements. This was obviously nonsense, and his army commanders who were clearly getting on top of the situation did not share Haig's views.[10]

On 15 April Foch told Clemenceau and Milner that Haig was paint-ing far too black a picture. GQG's excellent Deuxième Bureau and the French Military Mission attached to GHQ saw no reason whatsoever to modify the disposition of the GAR. Furthermore the enemy's reserves were such that they were in a position to mount an offensive at short notice at another point on the front, and they were waiting for a signifi-cant movement of reserves that would leave a sector undermanned.[11]

Meanwhile discussions continued about the consequences of the evacuation of Calais and Boulogne. The prospect was one that greatly alarmed the Admiralty who pointed out that ports to the west, such as Dieppe, Le Havre, Rouen and Cherbourg would have to be used as substitutes. They were much further away, and were thus out of reach for a number of smaller ships. Larger ships would have to be used, which would slow down the movement of supplies. Most serious of all, it would not be possible to maintain the blockade at Dover, which was the key to anti-submarine policy in the Channel.[12]

Lloyd George continued to pester Lord Reading in an attempt to frighten President Wilson into action. He wrote yet another urgent message to the ambassador on 14 April: 'There can be little doubt that victory or defeat for the Allies depends upon the arrival of the American infantry. Until the American infantry arrives the skeleton divisions will remain skeleton and useless in the field.'[13]

Things looked very different from the German point of view. The situation reminded Crown Prince Rupprecht of the First Battle of Ypres when the troops had been ordered to attack over and over again until they either could not, or would not, fight any longer. He thought it absurd that in such a situation both Hindenburg and the Kaiser issued orders urging 6th Army to take the heights of Mont Noir, Mont Rouge and Mont Kemmel. The Chief of General Staff at 6th Army, Lieutenant-Colonel Baron von Lenz, realized that the offensive had got hopelessly stuck. His army was left exceedingly vulnerable, and the offensive would probably have to be abandoned. Crown Prince Rupprecht was a trifle less pessimistic and still hoped that 4th Army might be able to bring some relief. He therefore sent word to the OHL not to demand the impossible of 6th Army.[14]

General von Lossberg, chief of general staff to 4th Army was slightly more optimistic. He argued that the British had been seriously weakened and at a number of points had been driven out of their strong defensive positions to flat ground which made observation difficult. But he also called for a pause of one week before continuing the offensive.

Ludendorff had to accept these arguments and with great reluctance agreed that there should be a pause for two or three days. The Germans had suffered heavy losses which had been particularly high in the officer corps. The troops were demoralized and there had been widespread drunken orgies as they fell upon the wine the British had left behind in their trenches. The British had recovered from the initial shock and were putting up a determined resistance as was seen at Bailleul. Without adequate supplies of ammunition for the artillery it would not be possible to silence the British machine-guns which had caused so much damage in the last few days.

In spite of this gloom and despondency the Germans made remarkable progress on 15 April. 4th Army advanced about two kilometres along the front from Bailleul to Wytschaete and Bailleul was once again in German hands. Further north they were also able to push forward in the direction of Ypres, but the British had already decided partially to withdraw from the salient on the night of 12 to 13 April.[15] To the south 6th Army made modest gains, improved its position and moved its headquarters from Tournai to Lille.

The Germans took the commanding positions on the high ground at Wytschaete and Metreen on the following day. 6th Army at Meteren was soon subjected to fierce counter-attacks in which a number of tanks were used, but they stood firm. Coupled with heavy artillery fire against the entire front of 6th Army this indicated that the British had brought up further reserves.

Crown Prince Rupprecht, having heard reports of the interrogation of British prisoners of war which indicated that the British army was in a state of disarray, was convinced that if only they could take Mont Kemmel the Ypres salient would fall.[16] Although 6th Army had got stuck in Flanders 4th Army's prospects still looked promising. On the morning of 16 April General von Kuhl again suggested a major offensive north of the Somme that would be co-ordinated with 'Georgette'. He was perfectly prepared to cancel 2nd Army's offensive south of the Somme if necessary. Ludendorff agreed, and encouraged by the results of the previous two days fighting, suggested to 4th Army that the offensive should go ahead. General von Lossberg was far less optimistic than he had been the day before and protested vehemently that this was out of the question. The infantry had suffered heavy losses and his divisions were seriously under strength. The British were in a formidable defensive position at Mont Kemmel and the surrounding high ground. 6th Army was still waiting for its artillery to move up. He concluded that to continue the offensive in these conditions would be disastrous. General Lequis, the dashing commander of 12th Light Infantry (*Jäger*) Division, suggested an attack at night, without a prior artillery barrage. This suggestion was turned down, and the Army high command argued that it was now clear that the offensive had once again degenerated into a battle of attrition and would have to be stopped.[17]

General von Kuhl took no notice of von Lossberg's objections, and reported to Ludendorff that he doubted that the British would defend

Mont Kemmel. The British had not defended Wytschaete very convinc-
ingly, and Wytschaete was the key to Mont Kemmel. Von Kuhl's main
concern was that the British would withdraw from the Ypres salient
before 'Tannenberg' was launched and that they would thus escape. He
therefore begged Ludendorff once again to send all available troops to
back up 4th and 6th Armies, even if this meant that 2nd Army would
have to halt its advance. 17th Army could also lend its support to the
offensive in Flanders. He insisted that if 'Tannenberg' were postponed
until 19 April it would be too late.[18]

Ludendorff was not convinced by von Kuhl's arguments. He did not
believe that the British were about to abandon the Ypres salient and he
did not want to cancel 2nd Army's offensive against Amiens. Although he
had previously dismissed the idea, he now agreed that 17th Army should
support 6th Army's efforts. General von Kuhl had the cold comfort of
being proven correct. While arguing with Ludendorff as to whether or
not the British would abandon the Ypres salient during the afternoon of
16 April he received news that the British Army was retiring, in which
case 'Tannenberg' would be irrelevant.

Preparations for 'Tannenberg' continued to meet the possibility of the
British only making a partial withdrawal from the Ypres salient. 4th Army
was to attack the salient from the north at Houthulst Forest. News that
the British were withdrawing from Poelkapelle to the east of Langemarck
enabled the Germans to take the high ground at Passchendaele, and
General Sixt von Arnim was straining at the leash. Since the British
seemed intent on defending Houthulst Forest he ordered 'Blücher' to
go ahead. He hoped thereby to divide the Belgians from the British by
seizing the bridges over the Yser canal. General von Quast agreed to
support this endeavour by attacking with his III Bavarian Corps and
the XIX Army Corps.

Pétain now decided to reorganize the French forces behind the battle-
front in Flanders so as better to meet this new threat. The resulting
Détachement d'Armée du Nord (DAN), was made up of General Robillot's
2nd Cavalry Corps, which had arrived in Flanders on 13 April, and five
infantry divisions placed under the command of General Mitry. Two
of these infantry divisions entered the fray on 16 April in support of
Plumer's army. They did not relieve the exhausted British troops, but
they did help hold the line.

Foch met again with Haig and Milner at Abbeville on 16 April, made a
tour of the battlefield and, having conferred with Wilson, agreed to pitch
in a further infantry division. At the same time he ordered two further
reserve divisions up behind the front. The French now had a total of
twelve divisions behind the British front.[19] Needless to say this was still
not enough for Haig, who continued to insist that the British front was
in imminent danger of collapse if he did not get still more help from

the French. Foch told him to stand and fight. Haig replied that he could only do so if the French sent him some extra divisions.

Foch had still not given up the idea of an offensive operation by I and III Armies. Pétain argued that he could not send the reinforcements that Foch had ordered and at the same time mount an effective offensive. Debeney's attacks on 11 and 18 April showed that he was correct. The first was a failure, the second only moderately successful. Foch was now placed in an awkward position between Haig and Pétain. Haig complained that he was not helping enough, Pétain argued that he was compromising the French Army by opening up a new front in Flanders at a time when he was facing a German army that was gaining in strength.[20]

'Blücher' began at 0900hrs on 17 April but met with surprisingly stiff resistance from the Belgians. They counter-attacked in the afternoon and forced the German right wing back to its starting position. Progress was no better elsewhere on the Ypres salient and it soon became clear that the Allies had no intention of abandoning the salient and had brought forward reserves, including some French units. They had merely withdrawn somewhat in order to improve their defensive stance, and the Germans made no progress against these stronger positions.

The French were now finally persuaded that there was not going to be an offensive in the Champagne, and somewhat belatedly admitted that the Germans had moved a number of rear divisions away to support the offensive on the Somme as early as 21 March. At the same time they noted that, although German forces on the Western Front may have increased in number, they had declined noticeably in quality since the beginning of the 'Michael' offensive.[21]

Both 4th and 6th Armies told Army Group Crown Prince Rupprecht that they needed several new divisions in order to continue the offensive. They were told that this would not be possible before at least 21 April and the OHL wanted to wait and see what happened on the following day before making a final decision. Orders were then issued down to the Corps level to get ready to halt the offensive and prepare for a second attempt. In that event a defence in depth would have to be carefully prepared.[22]

The results were again disappointing on 18 April. A surprise attack on Mont Kemmel ended in chaos as a result of a murderous British barrage. The 6th Bavarian Infantry Division in 4th Army proved to have no fighting strength left, having been severely mauled the day before.[23] It also proved impossible to cross the Steenebeek since the stream was strongly defended and 83rd Division which was designated to take part in the attack was unable to arrive in time, owing to the exceptionally difficult terrain. 4th Army almost managed to take Givenchy and Festubert, but was beaten back with heavy losses from machine-guns in their concrete nests. CIGS was able to report to Lloyd George that the

British Army had had a very good day, with these important successes at Kemmel and Givenchy.[24]

On 18 April Foch came part of the way to meet the repeated requests from Haig, Wilson and Plumer to send French Divisions north, by suggesting to Haig that tired British divisions should replace fresh French divisions on quiet sectors of the front such as the Vosges and Lorraine. Haig agreed, and Pétain ordered four infantry divisions to move to VI Army's zone on 25 April. The War Office was vehemently opposed to this move and wrote to Haig protesting that: 'This would eventually result in the complete intermixture of French and British Armies, destruction of identity of British Army and is contrary to instructions contained in first five lines of paragraph 3 of Lord Kitchener's memorandum Number 121/7711 December 28th, 1915, to you.'[25] Haig took heed of these objections, and Foch's suggestion thus did nothing to lessen tensions between GHQ and GQG. On 23 April Haig announced that he was only sending one infantry division, and that he had not decided what to do with the other three divisions: that would depend on the outcome of the battle. He added pointedly that he had already been obliged to disband five divisions and that he would have to dissolve four more.

Pétain was exceedingly angry about this note, and complained bitterly to Foch that the BEF had only received a trickle of reinforcements from home, whereas the French had supported the British Army with an average of fortry-seven divisions. He pointed out that the Germans might attack the French Army at any moment, and that not a single fresh British division would come to their aid. Pétain accused Haig of selfishly looking after British interests and ignoring the imperatives of the overall situation on the Western Front. He warned that GAN only had four divisions in reserve, and GAE nine.[26] By 18 April Foch had moved two entire French armies, the DAN and X Army made up of nine infantry divisions and three cavalry divisions, north of the Somme.[27]

Things were every bit as tense of the other side of the hill. 6th Army now called for a halt so that the troops could rest and plans were laid for a full-scale barrage in preparation for further attacks. Spirits were low at Army Group Crown Prince Rupprecht. Having discussed the situation with von Lossberg, General von Kuhl decided to halt the offensive either side of Bailleul which had clearly failed and which would bring precious few further gains. The major offensive against the Ypres salient, 'Tannenberg', was nevertheless to go ahead.[28] The campaign was threatening to degenerate into a battle of attrition, and this had to be avoided at all costs. It was therefore proposed that 6th Army should go on the defensive and that 4th Army should concentrate on taking Mont Kemmel.

The OHL agreed in principle with this assessment, but argued that since the British were putting up such a strong defence the offensive should now be directed principally against the weak French forces which faced 1st and 7th Armies.[29] 6th Army was ordered to take Givenchy and Festubert before adopting a defensive stance. The factories around Béthune were to be kept under heavy fire. 4th Army was to prepare the assault on Mont Kemmel.[30]

Lieutenant-Colonel Baron von Lenz, 6th Army's chief of staff, reported that, owing to a severe shortage of manpower, artillery and supplies, he would not be able to take Givenchy and Festubert.[31] In the following few days 6th Army was submitted to a series of powerful counter-attacks. General von Lossberg, chief of staff to 4th Army, insisted that 'Tannenberg' was too risky, and Ludendorff also had serious reservations about the operation. After further discussion the OHL ordered the cancellation of 'Tannenberg'.[32]

It was now essential for 4th Army to take Mont Kemmel. Even if they were to remain on the defensive this commanding position would allow the British artillery to cause serious damage and the Germans would be unlikely to hold on to their present positions. Were it to fall it might be possible to press on against Ypres and score a major victory that would get them out of the tactical impasse in which they now found themselves after the failure of 4th and 6th Armies' offensives.

An attack on this exceptionally strong position needed very careful preparation, and it was postponed until 25 April. The Allies were well aware that an attack was coming and General Foch ordered that the defence of Mont Kemmel justified a 'heavy sacrifice'. The parrot was not to leave its perch. He told Haig that, were it to fall, the British Second Army would have to withdraw to the west of Ypres. Fearing that this retirement was likely he requested that Plumer be ordered to prepare positions in anticipation of such a move. Preparations also had to be made for a retirement of the right flank of the Belgian Army on Plumer's left. Haig also urgently requested the flooding of the coastal region east of Dunkirk should Mont Kemmel be lost.[33]

Haig told Foch that he doubted whether Plumer had sufficient troops to be able to defend Mont Kemmel. Foch pointed out that he had five infantry and three cavalry divisions from the French Army under the command of General Mitry, a number of tired British units had been withdrawn to quiet sectors of the French front, and the Belgians had extended their front to his left, thus releasing a British division plus an entire brigade. Cognizant of the importance of Mont Kemmel, Foch arrange for a meeting between Plumer and the Belgian General Gillain to discuss the co-ordination of their defensive tactics, and issued instructions to the French X Army to prepare to intervene.

Ludendorff now began to consider his next move. The French had moved a division to Wytschaete and another to Hazebrouk. Four further Divisions were in reserve behind the British positions at Doullens. The

French Army had also relieved the British south of the Somme. As a result the French forces opposite the 1st, 3rd and 5th Armies had been significantly weakened. He therefore proposed to mount an offensive by 1st and 3rd Armies. General von Kuhl agreed in principal, but continued to insist that it would only result in a partial success. The objective should still be a major operation against the British.[34] Hindenburg told the Duke of Brunswick that the best strategy was to wear out the enemy with a series of limited offensives. General von Kuhl protested that this would bring no significant gains, and that only a well-prepared and large-scale offensive on a broad front had any chance of success.[35]

There were now alarming signs that the French were preparing a major attack on 18th Army's left flank between Montdidier and Noyon, as well as at the junction of the inside flanks of 18th and 2nd Armies around Moreuil. On 18 April the French attacked on the Avre and although they were beaten back the Germans lost 2,000 men, and the French took the high ground to the west of Castel which gave them a commanding position over the Germans in the valleys of the Luce and Avre.

General von Hutier was now very concerned about the vulnerability of his troops west of the Avre and the Trois Doms stream, but he did not agree with the staff at Army Group Crown Prince Rupprecht's head-quarters that he should place his main defences behind these obstacles. He insisted that the terrain to the west was more suitable for defence, and that were his army to withdraw it would indicate to the Allies that there would be no offensive in this sector for the foreseeable future. He proposed a continuation of the offensive in a westerly direction towards the Noye. OHL's liaison officer who examined von Hutier's defensive positions west of the Avre concluded that they were perfectly adequate. Intelligence reports showed that the French had moved large numbers of troops up to Flanders so that they were unable to mount a large-scale offensive south of the Somme. On 20 April Ludendorff therefore agreed that there was no need to make any major changes on the Avre, but he refrained from commenting on the possibility of 18th Army going on the offensive.

Serious problems were by now clearly apparent in the German Army. Any chance of taking Amiens had been wasted due to excessive looting, vandalism and drunkenness. In many units discipline was breaking down and officers were losing authority. One officer even went as far as argu-ing in favour of reintroducing flogging, but added sourly: 'but our weak social conscience considers the hide of these conscienceless fellows so important that it may not be tanned.'[36]

But not all Germany's weakness could be attributed to the breakdown of military discipline. The troops were utterly exhausted:

The physical exhaustion of the infantry during the period from April 4th to 10th, not until the end of which was a cessation of the fighting considered necessary here at the Front, was so great that finally the men could hardly fire their rifles; they let themselves be slowly wiped out by the enemy's artillery fire almost without caring, and would hardly move from the spot. They were just like used-up horses which stand fast in the shafts and duly take the blows of the whip without a movement. They could not advance; they could not shoot; they could not even get out of the way of the fire; they just stuck there.

The only compensation for the German Army was that the enemy was equally exhausted. As Rudolf Binding put it: 'Both weapons were equally blunt.'

The offensive at Villers-Bretonneux was first postponed until 23 April and then for one further day largely because British bomber aircraft had managed to destroy the railway line between Chaulnes and Guillaucourt by causing 50,000 rounds of ammunition to explode. This resulted in serious logistical problems, which could not be resolved earlier. During the preparations for this offensive the German air ace Baron von Richthofen was killed on 21 April while on a reconnaisance flight.

Seventeen under-strength divisions were designated for the attack along with 1208 guns, 710 aircraft and thirteen tanks. Of the ten divisions in the first wave only five were considered suitable for 'an assault with limited objectives'. The others were not fully prepared for the attack and were in need of rest and further training. These divisions had lost up to 4,000 men in the 'Michael' offensive and who had only been partially replaced. Some were short of up to 2,400 men. Divisional commanders reported that many of their men were sick and that morale was extremely low.[37]

The preliminary barrage began at 0445hrs on 24 April and lasted for two and a half hours. The infantry attacked at 0715hrs in thick fog. 4th Guards Infantry Division took Villers-Bretonneux after heavy fighting up the slope to the village and pushed on to the woods beyond thus reaching their day's objectives. The left wing of the attack was less successful and made precious little progress. A counter-attack from Cachy at 2100hrs caused a panic and the troops fled.

Foch immediately ordered Rawlinson to counter-attack. GHQ sent a hasty note to Foch (whom they tactlessly spelt 'Fosch', thus prompting a marginal comment in blue pencil 'boche') saying that every effort would be made to recapture Villers-Bretonneux, and asking for substantial French support for this endeavour.[38] After a few hours of hasty preparation two Australian brigades and a British brigade launched a fierce counter-attack at 0230hrs on the night of 24/25 April to the north of Villers Bretonneux and won back a substantial amount of lost ground.

The British 58th Division recaptured Hangard Wood. The counter-attacks continued in the morning and the Germans were cleared from the village. The British were somewhat contemptuous of the French contribution to the operation, thus further souring relations between the allies.[39] The Germans were now forced onto the defensive along the entire front of the offensive, and on the evening of 25 April the OHL called a halt. The Germans had taken 2,400 prisoners and four guns but they had only gained a trifling amount of ground at the cost of 8,000 casualties.

Ten tired German divisions had been thrown against seven fresh French and British divisions who were expecting an attack. The battle had resulted in general confusion and the poor fighting spirit of the troops was clearly evident when they failed to resist the counter-attacks and in places panicked. Reserves were not brought in quickly enough resulting in a further loss of morale. The wings of 2nd and 18th Armies were dangerously weakened and the staff at Army Group Crown Prince Rupprecht were increasingly worried about the possibility of a large-scale counter-attack on their exposed position west of the Avre. Troops had to be moved from Army Groups Gallwitz and Duke Albrecht in order to shore up the front at this weak point. Neither Ludendorff nor von Hutier thought that the situation was so serious that it necessitated a withdrawal to better defensive positions. They still wanted the Allies to believe that further attacks were imminent on the 'Michael' front.

At 0330hrs on 25 April the Germans gassed the British artillery emplacements in preparation for their assault on Mont Kemmel. The 156-metre-high hill, which dominated the Flanders plain, was subjected to a murderous barrage of high explosives at 0600hrs which caused heavy losses in the tightly packed trenches which were manned by the French 28th Division supported by Lieutenant-Colonel H.D. Bousfield's Kemmel Defence Force.[40] Infantry from 4th Army's XVIII and X Reserve Corps began their assault at 0700hrs, the Alpine Corps attacking Mont Kemmel head on instead of on the flank. By 0810hrs they had reached the summit and half an hour later they reported that it had been cleared of the enemy. Meanwhile 56 Division captured the village of Kemmel. Brigadier-General P.P. de B. Radcliffe, the new Director of Military Operations, understated the case when he informed the House of Commons that the situation at Kemmel was 'not satisfactory', but he added the sober warning that the positions east of Ypres were now in danger. He ended his report by reassuring members that the situation at Villers-Bretonneux was now 'satisfactory'.[41]

Shortly after 0900hrs General von Lossberg spoke by telephone with Ludendorff saying that he intended to continue the attack. Ludendorff warned of counter-attacks and told von Lossberg that he should wait until he had brought up his artillery. General Sixt von Arnim therefore issued instructions that the attack should continue as soon as his 4th Army had adequate artillery cover. The infantry dug in and waited for the artillery to get into position. The storming of Mont Kemmel, a remarkable feat of arms that an exuberant Kaiser toasted with champagne, proved to be the final act of 'Georgette'.[42]

Von Lossberg felt that Ludendorff was being far too cautious and telephoned the chief of general staff of the Guards Corps saying that he thought it possible that the Allies having lost Kemmel might now finally decide to abandon the Ypres salient. In such an eventuality the Guards Corps was to attack immediately. Having moved a reserve division forward von Lossberg again telephoned the Guards Corps at 1615hrs and repeated his conviction that the Ypres salient would soon be cleared and that the British and Belgians would move back to the line from Ypres to Bixschoote. If this were to happen the Guards Corps was to attack frontally. Were the Allies to fall back behind the Yser Canal they were to operate west of the canal. The chief of general staff of the Guards Corps tried to dampen von Lossberg's enthusiasm and pointed out that his patrols had met with very stiff resistance.

Aerial reconnaisance, the cross-examination of French prisoners and the deciphering of British radio traffic provided ample evidence that the Allies were indeed preparing a large-scale counter-offensive. General von Lossberg was finally convinced that Ludendorff's repeated warnings were entirely justified and he issued orders to prepare to meet a counter-attack. No further advances were made that day, but were to continue in the morning.

It could very well be that Ludendorff was overly cautious and that von Lossberg's initial confidence was justified. The French only had three battalions of severely shaken infantry on the four-kilometre front from Mille-Kruis to Locre, of which two were defending the Scherpenberg with the other two divisions kilometres to the rear. Had 4th Army maintained the momentum of their assault in the afternoon they would have made substantial gains and the Allies were as yet in no position to take effective countermeasures.

Foch feared that Haig would be tempted to retire having lost Mont Kemmel, and therefore telephoned GHQ on several occasions, ordering that there should be no withdrawals, and called for vigorous counter-attacks. General Plumer issued similar orders to Second Army and to the DAN, but could not resist blaming the French for the recent setback.[43] The resumption of the German advance on 26 April was pre-empted by a counter-attack by about three Allied divisions after a heavy artillery barrage. This was successfully warded off, but it meant that 4th Army could not begin to attack until the afternoon. Very little progress was made. The troops were exhausted and the artillery was short of ammunition. General Sixt von Arnim therefore ordered a pause until 29 April. In the course of the afternoon General von Lossberg postponed the attack until the morning on the advice of the chief of staff of XVIII Reserve Corps who then urged that it be postponed until 28 April. Finally at 1945hrs he convinced von Lossberg to wait a further day. His disappointment was somewhat alleviated by the knowledge that he had captured an important strategic point and had taken 7,000 prisoners and fifty-three guns.

General von Lossberg's assumption that the British were about to abandon the Ypres salient was not far wrong. General Plumer was considering withdrawing to the west of the town and establishing a strong defensive line to the west of the Yser canal. Foch sent a number of telegrams to Plumer telling him that Ypres should not be abandoned under any circumstances. Finally a compromise was reached and during the night of 26 April the British and Belgians withdrew between two and three kilometres.

There was a further flare up between the French and the British at a conference at Abbeville on 27 April. Clemenceau was outraged to hear that an agreement had been reached behind his back between Pershing and Milner that the British were to receive all the American effectives.[44] Lord Milner explained that the original agreement was that the Americans should be given experience with British divisions for about ten weeks before going back for training under American officers. In the emergency situation created by the 'Michael' offensive Generals Pershing and Bliss had agreed on 27 March that machine-gun and infantry units should be allocated to British divisions. At an Anglo-American conference on 7 April the American delegates stressed that this could not be regarded as a permanent arrangement, and that they intended to form an American group under Pershing. Clemenceau professed to be satisfied with this explanation. Foch however flatly refused to entertain a British suggestion that it might be necessary to retreat to the Channel ports. He continued to insist that the German attacks were diminishing in strength, and that the British had to stand and fight.[45]

The Germans hoped that it would be possible to close off the Ypres salient on 29 April. Seven divisions were placed in the front line of the attack and there were six further divisions immediately behind them. The attack, which began at 0640hrs after two and a half hours of artillery barrage, was not a success. The Allies had ten divisions against seven German divisions in the first wave and they were well prepared for an attack, thanks to information gleaned from prisoners. Poor visibility made it difficult for the Germans to spot artillery and machine-gun positions which caused heavy casualties. By 0800hrs it was becoming clear that the attack was in difficulty. At 1045hrs Ludendorff pondered whether to stop the attack. General von Lossberg was equally gloomy and reported to the OHL at 1200hrs that Allied resistance was solid and that their artillery and machine-guns were doing a lot of damage. By the evening it was obvious that the offensive had to be suspended and von Lossberg, von Kuhl and Ludendorff had independently reached the conclusion that 'Georgette' was finished and 4th and 6th Armies were exhausted. Lossberg reckoned that 4th Army needed ten or twelve fresh divisions in order to take Poperinghe, Mont Rouge and Mont Noir, and that since these were not available they would have go on the defensive.

At Army Group Crown Prince Rupprecht's headquarters General von Kuhl was bitterly disappointed by the failure of 'Georgette'. In many ways it was a highly skilful operation. The storming of Mont Kemmel was an outstanding achievement and the Germans had obliged the Allies to move nineteen infantry divisions and six cavalry divisions from other sectors of the front to meet the threat. This left Pétain's reserves dangerously depleted, and Foch felt obliged to send an urgent note to Haig asking for up to fifteen tired British divisions to be sent to quiet sectors of the French front.[46] The British Army had lost far more ground that it had gained in four months of the bloody battle of Third Ypres in 1917. The Germans had taken 30,000 prisoners and 250 guns. The Allies had lost about 112,000 men, the Germans 86,000.[47] But they had not scored the success for which they had such high hopes. They had failed to reach Saint Omer. They were not in possession of the strategically important line of hills from the west of Kemmel to Cassel, which would have presented a real danger to the left flank of the British army in Flanders. Nor had they been able to nip off the Ypres salient that had been further strengthened by a well-considered retirement. The British had been delivered a heavy blow, but they were not on the point of collapse, and nowhere near being driven back to the coast. Worst of all the German troops were now in a dangerously exposed salient to the west of Armentières, the left flank of which was strongly enfiladed.[48]

By now there were clear signs that Ludendorff was living in a fantasy world. Crown Prince Rupprecht was appalled when he told him on 4 May that he hoped that the British and the French would suddenly collapse just as the Russians had done.[49] Crown Prince Rupprecht was further convinced that Germany should begin negotiations for an armistice, but imagined that a guarantee of the frontiers of Belgium, plus the handing over of the predominantly French-speaking parts of Alsace and Lorraine in return for some colonial concessions by the Entente would provide an adequate basis for talks.[50] Prince Max of Baden was also of the view that peace negotiations should begin at once. Both men agreed with Stegemann, the prominent Swiss military commentator, who had written that Germany's position was 'brilliant but hopeless'.[51] They hoped that it might be possible to arrange a meeting between Stegemann and Ludendorff in the hope the he might be able to convince him that that the military situation was indeed hopeless, and that Ludendorff's insistence that Belgium would have to remain under German control after the war was utterly unrealistic.[52]

There was some concern that the fighting spirit of the troops had been undermined by Bolshevik propaganda, but further investigation showed that this was an unduly pessimistic view. At a conference held in Dresden on 17 May 1918 on 'Patriotic Instruction' in the XII and XIX Army Corps districts, it was reported that prisoners of war returning from Russia were not in the least bit affected by Bolshevik ideas. The OHL's top propagandist and head of the War Press Office (*Kriegspresseamt*), Major Nicolai, told the conference that the overall situation was most favourable for an effective propaganda campaign. He claimed that half the British Army had been destroyed, and pointed out that victory had been won in the East. Propaganda should now concentrate on the need to fight on for a final victory and for a peace that would leave Germany prosperous and powerful.[53]

In July 1917 a new office was created within the OHL responsible for propaganda abroad called the Military Bureau of the Foreign Office (*Militärische Stelle des Auswärtigen Amts* – MAA) in Berlin commanded by a highly accomplished empire builder, Colonel von Haeften.[54] The title of this office was changed to Foreign Department of the OHL (OHLA) in order to emphasize that it was subordinate to the military. Haeften not only controlled foreign propaganda but also formulated policy and vetted the reports that were sent to the civilians on the situation at the front. Haeften's organization became virtually independent from the Foreign Office and the military attachés and acted as the OHL's personal foreign service. Ludendorff had a very high opinion of him, although he disagreed emphatically with his views on the future of Belgium.

In March 1918, shortly before the offensive began, Haeften met secretly in the Hague with a senior official who was familiar with the situation in Washington and London. He listed what he considered to be the Entente's minimal peace terms. Belgium had to be restored to full sovereignty and integrity. The Germans had to evacuate northern France. Alsace and Lorraine should be autonomous, but not necessarily returned to France. Germany would have to become a constitutional monarchy. The question of an eastern settlement would be resolved at the peace conference.[55] On 19 December Lord Robert Cecil had given a speech in which he announced, much to the annoyance of the French, that the British government would not necessarily insist on the return of Alsace-Lorraine to France. The Germans thus had some indication that at this early stage of 1918 campaign the Entente might possibly have been willing to enter peace negotiations, and that Ludendorff's continued insistence that this was utterly impossible was unfounded. Certainly they would not have been prepared to discuss his totally unrealistic terms, but a compromise peace could not be simply ruled out as unacceptable.

Colonel von Haeften was widely denounced in military circles as a defeatist, and his arguments in favour of a compromise peace fell on deaf ears. The head of the War Office (*Kriegsamt*), General von Scheüch, tried to secure his dismissal, but Ludendorff stuck by him. Haeften assumed that Ludendorff had to demand extensive war aims in the west in order to keep up the army's morale, and that in his heart of hearts he knew that a compromise peace was unavoidable. According to Haeften Ludendorff would have liked the proposal for a compromise peace to come from the civilians and not from the OHL.[56] This is highly unlikely, as the furthest that Ludendorff would go was to say that he wished for an 'honourable' peace, and it was not until 11 September that he agreed to relinquish any claim to Belgian territory.

The belief that the demand for extensive annexations was good for the troops' morale was the reverse of the truth. To most soldiers the *Vaterlandspartei* of Admiral von Tirpitz and Wolfgang Kapp, which had been founded on 2 September 1917 as a response to the Reichstag's peace resolution, was a despicable organization. It called for the war to be continued so as to secure totally unrealistic annexations. As one farmer's son wrote, 'If these people merely earned 70 Pfennigs per day and could see the shrapnel flying things would be very different.'[57] A transport worker wrote in a similar vein, suggesting that the editors of newspapers who supported the Pan Germans and their annexations should be forced to spend a month in the trenches. He was convinced that that would change their tune.[58]

Ludendorff would not entertain any thoughts of peace and was determined to strike again on the 'Michael' front. During the 'Georgette' offensive only limited operations were possible on that front. On 5 April Ludendorff asked the general staff chiefs of 17th, 2nd and 18th Armies when they would be able to resume the offensive. 17th and 2nd Armies replied on the following day that needed three weeks respite. Ludendorff therefore ordered a massive bombardment of Amiens and local attacks in support of 'Georgette'. He ordered the left wing of 2nd Army, which was south of the Somme, to be ready to attack on 12 April by which time 'Georgette' would hopefully be showing signs of success. Army Group Crown Prince Rupprecht promptly issued orders to this effect.[59]

On 29 April von Kuhl discussed the situation on the 'Michael' front with Ludendorff at Douai. He argued that an offensive from Arras to the Somme in the direction of Doullens ('New Michael') was preferable to a renewed offensive in Flanders ('New George'). Ludendorff agreed with von Kuhl, and ordered that 4th Army should go on the defensive while preparations were made for an offensive on the broadest possible front by 17th Army in the direction of Doullens, supported by an attack by 6th Army towards Saint Pol. The offensive would not be able to begin before the middle of June.[60]

The OHL issued orders to this effect on 1 May and pointed out that the British had greatly strengthened their positions in Flanders so that 'New Michael' offered by far the best prospect. Army Group Crown Prince Rupprecht began to have second thoughts. The 'New Michael' front to the north of Bapaume in the direction of Doullens was dangerously narrow, with the strongly defended town of Arras to the right and the Somme to the left. At best this would only result in a modest tactical gain, and only if it were combined with an attack near Bethune in the direction of Saint Pol ('Hubertus') could a really damaging blow be delivered to the British. If successful this would result in a breakthrough on a broad front, Arras would be bypassed and the British would be forced back to the sea. The major problem was that this plan needed at least fifty-five divisions, and it was doubtful if they would be available. In that case a diversionary attack by Bethune and a feint in Flanders might possibly take the pressure off 'New Michael', but von Kuhl remained very sceptical. He argued that Army Group Crown Prince Rupprecht lacked the strength to carry out both 'New Michael' and 'Hubertus', and that 'New George' offered the best chances of success. 'New George' involved an attack on Hazebrouk and Poperinghe which would drive the British out of the Ypres salient, and would be followed by a push towards Calais and Dunkirk thus putting the British in an exceedingly difficult situation. A precondition for the success of the operation was that the offensive against the French Army would result in the French Divisions being withdrawn from Flanders. A feint against Doullens was also essential.[61]

On 2 May the OHL rejected this argument, and insisted that the British had concentrated their defences in Flanders and that 'New George' would therefore meet with much stiffer opposition than 'New Michael'. General von Kuhl agreed that the British were in a strong position in Flanders, hence it was essential to lure the French divisions away by means of a convincing feint. Once again Ludendorff seemed incapable of thinking in operational terms, and was obsessed with delivering yet another blow against the enemy that would result at best in a tactical gain. His proposal for 'Hubertus' was fraught with difficulty since it would involve an attack on the Loretto Heights. It could only succeed if it were combined with 'New Michael', but there was general agreement that the manpower and artillery was lacking to mount both operations.[62] The OHL therefore ordered Army Group Crown Prince Rupprecht to give priority to 'New Michael', but also to prepare 'New George'. No mention was made of 'Hubertus'.

General von Kuhl still hoped that he would be able to persuade Ludendorff that 'New George' was preferable to 'New Michael'.[63] He was unsuccessful. Army Group Crown Prince Rupprecht was ordered to prepare for 'New Michael' and simply lay the groundwork for 'New

George' so that should the overall situation change dramatically, thanks to a major success by Army Group German Crown Prince, it would then be possible to mount a further offensive in Flanders.

The British Army was preparing for the Germans to attack again in Flanders. Haig wrote to Foch on 4 May saying that he was unable to mount an offensive operation at the moment, as he was awaiting a German attack. He expressed his delight at the news that the French were preparing an offensive.[64] On the following day he told Foch that there would be no voluntary retirements anywhere, and that switch lines had been built in order to stop any breakthrough. He intended to give the Belgians a helping hand to build switch lines in order to avoid a breakthrough on their front.[65]

The Allies were getting increasingly impatient with the Americans. Both Lloyd George and Clemenceau spent two days trying to get Pershing to be more co-operative, but they achieved very little. Under the terms of the Abbeville Agreement between Milner and Pershing US troops were to be used 'under the discretion and at the discretion' of General Pershing. Lord Reading in Washington felt that the Allies should be dealing with the President over this issue, and not with Pershing. In the meantime he suggested that Foch and the Supreme War Council at Versailles should exercise the maximum pressure on Pershing. Meanwhile the ambassador's prodding began to produce results. Officials in Washington stated that 180,000 rather than 120,000 infantrymen would be shipped to France in May. This was subsequently reduced to 150,000 men for May, June and July, and then increased to 250,000 men for the next two months. The major problem now was that the lack of British shipping made it impossible for the Americans to reach the target of 100 divisions set for July.[66]

Foch wanted to launch an offensive against the German salient at Armentières in which the British First Army would act in conjunction with the French forces in Flanders (DAN). Haig insisted that this was not possible for the time being and Pétain, with his concerns about the French positions south of the Oise, objected vigorously to any operations in Flanders. The most Foch achieved was to veto Wilson, Pétain and Haig's proposals for further withdrawals, and since he did not envisage attacking before the middle of June the argument over the counter-attack was settled by Ludendorff's 'Blücher' and 'Yorck' offensives of 27 May.[67]

General von Kuhl met Ludendorff at Tournai on 4 May and raised the now familiar objections to 'New Michael'. The attack was on a dangerously narrow front and presented a number of serious tactical problems. By contrast the objectives of 'New George' were attainable with the existing strength of the Army Group, provided that the attack by Army Group German Crown Prince succeeded in drawing the French divisions away from Flanders. Ludendorff was convinced by these arguments and on the following day reversed his decision and ordered that 'New George' should take precedence over 'New Michael'. In order to make sure that the enemy did not get wind of this change of plan preparations for both offensives continued and final orders were to be given on 22 May. 'New George' was renamed 'Hagen' and 'New Michael' became 'Wilhelm'.[68]

General von Kuhl believed that Flanders was the point at which the British could be most severely hurt, and he continued to argue in favour of a renewal of the offensive on the 'Saint George' front. This time it was to be to the south of Ypres in the direction of Poperinghe and Cassel and on to Dunkirk and Calais, thus forcing the British back to the Channel ports. He felt that this was greatly preferable to an offensive both sides of Arras in the direction of Saint Pol and Doullens.[69] There were serious difficulties facing 'New George'. The French had moved between ten and twelve infantry divisions to Flanders along with a considerable amount of cavalry, but the situation on the 'New Michael' front was hardly any better.

There was an element of confusion in the OHL's revised orders. The professed aim of 'New George' or 'Hagen' was that a decisive blow should be delivered against the British, but the objectives set was too modest for this to be achieved. General Sixt von Arnim, who commanded 4th Army argued that the offensive should be on a broader front. He pointed out in a memorandum of 11 May that the narrower the attacking front the easier it was for the enemy artillery to concentrate their fire. When the artillery was attacked head-on it was difficult for them to fire from the flanks. It was also easier to exploit local tactical advantages on a wide front. He also argued that the tactical goals were too modest and that the OHL had not given him sufficient operational freedom should he meet with initial success. General von Kuhl was in agreement with most of Sixt von Arnim's arguments and wrote to the OHL to this effect on 13 May. The only of point of disagreement was that von Kuhl insisted that, should the offensive make slow progress in the early stages, it should be called off.

Ludendorff replied on 15 May saying that 4th Army would not have the strength to attack on a such a broad front as Sixt von Arnim had in mind, and warned that that the British would resist fiercely and would be able rapidly to bring in reserves. He warned that the German Army could no longer withstand heavy losses and that the chances of success were slim. General von Kuhl began to wonder whether much could be achieved with an offensive that had, at first sight, seemed so promising.[70] Army Group German Crown Prince would not be able to start its offensive until the end of the month, thus giving the British Army time to bring in reserves and improve their defensive positions.

General Mangin subsequently considered this to be a grave mistake on Ludendorff's part. He did not exploit the advantages he had won over the British and by embarking on a fresh offensive at Chemin des Dames he gave the British a valuable breathing space. General Buat agreed and suggested that it might have been possible to take Amiens and thus cut off the British and Belgian armies.

Time was certainly pressing. The British had suffered 250,000 casualties since 21 March. Twelve of their sixty-two infantry divisions were mere skeletons, and the two Portuguese divisions were out of action for the foreseeable future. The French had lost about 100,000 men, and forty-three of their 103 infantry divisions had been involved in the fighting, along with six cavalry divisions. There were only four American divisions, but fresh troops were beginning to arrive in large numbers. Although the Germans with their 206 infantry divisions still had a considerable advantage, they were tired and desperately short of recruits. They had lost more men in April than they had in March, and there was there was a noticeable decline in fighting spirit. Their artillery and airforce were worn down by constantly being moved from one battlefield to another, and both arms were inferior to those of the Entente. Many senior commanders felt that the war could not possibly be won, and pointed out that the large salients by Montdidier and Armentières were extremely vulnerable should they be forced onto the defensive.

8

'Blücher': The First Phase
27 May-30 May

W hen the 'Michael' offensive ground to a halt Ludendorff hoped that 'Georgette' would make it possible to resume 'Michael' in the form of an offensive against the British army in the direction of Doullens, and drive it back to the sea. Crown Prince Rupprecht and his chief of staff, General von Kuhl, enthusiastically supported this proposal. By 12 April, three days after the beginning of 'Georgette', it was obvious that this was hopelessly unrealistic. Although they had suffered a terrible beating, the British were far too strong for a German offensive to have any chance of success. This gave force to Colonel Wetzell's arguments in favour of an offensive against the French. But Ludendorff still thought of this as a means of opening up the right wing of the British army and forcing the French to withdraw their reserves that were shoring up the British Army. He remained convinced that a decisive victory could only be scored against the British.

As early as January the OHL had ordered Army Group German Crown Prince to prepare an offensive by 3rd Army in the Champagne code-named 'Roland' which would be launched if 'Michael' failed. The French were very thinly spread at the point where the German 7th and 1st Armies met near the Chemin des Dames, a spot that had seen some very bloody fighting in the previous year. Ludendorff, Colonel Wetzell and the staff at Army Group German Crown Prince agreed that this was an ideal place for a major offensive, even though the soggy terrain of the Ailette valley and the high ground of the Chemin des Dames presented formidable obstacles.

On 17 April the OHL ordered Army Group German Crown Prince to prepare an offensive against the Chemin des Dames although Ludendorff still hoped that the 'Georgette' offensive would further weaken the

British and that the attack on Mont Kemmel, scheduled for the following day, would be successful. Two days later a meeting was held at General Headquarters to discuss the offensive by 7th and 1st Armies. The staffs of both Armies outlined their plans which the OHL accepted in principle.[1]

On 20 April Colonel Wetzell wrote an appraisal of the overall situation.[2] He argued that the British sector of the front had become the 'united front of the Entente' where French and possibly American divisions fought alongside the British. This was because Foch was determined to protect the coalfields of Béthune, and in order to do so was forced to prop up the British Army, which had been so badly mauled in the past four weeks. This meant that he had to abandon any idea of a large-scale counter-offensive, and it was doubtful that he would even be able to mount limited attacks, given the parlous condition of the British Army.

Wetzell did not believe that it would be feasible to restart 'Michael' because the front had broadened, and a large number of men were needed to hold on to positions that had recently been overrun. This meant that it would not be prudent to withdraw inexperienced divisions to give them the necessary training. However, it might still be possible to prepare twenty-five to thirty divisions for an offensive on the Western Front by the middle of May.

He did not believe that a renewed offensive against the British would be successful, but he agreed with Army Group German Crown Prince that a breakthrough might be possible on the Chemin des Dames. In preparation for this offensive 18th Army was to attack in a south-westerly direction via Montdidier in order to tie down a significant portion of the French army. 4th Army would keep up its offensive, and some deceptive moves in Alsace by tired German divisions could also oblige the French to move some divisions away from the Chemin des Dames area.

Ludendorff welcomed the suggestion for an offensive along the Chemin des Dames, which was now code-named 'Blücher', as a means of drawing French divisions away from Flanders, but it was not until the end of April, when both 6th and 4th Armies got stuck, that he gave it any serious attention.

On 28 April Colonel Wetzell prepared a paper entitled 'Offensive Against the French' in which he argued that the offensive against the British could not recommence until the bulk of the French supporting divisions had been withdrawn.[3] This could be achieved by an attack by 7th Army code-named 'Yorck' which was designed to draw reserves away from 18th Army's front. 18th Army was then to advance to the line Domfront-Méry-Mareuil-Thiescourt and then on to Compiègne in an operation code-named 'Gneisenau'. 7th Army would then advance along both banks of the Aisne past Soissons, and continue in a westerly direction. French divisions having been moved from the British front, it should then be possible to mount another offensive against the British.

When the German offensive in Flanders was brought to a halt on 29 April Ludendorff immediately began a round of discussions with the army commanders on how the campaign was to proceed. Wetzell's basic arguments were accepted, and it was eventually decided that there should be an offensive on the Aisne, beginning about 20 May. It was designed to weaken the Entente's front facing Army Group Crown Prince Rupprecht and hopefully would create the preconditions for a successful offensive against the British in mid-June. Army Group Crown Prince Rupprecht was to transfer substantial amounts of artillery along with several reserve divisions to Army Group German Crown Prince to ensure the success of this operation. Some officers at the OHL warned that the German army could not continue with offensives on such a scale, but Ludendorff would not listen. He silenced one such officer, Colonel von Thaer, very brusquely: 'Stop bitching! What do you expect me to do? Make peace *à tout prix*?'[4]

Army Group Crown Prince Rupprecht immediately began to decide on the point where the British could best be attacked once the opposing forces were reduced. The staff had already decided that the proposed offensive on the wings of 17th and 2nd Armies in the direction of Doullens, code-named 'New Michael', was unlikely to bring anything more than a modest tactical success. They then proposed 'Hubertus', a much more ambitious plan in which 6th Army would push forward from Béthune to Saint Pol simultaneously with 17th and 2nd Armies' 'New Michael'. It was hoped that this massive encirclement of the British stronghold of Arras on a front of fifty-five kilometres would make it possible to force the British back to the sea.

The Army Group was well aware of the difficulties of mounting such an operation. Preparations for the 'New Michael' offensive in the open country around Bapaume and Albert could not be concealed from the enemy. It would thus be virtually impossible to catch the British off their guard, and surprise was the essential ingredient of success. It was also a matter of some doubt whether the Army Group would have sufficient forces to carry out such an ambitious plan successfully. An alternative strategy was therefore proposed in that the wings of 4th and 6th Armies should resume 'Georgette' and attack in the direction of Poperinghe and Cassel – a plan now code-named 'New George'.

It was estimated that 'New George' could only succeed if the Entente moved reserves to counter a threat to Béthune in a scaled-down version of 'Hubertus', and by a feint attack on the 'New Michael' front, but even then the results would not be decisive. The most that could be hoped for was to push the front forward sufficiently so that the British base at

Dunkirk would be within artillery range and Calais would be under serious threat.

On 2 May Ludendorff expressed his serious reservations about 'New George'. He pointed out that the British had concentrated on the defence of Flanders and that their defences were weaker on the 'New Michael' front. He did not want to abandon 'New George' altogether, but the emphasis was now to be on 'New Michael'.

On 4 May Ludendorff visited army Group Crown Prince Rupprecht's headquarters at Tournai where he addressed the staff.[5] He pointed out that the German army had so severely battered the British, whom he optimistically estimated had lost 400,000 men, that their divisions were reduced from twelve to nine battalions, and they faced a serious lack of fresh recruits. They had been obliged to raise the age of servicemen and were even thinking of introducing conscription in Ireland.[6] The French had been obliged to take over a section of the British front as well as send divisions to prop up the British army north of the Somme, and had been called in to help out at Kemmel. The French were thus in no position to mount a major offensive, had modest reserves of manpower and appeared to be content to wait for the Americans. Although the Americans had fought quite well in some severely limited operations, there were still too few of them to make much of an impact. The two Italian divisions that were on their way to the Western Front did not pose much of a threat. Ludendorff hastened to add that the Germans had also suffered very heavy losses in the 'Michael' and 'Georgette' offensives, but he hoped that it would be possible to mount another major offensive by the end of May.

In the course of these discussions von Kuhl persuaded Ludendorff to change his mind. He argued that the German offensive on the Aisne would oblige the French to move their reserves from Flanders and that this would give 'New George' a real chance of success, whereas 'New Michael' required far too many divisions to be feasible. 'New George' was now first on Ludendorff's list of priorities as a follow-up to the offensive against the French.

In preparation for the new offensive the OHL withdrew thirty-two of the best divisions to rest and be trained and equipped as 'Mob' Divisions. A substantial number of batteries and Luftwaffe squadrons were also brought back well behind the front for rest and training. The remaining troops at the front were therefore singularly hard-pressed.

Although the worst was over for the British Army, and for the next three months it was the French that had to bear the heavier burden, the setbacks in March and April begged a number of questions. How could an entire army have been wiped out, and the Entente come painfully close to a crushing defeat? Who was to blame? What had gone wrong? On 7 May Major-General Sir Frederick Maurice, who had been moved from his position as Director of Military Operations and was about to take up a command in France, dropped a bombshell. He allowed a letter to appear in the press which accused the Government of starving the BEF of forces, of sending white (and by implication superior) troops to distant theatres where they were of little use, and of forcing Haig to extend his front to the south.[7]

General Maurice had contravened the Official Secrets Act and the Army Act, and could very well have been court martialled, but Lloyd George wanted to avoid any official enquiry, and decided to settle the affair in a debate in the House of Commons. He put on a bravura performance on 9 May in which he used all manner of sophistry and dubious statistics in a successful piece of damage control, and scored a decisive victory over his rival Asquith. Although he knew from figures provided by the Adjutant General that this was blatantly untrue, he shamefacedly lied to the House of Commons by claiming that the British Army in France was stronger on 1 January 1918 than it had been on 1 January 1917 and that there was only one white division in Mesopotamia and three white divisions in Palestine.[8] He studiously avoided the issue of the extension of the British front and left it to Bonar Law, answering a question by George Lambert, to tell the House on 23 April that the issue had not been discussed at the Supreme War Council in Versailles and that no pressure had been put on Haig. None of this settled the fundamental questions: were the recent setbacks due to the interference of politicians, or the incompetence of generals? Or was it a fatal combination of the two?

The French mission to GHQ reported that the British felt humiliated by having to call upon the assistance of the French army in moments of crisis. Now that things had quietened down on their sector of the front, they very much regretted having given up so much of their independence of action to Foch. It was pointed out that General Maurice's letter, which had caused such a scandal, was part of an attack on the subordination of the British Army to the French. On the other hand British troops were fed up with Haig and his entourage, and were most grateful for the help that had been given them by the French. It was suggested that the French should exploit these sentiments, and that they should largely ignore the protestations of the British High Command. There was also an alarming increase in anti-war sentiment in the British Army. A number of British officers, some of them in senior positions, were complaining bitterly that the French were prolonging a war that could not be won and which, the longer it continued, was liable to ruin the economy and make post-war reconstruction virtually impossible.[9]

'Blücher', the offensive against Chemin les Dames, was scheduled to begin on 27 May and was to be proceeded by a series of diversionary attacks which were to continue until 2 June so that the Entente would be uncertain where the *Schwerpunkt* of the offensive was to be found. To further confuse the enemy, troops in the trenches were told that the attack would be in the direction of Doullens. The French were not taken in by these stratagems and did not rush in reserves from Flanders.[10] They did not consider that any of these moves were a prelude to a major offensive, and held themselves at the ready.

Plans for 'New George' and 'Wilhelm' (as 'New Michael' was renamed) were completed by 17 May, and the offensives were to begin in late June.[11] The OHL considered that 4th Army's first day objectives for 'New George' – an advance of about 10 kilometres – were overly optimistic. They proposed a line much closer to the starting point, and on a much narrower front. Both Army Group Crown Prince Rupprecht and the staff officers at 4th Army agreed that the offensive should be on a broad front so as to be protected on the flanks by the floodlands and the forest of Nieppe, and that it should not be tied down to obtain distinct objectives. Local commanders should be empowered to react as they saw fit, and exploit each and every opportunity as it arose. Army Group Crown Prince Rupprecht hoped that it would be possible so to shake the British that Ypres could be encircled.

Ludendorff agreed in principle with Army Group Crown Prince Rupprecht's assessment of the situation, but insisted that the breadth of the attack would have to depend on the number of divisions available. Similarly the depth of the attack would depend on the enemy's reserves and staying power. Unlike 'Michael' and 'Georgette' when the Germans met with feeble initial resistance and few reserves, 'New George' would encounter strong opposition and a wealth of reserves. German manpower was seriously deficient, so that Ludendorff could only hope against hope that the offensive against the French would draw reserves away from Flanders, otherwise he doubted that much progress could be made.

On 20 May Ludendorff finally agreed to von Kuhl's plan for 'New George' which had been curiously renamed 'Hagen' after the treacherous character who fatally stabbed Siegfried in the back. On the following day Wetzell issued a serious warning that the offensive had a slim chance of success. If 'Blücher' failed to draw enough reserves away from Flanders 'Hagen' was unlikely to make much progress. It would be the last chance in 1918 to achieve victory and thus it had to go ahead. If it were to get stuck in the early stages it would soon degenerate into a battle of attrition in which, as previous battles in Flanders had shown, the Germans would be at a serious disadvantage.

Wetzell now argued that if 'Blücher' failed to attract large numbers of reserves it should be followed by a further offensive against the French around Verdun where the French were relatively thin on the ground.

The French would be bound to bring in reserves from Flanders to defend Verdun, since after 'Blücher' they would have no others available. 'Hagen' would then deliver the *coup de grâce* .[12] There is no record of Ludendorff's reactions to Wetzell's paper, and it was ignored. He now turned his attention to the detailed planning of the offensive against the Chemin des Dames.

Meanwhile von Kuhl was insisting that the OHL had to make a final decision whether to go for 'Hagen' or 'Wilhelm'. During a railway journey from Zeebrügge to Kortryk on 20 May he repeated his argument that 'Wilhelm' was the more difficult operation and had no clear goal. 'Hagen' was easier and had an attainable objective. Ludendorff saw the logic in von Kuhl's argument and ordered him to go ahead with 'Hagen'. The German Crown Prince was to attack the French in 'Blücher' on 27 May and 'Hagen' could therefore begin in early July. General von Kuhl was delighted that a decision had finally been made, and on his arrival in Kortryk he immediately passed on the good news to Crown Prince Rupprecht. He found his superior officer in a deeply pessimistic mood, insisting that if the war continued into the winter there would be a revolution in Germany. Kuhl attributed this gloom and despondency to the influence of Prince Max of Baden who was visiting Crown Prince Rupprecht's headquarters.[13]

From the middle of April Army Group German Crown Prince was busy planning an offensive. Ludendorff supported Colonel Wetzell's proposal for an attack along a wide front towards the line from Compiègne to Soissons and Reims in which the 7th and 18th Armies would deliver successive blows in careful co-ordination. The Army Group did not like this suggestion. The chief of staff, Colonel Count Schulenburg, repeatedly argued in favour of an offensive along the entire front of 7th Army, rather than an initial attack by 7th Army with a follow-up offensive by 18th Army as Wetzell proposed.[14] This offensive could be supported by an eastward push by 1st Army designed to encircle Reims. Schulenburg became quite carried away with his plan, and suggested that the Army Group could then advance towards Paris. Ludendorff pointed out that this was totally out of the question as neither the manpower nor the artillery was available for such an ambitious operation.

The goals of the offensive were continually extended. Initially it was intended to reach the Aisne. Then it was extended to the high ground between the Aisne and the Vesle. After further consideration it was hoped that the Vesle would be reached. Finally it was decided to cross the Vesle and push on in a southerly direction to the Marne. Army Group German Crown Prince wanted an offensive on a broad front, the right wing to go along the Oise in the direction of Compiègne, the left wing to move around Reims to the forest to the south. This ever increasing optimism was occasioned by the fact that the Germans had a three to one superiority in infantry and a four to one superiority in artillery on 7th Army's front before the French brought in their reserves.[15]

Army Group German Crown Prince did not have enough men to carry out an offensive on such a broad front, and after the war Crown Prince William argued that had troops been sent from Army Group Crown Prince Rupprecht his offensive might have succeeded.[16] But this was hardly possible. Rupprecht's men were in exposed positions at Kemmel and on the Ancre and the Avre. Behind the lines troops were undergoing training for 'Hagen' – the main offensive for which the attack on the Chemin des Dames and Reims was merely a preliminary. They could not be spared without seriously compromising 'Hagen's' chances for success.

The 'Blücher' offensive by 7th Army had to overcome some major obstacles. The Ailette and the Oise-Aisne Canal had to be crossed. The battlefield was full of waterlogged bomb craters and marshy land. The steep slopes of the Chemin des Dames reached a height of 120 metres and offered the enemy an excellent view of the German army's deployment. There was an elaborate network of trenches, dugouts and obstacles, many of them built by the Germans all along the ridge. The only point in Germany's favour was that the area was relatively lightly manned.

Once the Germans crossed the Aisne and its broad valley they had to surmount another ridge similar to the Chemin des Dames. The strategically important town of Soissons was strongly fortified. Thus the Germans were called up to cross a river, two canals and two ridges, both of which were over 100 metres high until, after eighteen kilometres of almost impassable ground, they reached the Vesle at Fismes.

1st Army's prospects were hardly better. Their offensive, code-named 'Goerz' after the swashbuckling sixteenth-century mercenary best known for the expletive 'Lick my arse!', involved crossing the Aisne-Marne Canal and then fighting uphill in wooded country to the south of the Aisne which afforded the French an excellent view of the approaching forces. The Aisne is an average of thirty-five metres wide at this point, and thus presented a serious problem for the engineers. Furthermore the French occupied the same positions in which they had been since 1914, and were thus extremely well prepared.

The OHL studied the results of 'Georgette' with the utmost care and came to the conclusion that the artillery was the essential ingredient for success. Shelling the enemy's batteries with gas had proved most effective. Less satisfactory had been the rolling barrage, which proved exceptionally difficult to co-ordinate effectively with the infantry's advance, since the infantry had very few radio sets with which they could remain in contact with the batteries. This problem was partly overcome by allotting an artillery battery to each infantry regiment. But far more important was the insistence that the infantry should be more independent, and not rely on the artillery to do their work for them. The Germans had a tendency to crowd together when they met resistance, thus offering an easy target to the defenders. Furthermore it was reported that they seldom made use of their weapons as they approached the enemy. They were now trained to attack in waves and in smaller groups, making good use of their light machine-guns. The troops complained bitterly at having to undergo rigorous training in these new tactics, but they proved highly successful in reducing casualties.[17]

The Entente had large number of tanks, which was a matter of considerable concern to the infantrymen. Staff officers told the men that they presented no serious danger since they could easily be attacked from the rear with machine-guns and mortars, and could be immobilized by placing a grenade in the tracks. Large-calibre rifles with armour-piercing bullets and artillery firing over open sights proved more effective against these slow moving and unreliable behemoths.

At the end of April there were only seven divisions at the front and one division at the rear on the 'Blücher' and 'Goerz' fronts. This had to be increased to a total of thirty-six divisions before the offensives could be launched. Only eight of these divisions were fresh and one of these was designated for the defensive. The assault divisions all had to be trained and equipped up to a common standard. They were all short-handed; the battalions that normally numbered 850 men were missing between 150 and 200 men. The large amount of artillery foreseen for 'Blücher' had to be brought forward close to the front, and this could only be done on the eve of the battle. That it was done without detection is a tribute of German organizational skill.

There was, however, mounting concern about morale within the German army. Army Group Crown Prince Rupprecht reported that up to 20 per cent of the troops who were moved from the Eastern to the Western Fronts deserted. When caught they were usually given a four-month jail sentence which was exactly what they wanted, as it gave them a respite from being sent to the front. It was noted with approval that the British Army usually shot deserters.[18]

The French expected an attack, but they were at a loss to know where it would fall. So successful were the German deceptive moves that they first thought it would be in the Champagne or Lorraine. Some correctly suggested the Chemin des Dames and Reims, others Verdun and Nancy. Haig insisted that his armies would bear the brunt of the offensive which he believed would be around Arras or possibly in Flanders. The bulk of the Entente's forces were on the 280 kilometres of front north of the Oise. There were 107 infantry and seven cavalry divisions with forty-two divisions in reserve in this sector. On the 560 kilometres of front south of the Oise there were only sixty-six infantry and three cavalry divisions with eighteen divisions in reserve.[19] On 26 May, by which time it was clear that the Chemin des Dames was under a serious threat, the reserves south of the Oise were strengthened by seven divisions.

Marshal Foch issued a directive on 20 May in which he argued that the war could only be won with an offensive and that the Entente was in an excellent position to hit back. They had more guns than the Germans and an overwhelming superiority in tanks and aircraft. General Fayolle's Army Group was ordered to prepare an offensive at Amiens to relieve the pressure on this important rail centre. The British were to push the Germans back from the vital Béthune coalfields. Should the Germans attack before either of these offensives could begin, the Entente was to mount a counter-offensive as soon as possible.

The French VI Army under General Duchêne covering the front from Varennes to Reims consisted of eleven divisions with five at the rear. Of these divisions four were British, resting after having been severely mauled in earlier fighting, as were many of the French divisions since Foch considered this to be a quiet sector. The British divisions were part of Haig's *roulement* whereby exhausted British divisions were exchanged for fresh French ones. Only six of the French divisions were battle-ready, and Duchêne's army was suffering severely from the Spanish flu epidemic that was soon to cause millions of deaths, mainly of civilians.

General Duchêne was determined to hold the front line trenches, occupied by tired British infantry regiments, so as to stop the Germans from taking the high ground of Chemin les Dames which had been won at such very high cost in the Nivelle offensive in 1917. He had made the mistake of moving troops forward from the battle zone to north of the Aisne in the hope of holding the forward zone. Once this was overrun his battle zone was far too weakly held to offer any serious resistance. He had also failed to order the destruction of the bridges across the Aisne. He insisted that no ground should be given up so dangerously close to Paris, and he was confident that the position was so strong that it could be held. In this he found himself at loggerheads with General Pétain and General Franchet d'Espérey, who commanded the Group of Armies of the North to which VI Army was assigned. They both knew that given the precision of the artillery it would be impossible to hold the Chemin des Dames, and that Duchêne's tactics would greatly increase the initial casualties. They argued that the main line of defence should be in the battle zone where it would be much easier to mount counter-attacks. When the Germans attacked the French VI Army seemed unable to decide whether to concentrate on holding Chemin des Dames, or make a stand in the battle zone.

Duchêne had refused to organize his defence according to the principles outlined in Pétain's Directive Number 4 of December 1917 which called for a defence in depth with lightly held outpost positions. He had argued that this was not suited to the topography of his VI Army's front, and that were he to give way on the Malmaison plateau it would outrage public opinion.[20] Pétain's chief of staff, General Anthoine, was Dûchene's brother-in-law, and argued strongly in his favour. Duchêne was not persuaded by Pétain's arguments and the commander-in-chief was thus faced with the choice of firing him or giving way. With deep regret he decided to let his subordinates prepare in their own way a battle of which they would have the immediate charge.[21] Thus the argument between Duchêne and Pétain had not been resolved, and the consequences were disastrous. The Germans were quick to exploit the resulting confusion.

General Duchêne had some warning of the attack on Chemin les Dames from information gained from German prisoners taken in raiding parties on 26 May and he prudently moved his reserve divisions into the battle zone. But he scarcely had time to make any major changes, nor did he have any idea of the scale of the attack. General Franchet d'Espérey ordered the French IV Army to the right of Duchêne's VI Army to be ready to send in reserves and to prepare the defence of Reims. The German positions were heavily shelled in the night of 26/27 May causing some casualties, but this did not hinder the movement of troops forward in preparation for the attack.

General von Boehn's 7th Army aimed to seize the Chemin des Dames, cross the Aisne and reach the Vesle in one fell swoop. The other objective of 'Blücher' was to push forward towards Soissons and to encircle the town. The right wing of General Fritz von Below's 1st Army and the extreme left of 7th Army was to launch 'Goerz' one hour after 'Blücher' with the Aisne-Marne canal as its objective.

At 0200hrs on 27 May 7th and 1st Armies opened an intensive barrage on all the French positions that were within range. Once again it had been carefully orchestrated by Colonel Bruchmüller. It was of an even greater intensity than the preliminary barrage on 21 March, with between forty and forty-one batteries per mile, as opposed to 35.6 batteries per mile at the beginning of 'Michael'. For the first ten minutes the artillery fired gas ammunition at all targets within reach and as rapidly as possible. The next sixty-five minutes were devoted to counter-battery fire while the trench mortars concentrated on the front line defences and their wire. At the same time key traffic and communications centres and camps were kept under constant fire, so as to stop any reinforcements being brought forward. The next eighty-five minutes were devoted to concentrated counter-battery fire, mainly with gas shells while all available artillery crept back and forth over the infantry positions. At 0335hrs the batteries detailed for the creeping barrage put their fire down on the forward positions.[22]

The effect was shattering. At daybreak the infantry advanced, hidden by a light mist. The artillery had done its work, the forward positions were destroyed, and by 0530hrs the first German unit had reached the

Chemin des Dames. The French were caught completely off guard and the exhausted British divisions which had been sent to what had been assumed to be a quiet sector of the front offered little resistance. Allied reserves were concentrated on the Somme and the Lys where they remained in anticipation of an offensive. Haig subsequently claimed that he and his Director of Operations at GHQ, Major-General Davidson, had repeatedly warned the French that the Germans were about to attack on the Aisne, but that this had been pooh-poohed by Foch and Pétain's staff officers, Generals Weygand and de Barescut. Instead of heeding this warning Foch placed five tired British divisions on the Aisne which were instantly wiped out.[23] There is no evidence in the archives to substantiate this allegation.

General Mordacq argued that the Chemin des Dames offensive made absolutely no strategic sense, and therefore had to be a feint. Foch agreed, and insisted that it was important not to move any reserves from Flanders.[24] The French therefore clearly understood Ludendorff's original intentions, and by not moving men from Flanders frustrated his strategy. Once again the Germans were to have tactical successes that were eventually to land them in serious difficulties. Nevertheless, the French were extremely worried. With the Germans only sixty kilometres from the capital, Pétain once again thought of evacuating Paris, and even thought that the mighty fortress of Verdun might be lost. General Franchet d'Esperey ordered the evacuation of Reims, but General Micheler kept his head and refused to carry out the order.

In the centre of the offensive General Winckler's corps, made up of 1st Guards, 33rd Infantry and 10th Reserve Divisions met with precious little opposition and reached the Aisne without difficulty. By the early afternoon they had secured bridgeheads on both the Aisne and the Canal which ran beside it. By the evening Winckler's men had moved forward to the Vesle and had advanced an amazing twenty kilometres. The 1st Guards Division met somewhat stiffer opposition. They were held up on the Aisne and did not manage to reach the Vesle by nightfall.

To Winckler's left General Conta's 10th and 28th Guards Divisions had to scramble up the overgrown slopes to the Chemin des Dames, often on their hands and knees, but the French had been broken by the barrage, and by 1700hrs they reached their objectives on the Vesle. His 5th Guards Division advanced rapidly across open country, the British divisions having been so heavily bombarded that they could offer precious little resistance. Indeed they moved forward so rapidly that the few supporting tanks were unable to keep up. They found all but one of the Aisne and the canal bridges untouched, and by the early afternoon the division had crossed both obstacles. By 2000hrs they had crossed the Vesle and seized an abandoned airfield, with substantial amounts of fuel and a few planes, twenty kilometres from their starting point.

General Schmettow's corps on Conta's left met with stiffer initial opposition from the British positions around Ville au Bois, but by 1000hrs all his divisions had reached the Aisne, which was nearer to his starting line than it was to any of the other corps in the 7th Army. The retiring British had destroyed most of the bridges, thus causing further delays. Once over the Aisne and the canal Schmettow's divisions were held up again in the forest of Gernicourt where the British made a stand. It was evening before they were able to fight their way past this obstacle, so that by the end of the day they had advanced about five kilometres, a modest amount compared to the gains made along the Chemin des Dames.

The success of 'Blücher' guaranteed that 'Goerz' would reach its modest objectives from Moscou to Hill 83 and the Aisne-Marne canal without much difficulty. The OHL then gave permission for the advance to continue, but von Below's men soon came up against stiff resistance from the British, and by evening had only reached Cormicy, and that with great difficulty. General von Below sent in the 86th Infantry Division to plug the gap between his right flank and Schmettow's corps.

General von Boehn was understandably pleased with the day's work and was convinced that the enemy had not yet recovered from the initial shock. He was therefore keen to continue the advance during the night. The OHL agreed, and ordered General Conta's corps to take the high ground south of the Vesle while the neighbouring divisions were to move up to the river.

Foch still assumed that this was merely a diversionary attack designed to force the Entente to withdraw reserves from north of Amiens, but the commander of the Group of Armies of the North (GAN), General Franchet d'Esperey reported on the evening of 27 May that the situation was 'very dangerous'. Pétain then ordered in reserves from north of the Oise and told General Micheler, who commanded V Army, to prepare to lend a hand.[25] Foch still thought that a German offensive in Flanders was a distinct possibility, and was thus reluctant to send Pétain the help for which he was asking. As the Germans continued their advance he changed his mind. On 28 May told Haig that he was obliged to send V Army to the south, so that the four divisions of X Army were the only French units left that could lend assistance to the British Army should it come under attack.[26]

General Duchêne, whose army was rather thinly spread, having had to take over a further sixteen kilometres of front after the collapse of Gough's Fifth Army, was left with only five divisions intact with a handful of demoralized troops who had been driven back from the Chemin des Dames. He faced twenty confident German divisions. On the morning of 28 May, in spite of this somewhat precarious situation, Pétain ordered him to stop the German advance on the

Vesle. General Franchet d'Esperey promptly ordered seven divisions, of which one was British, to help him hold the line and hopefully to win back some of the lost ground. But only three of these divisions were in position on 28 May and they proved far too weak to hold up the German advance.

Pétain visited all the headquarters on the front under attack on 28 May, and came to the conclusion that the Vesle could not be held. He therefore ordered that the flanking positions on the left astride the Aisne by Soissons and on the right by Reims should be strengthened so that as the Germans pushed forward in the middle the resulting salient could be hit on its extended flanks.

By the evening of 28 May Duchêne's VI Army had seventeen infantry divisions behind them, of which four were British plus two cavalry divisions. A further eleven divisions, one of which was British, were on their way along with three and a half cavalry divisions. But the Entente was beginning to scrape the bottom of the barrel. There were now only eight divisions in reserve from the Swiss border to the Oise. One was Italian and three were untrained American divisions. North of the Oise to the Channel there were only ten French divisions alongside the British, Belgian and American divisions. The Germans had an impressive sixty-five divisions in reserve of which forty-seven were fresh. Forty-one of these divisions, of which twenty-eight were fresh, were in Army Group Crown Prince Rupprecht, and there were clear indications that they were poised for an offensive north of the Oise.[27]

On General von Boehn's right General François' corps was ordered to extend their bridgehead over the Ailette Canal at Leuilly on the following day, but he had insufficient artillery support for this to be possible. On François' left General Larisch requested support from 51st Reserve Division, but this was refused as the OHL had ordered that reserves should only be used in support of a major success. Larisch's advance on 28 May was held up by the difficulty of bringing up the artillery because of crippling French artillery fire. His offensive could not begin until the afternoon, and met with stiff resistance from the French, but they were unable to save Soissons which the Germans reached at 2100hrs. The town was encircled and soon was largely in German hands.

General von Kuhl attributed the German success at Soissons to the fact that the French were caught by surprise. He told Colonel Wetzell that this showed once again that Ludendorff's insistence that careful preparation was more important than surprise was a serious mistake. For von Kuhl the most carefully laid plans would come to naught without a large element of surprise.[28]

To Larisch's left General Wichura's 9th Division came under heavy enfilade fire from Fort Condé and was also unable to resume their attack until the afternoon when 14th Reserve Division captured the fort. In was not until 1945hrs that Wichura's men were able to cross the Aisne, most of the bridges having being destroyed. 37th Infantry Division of his right pushed on over the Vesle and advanced a further 5 kilometres in a south-westerly direction.

General Winckler's corps on Wichura's left also met with little serious opposition, and merely had to clear up isolated pockets of resistance. By evening all his divisions had crossed the Vesle and taken possession of the high ground to the south-west. General Conta also had few difficulties on 28 March except on his left where the 5th Guards Division came up against mixed French and British positions. They were further delayed by an Allied counter-attack which was beaten off. By the end of a day of relatively heavy fighting they had had crossed the Vesle and had advanced a total of some four to five kilometres due south.

On Conta's left the British had retired on the front facing General Schmettow's right wing, but were unable to offer much opposition from their new positions. 7th Reserve Division, placed on Schmettow's left, had much greater difficulties, and made only modest gains. At the end of the day his divisions formed an awkward right angle pointing south. To the left of General Schmettow's corps, which formed the left wing of 7th Army, the 1st Army forced its way south across the Vesle and made a modest advance in the direction of Reims.

The Germans had only met with serious resistance on the two wings of their advance on 28 May. They had thus had no problems with supplies. They had used up very little ammunition and had captured large quantities of food and drink as they moved forward. They had not made quite such dramatic territorial gains as they had the day before, but they had advanced thirty kilometres in two days, and had reached their objectives. Some units indulged in drunken orgies as they fell upon large supplies of *pinard* and discipline collapsed. But this only affected troops at the rear and did not present any serious problem at the front. The prospect of capturing staggering amounts of food and drink was a powerful incentive for troops on the attack; but it presented a problem when the momentum of an offensive was lost while men stuffed themselves, and military effectiveness and discipline were difficult to maintain when they were incapacitated by drink. For this reason in July every division appointed a Spoils (*Beute*) Officer and each regiment had a Spoils Troop, made up of an energetic officer and reliable men selected from each battalion. They were responsible for handing out captured food, clothing, alcohol and tobacco for immediate consumption by the troops. The remaining supplies were handled by Military Police patrols and were placed in the charge of a Divisional Collection (*Sammel*) Officer. He was made responsible for ensuring that rearguard troops, such as the artillery and engineers, did not get short-changed. They were also required to keep a certain amount in reserve for any later handouts. By such means it was hoped that indiscriminate plundering could be avoided, and that everyone got a fair share of the spoils of war.[29]

Food and drink was not the only form of spoils. Weapons and equipment were equally important. The OHL offered special premiums for units that showed particular expertise and initiative in collecting weapons and matériel and bringing it to the rear. This was often an extremely dangerous task, as it was frequently conducted under heavy fire. A considerable amount of valuable material was retrieved from abandoned positions that were still under enemy observation. The rewards for such action were generous. One Bavarian infantry company was given the princely sum of 2000 marks for a particularly successful operation.[30]

Ludendorff arrived at 7th Army headquarters at 0800hrs on 28 May accompanied by the German Crown Prince and his staff. He seemed uncertain what to do next. He wanted to advance westwards between the Aisne and the Oise-Aisne canal; but he also wanted to exploit the success of Winckler and Conta's corps as they pushed south. Once again he seemed in danger of dissipating his resources in pursuit of two contradictory goals. At 1300hrs he gave the go-ahead for General Winckler to continue his advance south. General Wichura's corps was ordered to take the high ground south of Soissons so that the French would be obliged to move divisions from the area between the Aisne and the Oise, thus opening up the way for a westward advance. Then 18th Army was to attack from Noyon along the southern bank of the Oise and head south-west in the direction of Compiègne. This was a modification of 'Gneisenau': an offensive in the direction of Compiègne from the line from Montdidier to Lassigny.

Ludendorff was now calling for a large-scale offensive that he had previously rejected on the grounds that he lacked the manpower. Reims was to be taken to secure his lines of communication. Winckler was to continue his advance in a southerly direction. The right wing of 7th Army was to drive westwards and 18th Army was to attack in the direction of Compiègne. His only hope was that he would meet with such success that he could do without 'Yorck'.

On the evening of 28 May the OHL was delighted to hear that the French were moving divisions from Flanders to meet the threat posed by 'Blücher'. The offensive was thus serving its purpose well and, given that the Germans had twice the number of divisions and superiority of artillery on the 'Blücher' front, they were confident that further divisions would be withdrawn from the north. On the other hand some staff officers began to worry that since the flanks of the advance had moved slower than the divisions in the centre they were now in a pocket that left them extremely vulnerable to flank attack. This was of course precisely what Pétain had in mind. The French troops at the bottom of the pocket offered little resistance to the Germans who were thus able to advance a further eleven kilometres, in spite of fierce fighting on the flanks, and were now less than five kilometres from the Marne.[31]

That evening Pétain issued order to the GAN to prepare two counter-attacks on the flanks of the German advance to begin on 31 May designed to push the enemy back to the Vesle and the Aisne. At the same time he admitted that there was little hope of stopping the advance in the centre of the attack until the Germans reached the Marne. Meanwhile a report from the French military attaché in Copenhagen suggested that the present offensive was a large-scale diversionary move in preparation for a major offensive between the Somme and the Oise, aimed in the direction of Paris. Pétain therefore asked Foch to place the four divisions of X Army, which was positioned between the Somme and the Lys, at his disposition. In addition he requested that the nine divisions of the DAN in Flanders should be relieved by British and Belgian troops. Foch, who still anticipated an attack in Flanders by Army Group Crown Prince Rupprecht, denied this request and merely ordered the detachment of some artillery from X Army.[32]

Generals François and Larisch who were positioned on 7th Army's right wing made only modest advances on 29 May, advancing an average of two kilometres. General Wichura's right wing had great difficulty in crossing the Aisne as the bridges had been destroyed and Larisch's corps had to lend a helping hand. Wichura's men crossed the Aisne by 1600hrs and advanced to the south of Soissons.

General Winckler's corps had fewer difficulties, and making skilful use of its artillery it advanced a considerable distance in a south-westerly direction. To his left General Conta made good initial progress until he was stopped by a counter-offensive by a French cavalry division amply equipped with tanks. Major-General Baron von Buchau who commanded 28th Division fell in this engagement. For the first time there were ominous signs that the supply lines were over-extended resulting in a lack of ammunition for the front line troops.

General von Boehn the commander of 7th Army felt that the front facing General Schmettow's corps was in a state of disarray because British and French troops were fighting side by side. He therefore ordered General Schmettow 'in accordance with the instructions of the OHL' to advance in an easterly direction so as to lend support to the right wing of von Below's 1st Army. It was soon clear that von Boehn's assessment of the situation was based on faulty intelligence and an overly optimistic assessment of General Schmettow's strength.

General Schmettow's corps was exhausted having fought through much of the night and was awkwardly placed. Whereas the main thrust of 7th Army's offensive was in a south-westerly direction his front faced south-east. The British had brought in fresh divisions to this sector and Schmettow's left wing was soon in danger of being separated from his right. Ludendorff was far from satisfied with 7th Army's progress on 29 May, and realized that as the French brought up their reserves it would be slowed down even more.[33] To Schmettow's left General Brimont of 1st Army also made little progress. In spite of the spirited resistance of French colonial troops his 242nd Division on his left was able with great difficulty to reach the outskirts of Reims.

General Wellmann, who commanded the 'Reims Group', was convinced that the French were about to abandon the town and asked General von Below's permission to attack. This was granted at 1235hrs, von Below warning that the town should not be taken by a direct assault but by encirclement. It was soon clear that Wellmann had been overly optimistic. The French had not retired, and he was only able to make modest gains.

Pétain went ahead with his preparations for a large-scale counter-attack designed to halt the Germans' push to the south, and drive them back across the Vesle and back to the Aisne. The Northern Army Group (GAN) was ordered to attack on a broad front from north of Soissons to west of Reims on 31 May.[34] American troops were on their way to help defend the bridges over the Marne, but they were very inexperienced and had to be given detailed instructions. Where possible they were to be assisted by French troops, in the hope that they would not be caught by surprise by small German units. This was a particular danger at night.

On the following day Pétain issued his Order of the Day Number 107:

> The enemy has struck another blow. He has been superior in numbers during the last three days and has managed to break through our front lines. But our reserves are arriving. You are going to break his will and hit back. Rise up heroes of the Marne! Forward for our homes and for FRANCE![35]

The counter-attack planned for the next day was ordered to go ahead.

These were brave words, but the mood at GQG was far from confidant. The head of the British mission to Pétain's headquarters concluded that the British Army would have to be evacuated from France, leaving up to 1 million prisoners of war behind. General Lawrence felt that Foch's blustering calls for a counter-attack were merely 'ridiculous'. Spirits remained low for several days. Back in London Hankey wrote in his diary: 'I don't like the outlook. The Germans are fighting better than the Allies and I cannot exclude the possibility of a disaster.' Wilson argued that there would indeed be a disaster if the British Army did not abandon Ypres and Dunkirk, and Foch's objections to this move would simply have to be overruled. He ordered detailed planning to begin for the evacuation of the BEF from the Continent.[36]

Clemenceau paid another visit to Duchêne's army on 29 May, having had to make a hasty change of venue when it was discovered that the Germans were already in possession of the town where they had arranged to meet General Degoutte, the commander of XXI Corps. The Premier was told that the battle had got out of control, the Corps was not fighting in an organized fashion and was merely marching to the rear. Clemenceau then went on to Duchêne's headquarters where he was told that no one knew quite what was going on. General de Maud'huy commanding XI Corps and General Chrétien at XXX Corps headquarters were equally unable to shed any light on the situation. Clemenceau was appalled and saw no alternative but to seek Foch's council.[37]

On 30 May Ludendorff insisted that the main aim of 'Blücher' should not be forgotten. If large numbers of troops were to be attracted from Flanders then the attack had clearly to be in a westerly and south-westerly direction so that Paris would be threatened. 7th Army's centre should therefore push on to the Marne and then move westwards, keeping its left flank along the river's northern bank. Reims would have to be taken so as to secure the railhead needed to supply the southern flank of the salient that the Germans had created since 27 May. This could be achieved by seizing the high ground of the Montagne de Reims to the south of the town, and by an attack to the east of the city which would help to provide a springboard for a further attack.[38]

The offensive at Chemin des Dames, which had been designed as diversionary move to draw reserves away from Flanders, had now become a full-scale offensive which had thrust forward well beyond its original goals, and resulted in the creation of a dangerously exposed salient. This left the German Army in an even worse position than they had been after the March offensive when they ended up in the Montdidier salient. Army Group Crown Prince Rupprecht had been obliged to send large numbers of labourers, transport and airplanes to support 'Blücher' with the result that preparations for 'Hagen' got badly behind schedule. It was now clear that this offensive could not possibly begin in early July.[39] In the course of the Chemin des Dames offensive Army Group Crown Prince Rupprecht had to send two Corps and the five best divisions designated for 'Hagen' to help Army Group German Crown Prince. 'Hagen' rapidly became a very remote possibility.[40] There was considerable satisfaction in the army with this remarkable achievement, but many agreed with the Brigade commander who told Admiral Müller: 'This is my ninth offensive. Now I've had my belly full.'[41] Success had followed success, but they were no closer to victory, and an increasing number of soldiers began to express similar sentiments.

9

'Blücher', 'Yorck' and 'Gneisenau': 31 May–14 June

The French were in exceptionally strong positions on both flanks of the new German salient pointing towards Château-Thierry. There was heavily wooded country at Villers-Cotterêts to the west and the high ground near Reims to the east.[1] It would seem that every successful offensive created fresh problems, and at each stage Ludendorff was diverted from his original concept. He was blinded by success and simply followed the line of least resistance. First he crossed the Vesle and then pushed on, exhausting his troops and dangerously exposing his flanks. His eye was no longer on Flanders, but on the prospect of taking Reims and destroying the French forces at Villers-Cotterêts. Preparations for the offensive in Flanders went ahead, but Ludendorff was now intoxicated by the glowing prospect of a major victory against the French.

The news of the German advance horrified the politicians in Paris and there were insistent demands that Generals Pétain and Duchêne should be 'sent to Limoges'. Duchêne, Degoutte and Maud'huy repeatedly told Clemenceau that they had virtually no artillery, and only had rifles and machine-guns with which to counter the German guns. Pétain remained remarkably cool amid this chaos. He realized that merely holding the German flanks was not enough to stop the enemy's advance, and he therefore ordered counter-attacks on both flanks of the Château-Thierry salient. At the bottom of the salient the Marne from Château-Thierry to Eperney was to be held at all costs, and troops that were still in training, including some Americans, were to be brought into position.

The pressure of the German forward thrust was such that it seemed increasingly unlikely that a counter-offensive would be feasible. The situation around Reims seemed critical, and on the afternoon of 30 May General Franchet d'Esperey told Pétain that he doubted that it would be possible to hold the western slopes of the Montagne de Reims. Pétain replied that he should be prepared to retire if the situation deteriorated further. The British 9th Corps, which had been moved to the Aisne to recuperate, was utterly exhausted after four days of intense fighting, each of the four divisions were reduced to one single battalion, and Lieutenant-General Hamilton-Gordon begged that it should be relieved.[2] General Foch felt obliged to release his last reserves from X Army, to support Franchet d'Esperey's hard pressed men. By the evening of 30 May the situation improved greatly, and it was clear that the German threat to Reims had subsided. Pétain now hoped it would be possible to go over to the offensive on the following day as he had previously planned.

The French launched a counter-attack in the early afternoon south of the Aisne near Soissons. It followed a murderous artillery barrage and a fierce aerial attack. Three French divisions attacked, supported by a large number of new tanks, which were small, relatively fast, and manoeuvreable and thus proved to be tricky targets. The Germans were able to contain the attack and pushed the French back beyond their starting positions, but they suffered severe casualties.

The Germans made better progress to the south where General Wichura's left was supported by General Winckler's corps. Winckler pushed forward quickly and reached his objectives with little difficulty, but this left a gap between him and Wichura's corps which had to be quickly plugged by 28th Reserve Division.

General Conta's corps also pushed rapidly forward and ended the day well to the west of Soissons. General Count von Schmettow faced much more determined opposition, particularly on his left wing and was only able to reach the Marne on his right. Nearer to Reims General Ilse was seriously short of ammunition and had to ward off a strong counter-attack and was only able to make modest progress. On his left flank the 242nd Jäger Division forced its way into the north-westerly suburbs of Reims. To the east of the city General Wellmann's corps made final preparations for an offensive to be launched on the following day.

Once again Ludendorff placed tactics before strategy when he analyzed the day's results. Forgetting his earlier strictures on the importance of Reims, he concentrated on the impressive advance made by generals Winckler and Conta. The OHL released three of their reserve divisions to support the advance to the south and south-east of Soissons which posed a direct threat to Paris.

At 1515hrs Ludendorff ordered the Army Group German Crown Prince to concentrate on advancing in the direction of Villers-Cotterêts and to the west of Château-Thierry. General Conta was to release two of his divisions to support this movement. In addition, Army Group Crown Prince Rupprecht was to send two divisions, and Army Groups Gallwitz and Duke Albrecht were each to send one division in support of this westward advance.[3]

Ludendorff had thus weakened Army Group Crown Prince Rupprecht which was preparing for the great offensive in Flanders for which the Battle of the Aisne was merely a preparation. Indeed there was some indication that the OHL was contemplating abandoning the offensive in Flanders and was about to concentrate on advancing towards Paris from the line from Villers-Cotterêts to Château-Thierry. Colonel Wetzell reminded General Schmettow during the afternoon that it was essential to secure the Reims railway so that the advance towards Paris could continue. At 1500hrs Ludendorff had told Army Group Crown Prince Rupprecht that Army Group German Crown Prince's operations were so promising that he should launch a series of feint attacks so as to lend their support. Clearly Ludendorff no longer saw the withdrawal of Allied divisions from Flanders as his principal goal. 'Blücher' was taking on a life of its own.[4]

'Yorck' had to be postponed for 24 hours in order to bring up the artillery, but the 'Blücher' offensive continued regardless. On the right flank a radio message was intercepted which indicated a withdrawal of the French 55th Division on the Oise east of Noyon. The OHL ordered General Hofmann's corps to pursue the enemy, but the temporary bridges across the Oise had been dismantled. Hofmann's men were therefore not able to cross the river until the afternoon, and then they met with unexpectedly strong opposition and soon got stuck. Clearly the news of a French withdrawal was mistaken.

On 7th Army's left the French had withdrawn during the night, which enabled General François' corps to make substantial progress towards the Aisne. General Larisch's division had a much tougher fight, but managed to cross the Aisne and take the high ground to the west and south-west of Soissons.

General Wichura's corps had to fight off a fierce counter-attack and thus made no significant progress. Only the 37th Division on his left was able to move forward without opposition, the French having withdrawn to a strong defensive position. General Winckler's corps advanced in a westerly direction, and since General Conta to his left headed south towards the Marne a dangerous gap between their two corps was created. Conta was thus obliged to plug the gap with his right flank, but nevertheless was able to reach the day's objectives. He now had the best part of two divisions placed between Brécy to the north of Château-Thierry and the Marne. They faced west in accordance with the OHL's orders. General Schmettow's corps had some fierce fighting along the road leading from Dormans, to the east of Château-Thierry and Reims, but by evening had reached the Marne. General Ilse, who had replaced General Brimont on the right of von Below's 1st Army had hoped to take Reims, but he was bitterly disappointed. He was suffering from an acute shortage of ammunition and the French beat back his attack on the town. At the end of the day he had captured a few French trenches, but at some points had actually lost ground. General Wellmann's corps to his left fared no better.

By the end of the fourth day of the 'Blücher' offensive the Germans had thus made good progress south towards the Marne and were well positioned for their westward drive towards Paris, but they were still dangerously weak on their flanks at Noyon and at Reims. The enemy's resistance was strengthening, and the troops in 7th Army were beginning to get desperately tired. The OHL were convinced that Reims would soon fall and thus did not think it was necessary to strengthen their forces around the town. They felt it was enough to detach General Schmettow's corps from 7th Army and place it under the command of 1st Army.

The atmosphere in Pétain's headquarters was getting extremely tense. Pétain was deeply shocked at how easily French troops had given way in the face of an attack by German troops who were in no way superior. The honour of France was at stake and had been seriously compromised by such *laisser-aller*. On reflection he felt that this was perhaps too harsh a judgment. The Germans, after all, were greatly superior in numbers, and he felt that this was the main cause of this extremely serious situation. He therefore wrote to Foch suggesting that he arrange a meeting with Clemenceau to discuss the emergency.[5] At 1049hrs Colonel Dufieux, the head of Pétain's Troisième Bureau, telephoned Weygand to say that the battle was brutal and casualties were very high.[6] The French divisions were badly mauled, and the moment had come to make some important decisions. Weygand asked what he suggested. Dufieux proposed sending Americans to relieve French units in the Vosges which could then be thrown into the battle. Weygand pointed out that this presented insurmountable logistical problems, adding that the Germans then might attack on such a seriously weakened front, and that the Reserve Army (GAR) had already been seriously thinned (*dégarni*). Dufieux said that the British army should help bring the Reserve Army up to strength. Weygand claimed that this was out of the question since not one of Crown Prince Rupprecht's divisions had gone into the battle, and it would not be possible to ask the British to weaken their front at this stage. Dufieux disagreed vehemently, saying that there were several of Crown Prince Rupprecht's units on the Aisne, and insisted that the threat was south of the Somme, not to the north.

Clemenceau, Foch and Pétain met that evening at the headquarters of VI Army at Trilport. Clemenceau had already spoken to Duchêne who complained that none of his superiors had visited his headquarters and claimed that all he had to oppose the Germans was the dust kicked up by his men as they retreated.[7] Foch told Pétain that the advance towards Paris had to be stopped whatever the cost. Any commander who showed the slightest signs of weakness was to be instantly dismissed. Foch wanted to send reserves north of the Somme, but Pétain was desperately short of reserves and felt that Duchêne had already made very poor use of the forces at his disposal. Haig was in no mood to help and resisted every effort to transfer divisions from the British front to help his hard-pressed ally. Having met Foch at Sarcus on the morning of 31 May Haig travelled to Paris to meet Lloyd George, Sir Eric Geddes (First Lord of the Admiralty) and Admiral Sir Rosslyn Wemyss (First Sea Lord) in order to discuss arrangements for the evacuation of Dunkirk. Their deliberations were rudely interrupted by an air raid.[8]

By 1 June thirty-seven Allied divisions had been involved in the battle since 27 May of which five were British. Seventeen divisions were worn out, two or three of them probably beyond repair. Sixteen divisions had been fighting for two to four days, and four fresh divisions had just entered the battle, with five more on the way. Pétain again suggested sending US divisions to the Vosges and Lorraine in order to relieve some excellent French divisions, which were badly needed in the battle.[9] Once again his request was turned down.

On 1 June Pétain told all his general officers that there were no more reserves available and that they had to hold fast, always keeping in mind that the honour of the country was at stake.[10] Colonel Dufieux made an urgent telephone call to Colonel Desticker, a staff officer at Foch's headquarters (EMA), asking when the British were going to send more help. Desticker replied that he had no idea, adding that he had not seen Foch for two days. Dufieux stressed that the situation was extremely serious, whereupon Desticker said he would speak to Foch the next day. Dufieux ended the conversation by urging him to do so without fail.[11]

Meanwhile the staff of V Army made plans for the evacuation of Reims, arguing that the high ground beyond Reims was strategically more important than the town itself. Given that the town was a vital communications centre, this is clear indication of how serious the situation had become. General Franchet d'Esperey felt that the situation conformed with the preconditions laid down for evacuation, and gave General Mazillier, who commanded 1er C.A.C., the order to abandon the town. Mazillier, who was well aware that there were considerable misgivings at headquarters about the decision, simply put the order in his pocket and calmly waited for it to be countermanded.[12] This piece of insubordination saved Reims, for Pétain was determined to keep the town. Franchet d'Esperey, his Army Group (GAN) having failed badly, was posted to Salonika to replace General Guillaumat, where he imposed singularly harsh terms on the defeated Bulgarians.[13] Clemenceau, who was facing increasing pressure from the Senate and the Chamber to remove Pétain, held General Guillaumat at the ready as the most suitable successor as commander-in-chief. Generals Duchêne (VI Army), Maud'huy (XI Corps) and Chrétien (XXX Corps) were all removed from their commands, and a court of enquiry was established to examine the causes of the Chemin des Dames debacle.[14]

Pétain, having been ordered by Clemenceau and Foch to halt the German advance at any price and to adopt a 'foot-by-foot defence to the last breath', now placed three more divisions between the Ourq and the Marne to block the bottom of the salient. He complained that there had been far too many retirements that had been excused by a need to realign the front. He therefore issued an order that the only effective way to realign the front was by counter-attack. No further retirements were permissible without the express orders of a superior officer.[15]

Back in Paris the British Ambassador prepared to evacuate the embassy. Maple and Company packed the archives at a cost of 1638.40 francs, and A. Lemoine et Fils were paid 3,840 francs for coal briquettes to fuel river-boats to ship this precious cargo down the Seine.[16]

Army Group Crown Prince Rupprecht observed that the Allies were sending in their reserves to the west of Soissons, strengthening their defensive positions around Villers-Cotterêts and were preparing a counter-attack, although it was still uncertain where the blow would fall. Crown Prince Rupprecht regarded the overall situation as extremely grave and there were obvious indications that the offensive was running out of steam. On 1 June he wrote to the chancellor, Count Hertling, insisting that peace negotiations should begin at once. He argued that it might be possible to deliver a few more punishing blows against the Entente on the Western Front, but Germany was in no position to deliver the *coup de grâce*. There would then be no alternative to a war of attrition which Germany could not possibly win because of the shortage of manpower.

Hertling gave a vacuous reply on 5 June. He expressed the confident hope that 'pacifist tendencies' would grow in the Entente as a result of German successes, and that this would oblige the enemy to seek a peaceful solution. The two men met a few days later in Brussels, but Crown Prince Rupprecht was unable to convince the chancellor of the gravity of the situation. Clearly he was completely under the influence of Ludendorff's unfounded optimism. The politicians stood passively by and waited for the OHL to provide the preconditions for a peace that would meet Germany's minimal desiderata.[17]

General von Boehn set ambitious goals for his 7th Army for 1 June, even though Ludendorff felt that they were unlikely to be achieved.[18]

The drive westward was to continue with General Conta's corps having to cover the most ground, moving to the north-west so as to straighten the line from Château-Thierry towards Villers-Cotterêts.

To the north General Hofmann had to abandon his attack for lack of artillery support against the reinforced French positions. On his left General François fared slightly better, and only managed to struggle forward some three kilometres. He was helped along by an aggressive General Larisch who finally came to a halt on the Aisne where all the bridges had been destroyed. Only his 6th division managed to cross the river, but soon came to a standstill on the opposite bank where the French offered tough resistance.

Larisch's left wing and General Wichura's corps also made little progress between the Aisne and the Marne. The French had counter-attacked the previous day, and were still an impressive fighting force steeled by Pétain's determination not to give ground. Wichura did somewhat better on his left where the French were much weaker, although he did have to beat off a spirited counter-attack in which a number of tanks were involved. General Conta's corps also managed to reach the day's objectives to the west of Château-Thierry, but only after a tough fight. He took the western portion of the town, but the east remained in the resolute hands of the French.

Operations around Reims brought disappointing results. To the west General Schmettow's corps had the greatest difficulty in holding its ground against a fierce counter-attack by the fresh French 120th division. General Borne's corps was desperately short of ammunition because Allied aircraft managed to destroy an important ammunition dump. They thus made precious little progress and the attacks by General Ilse's corps were unsuccessful. To the east of the town General Wellmann's corps made only modest progress as they had not been able to collect the mortars and ammunition that they needed for their assault. The aim of encircling Reims was not achieved and General von Below ordered a halt while ammunition was brought up to the front.

General von Boehn viewed the situation in a more positive light, and asked the Army Group to give him three or four extra divisions so that he could attain his more distant objectives. Ludendorff was sympathetic to this request. Two divisions were on their way from Army Group Crown Prince Rupprecht, and two more from Army Group Gallwitz, but the latter divisions were in poor shape and could only be used for defence.

Reims remained the key position without which 7th Army's left flank could not be adequately supplied. Ludendorff therefore ordered 1st Army to advance towards the Marne at Epernay. He was prepared to send four additional divisions to lend weight to this attack. Army Group German Crown Prince did not agree with Ludendorff and insisted that 'Blücher's' *Schwerpunkt* should be in the west with 7th Army. All efforts should be concentrated on that front so that the Allies would be forced to send in divisions that would make 'Gneisenau' easier.[19] An offensive in the direction of Epernay would meet very stiff resistance as the French would be able to bring in support via their railhead at Esternay some 36 kilometres to the south of the Marne. That would mean that 7th Army would not have the strength needed for its drive westwards. The OHL accepted these arguments and there was no more talk of an advance south of the Marne.

Thus 7th Army's orders for 2 June were to concentrate on the advance between Soissons and Villers-Cotterêts supported on the left down to Château-Thierry by an advance towards the Ourq. The army was unable to reach the day's objectives owing to a shortage of ammunition and a strong defence, which relied on the skilful use of artillery. There were also some dangerous counter-attacks in which tanks were used to good effect. General Wichura's fresh 47th Reserve Division was able to reach the road from Soissons to Villers-Cotterêts, but elsewhere General von Boehn's troops only got about halfway to their objectives.

It was now abundantly clear that the offensive was losing momentum. The troops were exhausted. Fifteen under-strength divisions had been fighting without a break for a whole week. Twelve of the fourteen reserve divisions had been used and there were only eight fresh divisions in reserve by 2 June, four of which immediately went into action. The French now had thirty-three divisions facing 7th Army's twenty-nine divisions. They had strengthened their artillery and used it to murderous effect, and their bombers continually attacked artillery positions and supply lines causing considerable damage.

In spite of the fact that the German offensive was beginning to slacken, Pétain was still seriously worried that they might be able to break through his front and threaten Paris. He estimated that the enemy had forty fresh divisions in reserve and he only had eight. Of the thirty-seven divisions on the Aisne front, of which five were British, seventeen were utterly exhausted. Five divisions were due to arrive by 2 June, but only one was fresh. Five more were to be added by 10 June. He therefore repeated his suggestion that American divisions in training in the north should be sent to the Vosges, and that British reserves should be sent south. Haig predictably refused this request. He pointed out that although the Belgians had agreed to take over a portion of the British front, they still need British artillery support. This meant that at most he could only withdraw one division from the front and place it in reserve. Only when the Americans provided five fresh divisions would he be able to take over a section of the French northern front. On 4 June Haig protested vigorously to Foch against any attempt to remove any part of the British Army from his command, at a time when not all of Crown Prince Rupprecht's forces were engaged in the battle.[20]

Foch was fast losing his patience with the British. In a lengthy memorandum to Clemenceau he pointed out that as early as January 1918 the Supreme War Council had complained that recruiting in Britain was hopelessly inadequate. Haig had said that he would probably lose about thirty divisions in the event of a major attack, since they were all seriously under-manned. In spite of this he had done nothing to strengthen his forces before the offensive on 21 March, and in April he had dissolved nine divisions. In the following month it had only been possible to reconstitute one division from fresh recruits from Britain. Then came the German offensive on the Aisne and Haig was obliged to dissolve two more divisions, thus leaving him with eight less divisions that he had in March. These could not be made up by the Americans who were bound to be slow in coming to the front. Foch insisted that if the British did not take drastic measures to rectify this situation the Entente could very well lose the war.[21]

The Supreme War Council held its sixth meeting at Versailles from 1 to 3 June. It very soon became exceedingly acrimonious. At a preliminary meeting between Lloyd George, Milner, Wilson and Du Cane, Haig claimed that the French reserves that had been thrown into the battle had 'melted away like snow' because the French Army had neglected both training and discipline after the disastrous Nivelle offensive and the mutinies of 1917. He therefore concluded that it would be simply a waste of good men to put them under French command. In a closed meeting between the British and French delegations Foch fiercely attacked the British for wanting to dissolve ten infantry divisions as a result of the heavy losses they had sustained during the previous three months. He pointed out that this diminution of the British Army was greater than the increase in the American forces, and this at a time when the Germans were mounting a massive offensive. Foch also called for an American Army totalling 100 divisions: twice the size originally envisaged.

This provoked a violent outburst from Lloyd George who protested that Foch was misinformed about the number of reinforcements sent from the United Kingdom to France, and suggested that he appoint an officer to visit Britain so as to get an accurate picture of the situation. Foch managed to keep his composure during this counter-attack, and continued to insist that the British could and should do much more.

The Prime Minister managed to ensure that this exchange was withheld from the plenary sessions which dealt with a number of issues such as intervention in the Russian civil war and the recognition of an independent Poland, but the main emphasis was on urging the Americans to speed up the dispatch of troops to France. It was estimated that there was sufficient shipping available to accommodate 250,000 men per month.[22]

British determination to remain on the defensive in preparation for another German attack was demonstrated in the publication of a paper by Major General Guy Dawnay, Haig's deputy chief of staff, on defensive warfare, which was promptly forwarded to the French. It echoed the German principle that the forward zone should be lightly held since concentrations of infantry to the front were subjected to murderous bombardment, obstacles were destroyed, wire was useless, the positions ruined and the troops incapacitated. On the other hand it was important to give the enemy the impression that one was prepared the hang on to the outpost zone, and all enemy patrols had to be stopped. Immediate counter-attacks were necessary in order to extricate men from the outpost zone. Local commanders should have discretion as to which positions had to be abandoned, but it had always to be remembered that 'there is only one degree of resistance, and that is to the last round and to the last man'.[23]

With great reluctance the British finally agreed to send three divisions to help out their hard-pressed ally. An argument now developed between Dufieux and Weygand as to how they should be transported. Weygand argued that they should go by rail. Dufieux insisted that they should go by road. The rail route went via Abbeville, while the route by road was direct. Furthermore, if they went by road and the British Army was attacked the divisions could simply do a left turn and join in the battle.[24] The British were characteristically slow in meeting this urgent French request, and Dufieux grew very impatient, asking Desticker when the British divisions were going to arrive. Desticker told him that they were on their way, to which Dufieux replied that it was about time, since it looked as if the Germans were about to launch an attack on the Reserve Army (GAR).[25] Lieutenant-General Pagezy, the head of Foch's Troisième Bureau, reassured Dufieux that three British divisions were on the way and would straddle the Somme. Dufieux asked under whose command they would be placed. Pagezy replied that he did not know, but assumed that they would remain under Haig.[26]

On 5 June it was finally agreed that the three British divisions should be placed west of Amiens so that they could quickly be moved either north or south of the Somme.[27] This assurance did little to appease Dufieux who complained bitterly of the bureaucratic obstacles that made it so difficult to get any help from the British.[28] The French were somewhat appeased when the British agreed to consider the possibility of sending nine infantry divisions south, including the crack Canadian Corps, along with some special forces such as motorized machine-guns. Meanwhile Foch moved three divisions from the DAN without bothering to inform GHQ, prompting General Plumer to protest .that he was unlikely to be able to defend the vital port of Dunkirk without adequate reserves.[29]

By 4 June Pétain was reasonably confident that the danger was over. He now concentrated on improving his defensive positions, and was ably supported in this task by General Fayolle, who commanded the reserve army (GAR). The main principles were to have lightly manned forward positions, and a strong main line of defence out of range of enemy artillery. The artillery was to be placed behind this line of defence. At the same time every effort was made to disrupt the enemy's preparations for an offensive in the Champagne.[30]

Foch was far less confident and ordered that the German advance towards Paris should be stopped at all costs, adding that any feeble commanders should be instantly dismissed. The army had to be imbued with the spirit of sacrifice, must be resolute and decisive. He told Pétain that the defence of Paris had the top priority, and that it was the most important and most dangerous task facing the French army. He repeatedly insisted that the army was not to give an inch.[31]

The British took the persistent French requests for help as a sign that they were about to crack. On 5 June Hankey, Sir Henry Wilson and Lord Milner attended an emergency meeting at Number 10 Downing Street to discuss the possibility that Ypres and Dunkirk would have to be abandoned, and were the French Army to collapse the entire British Army might have to be evacuated from France.[32]

The French were exceedingly angry with Haig for his refusal to even consider sending them any more help. Haig appealed to his Government, claiming that Foch was endangering the security of the British Army. At a conference in Paris on 7 June, attended by Foch, Weygand, Milner, Haig and Wilson, Clemenceau complained bitterly that although Haig had only been asked to consider the possibility of sending reserves south, he had protested vigorously even before he had received a letter to this effect from Foch. In reply Haig blurted out that he had been anticipating a German attack, and had any of his divisions been sent south he would have been left in dire peril. Foch replied haughtily that the offensive by the German Crown Prince, supported by Crown Prince Rupprecht, had been directed against his forces, and that he badly needed these reserves and could not be subjected to Haig's incessant reservations and objections. Clemenceau strongly seconded this attack on the British commander-in-chief. Haig complained that he had been robbed of five US divisions, along with a number of French divisions, which had left him very vulnerable, but Weygand pointed out that this had been agreed upon at a conference at Versailles, during which Haig's chief of staff General Lawrence had raised no objections.

Foch continued his attack on the British by repeating the accusation that if the British divisions were not kept up to strength the Entente was in serious danger of losing the war. Haig protested against the insinuation that the British were not pulling their weight, and Milner argued that Haig, unlike the French, only counted those divisions that were up to strength and were fully trained. These acrimonious exchanges ended when Wilson asked Foch which of the two objectives would the French defend in the event of a German attack on both Paris and the Channel ports. Foch, having been reassured by Pétain that Paris was no longer in danger, responded haughtily by saying that liaison between the two armies would remain intact, that Paris would be protected, and the ports would not be abandoned.[33]

Since 'Gneisenau' was due to begin on 7 June the OHL did not set any ambitious targets for 7th Army on 3 June, and Ludendorff insisted that casualties should be kept to an absolute minimum. Only limited attacks should be made, and they had to be carefully prepared. General von Boehn concentrated on the strong French position to the south-west of Soissons. The results of the day's fighting were again disappointing. 7th Army made no progress at all north of the Aisne. Between the Aisne and the Ourq they were only able to advance because the French withdrew to stronger defensive positions. General Larisch's left wing and General Wichura's corps forced their way through a weak point in the French defences and took 3,500 prisoners, fifteen guns and two aircraft.

On 4 June the Germans again made no progress north of the Aisne and only made modest gains south of the river, in spite of the OHL's insistence that an advance along both banks of the river was important for the success of 'Gneisenau'. General von Hutier, who spent the bulk of his time in early June doing the paper work for 'Gneisenau', was constantly pestered by Ludendorff about the smallest details of the operation. He felt that Ludendorff, by concentrating on the minutiae, saw only tactical trees and lost sight of the operational wood.[34]

On 5 June 7th Army made a few minor improvements to their position, but often at considerable cost. General Wichura's corps suffered terrible casualties and made very modest gains. The OHL suggested that only the three corps on the right wing of 7th Army – those of generals François, Larisch and Wichura – should continue with the offensive. All the others should go on the defensive.

Army Group German Crown Prince then ordered the advance to continue on both banks of the Aisne, but by the end of the day no progress had been made, and Ludendorff felt that the most that could be achieved were some minor improvements in the army's positions. The Army Group hoped that 'Gneisenau', now scheduled to begin on 9 June, would bring some relief, and that the offensive could then be resumed.

On the following day the Germans got a taste of things to come. The American 2nd division forced General Conta's men to abandon the village of Bouresches to the west of Château-Thierry and the Allies counter-attacked at other points, but to little effect. The Germans held their ground and made some advances. Ludendorff ordered 7th Army to concentrate on hitting the Americans so as to make it difficult for Pershing to form an effective army in France. General von Boehn ordered General Conta to prepare such an attack, but the difficulties were considerable. He was seriously short of ammunition and supplies and the Spanish flu, which had previously only seriously hit the Allied troops, had broken out on an alarming scale among the Germans. It would need extremely careful housekeeping for even these modest goals to be achieved. General von Boehn still hoped that 'Gneisenau' would cause the Allied front to collapse and ordered his army to prepare for a breakthrough.

Pétain remained alert to the possibility of another German offensive, but pressed ahead with his plans for a counter-attack. V Army was ordered to prepare an offensive to improve the positions between the Marne and Reims.[35] At the same time he thought the Germans might well attack IV Army on the Aisne, and General Debeney who commanded I Army sent urgent messages that an attack was imminent, and begged for American divisions to strengthen his defences.[36] While Foch ordered the construction of reinforced defensive positions behind the British and French lines to the south-east of Amiens, Pétain complained that he only had thirty-three infantry divisions in reserve. He hoped to build seven or eight new reserve divisions by the end of June, by which time the Americans would have relieved part of the French front in the Vosges and Lorraine. He warned Foch that I Army was exceedingly hard pressed, was exhausted and without reserves. If the Germans kept up their offensive it would be necessary to throw in all the Entente's reserves from Ypres to the Swiss border in order to hold the front.[37]

On 9 June General Fritz von Below's 1st Army attacked the high ground to the west of the town near Hill 240 at Vrigny to which Ludendorff attached particular importance. The attack was poorly prepared, supplies of ammunition were inadequate, the troops desperately tired. After some initial successes the Germans were driven back to their starting positions by skilful counter-attacks and heavy artillery fire.

Ludendorff insisted that the offensive against Reims should go ahead, but the staff at Army Group German Crown Prince argued that they lacked the strength to carry out such a mission. General von Below, an expert in offensive warfare, agreed but he fell sick and had to be replaced by General Mudra who reported back to the OHL that the attack on Reims would have to be postponed, but he still gave orders that preparations should continue. 1st Army went on the defensive, and the OHL began to think in terms of an attack on Reims involving 7th Army supporting 'Roland' with an attack from the south-west.

Ludendorff was fully aware of the importance of Reims but he refused to give General von Below and his successor the reserves, which

1 The German high command. Left to right: Hindenburg, the Kaiser, Ludendorff.

2 A captured German tank.

3 A German mortar.

4 German troops moving to the front.

5 German front-line troops prepare to advance.

6 The Kaiser converses with a field officer.

7 German troops moving to the front.

8 British soldiers clearing out front-line trenches taken over from the French.

Above left: 9 General Sir Henry Hughes Wilson, who took over as Chief of the Imperial General Staff in 1918.

Above right: 10 David Lloyd George: he and Haig were often at loggerheads regarding the conduct of the war.

11 An Irish battalion padre chatting with men in the previously French sector of the front.

12 German cavalry on the move in 1918.

13 Storm-troopers attack. Note the spacing between individual soldiers and the use of smoke to disguise their movements.

14 British soldiers wiring trees felled across a canal to hold up the German advance.

15 A British trench after a German assault.

16 German infantry and artillery in St Quentin.

17 German supplies move through Albert.

18 German troops fall on British supplies.

19 A German heavy mortar.

20 The devastated, cratered landscape that made it difficult for infantry, and virtually impossible for artillery, to advance anywhere fast.

21 German cavalry advance.

22 An impressive German gun. When the artillery could be moved to keep pace with the attack, the Germans' effective use of the 'creeping barrage' decimated enemy forces.

23 German troops in the debris-strewn streets of Bailleul.

24 A British artillery position near Albert.

25 The unique grave marker of the German flying ace Baron von Richthofen, with an epitaph inscribed in English and German on an aeroplane propeller. The 'Red Baron' was shot down by an Australian machine-gun crew on 21 April during a reconnaissance flight.

26 British flying officers put together a jigsaw-puzzle map to familiarize themselves with the geography of northern France.

27 Mont Kemmel, the strategically vital high point taken by the Germans on 25 April 1918.

28 Chemin des Dames.

29 German infantry in 1918. The Germans' overwhelming superiority in infantry and artillery occasioned the massive expansion of the 'Blücher' offensive.

30 German artillery in 1918.

31 Prisoners captured by the Germans in a wood near Reims.

32 A French 28cm mortar.

33 Walking wounded file past a battery on the Canadian Front.

34 German infantry on the attack near Montdidier, June 1918.

35 Young German soldiers captured by the Allies.

36 A German battery on the Marne, May/June 1918.

37 German infantry ready to attack on the Marne.

38 A German field dressing station.

39 A British 'Whippet' tank waiting to move forward.

40 A French company climbing a steep bank on the Marne front.

41 A French battery of 15.5cm howitzers in action.

Above left: 42 General Fayolle, commander of the French Group of Armies of the Reserve.

Above right: 43 General Gouraud, whose IV Army's inspired defence held up the German offensive east of Reims.

44 A French infantry company advancing through corn and brushwood on the Marne front.

VERY MUCH UP
A Champagne Counter-Offensive

45 *Punch* magazine's take on the Mangin counter-offensive.

"ACCORDING TO PLAN"
LITTLE WILLIE: "Well, Father wanted a war of movement, and now he's got it!"

46 A *Punch* cartoon from August 1918 marking the beginning of the German army's ignominious retreat from its hard won territory.

47 American troops marching German prisoners to the rear between Soissons and Château-Thierry in late July 1918.

48 Americans standing by a German barricade in Château-Thierry.

49 An abandoned British tank: given their failure to produce adequate numbers of decent tanks, the Germans relied almost entirely on captured British machines.

50 German soldiers with an 8.8cm anti-aircraft gun. These were also used in anti-tank warfare in the absence of an effective alternative.

51 A German soldier emerging from a dugout to surrender to advancing British troops.

52 British soldiers turn a captured German machine-gun against its former owners.

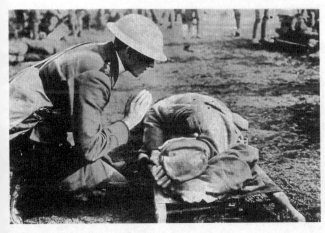

53 A British padre ministers to a badly wounded German.

54 Some of the 21,844 German prisoners captured by the British Fourth Army in the August offensive being marched to the rear in batches of a thousand.

55 Fourth Army officers processing German prisoners.

56 General Sir Douglas Haig thanking some of the Canadian troops who took part in the battle of Amiens.

they both deemed essential if the town were to be taken. The OHL had also failed to bring fresh troops forward to maintain the momentum of 7th Army's westward drive. Divisions were only withdrawn when they were utterly exhausted, whereas the Allies rotated their divisions rapidly.

Pétain was now overly pessimistic. The Germans were also exhausted and hopes that 'Gneisenau' would lead to a breakthrough proved to be wishful thinking. General von Boehn lacked the wherewithal to even make a halfway convincing feint attack in support of 'Gneisenau'. Admittedly this was not immediately apparent to the GQG. For the next few days the Allies mounted a series of counter-attacks which were successfully beaten back and on 11 June General François was encouraged when he noticed that Allies on his sector of the front had withdrawn. He ordered a pursuit and got as far as the Oise at Bailly where the Allies occupied old French trenches and stopped his advance. Elsewhere General Conta's attempt to drive the Americans out of the forest of Belleau failed, and the fresh American troops put up a surprisingly effective defence.

Meanwhile preparations continued for the advance along both banks of the Aisne. Given the shortage of artillery General von Boehn wanted to concentrate on the area south of the river in an operation code-named 'Hammer Blow'. If that was successful he hoped that he would be able to follow up with an advance along the north bank. The OHL agreed with this plan given that the Allied positions north of the river were particularly strong. The OHL's assessment of the situation on the Western Front on 5 June underlined that a major victory had been won south of the Aisne. The German Army had advanced well beyond their goals and it was nonsense to suggest that the offensive had ground to a standstill. On the contrary the preconditions for further advances had been achieved. Crown Prince Rupprecht could only shake his head at this overly optimistic assessment, and accused Ludendorff of refusing to confront reality.[38]

Haig was still very worried about the threat to his sector of the front, and continued to raise objections to the idea of sending any troops south to help the French. He insisted that he was only prepared to abandon the Ypres salient under severe enemy pressure.[39] By this time Foch had come to realize that Haig had good reasons for concern, since Crown Prince Rupprecht still had enough men to mount a major offensive against the British.[40] At the same time he urged Haig to ensure that his cadre divisions should be brought up to full strength, and that they should be given enough machine-guns and artillery.[41]

'Hammer Blow' began at 0500hrs on 12 June after a barrage that lasted one and a half hours. The Allies were ready for the attack and had moved their artillery back so that it was not touched by the preparatory barrage. German losses were heavy, and only on the left flank of the attack were they able to reach their objectives some two kilometres from the starting line. The Kaiser was so depressed by the initial results of the offensive that he ate nothing but a little chocolate mousse at lunch.[42]

The offensive continued on the following day but achieved nothing but a few corrections of the front. Army Group German Crown Prince suggested to the OHL that the offensive be called off since the losses were out of all proportion to the gains. The OHL ordered a halt on 14 June and 7th Army's offensive was thus ended.

General von Boehn gave a glowing account of the operation. The enemy had suffered a severe defeat and he had taken 60,000 prisoners and 830 guns.[43] He took great pride in having given the French army, for which he had the highest respect, such a thorough beating, even though he had fewer divisions at his disposal. He ordered 7th Army to go on the defensive, to do everything possible to save lives and prepare for a resumption of the offensive.

The most serious weakness of 'Blücher' was that Ludendorff seemed uncertain what it was designed to achieve. Initially the attack on Chemin des Dames was intended to draw Allied troops away from Flanders in preparation for a decisive blow against the British army. The battle then degenerated into a slogging match at Soissons and Reims, which tempted Ludendorff to abandon his original plan and to think of an offensive against Paris. Unable to make up his mind at this juncture, he waited for results rather than taking the battle firmly in hand. The OHL thus sent confusing and ambiguous orders that held up the advance around Soissons and led to a deadlock in the west.

The storming of Chemin des Dames was a brilliant feat of arms, the Germans having advanced up to 60 kilometres in a mere four days, but the offensive failed in its principal objective. 'Blücher' did not attract Allied divisions from Flanders and therefore there was no point in continuing it, unless it was clearly understood that 'Hagen' would be abandoned and full weight lent to the push towards the French capital. But this would have been a exceedingly difficult task. Pétain's defensive positions at the forest of Compiègne and at Villers-Cotterêts were formidable obstacles. Whenever the OHL sent divisions from Army Group Crown Prince Rupprecht to help out to the south this merely freed Allied divisions to meet the threat. Nor had the Germans inflicted any decisive damage on the Allies. The Allies suffered a total of about 135,000 casualties (about 103,500 French, 29,000 British, and 2,400 Americans) but they had lost 98,000 men. Allied casualties would soon be made up by fresh American troops, whereas the Germans had no means of replacing their losses.

It was simply not possible to score a decisive victory in this sector of the front, a victory that would end the war. Furthermore the very success of the offensive left Army Group German Crown Prince in a large salient with over-extended lines of communication which offered a tempting target for an Allied counter-offensive. The French had strong positions at Reims to the east and Villers-Cotterêts to the west of this salient whence they threatened 7th Army. Indeed the success of 'Blücher' further misled Ludendorff into thinking that he was on the right track. In his analysis of the operation he once again stressed the importance of pushing forward as fast and as far as possible, throwing in the reserves to support advancing troops. On the other hand he reminded the Army Group Commanders that the whole point was to inflict as much damage as possible on the enemy, not simply to gain ground. Ludendorff noted that many commanders in the later stages of the offensive had tended to attack with insufficient forces, with poor reconnaissance from the air, and with inadequate artillery support, simply to win ground which was without significance for the overall situation. The secret for success was to achieve the closest possible co-operation between the infantry and the artillery. Stiff pockets of resistance should be broken by the artillery, not by the infantry.[44]

Ludendorff had many reasons to be satisfied with the offensive. He had fought another superb battle, 7th Army had advanced an impressive distance, but the end result was unsatisfactory, and he was no nearer to striking the decisive blow for which he had worked so hard. On 25 June he reminded all senior commanders that the war could only be won by massive offensive blows, and that a defensive strategy was out of the question. He insisted that the principles applied in the previous offensives were tried and proven. This was admirably illustrated by 11th Infantry Division's attack near Noyon on 9 June in wooded, hilly country, against a determined defence. The attack had been highly successful, and casualties were minimal. However, the German army still had a tendency to bunch up too closely when attacking, and paid far too much attention to gaining ground, or taking some prestige object such as a hill, wood or village, even when little was gained by such operations. Counter-attacks were also not always strictly necessary, and often led to unacceptably high casualty rates. Army Group Duke Albrecht had shown that an elastic retirement could be most effective in such circumstances.[45]

There is an unmistakable note of desperation in Ludendorff's memorandum. The German army had delivered some shattering blows on the Entente, but it was beginning to get punch drunk, and it was increasingly obvious that it was most unlikely to be able to deliver a knockout blow. Germany was further away from victory at the end of June than it had been in March, and more of the same was unlikely to change the situation. Ludendorff tried to convince himself that British morale had been shattered by the defeats in March and April, and that they longed for peace. Interviews with prisoners of war indicated that the British placed the blame for their setbacks on the French and vice versa. Both had a poor opinion of the Americans. But he had to admit that the British had put up an impressive defence at Armentières, and many senior officers doubted whether the British could be made to crack.[46]

Ludendorff placed the blame for these recent setbacks on poor security. He called a meeting with the representatives of the Bavarian, Saxon and Württemberg armies at the OHL on 25 June and told them that the recent offensives had all failed because the enemy knew the Germans' plans. He regretted to inform the Military Plenipotentiaries to the OHL that he would not be able to give them detailed briefings in future, and that they would have to rely on the singularly jejune daily reports issued by his staff. In addition they would be given maps indicating any changes in the front. The Military Plenipotentiaries, who had precious little to do at the best of times, were left at a loose end.[47]

The poor performance of Duchêne's VI Army at Chemin des Dames caused outrage in Paris, and on 26 July 1918 Clemenceau set up a committee of enquiry on the Army's performance from 26 May to 3 June.[48] The commission established that there had been neither strategic nor tactical surprise, and that Pétain had placed four reserve divisions behind VI Army, with four more on the Oise ready to move at a moment's notice. The only element of surprise was the sheer force of the German attack. It was admitted that the Germans had pulled off a real *tour de force* in assembling such a large concentration of troops without detection by French military intelligence. Careful examination of VI Army's intelligence, particularly air reconnaissance, showed that everything possible had been done under the circumstances. The Germans had skilfully moved their artillery forward during the night shortly before the offensive began, and had made remarkably successful use of camouflage. The Commission concluded that the fault perhaps lay in the intelligence gathering by higher echelons such as General Franchet d'Esperey's Army Group (GAN), Pétain's GQG or even the Allied Supreme War Council in Versailles.

VI Army had been alerted on the evening of 26 May, and was thus ready to meet the Germans. The major difficulty was the overwhelming superiority of the German artillery. They had at least 4,000 guns, whereas the French only had 1,032 of which not all could go into action.

A fatal mistake had been the failure to destroy the bridges across the Aisne. General Duchêne told the commission that he had ordered the engineers not to place charges under the bridges until he gave the order to withdraw. He had been told that it would take less than an hour to prepare the bridges for destruction, and he did not want to run the risk of damaging any of the bridges prematurely. The overwhelming force of the German attack, and the skilful use of storm-troopers who pushed forward and seized a number of bridges, left the engineers no time to place their charges.

General Duchêne came under heavy criticism from Pétain, Maistre and Foch for ordering four infantry battalions north of the river Aisne thus weakening his second line of defence, and given the speed of the German advance they had no time to get into position. As a result the Aisne was lost. Duchêne laid the blame for this unfortunate state of affairs on the divisional commander who failed to carry out his orders properly. He claimed to have only ordered three battalions to cross the river, and they moved far too slowly and for this reason were easily overrun.

The central point of the enquiry was to determine whether General Duchêne had been ordered to hold the first or second line of defence at all costs. Pétain's Directive Number 4 of December 1917 and modified in January called for lightly held forward positions, the enemy to be stopped at the second line of defence. There was ample evidence that Pétain had made an exception in the case of the Chemin des Dames because of the peculiarities of the topography in his orders on 20 April. Both Foch and the commander of the GAN had agreed that the high ground on the Chemin des Dames offered the best line of defence. Therefore General Duchêne could not be charged with failure to carry out orders. Furthermore he insisted that his requests to both Pétain and D'Esperey for reinforcements had been turned down on the grounds that all available units were needed north of the Oise.

The Commission concluded that the setback on the Chemin des Dames was due to overwhelming superiority of the enemy in manpower and matériel against VI Army's over-extended and under-manned front of 90 kilometres. The divisions were tired, had been seriously afflicted by influenza, and a large number of men were on leave or in training. Foch and Pétain agreed that after the battles of March and April the Allies could not afford to give up any more ground north of the Oise and they had to begin preparations for a counter-offensive. If there were any serious mistakes made, they were at the highest level, but an investigation of the higher commands exceeded the Commission's brief.

10

The Aisne:
15 June–14 July

During the final days of the Battle of the Aisne the French High Command received reports of preparations for an offensive against General Humbert's III Army on a front from Montdidier to Noyon. The Germans were in an excellent position for an offensive in this sector as they occupied salients on both wings which General von Hutier's 18th Army had carved out of Gough's Fifth Army in 'Michael III' in late March. But French intelligence were puzzled by the quite untypical openness with which the Germans were making their preparations, and thought that this might well be a feint. Preparations for a continuation of the offensive north of the Somme were further advanced, but perhaps this was merely a sign that the Germans were hastily preparing to strike a surprise blow. Information gained from prisoners suggested that this was indeed the case, and some deserters spoke of an impending offensive. The French also saw the deserters as indicative of a further decline in the German army's fighting spirit.[1]

The problem of morale and desertion is an immensely complex issue, and it is all too easily to make hasty generalizations. As CIGS wisely put it in August 1917: 'As regards morale, it is essential not to attach too much importance to the statements of deserters and other prisoners or enemy correspondence…. Our own officers and men taken prisoner do not always express confidence in victory, while censored letters show that every man in our Armies is by no means possessed of good morale. This is only natural and to a greater or lesser extent is common to all armies and in assessing the enemy's condition it is necessary to approach the task with a perfectly unbiased and impartial mind.'[2]

One of the most remarkable aspects of the trench warfare of World War I, in which millions of men fought for years on end in appalling conditions, suffering frightful casualties, in a seemingly endless and increasingly pointless conflict, was the remarkably small number of deserters. The German army did not lose the war because of desertions, but the number of desertions increased dramatically when it was obvious that the war was lost. As Schopenhauer remarked sardonically: 'The more stubbornly one clings to an error, the more shameful the proof to the contrary. When an organization falls apart, such as a defeated army, the wisest man is the one who runs away first.' Many acted on this principle, for it was only when armistice talks began in October that the rate of desertions increased sharply.

Ludendorff bemoaned the fact that life in the trenches tended to reduce disparities of rank and thus undermine discipline.[3] Discipline certainly became much more informal in the German Army during the war. In part this was due to a reluctance to water down the officer corps. A German battalion at full strength had about twenty-five officers, five with each company and five more at battalion HQ. Later in the war many battalions made do with about seven officers: a captain serving as CO, a lieutenant as his adjutant, four second lieutenants as company commanders and a medical officer. Platoons were thus more often than not commanded by battle-hardened NCOs rather than inexperienced public school boys and chinless wonders, as was all too often the case in the British Army.[4]

In such a situation there was little room for what the Tommies called 'bullshit'. Men were all in the same boat, anxious not to let their mates down, and usually led by men whom they trusted. Morale in the German Army improved greatly during an offensive. Spirits dampened markedly when men found themselves shuddering in dugouts for months on end, badly fed and ill equipped, cowering under horrendous Allied artillery fire and bombing raids, strafed by low-flying aircraft whose machine-guns were mounted at an angle, cold and frightened, far away from their loved ones whom many feared they would never see again. For most German soldiers going on the offensive was a relief. They were excellently trained and confident of victory, but every bit as important they were active subjects rather than passive objects. An offensive might increase one's chances of being killed or wounded, but one had the feeling that one's destiny was in one's own hands, and one was no longer completely at the mercy of an Allied artillery man or pilot.

Ernst Jünger, as always, was a keen observer of this phenomenon. As late as October 1918 he wrote:

> This was the first time in a battle that I came across a man who caused dif-
> ficulties not because of cowardice but because he had simply had enough.
> Although such feelings were stronger and more widespread in the last
> couple of years, it was very rare that they found expression during a battle,

because action binds people together whilst inaction separates them. The most startling expressions of the increasing unwillingness to fight came from columns of troops marching back from the battlefield.[5]

It was perhaps for similar reasons that the number of desertions in the Bavarian Army was higher in 1917 than they were in 1918.[6]

The German and British Armies differed widely both in their attitudes towards the law, and in the severity with which it was applied. Only forty-eight men were condemned to death in the German Army throughout the entire war, and of these only eighteen were deserters.[7] The British executed 269 men. The German Army had professionally trained military lawyers, the British did not. In German military law the principle of *in dubito pro reo* applied. The British Army did not feel that military law was there to punish offenders, and certainly not to show justice. It was there for its deterrent effect and '*pour encourager les autres*'. As the Duke of Wellington said: 'I consider all punishments to be for the sake of example.'

The German Army was also somewhat more lenient in the definitions they applied. What in the German Army was considered AWOL in the British Army could well be deemed desertion. But in both armies the application of military law became less severe as the war dragged on. 248 Death sentences were revoked in the British Army in 1918. In April 1917 minimum sentences were reduced in the German Army, and there were general amnesties on the occasion of the Kaiser's birthday.

From the evidence provided by deserters who took advantage of an amnesty and returned voluntarily from neutral countries it appeared that most desertions took place from military depots. It was therefore ordered that a closer guard should be kept on these depots and that weapons should be used against anyone trying to escape.[8]

The number of desertions from the German Army in the first eight months of 1918 was remarkably low; and those who might have seemed most likely to desert, such as troops from Alsace-Lorraine, were no more eager to throw in the towel than were Prussians. Thus 3rd Army, which had a large number of men from the two provinces, reported twelve desertions in February 1918, two of whom were from Alsace-Lorraine, six from Prussia, three from Württemberg and one from Baden. In March there were only two deserters, both of them Prussians. In April there were seven, two from Alsace-Lorraine, four Prussians and one Württemberger. There were only two desertions in May, four in June, four in July, and four in August. In September the figure rose to fifteen, but in an army of some three-quarters of a million men, this was still a minute trickle at a time when many soldiers had come to the conclusion that the war could not possibly be won.[9]

Soldiers from Alsace-Lorraine were always viewed with deep suspicion, were frequently charged with disloyalty, and suffered from a number of discriminatory measures which were only removed in the summer of 1918, by which time it was too late to have any effect. At one point the OHL threatened to send all the relatives of deserters from Alsace-Lorraine to concentration camps. There was a mutiny in a training camp at Beverloo in Belgium in May 1918 in which troops from Alsace-Lorraine played a prominent role. They were second-echelon troops that had been moved from the Eastern Front, however, and this was a more important factor than the province from which they came.[10]

In the final stages of the war the OHL reached the conclusion that the reason why most soldiers from Alsace-Lorraine deserted was not because of cowardice, lack of strength of character, or discontent with conditions in the German Army, but purely and simply because they assumed that Alsace-Lorraine would soon return to France.[11]

By September 1918 the Prussian War Minister was complaining bitterly that there were far too many desertions. He suspected that this was due to people expecting to be granted a pardon on the Kaiser's birthday. The military authorities were ordered to find out whether or not this was true.[12] The German Army was far more lenient with their punishments for deserters than were the British who shot seven times more men for deserting the colours than did the Terrible Hun. Men from Alsace-Lorraine played much the same role in the German Army that the Irish 16th Division did in Fifth Army. But Gough stood up for the Curragh rebels, whereas in the German Army few senior officers were prepared to put in a good word for the *Wackes* who fought just as well, if not better.

Desertion was thus not a serious problem in the German Army in June 1918, and planning could go ahead without worrying about a serious decline in morale. 'Gneisenau' had originally been designed as a subsidiary action to 'Blücher'.[13] It was assumed that the French would move divisions to meet to threat to the south and thus offer 18th Army the opportunity to broaden the front. But 7th Army's right wing had been halted and General von Hutier was now ordered to help out by westward wheeling movement hinged on Montdidier to the north. He was then to cross the Matz, ending on the line from Montdidier to Compiègne, thus getting some movement back into 'Blücher's' right wing. Far from being a bonus derived from the success of 'Blücher' it was now imperative to launch 'Gneisenau' to save 'Blücher' from stalemate. For this it would need more divisions than the ten originally allocated, and would have to be helped out by the right wing of 7th Army.

General von Hutier had eleven divisions in the first line, and seven in the second and third. In addition the OHL held three divisions in reserve and one more was on its way. But most of these divisions were under-strength, tired and already hit by the Spanish flu. Lieutenant-Colonel Bruchmüller was made responsible for the artillery, much to von Hutier's delight; but there was considerable friction between the newcomer and some of 18th Army's senior gunners, led by Lieutenant-Colonel Stuckenschmidt who was posted elsewhere. This situation was made worse by the fact that many batteries arrived at the last moment from other points on the front, and thus had insufficient time to prepare.[14]

Bruchmüller's preparatory barrage for 'Gneisenau' began at 0050hrs on 9 June on a broad front that extended well beyond the wings of the offensive. At 0420hrs the infantry began their attack. They pushed their way forward through thick fog, across difficult terrain and through their own gas. The support artillery found it difficult to locate their targets, the rolling barrage was poorly co-ordinated, ammunition was scarce, and the French artillery caused heavy casualties in some 600 metres of no-man's-land. In spite of these difficulties the Germans made remarkably good progress. They reached the French battle lines on a broad front and advanced up to 9 kilometres. For the following day General von Hutier ordered his left wing to co-operate with General François' corps of 7th Army in order to nip off the French forces in the Carlepont forest directly to the south of Noyon, and then push westwards to straighten the front. General François was unable to oblige. He had precious little artillery left having lent much of it to support the 'Gneisenau' barrage, and most of the rest was to be used for 'Hammer Blow' which was due to start in two days time.

General Humbert's III Army defences were in a state of some disarray as a result of the ongoing differences between Foch and Pétain. Foch called for an inch by inch defence with a strong front line. Pétain's Directive Number 4 called for lightly held outposts with a strong second line of defence beyond the range of the enemy's trench mortars. Humbert's forward positions were almost complete and strongly held; his second line was hardly more than a mark on the map. Both Pétain and Fayolle, the Army Group Commander, ordered him to diminish the number of troops in the forward positions and to strengthen his second line. They pointed to the way in which the British had been broken by heavy artillery and mortar fire on the front line trenches on 21 March and again on 9 April. The same mistake had been repeated with disastrous consequences on the Chemin des Dames. Humbert reacted slowly and reluctantly to these orders, and was strengthened in his defiance of the orders from his superior by Foch's repeated insistence that every inch of the sacred soil of France had to be defended.[15] As a result the forward positions were quickly overrun and the French pushed back, but GQG remained calm. The retreat was orderly, and there was no repeat performance of the chaotic situation on the Chemin des Dames. Fayolle was quick to send in reserves, and Foch did not feel that the situation warranted sending an urgent request for help to GHQ.

The offensive continued at 0400hrs on 10 June. The battle swung back and forth with offensive and counter-offensive following in quick succession. Positions were taken at heavy cost only to be lost soon afterwards and regained at even greater cost. But at the end of the day the Germans had again made reasonable progress and although the French had brought in four new divisions they still had thirteen divisions to the French eleven.

On 11 June IX and XVII Corps on 18th Army's right wing attacked at 0500hrs but made no progress at all. VIII Corps to their left had hoped to attack at 1230hrs but the French launched a series of ferocious counter-attacks against the salient formed by IX and XVII Corps' advance in the previous two days, and the attack had to be cancelled. The French were eventually beaten back and lost sixty-three tanks, but German losses were also heavy and they lost some of their guns which they could ill afford to lose.

General von Hutier was somewhat more successful on his left flank where he exploited the opportunity afforded by the French withdrawal from the forest of Carlepont to make some modest gains. He was supported in this endeavour by General François' corps which, after an initial advance, was soon drawn to a halt.

The French bombarded the entire 'Gneisenau' front during the night of 11/12 June and continued in the morning. This was followed by further French counter-attacks that made it impossible for the Germans to attack the designated goals of 'Hammer Blow'. Where attempts were made, such as at Hill 155, they resulted in failure.

The French continued to counter-attack on the following day, but they were losing strength and Pétain ordered a halt since he lacked reserves, and wanted to stop any further losses. They were still enough to bring 'Gneisenau' to an end. 'Hammer Blow' also had to be aborted. The Germans had advanced up to ten miles and had taken 15,000 prisoners and 300 guns, but they had lost 25,000 men and sixteen guns. Total French losses amounted to 40,000. The French could afford to wait for the Americans, the Germans had been unable to improve their position against the British in Flanders, and thus could not yet deliver the decisive blow. Both sides were anxious to call off the fight for fear that it would degenerate into a battle of attrition.

Ludendorff was bitterly disappointed. For all their achievements 'Blücher' and 'Gneisenau' had failed to draw Allied divisions from the Flander's front and the butcher's bill had been high. He ordered the artillery to keep on hammering away at the front from Montdidier to the Marne and Reims in the hope that the Allies would think that an attack towards Paris was imminent. The OHL gave the press an optimistic account of the last three months fighting claiming to have taken 212,000 prisoners, 2,800 guns and more than 8,000 machine-guns. The Allies lost about 500,000 men (200,000 French, 290,000 British and 2,400 Americans).[16] The French had suffered a severe battering on the Aisne and the Matz, and were running out of reserves. They had barred the way to Paris, but they braced themselves for the next onslaught for which the Germans seemed to have ample reserves.[17] The fighting had been ferocious as Hans Spiess, now serving as a machine-gunner in the 2nd Bavarian Division, wrote to his parents. His division lost 3,400 men and 1,100 horses during the offensive. Airplanes had destroyed the division's baggage train, so that the men had to live off the flesh of the dead horses. Corpses rotted under the summer sun, letting off a terrible stench, and dead men and horses were piled up to make gun emplacements. Spiess' unit had to be withdrawn because the losses were so heavy.[18]

Pétain's intelligence staff assumed that the German aim in the Battle of the Aisne was to draw away reserves and then attack the British north of the Somme. The success of the operation had led them to change to objective and to push one towards Paris on the front from Montdidier to Noyon. They calculated that the decision to head for Paris was made on 28 May and put into effect on 9 June. The second stage of the offensive was improvised and poorly prepared, and was disrupted by a strong defence and determined counter-attacks. These counter-attacks, which began on 6 June, forced them to keep their storm battalions at the front, rather than withdrawing them for a rest and preparation for the renewed offensive. The Deuxième Bureau pointed out that the Germans were running very short of effective manpower. On 21 March they had 78 fresh divisions in reserve. By 27 March they still had eighty-five divisions, of which sixty-two were fresh. By 27 June they only had sixty-six divisions, of which thirty-nine were fresh. Most of these divisions were of poor quality, they were young and inexperienced. With remarkable accuracy they estimated that the Germans would not be able to attack again before 15 July. They were less accurate in their assumption that the offensive would be in the direction of Amiens and would be designed to divide the British and French armies.[19] The fact that the Entente was expecting an attack at Amiens was the major reason why it did not occur.

Ludendorff's attention now turned to Army Group Crown Prince Rupprecht whose staff estimated that at most four divisions had been withdrawn from Flanders by 1 June, and considerably more from the front near Amiens. This had not in any way reduced Allied defensive ability, and it was obvious that the British anticipated a major German offensive.

The OHL took a more optimistic view of the effects of the battle of the Aisne. In their 'Situation on the Western Front' of 2 June they reported that there were twelve French and two English divisions in the front line opposite 7th and 1st Armies. There were a further thirty-seven French and five British infantry divisions and three British cavalry divisions in the rear echelons. Most of these divisions had taken part in the fighting in March and April. It was estimated that only twelve of the French divisions were ready to do battle, some of which were on their way to the front. The British had seventeen such divisions in reserve between Amiens and the coast. It was assumed that American and Italian divisions would also be positioned on quiet sectors of the front.[20]

From the above the OHL deduced that the battle of the Aisne had not weakened the Allied front in Flanders sufficiently for it to be possible to go ahead with 'Hagen' – the decisive blow against the British in Flanders. They hoped that by continuing to hammer away at the French they would withdraw further divisions from Flanders. If necessary some of the 'Mob' divisions designated for 'Hagen' would have to be used against the French. On 3 June the OHL thus told Army Group Crown Prince Rupprecht that the offensive in Flanders would have to be postponed for a few weeks.

The OHL did not believe that the Allies were in a position to launch a major offensive, and thus were determined to keep the initiative with a series of limited attacks. Ludendorff rejected out of hand the widely held view that the offensive on the Aisne had simply got stuck, and had not resulted in the expected breakthrough. He insisted that the Allies 'had suffered one of their worst defeats which laid the foundations for our further successes'.[21]

Ludendorff was assuming that 'Gneisenau' would attract sufficient divisions away from Flanders to enable 'Hagen' to proceed. Failing that he still had an offensive in the Champagne up his sleeve. On 6 June Ludendorff conferred with General von Kuhl and the chief of general staff of 3rd Army, General von Klewitz, at Avesnes. At issue was whether to go ahead with 'Hagen' or 'Roland'. There was general agreement that 'Hagen' was far more important than 'Roland', even though the Allies had not yet withdrawn enough divisions from Flanders. Ludendorff announced that 'Hagen' could begin at the end of July and that it would be a decisive battle.

General von Kuhl was told to await the outcome of 18th Army's 'Gneisenau' offensive before a decision could be made to go ahead with 'Hagen', or whether there should be a more limited offensive by 7th and 3rd Armies across the Marne to the east of Reims code-named 'Roland'.[22] Everything depended on how much further the French positions in Flanders were weakened. Although von Kuhl had constantly complained that his best troops had been moved to Army Group German Crown Prince, he still believed that 'Hagen' was the only viable alternative. He was fully aware that the troops in the trenches were burnt out, that the replacement situation was chronic, that there was a desperate shortage of horses and fodder, but he insisted that were they not to launch another major offensive they would lose the initiative, and by implication be unable to win the war. It was noted that the German Crown Prince kept twelve sleek thoroughbreds stuffed full of oats at headquarters, while the artillery horse were mere bags of bones, but Rudolf Binding sardonically remarked that the oats of which they deprive other horses were not enough to win the war.[23]

Ludendorff, who appeared tired and depressed, gave his approval, and 'Hagen' was scheduled for the end of July. Ludendorff told von Kuhl that the offensive would have to be decisive, but von Kuhl was convinced that Ludendorff was grasping at straws.[24] The problem of replacements was so acute that 'Hagen' could not possibly be decisive. It would also be the last German offensive in 1918. Meanwhile the Americans were pouring into Europe and would soon be at the front in large numbers. On reflection General von Kuhl came to the sober conclusion that the OHL would have to face the political consequences, abandon their exotic war aims, and negotiate acceptable peace terms.

In the course of the following days it became likely that 'Hagen' would have to be further delayed. 4th Army reported that they were nowhere near ready, and that it would be unlikely that that they would be in a position to launch the offensive on the proposed date of 20 July. 4th Army had lost five Divisions for 'Blücher' and had been given no replacements. 'Hagen' could not begin until the artillery that had been lent to Army Group German Crown Prince was returned, along with the aircraft, labour and transport. Furthermore the men and material that were returned to the Army Group would be exhausted. Meanwhile further divisions were being given up in support of 'Blücher'. By mid-June it seemed that 'Hagen' was doomed. General von Kuhl was at the end of his tether. He bitterly complained that for weeks on end he had had to put up with Ludendorff's nervous excitement, his petulant scolding, his threats, his criticisms, his interference in the minutest tactical details, and the endless telephone calls that made careful planning and the issuing of coherent order a virtual impossibility.[25]

General von Hutier reached similar conclusions. At home social- ist and pacifist propaganda was beginning to have a serious impact. A train bringing replacements for the 2nd Bavarian Division had 'Red Guards' painted on the carriages. Infractions of military disci- pline were become ever more frequent. Agitation for reform of the Prussian three-class franchise was dividing the country. Food was in short supply, causing widespread discontent. Abroad the Germans only had enemies and no friends. This was due to the Entente's skilful propaganda campaign and to grave mistakes by politicians such as Bethmann-Hollweg, who had described a treaty as merely a 'scrap of paper' and had admitted that Germany had acted illegally in Belgium.

To cap it all the German Ambassador to London at the outbreak of the war, Prince Lichnowsky, had written a lengthy memorandum justifying British diplomacy during the July crisis, and arguing that Germany was responsible for the outbreak of war. It was published in the newspapers, causing a major furore, and the ambassador was obliged to resign from the diplomatic service.

Even more serious was the failure of the Army to score a decisive victory. Ludendorff was trying to wear out the Entente before the Americans could be deployed in large numbers, by a series of blows following in rapid succession. First there was the 'Great Battle in France' on the Somme in March which failed to divide the British and French Armies, then the offensive in Flanders which brought only limited gains. This was followed by the Battle of the Aisne, which also failed significantly to alter the situation. Lastly there was 'Gneisenau' which had been undertaken with forces that were insufficient to secure a major success. General von Hutier predicted that any future offensive would follow the same pattern: there would be initial gains, the enemy would bring in the reserves, and the German advance would be halted.[26]

'Blücher' and 'Gneisenau' did not seriously weaken the Allied position in Flanders largely because Foch, Haig and Pétain agreed that the next German attack was likely to come somewhere north of the Somme. Far too many of the troops designated for 'Hagen' were used up in these preliminary offensives. Since the Germans were unable to take Reims there were serious supply problems on the Marne. None of this worried Colonel Wetzell who, in a memorandum of 6 June, argued that the British had been so weakened by the spring offensive and were no longer supported by fresh French divisions. It should therefore be possible to deliver the decisive blow in Flanders. The French had suffered such a severe defeat on the Aisne that Foch would not be able to lend the British any help. The French would have to be deterred from sending troops to Flanders and should thus either be attacked in the Champagne ('Roland') or the inside wings of 7th and 1st Armies should advance towards Epernay so as to cut off Reims. 'Roland' was not practical because it would involve using a number of 'Hagen' divisions and would take too long to prepare. This would mean delaying 'Hagen' until the end of August which would give the French time to rest and the British time to improve their defences, or possibly mount a counter-offensive. It would also exhaust some of the divisions needed for this decisive blow.

An offensive on the Marne looked much more promising. French forces were relatively weak, the area was favourable to an offensive, and it would not be necessary to use any of the 'Hagen' divisions. Wetzell described this attack as 'daring but not difficult' and suggested it could begin between 20 and 25 June. On 8 June the OHL ordered Army Group

German Crown Prince to draw up plans for 'Marne Defence and Reims Attack'. They asked 7th Army how they envisaged such an offensive.

Army Group Crown Prince Rupprecht reported on the same day that the battle of the Aisne had resulted in the withdrawal of a significant number of French reserves from their front. Some 40,000 Americans had been sent to Ardres to the south-west of Calais. It also seemed that some tired French divisions had arrived at Doullens.

The more the OHL contemplated 'Hagen' the more difficult it seemed. On 12 June even the optimistic Colonel Wetzell argued that the French would have to be forced to withdraw more troops from Flanders before it could begin, and that Army Group German Crown Prince should therefore not give them any breathing space. An offensive either side of Reims by 7th and 1st Armies could create the preconditions for 'Hagen'. It would be supported by troops from Army Groups Gallwitz and Duke Albrecht, but not by Army Group Crown Prince Rupprecht, whose troops should prepare for 'Hagen'.

On 14 June the OHL ordered 7th Army to draw up plans for operation 'Marne' and 1st Army to prepare operation 'Reims'. This combined operation designed to encircle Reims was to begin on about 10 July. Army Group Crown Prince Rupprecht would launch 'Hagen' ten days later. Meanwhile the Allies should be led to believe that the offensive towards Paris would continue, and Army Groups Gallwitz and Duke Albrecht were to attack any points on the front occupied by the Americans.

Time was now of the essence. The OHL estimated that there were twelve American divisions in France. It was therefore essential that the Allies be hit hard before the Americans would be able to plug the gaps. The major problem, however, was that the Germans had suffered very heavy casualties since March and these could not be replaced except by using the lightly wounded and troops from transport and supplies. Spanish flu was taking its toll and the German army was losing both in numbers and in quality. The Austrian offensive in Italy had failed as many at the OHL had feared and thus would not bring any relief to the Western Front. Ludendorff now asked the Austrians to send five or six good divisions to the Western Front, along with sufficient artillery, pioneers, horses and petrol. The Austrians dragged their feet and finally agreed to send two divisions in mid-July, which would have to be sent to a quiet sector so as to grow accustomed to conditions on the Western Front.

Ludendorff now began to wonder whether it might be better to go on the defensive, but hastily ruled out this possibility.[27] The front contained too many salients after the 'Michael', 'Blücher' and 'Gneisenau' offensives and would be difficult to defend. The effect on Germany's allies would be unfortunate and above all the troops would become demoralized if they were to be asked to stay in their trenches. Frequent complaints when 'Michael' was stopped indicated that Ludendorff was perfectly correct in this assumption.

Ludendorff still hoped that it would be possible to fight a decisive battle in Flanders. Army Group Crown Prince Rupprecht was less sanguine. General von Kühl did not believe that it could be done, but vainly promised 'a great success'. The Army Group had been obliged to send thirteen 'Mob' divisions to Army Group German Crown Prince. They had been ordered to thin out their front line, which left it precariously weak. The British army had had a breathing space and time to bring in reserves. It was no longer possible to catch them by surprise. The OHL now suggested that a diversionary attack by 17th Army should precede 'Hagen' and that the 'Hagen' front should be extended southwards.

General von Kuhl put forward these ideas at a meeting in Roubaix on 14 June, at which the Army Groups' chiefs of general staff met with Ludendorff. He was unable to convince the Quartermaster General that the proposed attack by 17th Army was neither necessary nor even feasible. Ludendorff argued that the offensive at Reims was designed to draw in French divisions and reserved judgment on the proposed diversionary attack. He announced that since 'Blücher' had failed to draw reserves from Flanders he intended to launch 'Roland' to the east of Reims in order to straighten the front and to attract French reserves away from Flanders. He hoped that 'Hagen' could then follow on 20 July, in spite of the shortage of men and artillery.[28]

Heavy losses in 'Blücher' aggravated by the shortage of replacements meant that 'Roland' had to be further delayed. This in turn meant that 'Hagen' could not possibly begin before early August. The atmosphere at Army Group Prince Rupprecht's headquarters was increasingly gloomy. The men in the trenches were worn out and demoralized. They were losing one thousand men every day, and there were virtually no replacements. The 'Mob' Divisions that were to lead the offensive could not remain to the rear and allow the Divisions in the trenches to bleed white. Meanwhile the British had been given time to recover, and to bring up their reserves. General von Kuhl felt that the war had reached a turning point, and Germany's prospects were bleak.[29]

Two days later Ludendorff stated that there was not enough artillery either to support this attack or to permit a widening of the 'Hagen' front, but he was confident that Army Group German Crown Prince's offensive would force Foch to move both French and British reserves. The 'Hagen' offensive could begin at the end of July. On 19 June Ludendorff revised this schedule. Army Group German Crown Prince's offensive around Reims could not start before 15 July and needed support from 'Hagen' units. It would not therefore be possible to launch the offensive in Flanders with twenty-seven Divisions until the beginning of August.

Army Group Crown Prince Rupprecht did not like the idea of post-poning 'Hagen' so long since it would give the British about a month and a half to improve their defensive positions, and they might even go on the offensive, thus disrupting preparations for this critical opera-tion. There was reason to believe that the British wanted to win back Kemmel, Bailleul and La Bassée which they had lost in the Battle of Armentières because these were key positions which threatened the important industrial region of Bethune as well as the Channel ports. It was therefore necessary to consider reworking the plans for 'Hagen'.[30] They suggested that some of the 'Mob' divisions should be brought up to the front line to strengthen positions that had been heavily pruned. On 16 June Generals von Quast and Sixt von Arnim, commanding 6th and 4th Armies told Crown Prince Rupprecht that the war would have to be ended that year as it would be impossible to continue into 1919. Rupprecht was in full agreement and the news that the Americans now had at least twelve divisions in France confirmed his pessimism.[31]

The French were still deeply concerned about the vulnerability of Paris, and on 15 June Clemenceau, Pétain and Weygand met at Foch's headquarters to discuss plans for the defence of the nation's capital.[32] At the same time Foch proposed an offensive to seize the plateau to the west of Soissons which would cut the enemy's supply lines to the Aisne, and stop their thrust towards Château-Thierry.[33] Pétain immediately ordered the bombardment of Soissons by artillery and from the air in order to disrupt this important railhead and communications centre. He also drew up a plan to capture the high ground dominating the town.[34] The more cautious Anthoine ordered extra air reconnaissance in order to determine where the next German attack was likely to occur.[35]

The Germans were first able effectively to shell Paris on 23 March and this caused further friction between Pétain and the politicians. The politicians insisted that this indignity had to cease forthwith, and that the Parisians should be able to go about their daily business without such rude interruptions. The War Minister was furious that nothing seemed to have been done to put an end to this menace to his popularity. Pétain's headquarters' staff replied that it was exceedingly difficult to locate the long-range guns that were firing on Paris. They had been obliged to bring long-range artillery forward and had begun counter-battery fire as early as 24 March, but a considerable amount of artillery had been tied up by only two known German guns, and that artillery would have been better employed against the German offensive. Anthoine sourly pointed out to the Minister of War that stopping the German advance towards Paris was a higher priority than placating a politician.[36]

Relations between Foch and Pétain became increasingly strained. Foch believed that the next blow would be against the British and that French reserves should be sent north, but Pétain argued that Paris was more important than Ypres, and that he had no intention of weakening his defences on the Oise and the Marne in order to help the Belgians.[37] He threatened to refer the matter to the government should Foch persist in ordering French divisions to help out the British Army. Pétain also refused to pass on Foch's orders to the effect that two strong lines of defence should be maintained. Firmly believing in a more flexible approach to defence, he argued that it was only possible to do this in the British Army which had to defend a much shorter front, and that any changes in the present system would imply that the defences were inadequate and would have a shattering effect on morale.[38] He told Foch that he was fed up with the attitude of the British Army. Ypres was far less important than Paris, and therefore the northern army (DAN) should be withdrawn as soon as possible, even at the risk of seriously annoying the British and the Belgians. Ignoring the German offensive in Flanders on 9 April, Pétain insisted that the French Army had been fighting continuously since 21 March, and had born the brunt of the four main German offensives. The French army was very tired, while the British Army had been resting for two months, had had time to reorganize, and in any case had a far greater density on their sector of the front.[39] Pétain ordered a memorandum to be drawn up which would explain to Foch why it was impossible to send the British any more help. The British had a shorter front, and had had time to regroup. The French needed time to recuperate and to prepare for the inevitable offensive in the direction of Paris.[40]

For all their differences Foch had to agree with Pétain's low opinion of the British. At 2210hrs on 17 June Colonel Dufieux at Pétain's headquarters sent a telegram to Foch's staff officer Colonel Desticker saying that the French army was in desperate need of relief. 'At the moment', he said 'we are not alive, we simply exist'. The Poilus were fed up with the Tommies, and with good reason. 'You cannot deny that a ninth-grader who looks at a map of France can see that the British are holding a very small sector of the front, we are looking after the remainder, and the *poilu* has never had a moment of rest.' The French were very thin on the ground, and might well be unable to withstand the next German attack.[41] Desticker was slightly more favourably disposed towards the British since they too were expecting an attack at any moment, but was not unsympathetic to this outburst. Dufieux closed the conversation by complaining that the British were simply not pulling their weight.

Meanwhile relations between Haig and Foch improved somewhat, and agreement was reached that it was desirable that all British and French troops should be in the zones of their respective armies. It was agreed that the DAN should return to Pétain's command, along with the French reserve infantry divisions. All British divisions serving under French command would be returned to Haig.[42] But this did not mark the end of tensions between the two armies. Pétain continued to complain that he was short of manpower, and requested the help of British divisions. Haig resisted this as long as possible, and it was only when Foch intervened that he finally agreed to send one division within eight days, and a second division a week later.[43] Haig counter-attacked by complaining to Clemenceau that Foch's staff was incompetent, and was not large enough to handle the daunting task it had to face. He suggested that Foch should avail himself of Pétain's excellent staff, and that Pétain should be given a new staff.[44] Foch, getting virtually nowhere with the British, now placed his hopes in the Americans. He called for eighty American divisions by April 1919 and 100 divisions by July. He asked for gigantic divisions of 42,000 men, which would require the recruitment of 250,000 men per month. At this rate the Americans would have 5,426,000 men in France by September 1919.[45]

News of Kühlmann's speech to the Reichstag on 24 June, in which he said that the war could not be won by military means alone, was delivered on the same day that the Austrian offensive on the Piave was finally halted. These good tidings electrified Foch who immediately proposed an offensive within two months. A force of twelve American, ten French and seven or eight British divisions would attack using the German methods of attack that had been so successful since March, and which had been carefully studied from captured documents.[46] Pétain had already proposed a less ambitious attack by V Army to begin between 25 and 30 June the three essential principles of which were absolute secrecy, surprise, and an offensive spirit in all arms: infantry, artillery, air and tanks.[47] General Fayolle did not share in the general sense of optimism. He expected the Germans to drive in the direction of Paris by attacking around Villers-Cotterêts, and further north by Compiègne.[48] Concern was also expressed about the quality of the recent batch of recruits. Previously recruits were given six months basic training before going to special training battalions. The class of 1919 only got three months basic training and thus arrived at the training battalions with very hazy notions as to the relative geographic location of their arses and elbows.[49]

Pétain's main concern was still with the defence, and he issued detailed orders to the Eastern Army Group (GAE) to prepare a defensive plan. They were to consider reducing forces in certain sectors, to work out the details of retirements and concentrations at the divisional level, prepare for counter-attacks, be ready for a partial or general retirement, and have charges in place for the destruction of key facilities in such an eventuality.[50] At the same time he once again repeated his ideas on defensive strategy, insisting that the main line of resistance had to be out of range of enemy artillery, and that it was at this line that a defensive battle was to be fought. It had to be at least two kilometres from the enemy front line, had to be continuous so as to avoid infiltration, and have a number of well concealed strong points.[51]

On 26 June Pétain lost the right to appeal to his government against orders from Foch, the right that had been accorded to Haig and Pétain at Beauvais. His chief of staff Anthoine was sacked, but he only accepted this decision when he was replaced by his good friend General Buat. He was an outstanding officer who had served as Minister of War in the Millerand cabinet in the first two years of the war. He was then appointed to command the heavy artillery reserve (RGAL). He was an exceptionally hard worker who had excellent relations with the army commanders, and especially with Pétain. Although this was a setback for Pétain the effect was not quite so dramatic. Clemenceau was growing more critical of Foch and agreed with Pétain that his obsession with the north was unfortunate.

Pétain agreed with Fayolle that the enemy was aiming for Paris, but he felt that the Germans was very vulnerable on their left in the Château-Thierry salient. Here they were threatened by the French position on the Montagne de Reims. They could well attempt to improve their position by an offensive against this strategically important high ground. He therefore asked for three British divisions to strengthen the left flank of the French army so that he could move the 5th, 14th and 152nd Infantry Divisions to Saint-Juste and Crepy-en-Valois to strengthen the French right.[52]

The OHL replied to Crown Prince Rupprecht's concerns on 23 June by reassuring him that they did not think the British were likely to launch an offensive in the foreseeable future, and that the front line would have to be as thinly manned as possible, so as to enable the assault troops to be fully trained. Even if the British were tempted to attack, the Germans had sufficient reserves to beat them back. Since it was unlikely that casualties could be replaced these men needed a at least five to six weeks training, so that losses could be kept at a minimum.

Army Group Crown Prince Rupprecht agreed that the British were unlikely to attack, and all the indications were that they were preparing to meet a major German offensive. But they added the warning that if 'Hagen' were further postponed there was a very real danger that the British would attack and disrupt the offensive. They felt that their positions at Kemmel were particularly vulnerable.

Repeated warnings from Army Group Crown Prince Rupprecht convinced the OHL that the British might indeed attack in order to take the pressure off the French. Orders were therefore issued that preparations for 'Hagen' should go ahead.[53] Ludendorff's stop-go attitude caused endless confusion, and his forces in Flanders were uncertain whether they were to prepare an offensive, or get ready to meet a determined British attack.

At the end of the month the British attacked at Béthune, Albert and Moreuil and Army Group Crown Prince Rupprecht expected that there were more to come. The OHL agreed that the British were trying to disrupt the 'Hagen' offensive, but still refused to allow the 'Mob' divisions to halt their training and be brought forward for fear that this would seriously weaken the offensive's initial blow.

Foch was still worried about another German breakthrough. In his Directive Number 4 of 1 July he stressed that the most dangerous lines of advance would be towards Abbeville and towards Paris. An advance towards Abbeville would cut off communications with the north of France. An advance towards Paris would have a disastrous effect on public opinion, and disrupt the essential business of government by causing it to evacuate the capital. An advance towards Dunkirk, Calais, Boulogne or Châlons, which was a matter of such great concern to the British, would not be nearly so serious. For the moment every inch of the front from Château-Thierry to Lens had to be defended so that Paris could be spared.[54]

Pétain was also once again very concerned about the likelihood of yet another German offensive. He thought there were five distinct possibilities. The Germans might attack in the direction of Abbeville in order to separate the British and French armies; or in the general direction of Paris. Perhaps they would cross the Marne in order to separate V and VI Armies. On the other hand they might launch an offensive in the Champagne in order to seize the Montagne de Reims and push on to St-Hilaire-au-Temple and Châlons-sur-Marne. Lastly they might attack in Lorraine.[55]

Four days later Pétain knew that the Germans had decided in favour of option four: an attack by Reims in the direction of Éperney and Châlons.[56] He had arrived at this conclusion thanks to the excellent intelligence provided by his Deuxième Bureau. On 1 July they reminded him that concentration for the 'Battle of Picardy', as they called the 'Michael' offensive, had begun on 1 March and lasted for eighteen days. The offensive began on 21 March. If the Germans took the same length of time to prepare the offensive at Reims, an offensive would begin on 14 July.[57] Their estimate was accurate to within twenty-four hours.

In spite of mounting evidence of an imminent attack Pétain ordered preparations to go ahead for an offensive by X Army from the forest of Villers-Cotterêts to be led by General Mangin, a dashing commander and protégé of General Nivelle, known in the French Army as 'The Butcher' for his key role in the ill-fated offensive in 1917 which had led to his dismissal.[58] Pétain was now misled into thinking that the offensive would be west of Reims against his VI and X Armies, and that it would begin at 10 a.m.. He therefore sent an urgent message to Foch, asking him to get artillery reinforcement from the British Army.[59]

Faced with such overwhelming evidence, Foch now agreed with Pétain that the Germans were about to launch a major offensive around Reims. GHQ was still not convinced. They believed that the offensive in the Champagne would be a feint, and thus they resisted Foch's attempts to move a large number of British divisions south. Haig had the full support of the War Cabinet which told him that he should use the discretionary powers vested in him in the Beauvais agreement should he feel that the British Army was endangered.[60]

Counter-attacks north and south of the Somme on 4 July were a matter of some concern to the Germans. Tanks were used to great effect, and north of the river the British succeeded in seizing the high ground near Hamel. There was also evidence that the British were preparing an attack on 6th and 4th Armies in order to take the pressure off the offensive at Reims.[61] 15,000 men in 6th Army were reported down with influenza and it seemed likely that 'Hagen' would have to be postponed. It was felt vital that 'Hagen' should follow 'Reims' and 'Marne' as quickly as possible so as to catch the Entente forces off balance.[62]

On 11 July the OHL told Army Group Crown Prince Rupprecht that 'Hagen' would begin on 1 August. None of the thirty-one 'Mob' divisions designated for this attack should be used to counter British attacks, unless they managed to make a major breakthrough as at Cambrai in 1917. They should be as fit as possible for an offensive on which Ludendorff placed such high hopes.

Everything now depended on the success of the German offensive both sides of Reims, otherwise 'Hagen' was doomed to failure. Many of the higher commanders were beginning to have their doubts, and felt that Ludendorff was overly optimistic. He appeared to be convinced that the offensive at Reims followed by a major blow in Flanders would bring victory. On 18 June he had confidently predicted that France would soon collapse.[63] General von Kuhl was not convinced. He believed that a tactical success was the most that could be hoped for.[64] By the end of June the OHL turned its attention to the possibility of 'Hagen' failing to be a decisive victory and asked themselves where else they could attack. All four Army Groups were ordered to make preparations for further offensives: Army Group Gallwitz's nine divisions in 'C' Detachment, Army Group Duke Albrecht's on the Rhine-Marne canal, and Army Groups German Crown Prince and Crown Prince Rupprecht between the Somme and the Marne were singled out as key areas for further offensive action. Ludendorff was still uncertain where to strike a blow as a diversionary move to relieve the pressure on the offensive either side of Reims. Should it be an offensive by Army Group German Crown Prince in the direction of Paris, or towards Amiens or perhaps in Flanders?

Amidst all this confusion and uncertainty Ludendorff dropped another bombshell. He now announced that preparations should begin for a major offensive between the Somme and the Marne in the direction of Paris and Amiens, which would begin once 'Marne Defence', 'Reims' and 'Hagen' were completed.[65] The staff at Army Group Crown Prince Rupprecht were appalled. How would it be possible to assemble the forces for this offensive at the end of July, before 'Hagen' had even begun? How would it be possible to attack on such a broad front from the Marne to the Somme? An attack in the direction of both Amiens and Paris was out of the question. It would be utterly impossible to mount an attack on this scale after 'Hagen'.

General von Kuhl assumed that the proposed offensive was an alternative to 'Hagen' in the event that the British positions in Flanders were too strong, and that the attack failed to achieve the essential element of surprise. Since von Lossberg's preparations for 'Hagen' were hardly concealed, surprise was most unlikely. Once again Ludendorff kept his intentions to himself, his options open, and the Army Groups were left to speculate as to his next move.

There is more than a hint of desperation in these ideas, and the main consideration seems to have been to maintain the offensive spirit of the troops who loathed the prospect of returning to defensive trench warfare. Colonel Wetzell however did not believe it would be possible to mount any further offensives in the autumn, and proposed an offensive in Italy instead. It would have to be under a German commander and include twelve to fifteen fresh divisions from the Western Front. At least it would lead to a significant shortening of the front; at best it would end in the destruction of the Italian army. The Allies would be obliged to send troops to prop up the Italians so that they would not have superiority on the Western Front in 1919.[66]

Ludendorff did not share the view that a major success could be achieved in Italy relatively cheaply, and rejected Wetzell's proposal. Having thus been snubbed Wetzell returned to a consideration of the Western Front. He came to the conclusion that if 'Hagen' did not bring any significant results the only possible course of action was to continue with the 'Blücher' and 'Gneisenau' offensives in the direction of Paris. He still assumed that the offensive around Reims and 'Hagen' would draw French divisions away from this sector of the front, and that it would be able to strike a blow in mid-September with forty to fifty divisions from 18th, 7th and the newly formed 9th Armies. If these forces were not available then Wetzell again suggested an offensive in Italy.

The OHL rejected Wetzell's basic argument and on 2 July ordered Army Groups German Crown Prince and Crown Prince Rupprecht to prepare operation 'Elector' (*Kurfürst*). This involved an offensive in the direction of Paris between Breteuil and Villers-Cotterêts supported by a thrust towards Amiens. Army Group Crown Prince Rupprecht set to work, and the plans for General von der Marwitz's 2nd Army made it obvious, even to the OHL, that it would be impossible to attack towards both Paris and Amiens. There were simply not enough Divisions available to attack on both sides of the Somme. General von Kuhl suggested that even if all forces were concentrated to the south of the river they would still be insufficient. The more he studied the problem the more he doubted whether Ludendorff knew what he was doing. The OHL took no notice of von Kuhl's objections and ordered Army Group Crown Prince of Bavaria to plan an attack on Amiens, straddling the Somme. Army Group German Crown Prince was told to prepare an offensive in the direction of Paris. General von Kuhl argued that it would be impossible to carry out both offensives simultaneously, and continued to stress that he doubted whether either could be realized.[67]

An offensive along both banks of the Somme presented formidable difficulties, not least of which being that it left both flanks dangerously exposed. Even the OHL began to wonder whether it was feasible. General von Kuhl then proposed an attack towards Doullens, with the left flank on the Somme, but he did so with a singular lack of enthusiasm or conviction.[68]

Neither of the two Army Groups concerned with planning 'Elector' showed any enthusiasm for the idea. Initially General von Kuhl thought that Ludendorff was giving up the idea of 'Hagen' and wanted to concentrate on taking Amiens. He repeatedly pointed out that they did not have the available forces for two major offensives, one towards Paris and the other towards Amiens. The OHL had eventually to concede that they were correct, and said that they would decide which of the two offered the best prospect after 'Reims' and 'Hagen'. In any event the offensive would not begin before the middle of September. There was bitter disappointment in 18th Army when they heard that their offensive had been cancelled.[69] The prospect of remaining in their exposed positions, at the mercy of the enemy artillery and bombers, was far from encouraging. The defences were further weakened by the removal of a number of divisions to support the offensive around Reims, leaving 18th Army in a very precarious position. The French were able to break through on a two- to three-kilometre front and advance up to 1,000 metres, with the desperately under-strength 84th Division offering precious little resistance. The large number of prisoners and machine-guns captured was testament to an alarming loss of morale.[70] As it turned out neither offensive on the Somme could even be considered, as the fortunes of war turned against the Germans.

In the course of June a series of discussions were held between the OHL and Army Group German Crown Prince on the details of the 'Reims' offensive. The front of the attack was broadened eastwards in spite of the objections of Colonel Wetzell who felt that it would lead to serious delays that would place 'Hagen' in jeopardy. 7th Army was to head for the Marne at Epernay. 1st Army was to advance to the east of Reims to Châlons and then join up with 7th Army on the Marne. 3rd Army's task was to protect the left flank of the operation. The advance was then to continue south of the Marne. A total of thirty-nine divisions were allotted for this ambitious offensive.

Ludendorff was confident that the offensive would succeed, although he was worried about the serious problem of replacements. He managed to convince himself that a victory on 15 July would restore unity at home and undermine French morale to such an extent that they might well sue for peace.[71] But the Army Group had to overcome some serious tactical difficulties, particularly the co-ordination of 7th and 1st Armies in the difficult terrain south of Reims with its hills, woods and streams. The Marne was also a formidable obstacle. The quality of the troops was a matter of concern and almost all units had been hit with the Spanish flu. To the west 7th and 9th Armies had been thinned out and were thus vulnerable to attack around Villers-Cotterêts as Colonel Count Schulenburg and General von Boehn repeatedly pointed out to Ludendorff. He replied that the French could not possibly attack on this sector once the offensive began. Concerns were also expressed that the Army Group lacked sufficient reserves to cope with a serious counter-attack. Yet in spite of all these reservations Army Group German Crown Prince trusted the OHL's assessment of the overall situation on the Western Front, and raised no fundamental objections to the offensive.

Ludendorff was playing for very high stakes. The offensive at Chemin des Dames had drawn some French reserves from Flanders, but the British were still in a very strong position, and the doggedness of the British defence was both admired and feared. He kept on hoping that an offensive both sides of Reims would oblige the British to move reserves from Flanders and that these operations – 'Marne' and 'Reims' – could be followed by a decisive offensive against the British in Flanders. It was highly questionable that the German Army would have the strength, even after a successful offensive around Reims, to mount another major operation within such a short space of time. Even if the British moved substantial numbers of reserves to the Reims front, an exhausted German Army would still come up against stiff resistance. The longer they waited to regain their strength the easier it would be for the British to improve their defences in Flanders. To many senior officers the Reims offensive only made sense because the alternative was unacceptable. The prospect of retiring to the positions they had held on 21 March and a continuation of a war of attrition was something no one could contemplate with equanimity. Those who argued in favour of a compromise peace had totally unrealistic views as to what might be acceptable conditions for the Entente. The OHL still hoped that a left hook and a right jab

would knock out the enemy, but there was more than a hint of desperation in the air. A diversionary strategy that had failed at Chemin des
Dames, which had left the Germans in a dangerously exposed position,
was now being repeated.

On 12 July Wilson proposed to Foch, whom he addressed as 'My Dear
Friend', that the Americans could man Second Army's guns which had
been left when the British withdrew from the French northern armies
(DAN) arguing that:

> These men could carry out their practice and training against live Boches
> instead of against inanimate targets at Mailly and other camps and could
> then rejoin Pershing's command when Second Army is, in his opinion,
> trained and ripe for movement.[72]

At this point Lloyd George rushed in to support Haig by writing to
Clemenceau saying that there were clear signs of an impending German
attack at Kemmel. He pointed out that of the 100 German batteries that
had been moved from the east to the west, eighty-eight of them had
gone to the British sector of the front. What was more, the British now
only had forty-five divisions facing a possible 100-110 enemy divisions.
Furthermore the Belgian army was hopelessly weak, and there was thus
the distinct possibility of a breakthrough that would threaten the vital
Channel ports. The Prime Minister suggested that far more American
divisions should be placed behind the British front. There were only
five American divisions behind the British Army, whereas there were
twenty-five behind the French. The British War Cabinet was deeply
concerned about the implication of this serious imbalance.[73]

Planning had be going on for some time by the British section
of the Supreme War Council at Versailles about what action to take
should the Channel ports be lost. If Dunkirk, Calais or Boulogne fell
British and Belgian troops would have to be supplied via Dieppe, Le
Tréport, Fécamp, Rouen and Le Havre. There was a serious question
whether these ports had the capacity to supply the BEF, and were the
Germans to use Dunkirk as a naval base cross-Channel communications would be seriously endangered. In a worst case scenario the
Admiralty was requested to work out how quickly the British Army
could be evacuated from France.[74] Although these were contingency
plans, they give some indication of the gravity of the situation as per-
ceived by GHQ. Ever since Chemin des Dames the War Cabinet had
feared that Paris might fall and that France might sue for peace. At the
end of June Lloyd George had asked Milner to examine the question
whether Britain could continue the war without France. Such contingency planning only ceased with the success of the Mangin offensive
at Villers-Cotterêts in July.

Crown Prince William was understandably concerned about the exposed position of his 7th Army in the salient between the Aisne and the Marne to the west of Reims. If successful the new offensive would relieve the danger to the eastern flank, but in the west the French at Villers-Cotterêts still presented a serious threat. Even if it were possible to mount an offensive in Flanders, which the Crown Prince doubted as it was so far distant from Reims, the French were still likely to counter-attack at Villers-Cotterêts. In his memoirs he claims to have drawn the conclusion that the offensive at Reims should also have included an attack on the French positions at Villers-Cotterêts in an attempt to shorten the front in a forward position.[75] There is no supporting evidence that he raised this objection at the time, in fact his Army Group along with the OHL refused the requests from 9th and 7th Armies for reinforcements. They did not think that the rumoured counter-attack, which was expected on the French national holiday on 14 July, was too serious a threat, and they were concentrating their attention on the forthcoming attack either side of Reims.[76]

The OHL insisted that the success of the initial stages of 'Blücher' had been due to energetic attacks by small groups, which pushed ahead and did not wait for their neighbours to keep pace. Where gaps in the enemy lines were made the stragglers would soon catch up. Above all the attacking troops had to avoid bunching up and thus offer an easy target to the defenders. The fundamental object was to inflict greater damage on the enemy than that suffered by the attacking troops. That was far more important than winning ground at any cost. Losses had to be kept to a minimum. Surprise was of the utmost importance, but this was where the Army Group came unstuck.

German prisoners of war showed a remarkable enthusiasm for betraying their brothers in arms. French Military Intelligence heard rumours of an impending offensive east of Reims, which were confirmed by the interrogation of prisoners taken from 228th Division.[77] This was corroborated by a group of escaped French prisoners-of-war who reported that preparations were being made for an attack between Reims and Château-Thierry. A captured German aviator admitted that this was indeed the case. In the first two weeks of July numerous similar sources convinced the French that an attack was imminent. The Deuxième Bureau knew that as early as 27 June no leave had been granted in 3rd and 7th Armies, and the movement of large numbers of ammunition trucks had been observed. One group of prisoners told the French that their barrage would begin shortly after midnight. Therefore at 0040hrs on 15 July the French opened fire along the whole 100 kilometres of the 'Reims' front, but they soon stopped. This allowed the Germans to begin their preparatory barrage as scheduled at 0110hrs with 6,400 guns and 2,200 mortars. 900 aircraft stood at the alert.

11

'Reims', 'Marne' and the Mangin Offensive: 15-31 July

The French were well prepared to meet the new German offensive. They had adopted a flexible defence with a thinly held 'observation line' ('Red'), which was designed to observe the enemy front, stop minor encroachments and which was ordered to retire to the principle line of defence ('Yellow') when an attack began. The main line of defence was to be at least 2,000 metres from the enemy lines, thus out of range of the bulk of enemy artillery and mortars. It was to be a continuous line, with strong-points at regular intervals. Two-thirds of the infantry and three-quarters of the artillery was to be concentrated in this main line of defence. If necessary it could be reinforced by troops from the second line of defence ('Green'), their positions being taken in turn by reserves. The reserves were to be placed behind some natural obstacle which would stop any further advance by the enemy, and from which counter-attacks could be launched.[1]

They knew that the Germans were preparing an offensive in the Champagne, and were therefore confident that there was less of a threat north of the Somme. Foch therefore ordered Pétain to move his reserves behind his positions in the Champagne.[2] He then repeated this message to Haig, adding that British divisions would probably be needed to hold the line and to launch counter-attacks. He also suggested that the British could attack the German forces which had been thinned out in preparation for the offensive in the Champagne. To this end he revived plans which had first been drawn up on 24 May 1918 for an attack between Festubert and Robecq which would free the mines at Bruay and disrupt the import communications centre at Estaires.[3]

Pétain's initial reaction to the German attack was to order General Fayolle to keep the Mangin offensive on hold in order to send reserves into the battle.[4] The French commander-in-chief asked Haig to send two additional divisions, but certain of his Prime Minister's support Haig told Foch that he was averse to sending any men to the Champagne for the time being, since the threat to his sector of the front was every bit as great as it was to that held by the French. Pétain slyly justified the postponement and scaling down of the Mangin offensive by expressing his agreement with Foch's Directive Number 4 which claimed that the main blow would fall between Lens and Château-Thierry. Haig also used the same directive to argue against sending British troops to the Champagne.

In a second note to Foch on 14 July Haig begged to be allowed to defer sending any troops south until they met the following morning to discuss the situation.[5] Foch, who had been longing to seize the initiative ever since April, told Pétain that nothing, not the German offensive, nor British reluctance to lend a helping hand, should be allowed to slow down or stop the Mangin offensive.[6] At 1300hrs therefore Pétain ordered that the Mangin concentration should go ahead, and that it should include the 2nd US division.[7]

Foch then told Pétain that General Mangin should attack between the Aisne and the Marne so as to neutralize the German offensive to the west of Reims, and enable the French forces to concentrate on dealing with the German push east of the town.[8] Haig sent a stinging rebuff to Foch, and flatly refused to send him any reserves. Why, he asked, had Foch changed his mind since Directive Number 4 of 1 July in which he had said that British reserves would only be required to support the French army if there was a direct threat to Paris? The British front was every bit as much endangered now as it was then. They were anticipating an attack between Ypres and the La Bassée Canal, although there was an equally serious threat of an attack to the south, between the La Bassée Canal and the Somme. There was no threat whatsoever south of the Somme, and the enemy was only in a position to mount minor offensives in the Champagne or in Flanders which would be designed to weaken the reserves prior to launching a main attack between Lens and Château-Thierry. Under these circumstances Haig flatly refused to send any reserves to the Champagne.[9]

Haig and Foch met at Mouchy-le-Châtel, half way between GHQ and the Generalissimo's château, on 15 July and in the course of a somewhat acrimonious discussion the British commander-in-chief, with great reluctance and under considerable protest, agreed to send 22nd Corps and two further divisions to the Champagne.[10] Since the German offensive had already begun Haig could hardly refuse even token support, but he was still convinced that the main offensive would be on the Kemmel front.

At 0450hrs that day the German infantry began their advance on either side of Reims following behind a rolling barrage. Two divisions waited before attacking the town. 7th Army faced the awesome task of crossing the Marne which was up to seventy metres wide, four metres deep, and ran through a valley two kilometres wide the wooded slopes of which were up to 200 metres high.

Units of 7th Army had begun the carefully rehearsed building of bridges across the Marne as soon as the barrage began. The river was crossed with relatively light casualties in spite of heavy artillery and machine-gun fire, but once over the Marne the Germans met with stiff resistance, though they were still able to advance some four kilometres to the south of the river. To the north of the Marne they broke through the main lines of defence even though the Italians put up a fierce resistance.[11] By evening 7th Army's staff decided that the French V Army had abandoned their forward line of defences and had fought their way back to their battle area.

V Army had gone through two changes of commander since 12 June, General Buat replacing General Micheler, only to be appointed to GQG only three weeks later and his place taken by General Berthelot. The Army had a front of some sixty kilometres to defend, and they had had insufficient time to prepare adequate defences having been forced into new positions during Battle of the Aisne. Furthermore V Army had been ordered on 8 June to prepare an offensive in the direction of Fismes, and was thus in an offensive rather than a defensive stance. V Army's defence in depth had been spread out too thinly. Troops had been dispersed in the outpost position, in strong points, in the main line of resistance, and in the second and third positions. There were simply not enough resources to man any of these positions effectively so that although there was plenty of depth, nowhere was there sufficient strength. In short V Army was not nearly so well placed to fight a defensive battle as was IV Army.[12]

Given the weakness of his defences Berthelot wanted to give ground when the Germans attacked and then immediately counter-attack, but General Maistre, his Army Group commander, felt that this was altogether too risky, and ordered him to remain strictly on the defensive. By 15 July the German advance had been halted and Bethelot immediately ordered a counter-attack. In his orders to his corps he wrote: 'An aggressive attitude is the only effective way to stop the enemy's advance, by inflicting serious losses and undermining his morale.' Apart from a spirited counter-attack by the American 3rd Division which drove the Germans back to the main line of resistance and in some spots even beyond it, V Army was not able to launch its counter-offensives until 17 July when they lent valuable support to the attacks on the following day by Degoutte's VI Army south of the Marne and to its left by Mangin's X Army from Villers-Cotterêts.[13]

General von Boehn cast an anxious glance at his western flank but was reassured that all was quiet. He knew that the next line of French defences would be exceedingly difficult to break but ordered the offensive to go ahead the following day. Pétain issued orders for the Germans to be forced back across the Marne, and for the artillery to destroy the bridges across the river. The Germans were subjected to a series of fierce counter-attacks and the Marne bridges were soon under heavy fire.[14] The French could also rejoice in the fact that the Germans had completely failed to penetrate their main line of defence.[15]

Fighting that day was particularly ferocious. Paul Knoch, freshly promoted to the rank of Lieutenant, told his parents that 'The Frogs put up an incredibly tough defence'. He had to tackle a machine-gun nest commanded by a colonel who refused to surrender, although it was now some three kilometres behind the German lines. The colonel and his men were forced out by flame-throwers, but he refused to surrender. He smashed a grenadier's teeth in with his revolver, and then shattered his skull with a hand-grenade, whereupon he was grabbed by the rest of the company and beaten to death. Of some 150 Frenchmen most were killed rather than taken prisoner. Lieutenant Knoch felt that the gallant colonel, who was the owner of the château that he had defended so valiantly, deserved a better fate.[16]

To the east of Reims the natural obstacles facing the attackers were less formidable. The Vesle had to be bridged and the flat land offered the French excellent visibility. The most serious problem was that this was a cratered landscape full of all manner of obstacles left over from previous battles which made it exceedingly difficult to bring artillery and supplies forward. In spite of these problems 1st Army made good progress and overran the French front line trenches according to plan. At some points the army command noted that the infantry had not been able to keep up with the rolling barrage, but by midday they had reached most of their objectives. General Mudra ordered the second wave forward but it soon became clear that the offensive had got stuck. Here too the French IV Army had withdrawn under the inspired leadership of General Gouraud to exceptionally strong positions to the rear. General Gouraud had paid meticulous attention since December to the preparation of IV Army's defences according to the principles laid down by Pétain in Directive Number 4. It now proved to have been an excellent investment. The American 42nd (Rainbow) Division fought in IV Army's intermediate position with great distinction, and General Mudra seriously doubted that it would possible to continue the offensive for several days.

To the left 3rd Army had to attack wearing gas masks since a strong southerly wind blew the gas back towards the German positions. Once again the army made excellent initial progress only to be stopped at the main French line of defence. In the afternoon General von Einem's men forced their way through the battle line near Perthes and he brought in support to widen the gap. Few further gains were made, and the Germans had made very little impression on the French battle zone.

Ludendorff was bitterly disappointed with the day's results. 7th Army had managed to penetrate the main French defences at some points but the French had retired in front of 1st and 3rd Armies and could not be dislodged from their carefully prepared and deep defensive positions. Ludendorff called von Kuhl that evening and complained that the offensive had brought such modest gains. General von Kuhl urged him to continue with the offensive by 1st and 3rd Armies, reminding him that although 2nd Army had got bogged down on 21 March, they had managed to push forward the next day. Ludendorff replied that he could not afford to risk the casualties involved in continuing the offensive. Kuhl pointed out that nothing significant could be achieved without suffering losses.[17] After further discussion the OHL ordered the operation to continue, but with the more modest goal of encircling Reims by cutting off the French salient. To the west of the salient 7th Army was to advance along both banks of the Marne. To the right the left wing of 1st Army was to push forward to Mourmelon le Petit. Two infantry divisions were to be sent as planned to Army Group Crown Prince Rupprecht for 'Hagen'.[18]

On further reflection von Kuhl came to the conclusion that the Crown Prince's offensive had failed, largely because the enemy were now fully familiar with German tactics, but also because the German Army was no longer what it had been in March. As a result the British had not found it necessary to send support to the French and their reserves in Flanders were intact. This would make 'Hagen' even more difficult, which in turn meant that the feint attack 'Nuremberg' was essential if 'Hagen' were to have any chance of success. Worst of all von Kuhl was strengthened in his conviction that 'Hagen' would not be a decisive battle and that it would result in the scales turning against the German Army. The Germans realized that the French had learned from Ludendorff's defensive tactics, and as a result the attack was a disaster.[19]

During the evening of 15 July the French launched a series of ferocious counter-attacks south of the Marne preceded by murderous artillery fire and supported by large numbers of tanks.[20] These continued on the following day. They were beaten back, but at exceedingly high cost so that it was impossible to continue the offensive in the morning. Constant artillery fire and bombing from the air made it extremely difficult to bring supplies across the river as most of the bridges were destroyed. The sappers lost a lot of men as they desperately tried to repair the bridges, among them General Unverzagt. The ever perceptive Rudolf Binding noted: 'Owing to our inability to defend ourselves the attacks from the air are becoming a great plague for the slowly retreating troops, even for HQ itself.'[21]

North of the Marne the situation was hardly better for 7th Army. They made only modest progress in some fierce and rather chaotic fighting. 1st Army was also unable to make much progress and there could be no question of closing off the salient.

The OHL calculated that the French had twenty-seven divisions against their forty-five. The ratio was favourable enough to continue the offensive, but given that they had to fight their way through extremely strong defences any further assaults would have to be carefully prepared. Even then the enemy would bring in large numbers of reserves and the battle would degenerate into a protracted slogging match, which the Germans wanted to avoid at all costs. Since the French had sufficient reserves elsewhere they would not need the help of divisions from Flanders and thus 'Reims' would serve no useful purpose. The most that Ludendorff could hope for now was to cut off Reims at the tip of the salient, but at a conference with 1st Army's staff he was told that several days of preparation were needed for this operation. Ludendorff sourly remarks in his memoirs: 'all I could do was to reject the idea'.[22]

Surprised by the intensity of the German offensive in the Champagne, Haig with singular ill-grace sent two more divisions to help out the French, but having done so he warned that he would now no longer be able to mount an offensive on the Festubert-Robecq front. This he did not greatly regret, as it was flat and damp country that was unsuitable for an attack. Taking Kemmel would make much more sense. Foch told Pétain that these two divisions, the 15th and 34th, were to be placed among the reserves (GAR) and could either be used in X and VI Armies' offensives, or defensively with General Humbert's III Army. Later that day Haig placed two further divisions, the 51st (Highland) and 62nd, at Foch's disposal.[23]

In surveying the options for further operations he concluded: 'The operation which to my mind is of the greatest importance, and which I suggest to you should be carried out as early as possible, is to advance the allied front east and south-east of Amiens so as to disengage the town and adjacent railway lines. This can best be carried out by a combined French and British operation, the French attacking south of Moreuil and the British north of the river Luce.' He had issued orders for operations to improve the front line south of the Scarpe which he hoped would mislead the enemy as to his real intentions. Here was the outline of the hugely successful offensive at Amiens on 8 August, which was to prove to be Ludendorff's 'blackest day'.[24] As soon as the pressure on the French slackened Haig again returned to the theme of an impending attack in Flanders and demanded that the four divisions that he had sent south be returned immediately.[25] With his low opinion of the French Army he entertained small expectation of Mangin's forthcoming counter-attack

Pétain was fully confident by 16 July that the enemy had been stopped and the Mangin offensive could go ahead as scheduled on 18 July. Pétain's pride in the achievement of his armies was in sharp contrast to his intense annoyance with the behaviour of the British. Foch had asked Haig for two British divisions but Haig announced that he had no intention of sending units to the Champagne. Foch then said that they would be placed in reserve, would only be used in a real emergency, and would be returned to the British Army immediately should the Germans attack. Haig had eventually accepted these conditions and with much reluctance had agreed to send two divisions. They arrived too late to take part in the battle.

Pétain's Troisième Bureau made an analysis of the fighting since 21 March which served to fan his annoyance with his reluctant ally. On 21 March the British were responsible for 170 kilometres of the front, the French for 530. On 16 July the British only had 150 kilometres, the French front had increased to 570 kilometres, and the Americans had sevenety-five kilometres. Since 21 March the French had participated in the Battle of Picardy with thirty-four divisions (one of them used twice), the Battle of Flanders with eighteen divisions (two of them twice), the Battle of the Aisne with forty divisions (two of them twice), the Battle of Montdidier and Noyon with seventeen divisions, and twenty-two divisions were involved at the moment in the Battle of the Marne and Champagne. By contrast the British had not taken part in any major engagement since the end of April. They had one division per two and a half kilometres of front, whereas the French had one division per six kilometres of front. The British had forty guns per kilometre, the French only seventeen.[26]

On 17 July the chief of general staff of 7th Army, Colonel Reinhardt, reported that 70 per cent of the bridges across the Marne were destroyed so that it had become almost impossible to supply his forces to the south of the river. He suggested they be withdrawn. The staff at Army Group German Crown Prince agreed and asked permission of the OHL to retire to the north of the Marne. This was granted. 'Reims' had now come to a halt and it seemed likely that 'Hagen' would have to be cancelled. The Germans had attacked at Beaumont and made five successive attacks east of Suippe but they were all repulsed. They made some progress west of the Main de Massiges, but once again they were pushed back in a determined counter-attack.[27] So ended the last major offensive of the imperial German army and with it all hope of a final victory.

3rd Army Headquarters issued detailed orders for the defensive on 17 July.[28] The first line of defence was to be held at all costs, unless Army HQ ordered a retirement. The same was true for the second line of

defence where the artillery was positioned. At the same time preparations were to be made for an overnight retirement to the second line
of defence. Particular attention was to be paid to anti-tank defence, and
light and highly mobile forces were to be posted in front of the first line
of defence. They were to adopt storm-trooper tactics.[29] Supporting battalions were to be placed behind the first line of defence, and battalions
resting in the rear echelons were to be brought forward to the second
line of defence in the event of an attack. Anti-tank guns, mounted on
trucks, were to be placed between the first and second lines of defence.
Trenches and dugouts were to be built as quickly as possible and well-
protected lines of communication to the rear established. Particular
attention was to be paid to maintaining close contact with flanking
armies. Careful reconnaissance, particularly of the positioning of the
enemy's guns, was to be carried out, and the enemy was to be misled
into thinking that a further attack was imminent by shelling the enemy's
artillery with gas combined with a barrage on their front line.

3rd Army's chief artillery officer doubted whether this would be possible.[30] The enemy's main line of defence was now so deep that it could
only be reached using very high trajectory shells. If all high trajectory
artillery was to be used against the artillery it would not be possible to
do enough damage to the enemy infantry and an attack was bound to
fail. The memorandum went on to point out that it would be virtually
impossible to achieve the same degree of surprise as in March. The
enemy was concealing its artillery, which was kept well back to the rear,
by not firing a number of batteries so as not to reveal their positions.
The main lines of defence were much better defended, and were far less
susceptible to damage by artillery fire.

This gloomy prognosis was confirmed by Ludendorff who announced
that 13 per cent of German artillery on the Western Front had been
destroyed in the month of July. He urged the artillery to pay renewed
attention to the vital question of counter-battery fire.[31]

Confident that the German advance had been halted Pétain now
ordered a counter-offensive by X and VI Armies positioned between
Villers-Cotterêts and Dormans to the east of Château-Thierry. They
were to be supported by offensive action to their right by General
Maistre's Group of Armies of the Centre.

For the first time in 1918 a German offensive had failed and 7th Army
was still dangerously exposed. The French had adopted the German
method of defence to great effect. The front line was relatively lightly
held, the main defences were in the battle line. This system had not
been properly used before by the French, though its adoption had been
ordered by Pétain since December 1917. One notable exception was
in a small section of the front near Noyon on 9 June. This came as a
surprise to the Germans because they had not sent out any patrols or

raiding parties for fear that prisoners would be taken who would betray their plans to the enemy. The eagerness with which German prisoners of war revealed all they knew is truly surprising and was a matter of grave concern. How far this was an indication of the demoralization of the German army in 1918 is impossible to judge.

In addition to this valuable source French intelligence had picked up a substantial amount of information about the forthcoming offensive. Loose tongues in Germany had been wagging and intelligence was passed to French agents in Switzerland who forwarded it to Belfort. Hertling's son reported that Brussels had been full of talk of a forthcoming German offensive in the Champagne. Reports of conversations overheard on the trams in Munich indicated that rumours were rife. Ludendorff received a number of letters warning him of gross breaches of security. A captured German officer provided the French with a considerable amount of false information. But when told that he had a perfect right to remain silent but that if what he said proved to be false he would be shot as a spy, he immediately told all he knew. Thus, German troops who were already tired after the attack on Chemin des Dames ran up against troops that were well prepared to meet them. Foch moved eight of his divisions from Flanders to meet the threat, and Haig reluctantly allowed four divisions to go in support and a further four divisions were sent to guard the crucial railhead at Amiens. Foch's powers of command were such that he was able to force the British to act against their own immediate interests and thus strengthen the French defences. Here was proof that the decision made at Doullens had been absolutely correct.

The attackers thus forced their way through an open door, advanced through a storm of artillery shells and then reached strongly held defensive positions that had been scarcely affected by their preliminary barrage. The French knew of the German plans, so the essential element of surprise was lost. The OHL were at a loss to know how to deal with this form of defence. The suggestion that the artillery could be brought forward for counter-battery fire proved too difficult to realize. Some staff officers grumbled that they did not have enough tanks to smash their way through defensive positions, but the number of tanks lost by the French on 11 June suggested that they were a dubious asset.

It soon became clear that the Entente was fully aware that the offensive at Reims was designed as a diversionary attack and that the main German offensive was to be expected in Flanders. Thus the front facing 'Hagen' was strengthened rather than weakened.[32]

Once the 'Gneisenau' and 'Yorck' offensives were finished the French immediately began a series of small-scale attacks in an attempt to force back the Germans' forward positions. Time and time again the French attacked between Soissons and Château-Thierry and scored some successes against tired German troops, most of whom had been involved in heavy fighting during 'Blücher' and 'Gneisenau'. The Germans were under almost constant artillery fire, were hard hit by the Spanish flu and had to undertake a number of retirements. They had been obliged to send units to support 'Marne Defence, Reims Offensive' and these had either not been replaced or if they had it was by distinctly inferior troops. With the railway at Reims still in French hands they were faced with serious logistical problems. The line from Laon to Soissons was out of service since the tunnel at Lassaux had been destroyed and it took some time to build a line around this spot. Ammunition was in short supply. That a fresh offensive was possible in this sector was almost unthinkable. Most worrying of all was a marked decline in the troops' quality and morale.

General von Boehn ordered his troops to adopt a flexible defence whereby an attack was to be held up at the front line and then driven back when off balance. In his words 'waiting for the enemy must be turned into threatening the enemy'.[33] In an army order of 6 July he vented his frustration at 7th Army's poor performance. He wrote: 'It is a disgraceful and outrageous state of affairs that the French, who have just been beaten, should be more efficient than we are!' He reminded his men that the point of the new defensive tactics was not to retire gradually but to hit back. The problem was, as General von Eben of 9th Army pointed out, that troops were simply too exhausted to be able to react so quickly. The troops were in no state to fight in such a manner, especially if they were also being called upon to prepare for yet another offensive. Attempts were made to strengthen the front line and give it more depth, but given the poor quality of the troops it was doubtful that this would be enough to halt a determined attack.

At first General von Boehn thought that these attacks were merely for reconnaisance, but Army Group German Crown Prince insisted that the French were preparing a major offensive and that his troops around Château-Thierry should be on the alert. This placed von Boehn in an awkward position as the OHL had ordered him to prepare to go on the offensive. Renewed French attacks obliged him to request reinforcements, which were readily granted. His position improved significantly when the new 9th Army under General von Eben, with Lieutenant-Colonel Baron von Esebeck as his chief of staff, was placed on his right to guard the strategically important town of Soissons. The battle zone was strengthened, troops were held ready for counter-attacks and XVII Corps at Laon was ordered to move up to Soissons and form a battle group that could respond swiftly to an imminent danger.

9th Army was hardly in position before it was subjected to heavy artillery fire from French batteries in the forest of Villers-Cotterêts followed by some determined attacks on 10 July. It soon became clear that the French were strengthening their positions opposite 9th Army and were bringing in a large number of tanks in preparation for an offensive. Army Group German Crown Prince were fully cognizant of this danger and General Count Schulenburg pointed this out to Ludendorff on several occasions. After repeated promptings the Quartermaster General ordered one division designated for 'Hagen' to be ready to lend a hand at a moment's notice.

9th Army expected the French to celebrate their national holiday on 14 July with an offensive, but the day passed quietly. 'Reims' began the following day and Ludendorff was convinced that the French would not attack between the Oise and the Marne. General von Eben felt that the danger was over for the moment and told his army group that he no longer needed the four extra infantry divisions he had requested on 11 July. On the other hand, since his army was placed only three days' march from Paris he knew that he could not relax and asked that his men might be regularly relieved with top quality troops.

Von Eben had hardly spoken before 'Reims' had to be called off and once again he was in seriously danger. Ludendorff agreed that his right flank and the left flank of 18th Army needed strengthening. In other words he felt that the blow would fall to the north of Villers-Cotterêts.

'Reims' had not led to any reduction of the Allied forces in Flanders, but Ludendorff was determined to go ahead with 'Hagen' even though the preconditions for its success clearly did not exist. The failure of 'Marne' and 'Reims' meant that 7th Army remained in a salient that was dangerously exposed to counter-attack. Nevertheless, on 16 July the first batch of troops were moved to Flanders and Ludendorff moved his headquarters to Tournai in preparation for the new offensive. It was a nonsensical decision, but Ludendorff's total reluctance to go on the defensive and thus allow the Allies to seize the initiative left few alternatives.

On 17 July, on the eve of the French counter-attack, the OHL discounted the possibility of such a move and planned the regrouping of forces after the attack at Reims. At a conference with the headquarters staff of Army Group Crown Prince Rupprecht at Tournai on 18 July Ludendorff dismissed the idea that the French were massing forces in the forest of Villers-Cotterêts as a mere 'rumour' and 'legend'. He assured the assembled officers that the OHL had absolutely reliable information that the French did not have large numbers of reserves in place, ready to do battle.[34] He then turned to a discussion of how to conduct the 'Hagen' offensive if the British adopted the same defensive posture as the French had done around Reims.

He was suddenly interrupted with the news that the French had attacked in full force with large numbers of tanks to the south-west of Soissons. At some points there had been no preparatory barrage and the

Germans were caught completely by surprise. According to his own account he finished his remarks in a state of great nervousness and then left for Avesnes where he was met by a very worried Hindenburg.[35] The Field Marshal told him that the French had broken through the left wing of 9th Army and the right wing of 7th Army and were threatening the vital rail link to Soissons. The OHL had sent some of the troops designated for 'Hagen' to help plug the gap.

Ludendorff still hoped that 'Hagen' could go ahead even though it was clear to most staff officers at the OHL that the Allies had seized the initiative. In the evening he telephoned General von Kuhl at Army Group Crown Prince Rupprecht's headquarters and anxiously asked whether it would be possible to launch a slightly less ambitious offensive given the shortage of artillery and fresh troops. It would seem that he was gradually beginning to realize that 'Hagen' was an impossibility. His tone was certainly noticeably less forceful than it had been in the morning.[36]

General von Kuhl concluded that 'Hagen' was doomed. A watered down version of 'Hagen' was pointless, and even if the divisions were at full strength it would still not be a decisive battle. It would use up the few good divisions that were still intact, and the enemy would then be in an excellent position to launch a major offensive. He was convinced that Ludendorff would cancel 'Hagen', leaving the German Army to go on the defensive and remain so, waiting for the enemy to make the next move. General von Kuhl placed the blame for this alarming situation on Ludendorff's 'hammer blow' tactics, which had stretched the army to breaking point and had necessarily failed to achieve a decisive result. Ludendorff appeared to be extremely nervous and the Kaiser spoke sharply about the failure of the offensive and the effect it would have both at home and abroad.[37]

It was now painfully apparent that the French offensive at Villers-Cotterêts was neither a myth nor a legend. General Fayolle, who commanded the Group of Armies of the Reserve (GAR) between the Aisne and the Marne, had planned an offensive at Soissons which, in co-operation with General Degoutte's 6th Army in General Maistre's Army Group Centre around Château-Thierry, was designed to cut off the westward German salient. Foch planned to use large numbers of tanks and relatively few infantry in the attack on Soissons from the forest of Villers-Cotterêts. The planners were encouraged by the relatively feeble opposition offered by the Germans in recent attacks and the fact that they had overcome some major obstacles for the tanks, and ordered the offensive to begin on 18 July.

In the night of 17/18 July the German troops in the front line were alerted by the unmistakable sounds of motor vehicles moving forward on the opposite front. In the early morning hours two French deserters crossed no-man's-land with the news that the French would attack between 0500 and 0600hrs. The storm that had raged during the night had put a number of telephone lines out of order so that this intelligence could not be relayed to headquarters before the attack began.

Thirteen French and three US divisions, supported by 400 tanks, stood ready on the 40 kilometres of front between the Aisne and Château-Thierry. Seven infantry and three cavalry divisions were in reserve. General Mangin's X Army from General Fayolle's Army Group attacked at 0535hrs without a preliminary barrage. The infantry followed behind a rolling barrage after a short burst of artillery fire. Massed formations of tanks were intended to achieve the essential element of surprise. Two hundred of them spearheaded the attack. Overhead, in Pétain's words, there was a 'thick cloud' of aircraft.[38] General Degoutte's VI Army in General Maistre's Army Group Centre (GAC) began their attack after an hour and a half of preliminary barrage and was supported by 100 tanks.

Mangin's sixteen French divisions with a large number of tanks attacked ten German divisions of which only two were battle-ready and four were exhausted. Six divisions stood behind the front and in the area between Laon, Soissons and Château-Thierry there were a total of ten reserve divisions. The OHL's overly optimistic assessment of the situation in this sector of the front was thus shown to be seriously misplaced.

South of the Aisne the French attacked as soon as the artillery opened fire and threw six infantry divisions and nearly 150 tanks against General Watter's tired corps. They quickly overran the lightly held forward positions and penetrated the main line of defence at several points. Having advanced up to five kilometres they were finally halted at about 1100hrs. The tanks caused some initial panic but were soon put out of action. Sixty-two of the 150 tanks were shot to pieces; a further forty broke down. Further French attacks were held up while they waited for new tanks to be brought forward and the offensive thus lost momentum at a critical moment. The tank was yet to become a decisive weapon, although many German military historians and tank enthusiasts attribute most of Germany's set-backs in 1918 to the overwhelming strength of Allied tanks. North of the Aisne General Staabs' corps were able to hold their ground against a secondary attack and prepared the bridges across the river for demolition so as the protect the German flank to the south.

The French resumed the offensive after a few hours pause but the Germans had used this breathing space to improve their defences and bring up some reserves. The French attacked again in the evening after a heavy barrage but made little or no progress.

Seventh Army to the south was not attacked as forcefully and Generals Winckler and Schoeler on the army's right wing were able to stand their ground. The French had managed to make a significant dent in the

German lines on a 15-kilometre front from the Aisne to the Ourq where they had broken through strong defensive positions that had been the particular concern of the OHL in previous days. 11th Bavarian Infantry Division had been wiped out.[39] Soissons, which was of vital importance for supplying 7th Army, was now under serious threat. The railway from Laon to Soissons, which had only been able to resume operation on 7 July, was now within range of French artillery and an important branch line was only 13 kilometres from the new French front. In the course of the afternoon Foch ordered Pétain to throw all his reserves into the battle, but this did not prove possible because IX and V Armies were unable to adopt an offensive stance without considerable reorganization, and thus X and VI Armies were left to their own devices.

General von Boehn hoped to repair some of the damage with a counter-attack and at 1900hrs ordered General von Etzel's XVII Corps to prepare to strike back. The staff at Army Group German Crown Prince were fully cognizant of the importance of Soissons and transferred three divisions from around Reims to help 7th Army hold the line from Soissons to Château-Thierry which they were determined to hold at all costs.

On the following day the French opened fire at 0500hrs along the whole length of the front they had attacked on 18 July. Although French prisoners had said that there would be a particularly strong attack north of the Aisne this was not the case. A rather feeble effort was easily beaten off and the few gaps made in the German lines were filled by evening. The French also made little progress immediately south of the river, the German machine-guns hidden in the high crops and bushes being highly effective, but further south they made significant gains in a determined attack supported by numerous tanks and aircraft. The Germans finally brought the advance to a halt in the evening having lost a considerable amount of ground. General von Etzel was in no position to mount his counter-attack and had to send a number of his men to help hold the line.

Once again the main French thrust had been against General Watter's corps and they had reached the main road from Soissons to the south. On Watter's left they initially made little leeway but in the late afternoon both von Etzel and Winckler lost ground before bringing them to a halt.

9th Army was convinced that the next serious blow would fall north of the Aisne as a number of French prisoners had averred. General von Eben therefore ordered a defence in depth. The situation around Soissons was also a matter of grave concern. 9th Army reckoned that they would be unable to hold the high ground to the west of the town as they lacked fresh reserves.

The Germans were uncertain what to do for the best. The withdrawal in the face of the French advance had created a logistical nightmare. If the rather weak defensive line covering the retirement failed to hold, a critical situation would arise. Hindenburg suggested an attack across the Aisne against the flank of the newly formed salient, but Ludendorff ruled this out as it would take far too long to prepare, and halting the French advance had absolute priority.[40] Army Group German Crown Prince ordered 7th Army to prepare for a retirement, but insisted that they should not yet give up any ground without a fight.

Crown Prince Rupprecht met the Chancellor in Brussels on 19 July and once again told him that the military situation was desperately serious and that nothing could be achieved by prolonging the war. Hertling replied that he would do all he could to reach a peaceful resolution by the autumn. He added that Hindenburg had replied to his question as to whether it was possible to defeat the British Army by shrugging his shoulders. Both still imagined that a guarantee for Belgium and a frontier strip in Lorraine for France would be a generous enough offer to bring the British to the negotiating table.[41]

On 20 July the German retirement across the Marne was successful. In a skilful operation the thinly manned flank held off the French while the bulk of the forces pulled back from the Château-Thierry pocket. To the north French attacks against 9th Army brought only modest gains, but the major push north of the Aisne which General von Eben expected did not materialize. The attacks against General Watter's corps of 7th Army continued throughout the day, but they were badly co-ordinated and were beaten off. Counter-attacks won back much of the lost ground so that at the end of the day the French had only advanced one kilometre and at very heavy cost. The French made slightly better progress against 7th Army's left wing but at the end of the day it was clear that the worst danger was over and the army had fought a skilful defensive battle with energetic counter-attacks.

The Allied attack south of the Marne disrupted General Borne's plans for an attack on the high ground to the south-west of Reims. An attack on the Fort de la Pompelle to the east of the town had to be postponed until 24 July. By 20 July, IX and V Armies had joined in the battle so that the Germans were forced to fight all around the Château-Thierry salient from the Aisne almost to Reims. The French were most successful on the Soissons side where Mangin's men had taken more than 15,000 prisoners and 400 guns.

The OHL received a number of alarming messages on the evening of 19 July and Ludendorff ordered General von Lossberg, chief of staff to 4th Army and the leading specialist on defensive warfare in the German army, to report to his headquarters at Avesnes on the following day.[42] Lossberg found Ludendorff in an alarmingly nervous state and suggested that 9th and 7th Armies should be withdrawn as quickly as possible behind the Aisne and the Vesle without worrying about saving equipment and supplies so as to spare the forces for 'Hagen'. Although Army Group German Crown Prince, Army Group Crown Prince Rupprecht and Colonel Wetzell were in full agreement with this suggestion Ludendorff turned it down flat and sent Lossberg off to advise General von Boehn how best to organize his defence.[43]

Hindenburg felt that the Germans should strike at the flank of the French attack across the Aisne from the high ground north-west of Soissons.[44] This led to a fierce exchange between the Field Marshal and Ludendorff during lunch at headquarters on 19 July. Hindenburg's proposal would involve bringing troops from Flanders, but Ludendorff still imagined it would be possible to go ahead with 'Hagen' and thus dismissed the suggestion out of hand. Later that day Ludendorff described Hindenburg's scheme as nonsensical, whereupon the Field Marshal called his subordinate aside and reminded him that he was speaking to a superior officer and that his comments should at all times be strictly professional.

Lossberg arrived at the headquarters of 7th Army during the afternoon of 20 July and was encouraged to find a calmer and more resolute atmosphere. The staff agreed entirely with his assessment of the situation. On the following day he reported to the OHL that the main problem was that most units were seriously below strength, so that companies were often made up of twenty or thirty men. They were exhausted, ill-fed and short of ammunition. He recommended a retirement so as to shorten the front but Ludendorff again refused, arguing that fresh divisions were on the way and that they would bring relief.

It was now clear to Crown Prince Rupprecht that a turning point in the war had been reached and that the German Army would have to go on the defensive. This meant that they had now lost the tremendous advantages that had been gained since 21 March. He felt that his troops had to be pulled back behind the Ancre and the La Bassée Canal and that the salient at Merville would have to be evacuated. It was obvious that 'Hagen' would have to be abandoned.[45]

Ludendorff would have none of this. He insisted that there should be no withdrawal behind the Ancre and the Avre so that the enemy would remain uncertain as to his intentions. But there were signs that he was at last beginning to realize the seriousness of the situation. He was prepared to forego a claim to the coalfields of Briey and to concede part of Lorraine to the French as a basis for peace negotiations. This totally unrealistic proposal was clear indication that his nerves were becoming very frayed. He then demanded of the Chief of the Admiralty Staff that an all-out effort should be made to sink American troop ships, otherwise the war would be lost. He was bluntly told that such a policy would only serve to stiffen the Americans' resolve and would do nothing to improve Germany's position.[46]

Ludendorff gave the impression that 'Hagen' would still go ahead. He moved units from all over the front to make up for those that had been sent to help Army Group German Crown Prince. General von Kuhl warned that it would not be possible to carry out 'Hagen' with limited forces and argued that it would be best to set more modest goals such as capturing the high ground from Dickebusch to Strazeele, as this would leave troops free to strengthen other sectors of the front and to relieve exhausted front-line troops.[47] Prospects for 'Hagen' dimmed further when Ludendorff called von Kuhl in the afternoon of 20 July ordering two more divisions to be sent to help out 7th Army. Colonel Wetzell then called to say that 'Hagen' would probably have to be cancelled. This was confirmed the same evening.[48]

General von Kuhl felt that Ludendorff had now gone to the other extreme, and attributed this change of heart to the influence of General von Lossberg who had always argued that a limited 'Hagen' would need just as many troops as the full-scale version. He therefore decided to visit Ludendorff at Avesnes and present his case that a limited operation was essential so as not to leave the initiative to the British, who had been obliged to send five Divisions to support the French.[49]

Ludendorff explained that even a limited 'Hagen' was out of the question. The situation on the Marne was critical, even if the French offensive were stopped. The German Army was now in a deep salient with both flanks dangerously exposed. Further offensives were needed to improve the situation, and they would require an extra five divisions. Ludendorff was deeply depressed. His hopes were dashed that he might win a decisive victory in 1918, and the army would now have to go on the defensive along the entire length of the Western Front.

On 21 July the French attacked General Watter's corps once again in full force. Having gained some ground the advance was halted. They also made little headway against General Etzel's corps. General Winckler's men were caught off guard in the early morning before they had been able to reach their new defensive positions, but they regained their balance and held their ground. General Schoeler's corps also held fast. Since the 1st Army front was relatively quiet Ludendorff ordered General Borne's group to attack the following day, two days earlier than previously agreed.

At the end of the day the OHL concluded that the defensive battle was over and that the French had suffered heavy losses. The Germans had also paid a high price and faced serious logistical problems with vital stretches of railway now under artillery fire. General von Hutier, who hated being on the defensive with inadequate forces, suggested that his 18th Army should launch an offensive to take the pressure off 7th Army. Ludendorff seemed to be receptive to the idea.[50]

Further French attacks on 22 July showed that the OHL had been over-confident. They were particularly heavy against General Winckler's corps and further ground was lost. Ludendorff began to panic, muttering to Colonel von Mertz, 'I hope the dear Lord will not abandon us!'[51] He now decided that a retirement was necessary, but did not agree with Lossberg that it would have to be as far back as the Vesle. Hindenburg informed the Kaiser of this decision during the afternoon, softening the blow by remarking that Frederick the Great had often been obliged to retire but had always emerged victorious. General Borne's offensive was now out of the question, and von Hutier was obliged to remain on the defensive with his army seriously undermanned, his troops exhausted by frequent guard duties and frantically building shelters. On top of all this the 'Spanish fever' had begun to take its toll.[52] By July 500,000 German troops had been infected. Manpower shortages were acute. In March average battalion size had been 850 men. It was now under 600.

The Kaiser visited the OHL at Avesnes that day and was for once told the bitter truth. Hindenburg attributed the failure of the offensive to a betrayal of the plans. At dinner that evening a deeply depressed Kaiser spoke of himself as a defeated warlord for whom due consideration had to be shown. That night he dreamt of his English and Russian relatives along with all his generals mocking him. Only the little Queen of Norway had been friendly towards him.[53]

7th Army seemed to regain some of its fighting spirit on 23 July and beat back an Allied attack, but some ground was lost on the eastern wing to the north-west of Epernay. The troops were now utterly exhausted and Army Group German Crown Prince announced that twenty-one divisions of 7th Army were in no condition to continue to fight and would have to be replaced. They saw no point in continuing to fight west of the Vesle. Retirement behind the Vesle would solve the chronic problem of supplies and would require only fourteen divisions to defend instead of the present twenty-seven divisions in the bulge.

Lieutenant Knoch wrote home that day and expressed his frustration at the failure of the offensive:

> Once again we are back on the defensive. Our offensive has failed completely. That will be the last for some time. I have become very pessimistic after this latest flop. How will the war end? Now the fellows on the other side will start their offensives, then it will be exactly as it was a year ago. Will we be able to keep going? It is best not to think about the future, and enjoy the few pleasant times as they come.[54]

Foch was far from pleased with the progress made since Mangin launched his counter-offensive. On 23 July he visited Pétain at Provins and gave him a long letter in which he outlined his concerns.[55] He complained that the enemy had managed to slow down the battle by strengthening their flanks with fresh divisions supported by artillery and at the same time delaying progress against the front by bringing in rearguards amply equipped with machine-guns. Foch insisted that the flanks had to be broken, and to that end an even dispersal of forces along the front had to be avoided.

Pétain promptly acted on these instructions and modified the orders he had given to Generals Maistre and Fayolle so that each Army Group was to make a concentrated attack with the maximum numbers. The GAR was to attack in a south-easterly direction towards a point north of Fère en Tardenois, while V Army of GAC was to push along both banks of the Ardre. Between these two offensives the centre was to push forward relentlessly while carefully guarding the flanks against counter-attacks.

While Foch thus urged his men on, Ludendorff still refused to accept the inevitable, and pinned his hopes on an offensive by 1st Army to the west of Reims which was planned for 25 July. He also ordered 9th Army to prepare to attack across the Aisne, past Soissons and westwards. Colonel Wetzell was appalled at these suggestions. He accurately anticipated Allied attacks on the right wing of 9th Army and the left of 18th Army and therefore suggested a withdrawal north of the Aisne.[56]

Further Allied attacks on 25 July made a withdrawal imperative, but still Ludendorff refused to allow it. His main concern now was the effect that abandoning all the ground won in the 'Blücher' offensive would have on Germany's allies. Colonel Count von Schwerin, chief of staff to Army Group Scholtz in Macedonia, was visiting the OHL and reported that the situation on the Bulgarian front was extremely grave. The Bulgarian military plenipotentiary, General Gantschev, had just returned from Sophia with a request for German divisions. At such a moment Ludendorff felt that the effect of such a massive retirement would be shattering not only in Sophia but also in Vienna and Constantinople, to say nothing of public opinion at home. Furthermore Ludendorff was reluctant to admit that the magnificent achievements of German arms had brought no rewards and that his strategy had failed. After such an immense effort Germany had finally lost the initiative.

News that 1st Army's offensive had merely resulted in a very minor adjustment of the front obliged Ludendorff to change his mind. At 2230hrs on 25 July he bowed to the inevitable, and to the advice of General von Lossberg. At midnight the orders were issued for a retirement behind the Vesle. The OHL announced that the operation was designed to 'win operational freedom'. General von Kuhl sourly noted that this was a polite way of saying 'in order to get out of an untenable position'.[57]

By this time Foch was certain that the Germans would be forced back behind the Vesle which would leave them in a very strong defensive position. He therefore began to plan an offensive by the French V Army and the British Fourth Army. The planning was kept so secret that not even Pétain was informed that there was anything in the works until 29 July, and even then it was in the very vaguest of terms. Pétain was now obliged to give the battle in the Château-Thierry salient a new turn (*allure*), since he had fewer forces at his disposal. He therefore issued instructions that all efforts should be economized and that the American divisions in VI Army should gradually assume the principal role.[58]

Reports on 26 July that the French infantry was weak and that advances were only possible because of constant artillery bombardments raised Ludendorff's hopes that a retirement might not be necessary after all. He repeated his concerns about the effect that it would have on Germany's allies. But at the end of the day he realized there was no alternative.

The retirement to the 'Blücher Line' began on 27 July, at first to the intermediate 'Big Bridgehead' line that Ludendorff had proposed on 22 July. He hoped that it might be possible to stay there and not go all the way back to the Vesle, but Crown Prince William said that this was utterly impossible as too many divisions were required to hold so long a front. The OHL agreed and ordered the 'Blücher Movement' to begin in the night of 1/2 August.

It was an immensely daunting task that involved bringing enormous amounts of equipment and supplies back over several miles. The Allies did little to disrupt the operation and by 3 August the Germans were safely installed in the 'Blücher Line'. 9th, 7th and 1st Armies now defended the front from Soissons to Reims with twenty divisions protected from Allied tanks by the Aisne and the Vesle. The defence of the bulge down to the Marne, which they had finally abandoned, had required thirty-three divisions at the front. Crown Prince Wilhelm looked forward with confidence to an Allied attack on this formidable defensive position. Thus ended what the French called the Second Battle of the Marne.

The OHL made a detailed study of the defensive battle and came to the conclusion that the army had failed miserably on 18 July. It was clear that at points where the Allies had broken through the German lines they had surrendered *en masse*. This alarming decline in the army's morale was attributed to the defence being too thin and lacking in sufficient depth. The troops were tired and poorly fed. Some senior officers complained of the ill effects of bellyaching (*Flaumacherei*) in the Reichstag and in the press.[59] 17th Army reported that fresh recruits showed an alarming reluctance to fight and German prisoners of war released from Russian camps refused to fight on the Western Front. They were organized into labour battalions which worked under fire. The morale of the home front was in serious decline.[60] On the other side of the scale many units had fought very well and the Allies had suffered 160,000 casualties to 110,000 Germans. The main reason for the withdrawal was not the morale of the troops so much as the worsening logistical problems that made it well-nigh impossible to hold such a long front.

Ludendorff must bear heavy responsibility for the setback on the Marne. By desperately clinging to the absurd hope that it might be possible still to launch 'Hagen' he held back reserves that could have been used in a powerful counter-attack along the lines suggested by Hindenburg, his nominal superior, on 19 July. When they were finally released it was too late and they were placed behind the front as defensive reserves.

Unlike earlier retirements on the Vistula in 1914 or to the Siegfried Line in 1917 the Germans were not in a favourable position behind the Aisne and the Vesle to launch a fresh offensive and it is partly for this reason that Ludendorff was so reluctant to agree to this withdrawal. But it was highly questionable whether the German Army would be able to continue on the offensive. They had won a series of brilliant tactical victories, but in doing so used up so much of their fighting power that an operational success became increasingly remote. Crown Prince Wilhelm and his chief of staff Count Schulenburg had the uneasy feeling, even before the offensive at Reims and on the Marne began, that this would be their last offensive. The German Army would be left exhausted, replacements were scarce and of poor quality, supplies running short.[61] The offensive at Chemin des Dames, although a brilliant tactical success, left the Germans dangerously exposed and failed to attract significant numbers of reserves from Flanders. The subsequent attack at Reims and on the Marne, designed in part to rectify the precarious position resulting from 7th Army advancing too far over the Aisne and Vesle, was a failure. Foch remained cool, the well-prepared French defences held and he concentrated on a counter-attack that was to result in the first major setback to the Germans in 1918 – and turn the tide of war.

Ludendorff refused to accept the uncomfortable fact that the French had scored a major strategic success with their counter-attack on 18 July. It did not matter that the Germans had lost ground, and their losses were within acceptable limits, but it meant that all the gains that had been made in May had to be abandoned and the 'Hagen' offensive in Flanders would obviously have to be abandoned. The Germans had lost the strategic initiative and on 24 July Foch discussed his plans for a general Allied offensive with Haig, Pétain and Pershing. The Germans were now forced onto the defensive and their hopes for a decisive blow against the British Army were dashed. Mangin's counter-attack on 18 July was thus as decisive an operation as the battle of the Marne in 1914, and was far more important that the tactical success of the British at Amiens on 8 August against the 2nd Army. As Pétain said, the success of the attack had 'broken the spell'.[62] Colonel Bauer, Ludendorff's close associate at the OHL, agreed. He considered that the failure of the Reims offensive marked the tactical turning point in the war.[63]

Hindenburg attributed the setback in part to the tanks but also to the French colonial troops. He wrote in his memoirs:

> Where there were no tanks the enemy drove a black wave towards us made up of African bodies. Pity those defenceless men they murdered and, even worse, martyred when they broke through our lines! Indignation is not directed against the Blacks who committed these horrors, but those who brought these hordes to the European continent ostensibly to fight for honour, freedom and the rule of law.[64]

The Germans had failed to realize that the French had been preparing an offensive between Soissons and the Marne from the forest of Villers-Cotterêts several weeks before they launched their offensive on 15 July. Given their exposed position, and the persistent warnings of a number of officers, it was the height of folly to press on over the Marne.[65] Ludendorff refused to heed any such warnings, insisting that the French were in no position to mount an offensive and that by crossing the Marne they would necessarily relieve any pressure on the flanks. Some placed the blame on Colonel Wetzell, who had hoped to seal off Reims with 'Marne'. The staff at Army Group German Crown Prince pointed out that this would only be possible in conjunction with 'Reims' to the east of the city, but added that they did not have the troops available to carry out both offensives effectively.

When the French attacked on 18 July Ludendorff was urged to retire behind the Vesle as quickly as possible. This he refused to do, largely for fear of a loss of prestige. As a result German casualties were unnecessarily high. The 11th Bavarian Infantry Division was completely wiped out that day.[66] Ludendorff once again meddled in the smallest tactical details, spending hours on the telephone talking to senior commanders, bombarding them with questions so that they were unable to give any effective leadership. As a result of these glaring mistakes Ludendorff and the OHL lost a great deal of their prestige. Official press releases that spoke of great victories were in sharp contrast to the reality clearly shown in the maps which showed that the Germans had retired behind the Aisne and the Vesle. The entire operation was thus a costly failure; the manpower problem was now acute, troops in the front-line trenches could not be relieved, morale among the troops and at home were at an all time low. By contrast the Entente had renewed confidence.

Ludendorff still refused to face reality. When Major Niemann took on his new position as liaison officer between the OHL and the Kaiser at the beginning of August he asked Ludendorff whether he should prepare William II for a general retirement in order to shorten the front. Ludendorff was outraged. The French had been unable to follow up their attack at Villers-Cotterêts and he was now preparing an offensive at Amiens once the troops had rested.[67] Many senior commanders were now convinced that Ludendorff had lost his grip. In an interview given to Associated Press shortly after the war the Crown Prince said that he and Schulenburg had been opposed to the whole idea of the 'Reims/Marne' offensive, which they regarded as pointless and thought would weaken Germany's overall position, and went on to denounce Ludendorff's 'dictatorship'.[68] This was something of an exaggeration. The two men did raise a number of objections to the plan, but were misled by the OHL into believing that the overall situation on the Western Front was such that it had a good chance of success.

Considering the glaring mistakes made by the Germans it is somewhat surprising that the French advance was so slow. They took twenty-one days to regain ground that the Germans had captured in less than a week. The French Army was so used to trench warfare that it lacked experience of a war of movement. The initial surprise achieved by the tanks that led to the collapse of the German front line could not be repeated. The Allies were far from confident and as late as 31 July Milner sighed, 'We shall never thrash the Boches.'[69]

12

Germany's Prospects: May–August

The initial success of the 'Michael' offensive had a dramatic effect on public opinion in Germany, as the Commanding Generals recorded in their monthly reports. January and February had seen an alarming number of strikes which had been watched with glee in Britain and France; now there was industrial peace and a general feeling of confidence. This could clearly be seen in the sale of war bonds. There were nearly 7 million subscribers to the eighth war loan, who contributed a record 15 billion marks. There was a widespread feeling that only a resounding victory would solve the many outstanding problems and the Austrians, Bulgarians and Turks knew that the German army alone was in the position to deliver the final blow. Thus the vast majority of Germans and their allies were determined that 'Michael' should succeed.

Meetings between the German Chancellor Count Hertling, the Austro-Hungarian emperor Karl and his General Staff and the OHL, held at the latter's headquarters at Spa in early May, went smoothly and there was general agreement with Ludendorff's assessment of the situation.[1] The Quartermaster General estimated that the British had lost 500,000 men in the two recent battles and that these could not be replaced without seriously disrupting the British economy. The French had been obliged to take over the entire front up to the Somme and had also to send large numbers of troops to prop up the British to the north of the river. Very few American troops had made an appearance.

Elsewhere the situation was most encouraging. Operations were nearing a satisfactory conclusion in Finland, the Ukraine and the Crimea. Grain supplies from the Ukraine had to be protected from 'bandits and

Red Guards', and the Bolshevik fleet in the Black Sea had to be rendered harmless. The Turks were negotiating a peace at Batum with the newly formed Transcaucasian Republic. The Germans were playing an active role in these negotiations. Peace had been concluded with Romania at Bucharest, leaving the problems between Turkey and Bulgaria over the Dobrudscha and Adrianopel unresolved. An agreement had been reached with Holland for the export of gravel and the free use of Dutch waterways for everything except war matériel.

The chancellor did not entirely share this mood of optimism.[2] He was very concerned about the problem of replacements. He somehow managed to convince himself that losses so far had been 'light to acceptable', but he had to admit that when the Allies counter-attacked they had been alarmingly heavy. Hertling did not believe that Germany was any nearer to winning the war, but he was not made of the stuff to stand up to Hindenburg and Ludendorff. He expressed his full agreement with their strategy, and made no effort to moderate their exotic war aims. Thus his informal peace feelers via Switzerland were bound to be fruitless.

King Ludwig of Bavaria, who was also present when Ludendorff made his *tour d'horizon*, was most alarmed at what he heard. His son, Crown Prince Rupprecht, shared his 'deep concerns' at the overall situation. His chief of staff, General von Kuhl, fully agreed that the situation gave cause for grave concern. So did Crown Prince Wilhelm and his chief of general staff General Count Schulenburg.[3] In an interview with Associated Press shortly after the war the Crown Prince said that he and his chief of staff were sharply critical of Ludendorff's tactics, dictatorial methods and excessive war aims.[4]

General von Kuhl was fully aware that Germany was in a very serious predicament. Troop replacements were no longer adequate, so that once the offensives by Army Groups German Crown Prince and Crown Prince Rupprecht were over it would not be possible to mount any more large-scale offensives. Furthermore the Army suffered from a chronic lack of horses and fodder, and would soon have to face the Americans. Since it was highly unlikely that the forthcoming offensives would result in a breakthrough, the consequences had to be faced. He believed that it would be impossible not to guarantee the integrity of Belgium. Concessions would have to be made over Alsace-Lorraine, and some of Germany's colonies would probably have to be lost. The OHL would have to abandon their totally unrealistic annexationist ambitions in Russia, the Baltic States and Poland, which were predicated on the success of the March offensive. This was an absurdity since the offensive had no clear operational goals and had only been planned at the tactical level. Ludendorff had only acted on the principal of attack and then see what happened. No decisive victory could be achieved by this hand to mouth approach.[5]

It soon became clear that Ludendorff was putting altogether too optimistic a gloss on the situation. A few days after this top-level meeting at Spa he told Colonel von Haeften, the OHL's representative at the foreign office, that only if he got 200,000 decent recruits could he hope to win the war. He insisted that he had told both the chancellor and the minister of war that the situation was very serious, but they seemed unable to do anything about it. Colonel von Haeften had already reached the conclusion that the war had to be brought to an end, and had suggested to the secretary of state for foreign affairs, Richard von Kühlmann, that he should meet Ludendorff and discuss with him the possibility of ending the war. Haeften proposed to Ludendorff that the pauses between offensives could be used to launch a propaganda initiative to test the waters. Ludendorff blandly replied that he had repeatedly suggested this to Hertling because of the serious problem of manpower. There is not a shred of evidence to suggest that he ever did so, and no one at the OHL had mentioned the possibility of peace talks at the recent meetings in Spa.[6] On the contrary, they fed Hertling with all manner of optimistic reports and discounted the fears of the more perspicacious of the generals.

Haeften was shattered by this interview and returned to Berlin convinced that diplomatic and political measures should be taken immediately to relieve a military situation which he believed was desperate. He therefore began work on his 'peace offensive'. The success of the offensive on the Chemin des Dames encouraged him to believe that the Entente might be receptive to a German initiative. He completed his important memorandum on this topic on 3 June.[7]

Haeften's paper is testament to an almost total lack of a sense of reality among the ruling elite in Germany in the summer of 1918. He proposed a political offensive that would undermine the enemy's morale and would support the military offensive currently underway. At the same time it would be possible to control and manipulate the German peace movement and render it harmless. The peace movement in Britain had to be given every encouragement to believe that there was a strong desire for a negotiated peace in Germany along the lines that had been suggested by Landsdowne. Leading figures from the aristocracy, the diplomatic service, industry, finance and the 'national' political parties should address public meetings and outline the kind of peace Germany desired.

In the east the emphasis was to be on saving the peoples of Eastern Europe from Bolshevik tyranny – Germany's mission in Europe was to defend 'basic human rights' and common 'moral and economic values' against the Red Menace. The Treaty of Brest Litovsk was negotiated in this spirit and far from leading to an annexationist peace, as the Entente insisted, it had guaranteed 'order and freedom'. Germany must be able to protect the German minorities in the area, and those who had lost their property to the Bolsheviks should be settled in the Baltic States. Furthermore, Germany had the essential right to secure adequate supplies of foodstuffs in the east so that it would never again be subjected to a blockade. Freedom of the seas would have to be guaranteed so that seafaring peoples would no longer have to seek England's permission to continue to exist. Germany's exemplary labour laws should become an international norm, a demand that would win Germany 'the sympathy of the working classes of the entire world' and encourage the stalwart British proletariat to strike and to stage a revolutionary upheaval that would bring down the government. A moderate position would have to be taken on the Belgian question and the question of war guilt sensitively handled so as to undo the immense harm done by the Lichnowsky memorandum. The glaring hypocrisy of the Entente must be exposed. All this would enable Germany to achieve what Haeften euphemistically called 'a statesmanlike peace'.

Haeften was worried that Ludendorff might reject his proposal out of hand and gave it to him with some trepidation. To his surprise and delight he enthusiastically seconded the memorandum and forwarded it to the chancellor without any changes, adding that the new offensive in the direction of Compiègne would soon begin so now was the ideal time to go ahead with the initiative. The Kaiser and the chancellor along with Hindenburg and Ludendorff were convinced that victory was near and refused to listen to the concerns of the likes of Crown Prince Rupprecht. On 1 June Prince Rupprecht had written to the chancellor telling him that he did not believe that Germany could possibly defeat the Entente. Peace negotiations should begin at once since once the new offensive began there would be nothing with which to threaten them. Prince Rupprecht claimed that even Ludendorff in his heart of hearts no longer believed a military victory was possible and hoped for some *deus ex machina* such as the internal collapse of France and Britain. This he thought was absurd, since neither country could be compared with Russia.[8] He suggested that peace might be possible on the basis of preserving the *status quo ante bellum* in the west and with unspecified territorial gains in the east. Hertling still believed that military success would force the Entente to the negotiating table, and that all he had to do was to open the dialogue. He had thus refused to grant Prince Rupprecht an interview.[9] But it soon became obvious, even to military amateurs like Hertling, that the Allies were not going to come begging for peace now that 'Blücher' and 'Gneisenau' had come to a standstill, the Austro-Hungarian army had failed in Italy and Bulgaria was in crisis. On 19 June, at Kühlmann's suggestion, he entrusted Colonel von Haeften with the propagandistic preparation for a 'peace initiative'.

That anyone seriously thought that Lloyd George and Clemenceau would find themselves in serious difficulties when a few worthies stood

up on their hind legs and extolled the virtues of Bismarck's social leg-
islation, Germany's innocence in the July crisis of 1914 or its civilizing
mission in eastern Europe, beggars the imagination. There were precious few dissenting voices. The press secretary to the foreign office,
Deutelmoser, felt that Haeften's suggestions were excessively crude and
wondered why the OHL had not made a peace initiative earlier. He
agreed with Kühlmann that the OHL's refusal to come clean on the
issue of the Belgian frontiers was a major weakness. He was convinced
that political unity at home was an essential precondition for any peace
initiative and that this could not be achieved until the OHL agreed to
electoral reform in Prussia.[10] But Deutelmoser could be discounted
as a prejudiced witness. He had been head of the War Press Office
(*Kriegspresseamt*) in the War Ministry, but had been fired by Hindenburg
and Ludendorff soon after their arrival at the OHL in 1916 for being
too sympathetic towards the chancellor, Bethmann Hollweg.

On 24 June Hertling was scheduled to address the Reichstag on
foreign affairs, but two days beforehand he begged Kühlmann to take
his place as he felt too tired to speak himself. Kühlmann's speech
was hardly remarkable. He underlined Germany's determination to
be the hegemonic power in Eastern Europe and made no mention
of concessions in the west. There was a hint that discussions in The
Hague with the British over the exchange of prisoners of war could
lead to peace talks between the two countries. The speech also contained a couple of sentences in which he gave a gloss of the Haeften
memorandum:

> As long as every attempt to open talks is immediately and roundly con-
> demned by the opponents of any discussion in the various countries, it is
> impossible to see how any exchange of ideas can begin that might lead
> to peace. With the incredible magnitude of this coalition war and the
> number of powers, including overseas powers, that are engaged in it, a
> purely military decision without diplomatic negotiations can hardly be
> expected to bring about a final end.

Loud applause from the left marked the end of von Kühlmann's political career.

The conservative politician Count von Westarp, a confidant of the
OHL and a man who had publicly complained that the Treaty of Brest-
Litovsk was a feeble peace, immediately left the chamber and telephoned
the OHL from the Reichstag building.[11] He then returned to the debate
to deliver a blistering attack on the secretary of state for failing the see
that the war was a question of 'to be, or not to be' between two diametrically opposed *Weltanschauungen*. Furthermore, the Flanders coast and
Belgium would have to be within Germany's sphere of influence. Peace

could not be brought about by negotiations, but only by a resounding military victory.[12]

Westarp's outburst was based on the Kaiser's bilious remarks in his notorious jubilee speech of 1901 in which he contrasted the 'Prussian-German Germanic *Weltanschauung*' based on 'justice, freedom, honour and morals' with the base Anglo-Saxon worship of Mammon, and went on to tell his entranced audience that in the inevitable struggle between these two world views one was bound to be destroyed. The right-wing parties gave Westarp a rapturous ovation. Gustav Stresemann assured the Reichstag that there had never been less reason to doubt a German victory, and added that he found Kühlmann's speech 'shattering'.

The conservative politician and banker Karl Helfferich was disgusted at Kühlmann for discounting the 'wonderful achievements of our offensive' and dismissed the speech as a 'testament to complete despair and resignation' which offered no political solutions.[13]

Hindenburg and Ludendorff intensely disliked the cunning, suave and dandified Kühlmann. They felt that he had not been nearly forceful enough in furthering Germany's interests in the treaties of Brest-Litovsk and Bucharest to which charge Kühlmann character-istically replied: 'I would rather be attacked for apparently granting too favourable conditions for peace, than let the public know the real nature of the agreements.'[14] Such duplicity was wasted on the OHL who loathed the 'ink pot men' of the foreign office. During the negotiations for the treaty of Bucharest Ludendorff had instructed his personal representative Major von Kessler to collect as much dirt on Kühlmann as he could. The good major was horrified to report that the secretary of state had played 'an American game of chance by the name of poker' and had attended a duck shoot. He added that a photo-graph was being circulated among German officers apparently showing Kühlmann happily swinging a champagne glass in the company of a notorious Bucharest whore. Subsequent investigations showed that the merry-maker was not Kühlmann but a young secretary from the German delegation.[15]

Kühlmann was certainly a *bon vivant*, but he spent his free time not in brothels and shooting lodges but rather, being a highly cultured man, visiting the museums and art galleries in the Romanian capital. His principal vice would seem to have been a passion for caviar, vast quanti-ties of which he consumed from stocks confiscated by the German army on the Black Sea coast.[16]

Hindenburg seized on Stresemann's remarks and sent two tele-grams to Hertling in which he referred to the 'shattering' effect of Kühlmann's speech on the troops' morale and expressed his outrage that Haeften's brilliant peace initiative had been ruined by his blundering. He demanded to know whether the chancellor shared the secretary of state's view that the war could not be won by military means alone.[17] Hertling loyally supported Kühlmann against these absurd charges in his reply to Hindenburg.[18]

On 25 June a spokesman of the OHL, Major Würz, announced that Kühlmann's claim that a military victory was not possible was not shared by the OHL. On the same day the army banned the Social Democratic newspaper *Vorwärts* whose headline read 'No End to the War by Military Decision'.[19] Hertling made no objection to the OHL's attempts to censor the secretary of state, and began to disassociate himself from a man whose days were clearly numbered.

Kühlmann's next speech in the Reichstag was a feeble affair and he almost apologized to Westarp for his previous gaffe. The Social Democrat Reichstag member Scheidemann remarked that he seemed to have given way to pressure from 'the gentlemen at supreme head-quarters'. Karl Helfferich commented that after these two disastrous speeches Kühlmann was finished and all that was left was a 'struggle over his political corpse'.[20]

Hertling visited the OHL at Spa on 1 July to discuss the Kühlmann affair with Hindenburg and Ludendorff. Hindenburg accused the sec-retary of state of being involved in a sinister liberal plot to undermine the war effort, which involved the *Frankfurter Zeitung,* the *Berliner Tageblatt* and the majority parties in the Reichstag. Hertling's pathetic reply was that Kühlmann's poor performance on 24 June was due to the fact that he had not had time to have a decent breakfast. His feeble protest about Major Würz's press conference was simply ignored, and Hindenburg announced that he could no longer work with Kühlmann.[21]

Hertling told Hindenburg and Ludendorff that although he had 'absolute confidence in our strength and our will to victory' he had to ask how the war was to continue and whether it was possible to defeat England. The alarming reply was that it was not possible to defeat England, but that it would be possible seriously to weaken its forces.[22] Hertling then asked whether in these circumstances it would be possible to begin talks with the British, given that they were unlikely to want to become totally subordinate to the Americans. The OHL replied that they had no objections whatsoever. Hertling again repeated the ques-tion and the OHL answered that the Entente had suffered such severe blows since March that the English must be thinking that they had a lot to lose. Should they make an approach the OHL would have no objection to opening discussions, provided that they were conducted with the 'dignity and energy that is commensurate with Germany's achievements'.

None of this had any influence on the discussion of war aims, to which Kühlmann was not even invited and which began the following day. During two days of talks the warnings of army leaders such as Crown Prince Rupprecht of Bavaria were ignored. The Haeften memorandum was thrown aside. Kühlmann's efforts to clothe expansionist ambitions in a moderate guise were scorned. In spite of the failure of the German offensive on the Marne, the meeting endorsed an expansionist programme including demands on the Flanders coast and in Belgium which could not possibly be achieved either by force of arms or by negotiation. The OHL was living in a fantasy world and seemed to imagine that the 'Reims' offensive, which was designed to provide relief for the logistical difficulties of Army Group German Crown Prince, would somehow provide the key for a such a decisive victory that an annexationist peace would be possible. [23]

After this *Alice in Wonderland* performance Hindenburg and Ludendorff departed for their operational headquarters at Avesnes. Kühlmann arrived in Spa on 6 July and it was clear to him that Hertling had no fight left in him and would not lend him any support. In the course of a stroll through the park on 8 July the Kaiser told him that their ways would have to part. Kühlmann took his leave with the antiquated and flamboyant gesture of kissing his sovereign's hand. [24]

Kühlmann's replacement was Admiral von Hintze, a sailor with considerable diplomatic experience and one of the Kaiser's favourites. He enjoyed a reputation for being a fervent nationalist who was close to the Pan-Germans, but Haeften was closer to the mark when he told Ludendorff that this toadying opportunist was unreliable and 'an extremely dangerous and ambitious opportunist who always puts his personal interests above those of the fatherland'. [25] Hindenburg was slightly more positive in his judgment of the new secretary of state: 'Hintze is a cunning, clever, ruthless but sympathetic personality. In addition he is a dyed in the wool Prussian, so I am satisfied.' [26]

Hintze proved to be every bit as devious and blasé as his predecessor and managed to continue along the same lines without alienating the OHL. He was appointed to be the political architect of a 'victorious peace' which would realize the fantastic expansionist dreams expressed in the Spa conference. The mood at headquarters on the eve of 'Reims' was so overly optimistic that the Kaiser refused to reply to President Wilson's request for Germany's conditions for peace. Ludendorff responded to Hintze's question as to whether the forthcoming offensive would result in a decisive and final victory with an emphatic affirmative. He imagined that Germany's totally unrealistic war aims were assured. [27] But there were those who made a more realistic appraisal of the situation. General Bartenwerffer, head of the Political Section of the OHL, complained to Lieutenant-Colonel Baron Mertz von Quirnheim, the head of Operations Section B, about what he called 'this shocking state of affairs', and both men agreed that Ludendorff was so vain that he could not bring himself to put the secretary of state fully in the picture.[28] The mood soon changed and Admiral Müller, the head of the Naval Cabinet, noted in his diary that the Kaiser was 'slightly less ebullient than usual. I have the impression that the day's objectives have not yet been reached'.[29] Hintze, ever the trimmer, began to adopt a more moderate policy, particularly with regard to Russia.

There were a number of incidents on the demarcation line with Russia which the Germans found hard to master for lack of troops. The Entente was hard at work stirring up anti-German sentiments among the Whites and the numerous Czech prisoners of war. This obliged the Germans to negotiate with the Bolsheviks, however distasteful that might have seemed. Areas of particular concern were the Baltic states and Trans-Caucasia where the oil from Baku was of particular significance.[30] Given the difficulties facing the Germans in Russia, particularly in the Ukraine, there could be no question of further reducing the 600,000 man Eastern Army in order to strengthen German forces on the Western Front.

Bulgaria was also an area of grave concern in the summer of 1918. Minister President Radoslavov, who had led the country into the war, was forced from office on 16 June having failed to achieve a satisfactory solution to the Dobrudscha question. His successor, Malinov, toyed with the idea of reaching an understanding with the Entente. He was greatly encouraged by the efforts of the American consul in Sofia who remained at his post and did much to undermine any remaining faith the Bulgarians might have had in a final German victory. In these circumstances it was hardly surprising that the Bulgarian army on the Macedonian front was losing the will to fight, and the German government therefore felt it unwise to withdraw the three battalions of German infantry and fifty batteries, along with some aircraft and staff officers, that gave the Bulgarians some backbone. The OHL, however, insisted that they were needed on the Western Front. Given that the situation in Romania was tense, since the army had not been demobilized and the peace of Bucharest had not yet been ratified, the Central Powers were in a precarious position in the Balkans.

The success of the offensive at Chemin des Dames acted as something of a boost to civilian morale, but this did not last for long. The end of the war was still not in sight. Casualties had been excessively heavy. Food was again in short supply, in part because deliveries of grain from the Ukraine had not been forthcoming. The daily ration of flour had to be reduced from 200 to 160 grams per head, there was a severe shortage of fruit and vegetables and it was announced that there would be 'meatless weeks' in future. It was forecast that the harvest would be disappointing and thus no relief was in sight. Shoes and clothing were also in very short supply.

The Social Democrats (SPD) and Independent Social Democrats (USPD) gained in popularity, and there was little that the government could do to counter their appeals for an end to the war since they were partially dependent on maintaining a majority in the Reichstag. The unions demanded higher wages and shorter working hours and there were a number of strikes, the most important of which was by the miners in Silesia in July. There was considerable discontent in rural areas where fodder had been requisitioned for the army's horses, and in May the amount of grain farmers could consume themselves was further reduced.

The failure of the 'Reims' offensive resulted in widespread calls for peace. With no hope of victory there seemed little point in soldiering on. That the army did not collapse was due in large part to Hindenburg's stoic calm and Ludendorff's frenetic energy. But Hindenburg began to seem out of touch with reality, Ludendorff was hovering on the brink of a nervous breakdown, and there was a growing conviction among senior officers, particularly after the Mangin offensive on 18 July, that the war could not be won.

The German army had paid a very high price for four months of very heavy fighting which had brought precious little gain. In April alone they had suffered 55,000 dead and missing and 488,000 wounded. This was the highest monthly loss in the German army since the beginning of the war. From March to July the figures were 227,000 dead and missing, 765,000 wounded and 1,960,000 sick, of whom an increasing percentage suffered from influenza. Of this total of 2,952,000, some 2,001,000 were able to resume their duties, leaving net casualties at 951,000. This meant that the army was reduced by one fifth from just over 5 million in March to slightly over 4 million in July. Army Groups German Crown Prince and Crown Prince Rupprecht, which had born the brunt of the fighting, were naturally hardest hit. The normal strength of an infantry battalion (without the machine-gun company) was 850 men. By July the average had sunk to 600 men. Similar losses had been incurred in the artillery.

Given the desperate shortage of suitable recruits, these deficiencies could not be made up. Each month on average 70–80,000 of the wounded and sick were able to go back to the front. Of 2,500,000 workers who were eligible for military service 1,200,000 were considered unsuitable. Very few of those who were physically fit for service at the front could be spared from industry, particularly the munitions industry, since there was already a shortage of skilled labour. Four million women were already employed as munitions workers along with 130,000 workers from Eastern Europe and 170,000 from Belgium. If men were taken from industry to serve in the army it would be at the cost of a reduction in the output of munitions. This placed the OHL in an agonizing dilemma. Which was more important – the output of munitions or the size of the army in the field? Which was decisive – manpower or weapons? The OHL made some savings in weaponry to win a few extra men for military service, but there was clearly a strict limit to the number of men they could enlist without seriously reducing the army's firepower.

There were 152,000 German prisoners of war in Russia who were due to be returned. By mid-May only 26,000 had come home, but they were in poor physical and mental condition and needed time for rest and training. The army noted with alarm that some had been infected with the Bolshevik virus.[31] Clearly there was not much relief to be found here. Attempts to find volunteers in Eastern Europe, particularly in Poland, were a failure. Few showed much enthusiasm for running the risk of being blown to pieces on the Western Front for the glory of the German Reich, and promises of independence for Poland or the Baltic states after the war were treated with the deep suspicion they amply deserved.

The situation in Germany itself was hardly better. Of the 400,000 young men born in 1900 who were eligible, only three-quarters were deemed suitable for military service. But they would only be ready to serve at the front by late autumn.

A concentrated effort was made to find men who had managed to find a relatively safe position behind the lines but who were able to serve at the front. By weeding out the general staff and support troops 90,000 extra men were found by the end of April and a further 42,000 by the end of July. In May 62,700 men were transferred to the infantry from the air force, transportation and signals, but it proved difficult to find suitable replacements and logistics suffered as a result.

Hindenburg informed Hertling of this alarming lack of replacements in a memorandum of 18 June drafted by Colonel Bauer. He insisted that the only chance for improvement was if the economy were brought under stricter control and if the Auxiliary Labour Law and the Hindenburg Programme were made more rigorous.[32] He proposed strict wage and price controls and demanded that war profits be ruthlessly taxed. Workers should not be able to change their jobs without permission, women should be obliged to do labour service and the age for military service should be increased to sixty. This was a key document in the preparation of the 'stab in the back' legend whereby Germany's defeat was attributed to treacherous and selfish behaviour on the home front.

Hindenburg was grasping at straws. It was unthinkable that these measures would be approved by the Reichstag, and even if they were, precious few workers could be released for military service without seriously endangering armaments production.

On 1 July the chancellor discussed these proposals in a meeting with the minister of war, General von Stein, the heads of relevant departments and the immensely powerful Colonel Max Bauer, head of the OHL's Operations Department II responsible for industry and economic affairs. There was general agreement that the measures were impractical. The Reichstag would find them unacceptable. It was doubtful if more than 100,000 recruits of dubious value would be found among the fifty- to sixty-year-olds. General Scheüch, the head of the War Office (*Kriegsamt*), which was responsible for munitions production, argued that an increase in the age of liability for military service to sixty was politically unacceptable. He saw a major problem in the reluctance of employers to replace experienced male workers by women. There were plenty of women eager to work in the munitions industry, but there was a general fear that this would lead to a reduction in productivity. Hertling concluded the meeting by remarking that the proposed measures would have a disastrous effect on morale.

The industrialist Dr Duisberg from Bayer Leverkusen held a meeting of fellow industrialists which was also attended by Colonel Bauer. They were in full agreement with General Scheüch's concerns about the effects of replacing skilled male workers with unskilled women. The meeting was unanimous in claiming that the main problem was that the military authorities were feeble in their dealings with the unions. They called for 'drastic measures' against 'agitators'. In spite of these objections the war ministry continued to enlist munitions workers, but the numbers were hardly significant. The problem of replacements for the army in the field was no closer to a solution, and remained a question of deep concern.

General von Kuhl sent a thoughtful memorandum on the problem of replacements to Ludendorff in mid-June. He strongly opposed the idea of reducing the size of infantry battalions from four to three companies. He argued that although their firepower had been increased by the addition of machine-gun companies, the number of men on a given length of front should not be reduced. He suggested that it would be better to do away with entire divisions so as to keep the remaining units up to strength.

Ludendorff rejected von Kuhl's suggestions out of hand. He felt that were the number of divisions to be reduced the Entente would take this as clear indication that Germany was facing a manpower crisis. The setbacks on 18 July, however, forced even Ludendorff to reconsider. Many infantry battalions were now reduced to only 200 men at the front gun in hand, the rest were clerks, stretcher bearers, cooks, drivers, runners, otherwise employed or on leave. On 29 July the OHL reluctantly ordered the dissolution of nine divisions, one having already been reorganized in June.

Equally alarming was the steady decline in the troops' morale. From the beginning of the March offensive there was a increase in the number of mutinies, desertions, attacks on superior officers and cases of insubordination, although the aggregate figures were still remarkably low – in the first six months of 1918 there were only 1,000 reported cases of desertion. The number of Germans taken prisoner was also rising as were cases of self-mutilation. The prisoners of war who had been released from Russia were particularly loath to continue fighting and many were spreading the Bolshevik call for an end to an imperialist war: a message which appealed to many war-weary soldiers who were otherwise impervious to communism. There was a shortage of experienced officers, and the overall quality of the army was falling as recruiting stations scraped the very bottom of the barrel.

On 3 August Crown Prince Rupprecht noted in his diary that post censorship showed an alarming decline in morale. The following excerpts from soldiers' letters were representative of a widespread discontent:

It's about time that our government began to negotiate a peace. More and more Americans are coming and we are in a lousy situation. Too many hounds mean death to the hare.

The war won't end until all the capitalists have been killed.

The war is only being fought for the capitalists. When one realizes it's all a swindle one wants either to do something else or run away.

The people at home must go on strike resolutely and make a revolution. Only then peace will come. This would have happened in 1916 had it not been for Hindenburg and Ludendorff. Enemy planes are a real menace and our defences against them are completely inadequate.

The air is literally infested with English planes. Goodness knows where the newspapers get all these stories of the heroic deeds of our pilots.[33]

Military law had become markedly milder during the course of the war. Death sentences were exceptional and courts martial were increasingly reluctant to hand out prison sentences. On 8 July the OHL wrote to the ministry of war complaining about the decline in military discipline. They insisted that officers should be made responsible for maintaining strict discipline and obedience. The courts martial should set an example by demanding the harshest possible punishment for any infractions of military law. On 22 July General von Stein issued an order to this effect.

It remained to be seen whether this was too little and too late to halt the decline in the army's effectiveness.

The German army proved unable to overcome the manpower shortages by any significant technical improvements. The production of machine-guns was more than satisfactory and each machine-gun company had five guns. Light machine-guns for the assault troops were also available in large numbers. The A7V tank proved to be a disaster and eighty of them were converted into use as transport. Only twenty were still used as tanks. The Germans relied almost entirely on captured British tanks of which they had 170. They rated them more highly than the faster French models.

Nor had the Germans developed an effective anti-tank weapon. The 13mm anti-tank rifle was cumbersome, of dubious efficacy and in short supply. Assault troops were not properly trained in the use of the 2cm cannon which had been designed as an anti-aircraft gun. All 200 of these weapons were withdrawn to be used in their former role. That left the infantry relying principally on armour-piercing artillery shells and machine-gun bullets, as well as mortars firing directly at the oncoming tanks.

The Luftwaffe hoped that they could overcome their numerical inferiority by superior technology. They were confident that their machines were better than anything produced by the Entente, but in the summer of 1918 they knew that the Entente's superiority in numbers was increasing and it would need some major technical breakthrough to correct this imbalance.[34]

The OHL made few changes in their defensive tactics ,which were still based on 'Principles for the Leadership in Defensive Warfare', written in the winter of 1916-17.[35] Some changes were made to take account of the shortage of manpower. Where necessary the front line did not have to be continuous but would be made up of pockets of resistance. Since they had lost so many prisoners, particularly in 7th Army, a policy of 'elastic retirement' was adopted. The use of artillery had to be kept at a minimum in order to save ammunition.

On 6 July the general staff at Army Group German Crown Prince ordered that the depth of 7th Army's forward zone should be increased from an average of between 100 and 200 metres to 500 to 1,000 metres so as to lessen the effect of a sudden barrage. The forward positions were to be abandoned in the event of a major attack and the entire forward zone should be ready to retire since 'this is more acceptable than the losses likely to be incurred by unnecessary forward defence'.

After the setback on 18 July the OHL was obliged to pay considerably more attention to the problem of defence. They no longer occupied well-prepared defensive positions and had to face an increasing number of tanks against which they had inadequate protection. They knew that there was precious little one could do to avoid being caught by surprise, but it was possible to minimize the effects of the initial shock. It was agreed that the forward zone should be held as long as possible, but this was only feasible if the troops were highly trained and motivated, determined to fight to the bitter end. This was no longer the case in most units of the German army in the summer of 1918.

Some officers at the OHL suggested that units should be prepared to retire up to ten kilometres in order to force the attacker to prepare a fresh assault, but Ludendorff objected vigorously and insisted that armies should have the discretion as to how far they should retreat. At least Ludendorff now accepted the idea that ground that had been won since 21 March could be abandoned if that seemed to be the most prudent course of action.[36]

Since they lacked the manpower it proved impossible for 7th Army to have a forward zone that was 1,000 metres deep. And without sufficient depth a flexible defence was hardly possible. The OHL therefore ordered that in places where a major attack was expected the defence would have to be several kilometres deep, with the artillery withdrawn so far that it would just be able to reach the front line. This would mean that were the Allies to break through the forward positions no great harm would be done, and a flexible defence would be possible. The decision to fight or retire would be taken by the army commands.

On 8 August the OHL published a paper on defensive warfare which was circulated down to regimental level. It urged units to be particularly alert so as not to get caught by surprise. When the Entente attacked the blow would have to be absorbed and then a counter-attack launched. Forward positions should make a fighting withdrawal to the main line of defence. Tanks should be allowed to move forward so as to separate them from the infantry, thus allowing them to be destroyed by artillery and mortar fire. The artillery had to be withdrawn in the event of a breakthrough. Otherwise it would have to lay down a heavy barrage in front of the main line of defence.

The OHL's memorandum of 8 August, the 'Black Day of the German Army', was little more than an admission that they were at a loss to know how to fight an effective defensive campaign. They lacked the manpower for an adequate defence in depth. As the Americans poured into Europe they were increasingly out-numbered. They had no real defence against tanks, although they were not quite so much of a threat as they were subsequently made out to have been. Their defensive positions were rudimentary, and this was no longer traditional trench warfare. The Entente now had the overwhelming superiority in men and matériel.

In April the Germans had 4,000,000 men on the Western Front. By July this had dropped to 3,582,000 and there was little chance of making up the deficit. Urgent appeals were made to Austria-Hungary to send the divisions which had been promised in June, but Vienna was slow to react. Lacking the manpower and still reeling from the shock of the Allied victory on 18 July it now seemed highly unlikely that the Germans would be able to mount another offensive and thus regain the initiative.

13

Amiens: 8-14 August

Ludendorff asked Army Group Crown Prince Rupprecht on 18 July whether it would possible to go ahead with 'Hagen' or whether it would have to be drastically modified. The army group's staff replied that it would still be possible to attack across the line from Cassel to Poperinghe and aim for Dunkirk, but the offensive to the north of Ypres would have to be cancelled. If still more troops designated for 'Hagen' had to be sent to support 17th Army or Army Group German Crown Prince then even this modified version would be out of the question and only a minor offensive would be feasible.

The morale of the German troops in Flanders was very low. They hated being on the defensive since it was generally believed that losses tended to be higher than during an offensive. Exhausted divisions, chronically below strength, ill fed and wracked with influenza, cowered in the trenches and dugouts as the British artillery blasted away at them and the airforce rained bombs upon them. There was a desperate shortage of relieving forces and the troops designated for the attack had little time for rest and training. Crown Prince Rupprecht was now losing about 1,100 men per day and some of his divisions had up to 2,000 men sick. The divisions in the trenches on average lacked 2,500 men. By July the average battalion strength was down to 673 men. The longer 'Hagen' was postponed the more the situation deteriorated. Weeks and months went by until the situation became critical. Without large numbers of fresh troops an offensive was unthinkable and these were nowhere to be found.

Morale in the German Army continued to decline and by August had become a matter of serious concern to the authorities.[1] There was an alarming increase in the number of deserters and scrimshankers, crime was rampant and censors reported that letters from the front revealed a widespread feeling of despondency. Many factors contributed to this dangerous decline in morale which could not be overcome by rousing words, or appeals to patriotism. The root causes of the problem had to be tackled head-on.

The principal causes were not difficult to identify. The food situation was chronic and was a major source of complaint. The high hopes that had been placed first in unrestricted submarine warfare in 1917 and then in the great offensives of 1918 had been cruelly dashed, resulting in resignation and ever stronger suspicions that the war could not be won. Troops complained bitterly that they did not get enough leave and that orders and decorations were unfairly distributed. There had been an alarming decline in the quality of the officer corps and of non-commissioned officers as draft boards scraped the very bottom of the barrel. Common to all armies in the Great War there was great resentment among the men in the trenches of the comfortable and privileged life of staff officers who stayed well out of harm's way miles from the front lines.[2] Training was often overly rigorous, and too little consideration was paid to the needs of exhausted men who had spent long and taxing spells at the front. There was deep resentment of spiraling wages at home which were out of all proportion to the miserable pay in the army, and which were compounded by the constant belly-aching among civilians.

Inadequate rations were a fundamental cause of declining morale and were having a marked effect on physical fitness and endurance. There was no easy solution to this problem since it was not possible to increase the rations. There were, however, some areas where improvements could be made. Whereas beer was readily available at home, it was seldom available at the front. Bavarian troops were said to suffer particularly from the desperate shortage of their national tipple. Similarly troops got none of the variety of breads that were available at home. Another major grievance was that the army issued beech leaves as an ersatz tobacco, whereas cigars were available at home, although admittedly in limited numbers. More could be done to provide the troops with fresh fruits and vegetables. A suggestion was also made that men could prepare some of their own foods. While this was not the most rational and economical way of feeding an army, it would result in fresher, warmer meals and give the men the satisfaction of fending for themselves.

Soldiers are by nature optimists as long they are not taxed too hard and too long. The first serious signs of trouble were in May 1918. The Germans offered virtually no resistance to an attack by the under-manned 2nd Australian Division at Ville sur Ancre on 19 May. General von Kuhl sent an officer to investigate. His report was not encouraging. Morale was extremely low as the troops had been given no rest and were expected soon to go on the offensive. 2nd and 17th Armies were in miserable positions in the old Somme battlefield and the Alberich

positions which had been destroyed the previous year. There were precious few dugouts, it was extremely hot and the troops were seldom
able to find any shade. They were exhausted, apathetic, and discipline
was hopelessly lax.[3] By early August this malaise had spread to the entire
German Army. They had been on the offensive for four months, had
suffered terrible casualties and were exhausted. They badly needed a rest
in which to restore their spirits.

The great mistake in the past had been to talk of an early end to the
war, thus raising hopes which were soon to be crushed. In the spring
of 1917 it was announced that unrestricted submarine warfare would
bring peace by the autumn. This mistake was repeated in the spring of
1918 when it was claimed that the great offensive on the Western Front
would again bring victory by the autumn. During the preparations for
the 'Michael' offensive morale had been remarkably high, since it was
widely believed that the war was entering its final stages. Now it was
felt that the war would last for at least another two years, thanks to the
United States entering the conflict. Some argued that this sentiment
could be exploited so that hatred of the United States might grow in
intensity, and that this would help soldiers accept the fact that the war
was likely to continue for a considerable time to come. Perhaps soldiers
might then come to terms with the sacrifices this would entail.

The gross disparity between the incomes of soldiers and civil servants
on the one hand and workers at home on the other was seen as a major
cause of discontent, particularly among married men who found it virtually impossible to support a wife and children with such meagre means.
Workers lived comfortably at home with their families, many earning
as much as, sometimes even more than, a battalion commander, while
soldiers faced death and serious injury, lived in appalling conditions and
were seriously undernourished. Clearly it was not possible to reduce the
wages of civilians, and thus the only possible way to improve the situation was to have a significant increase of soldier's pay, particularly that of
married men. Although such a measure would cost the Reich billions of
marks, if it were not put into effect the consequences would be dire.

To avoid giving front-line soldiers too much money in hand, which
they readily frittered away paying absurd prices for needless pleasures, it
was suggested that the married men's allowances should be paid directly
to the families. The tendency to make extravagant promises of a wonderful life once the fighting stopped should be avoided. The hopes that were
thus awoken were bound to be dashed, and the resulting disillusionment
would likely have dangerous consequences.

Lack of transport was the major reason why leave had been reduced,
and recently stopped altogether. The ordinary soldier had absolutely no
understanding of the problems involved, and this was a major cause of
complaint. It was assumed that the OHL would soon give the order

for the army to go on the defensive, and that should make it possible to grant more leave. Hopefully it would be possible to give each man two leaves of a fortnight each per year. Even though soldiers on leave would necessarily hear a large number of complaints from disgruntled civilians, it was absolutely essential that they be given adequate time away from the front. Extra leave should also be granted to men who distinguished themselves in the field. Thus men who carried out a successful patrol should be given fourteen days leave as a reward. This would prove a powerful incentive and boost morale.

There were numerous reports of less than satisfactory behaviour by troops on leave, particularly German troops who spent their leave in Austria-Hungary. Both officers and men behaved so badly in Vienna and Budapest that the War Minister in Berlin felt obliged to order that only soldiers from Austria-Hungary would henceforth be allowed to go there on leave.[4]

Soldiers who in civilian life worked in the agricultural sector were given 'Agricultural Leave' (*Landwirtschaftlicher Urlaub*) at harvest time. This was the source of much ill feeling among those who did not have this opportunity to escape duty at the front. Furthermore there were a number of cases reported where men on such leave had not worked at all, and had simply had a holiday. Clearly officers had to explain to their men that such leave was absolutely essential, given the serious difficulties faced in feeding a nation at war under an Allied blockade.

The army was relatively generous in granting compassionate leave when there was a death in the family, serious illness in the immediate family, or when pressing family affairs had to be settled. Care was taken to ensure that officers were not favoured in this respect, since in rare cases when this did occur it created a very bad impression on the men and undermined morale.[5]

The lack of medals and decorations was a constant cause for complaint. Officers who had been fighting on the front under the most taxing of conditions frequently had not been awarded the Iron Cross First Class. Many of those who have been given this medal in 1914 had been given no further recognition. Austrians and Saxons were given far more decorations than those serving in the other German armies, and as a result were the objects of considerable envy. Prussians received the fewest medals of all and this was a source of widespread discontent. It was argued that it would not be difficult to award more medals and that this would have a very definite effect on morale. Only the Prussian authorities appeared to be deaf to the need to boost morale by such means. Under these circumstances it is doubtful whether the King of Saxony's desire to be promoted to the rank of Field Marshal met with much sympathy. Although he was already a Field Marshal in the Prussian army he had not yet reached this exalted rank in his own forces. In order to make this possible the Saxon War Ministry suggested that every officer in the Saxon army should contribute 50 pfennigs towards the purchase of a Field Marshal's baton. Should this not prove sufficient, the additional money would be taken from a charitable fund.[6] History does not record how this preposterous suggestion was received, but within less than a year the King was to lose his throne and the Saxon Army was dissolved.

That medals were awarded to the wounded was a popular measure, but there was a certain injustice involved. Many men had served for a long time at the front without being wounded and yet had received no recognition. Getting wounded was hardly a sign of particular merit, and was often the result of carelessness or stupidity. The Austrians, on the other hand, awarded the Karl's Cross to all soldiers who had served at the front for more than a year, and the suggestion was made that a similar medal could be struck for German units.

According to newspaper reports 51,386 Iron Crosses First Class had been given to staff and other officers, 16,713 to NCOs and men and 472 to service personnel. Since NCOs and men made up the bulk of the army this was clearly an unjust distribution. Furthermore, most medals were handed out by divisional commanders. It was greatly appreciated when they were awarded by more senior officers. When Field Marshal von Hindenburg awarded eighteen Iron Crosses Second Class to men in 233rd Light Infantry Division the effect was most impressive. Captain Bosl, the author of the report on morale, argued that these gallant soldiers would never become Social Democrats.

The close relationship between senior commanders and their men that was present at the outset of the war no longer existed. When XXI Army Corps took Luneville in August 1914 General Fritz von Below had been strewn with flowers by men as they gave him rousing cheers. Such a scene was now unthinkable. In part this was due to men who had served a lengthy stretch at the front being so hardened that they felt their officers would better employed teaching their grandmothers to suck eggs than issuing them with orders and offering advice. In trench warfare, officers, NCOs and men lived in very close proximity and although this often engendered a close feeling of comradeship the hierarchical structure of command was weakened, discipline suffered and a general sloppiness took over. Many of the best officers and NCOs had been killed, seriously wounded or taken prisoner and of necessity were replaced by men who were often lacking the essential military virtues and, in the case of officers, the desirable social standing that had been the norm when the war began.

It was frequently noted that the problem of discipline was particularly serious behind the lines. Troops in the front line were under strict discipline and control and presented no problem. Young officers, civil servants and medical and veterinary officers were appallingly sloppy. They slouched around with their jackets unbuttoned and their caps askew, and overlooked gross breaches of discipline by the other ranks.[7] The headquarters of 19th Army reported that of thirteen recently commissioned lieutenants nine had gone absent without leave to visit relatives, even though they had been expressly told by the transport officer that this was not permissible.[8] The miscreants were given the modest punishment of four weeks house arrest on returning to their units.[9]

Training both for officers and NCOs had to be thorough and intensive, but the emphasis, it was argued, should be less on drill – important though this was – and more on encouraging initiative, independence, and swift judgment. Proper training brought knowledge, which in turn raised self-confidence and inspired the trust of subordinates. This needed great skill, and thus only the best officers and NCOs should be entrusted with training duties. Promotion to the rank of NCO should not be based on length of service, but purely on ability and character. It was a serious mistake to select men for promotion on the basis of good behaviour and conformity since such people were often lacking the character, drive and the authority required to be an effective NCO. There were complaints that the newer officers frequently lacked the character and the necessary upbringing to have a true understanding of what it means to be an officer and had no notion of the traditional conception of honour. The usual punishments meted out to officers in peacetime, such as house arrest or extra turns as duty officer, no longer had any effect. Much harsher punishments, such as a dishonourable dismissal, were needed for failure to carry out duties. Older officers bore much of the responsibility for this state of affairs. They tended to ignore the social side of an officer's life, and concentrated exclusively on the performance of prescribed duties. There was a widespread feeling of 'here today, dead tomorrow' which made many officers indifferent to the future of the officer corps and they no longer cared about their social status within the army or society. Frequent and rigorous training of all officers had to continue, and particular emphasis placed on behaviour appropriate to the officer class.

By July there were signs that discipline was beginning to slacken, even in the front line. The War Ministry in Berlin found it necessary to remind all units that discipline must be maintained in the field at all times, and that officers were perfectly justified in using their weapons where necessary. Punishments should be made to fit the crime, and the death penalty was quite appropriate in cases where an order was refused.[10]

In August the Prussian War Ministry received a detailed report on the troops' morale from the German Foremen's Association (*Deutscher Werkmeister-Verband*) in Düsseldorf.[11] It was a national association, with more than 13,000 members, which enjoyed Ludendorff's enthusiastic support. They reported that the degree of ill feeling among men serving on the Western Front was so intense that it gave rise to grave concern. They complained that they were often badly treated by their officers. There were very few older and more experienced officers at the front. Officers were either very young, or they were recently promoted from the ranks (*Feldwebelleutnants*). Mutual respect and camaraderie between officers and men had declined markedly, and the men had become increasingly disgruntled and disillusioned. The front line was thinly held, but when the men were withdrawn they found the rear echelons packed with officers and men. There were frequent complaints about the unequal treatment of officers and men. Officers got fresh white bread, while the men had to make do with standard army issue square loaves of rye bread (*Komißbrot*) that were scarcely edible. Men paid three or four times more for cigarettes than did officers. Officers were able to send butter and fat home, and in the Ukraine they bought butter for 2 marks 50 per pound, whereas the men had to pay between 8 and 18 marks. The report concluded by arguing that the level of bitterness among the troops was 'incredible' and posed a grave danger to the security of the Reich.

Ludendorff appeared to pay little attention to these ominous warnings. Having analyzed the extent of the damage inflicted on the Marne front he concluded on 19 July that 'Hagen' would have to be cancelled and that Army Group Crown Prince Rupprecht would have to send more troops to plug the gap in the German front. He refused to accept any responsibility for this disaster, blaming it all on Colonel Wetzell and on the miserable failures of 7th Army. He managed to convince himself that this was merely a local failure rather than a fundamental reversal, and that this was the last desperate effort by the French to seize the initiative which had left them a spent force.

General von Lossberg, who as chief of the general staff to 4th Army was responsible for planning 'Hagen', arrived in Avesnes on 20 July and was appalled by what he saw. The Entente had clearly seized the initiative and the morale of the German army was alarmingly low. He suggested an immediate withdrawal of 9th and 7th Armies behind the Aisne and the Vesle to be followed by a slow retirement to the Siegfried Line within the next three weeks.[12] 'Hagen' should go ahead but Lossberg insisted that it would not be a decisive battle and would only bring a tactical success. If it was decided to cancel 'Hagen' 4th and 6th Armies should also be withdrawn and the entire Western Front should go on the defensive. A defensive line should then be prepared from Antwerp to the Meuse behind places that could be easily flooded, as well as from Metz to Strasbourg and the Rhine.[13]

Ludendorff replied that Lossberg's proposals were militarily correct but politically unacceptable. According to Lossberg's unconfirmed account he told Ludendorff that it would be a dangerous mistake to sub-ordinate military imperatives to political considerations. Ludendorff then dramatically threatened to resign and stormed off to see Hindenburg. Later he told Lossberg that the Field Marshal had refused to accept his offer of resignation. Lossberg concluded from this bizarre behaviour that Ludendorff had lost his grip.[14]

General von Kuhl was in broad agreement with Ludendorff. He felt it would be a mistake to adopt a purely defensive posture as Lossberg had suggested, since that would hand over the initiative to the Entente. Although he knew that the German army could no longer fight a decisive battle, he was in favour of a modified 'Hagen' that would help spoil the Entente's plans for a further offensive.

Having received more worrisome news from Army Group German Crown Prince, Ludendorff cancelled 'Hagen' for the time being and ordered Army Group Crown Prince Rupprecht to go on the defensive. Von Kuhl felt this was a bad mistake. The British had already sent five divisions to support the French offensive and further divisions were bound to follow. Ludendorff replied that the situation facing Army Group German Crown Prince was so serious that von Kuhl's Army Group would have to send five more divisions. This would make it impossible to mount even a small-scale offensive. Ludendorff added that he hoped to attack the left and right flanks of the French advance. He also ordered Army Groups Gallwitz and Duke Albrecht to plan offensives and insisted that the army should be ready at any time to go on the offensive anywhere on the Western Front wherever an opportunity arose.[15] Ludendorff was now indulging in fantasy and refused to face the unpleasant truth that he had lost the initiative on 18 July.

On 20 July the OHL announced that they expected the Entente to attack 9th and 18th Armies north of the Aisne. The British might possibly be tempted to attack in Flanders. Two days later 2nd Army and the right wing of 18th Army were withdrawn from the bridgeheads across the Ancre and the Avre where they had suffered severe losses in a series of attacks and which could only be held if they were greatly strengthened. No reserves were available.

By 27 July the OHL was reasonably confident that the Entente would not mount any major offensive for the time being. They expected the fighting around Reims and Soissons to continue and thought that the Entente might attack between the Aisne and the Oise. The retirement behind the Vesle had been ordered 'so as to regain operational freedom'. The main task now facing the army was to build up its divisions to full strength, if necessary by dissolving some of them. Assault troops were to be rested beyond the range of enemy guns.

General von Hutier was less sanguine. He made preparations in antici-pation of a major attack by the French, which he was convinced could start at any moment. He was gratified that the OHL had sent him some replacements both of men and artillery, his army having been stripped bare during 'Marne' and 'Reims', but he feared that it could well be too little too late.[16]

On 2 August Ludendorff wrote to all the Army Group commanders on the Western Front telling them to go on the defensive, but also to prepare a number of attacks. These included a modified 'Hagen', an attack on both sides of the Oise towards Montdidier and Soissons ('Elector'), a small offensive at Fort Pompelle to the east of Reims, and an attack by Army Group Duke Albert. All these operations were to be seen as defensive moves and were not considered as proper offensives.[17]

Although Ludendorff did not expect a major Allied offensive it is clear that he was now adopting a defensive posture, and that the Entente had thus won the initiative. Planning was now begun for a general retirement as suggested by General von Lossberg, but Ludendorff insisted that this would only take place if the existing front proved untenable. General von Hutier noted that the OHL was getting increasingly nervous and uncertain, and that this manifested itself in frequent accusations that Army Group commanders were making grave errors, when this was manifestly not the case.[18] He had now reached the conclusion that nothing short of a miracle would make it possible for Germany to win the war, and that a negotiated peace was thus the only alternative.[19]

There was considerable reluctance among senior commanders to go on the defensive and thus hand over the initiative to the enemy. Army Group Crown Prince Rupprecht continued to insist that a modified version of 'Hagen' was possible, and Army Group Gallwitz reported to the OHL on 6 August that a purely defensive strategy was unacceptable. It was argued that men and matériel were used up just as quickly in defence as in the offense and that the German Army could not afford simply to react to the Entente's moves.[20]

Crown Prince William did not share these views. At the end of July he wrote to his father the Kaiser pointing out that the German Army was running desperately short of both men and matériel, with no likelihood of an improvement. The Entente was getting stronger, and with the Americans arriving in Europe in large numbers they would soon have an overwhelming superiority. Germany would now have to go on the defensive and although it would be possible to hang on for a considerable time, certainly well into 1919, the effect on morale would be disastrous. 'Radical democrats' and 'pessimists' would have a field day and the demand for a peace at any prize would grow louder. If Germany were to be defeated a situation analogous to that in Russia was likely to occur, and the Hohenzollern dynasty could well be toppled.[21]

There was more than a hint of desperation in this note. The Crown Prince insisted that the war had to be continued, but he offered no suggestions as to what should be done. Furthermore he implied that in the long run there could be no hope for victory. General von Hutier was in full agreement and did not believe that it would be possible for Germany to go on the offensive again in 1918, in spite of von Kuhl's argument that the army should pause, regroup and continue the struggle.[22]

The retirement behind the Vesle greatly strengthened the German position. The French were reaching exhaustion after two months of heavy fighting. On 4 August the front was reorganized with 2nd, 18th and 9th Armies forming a new Army Group under General von Boehn with General von Lossberg as chief of staff. General Heuser replaced Lossberg as chief of staff to 4th Army.[23] The staff at Army Group Crown Prince Rupprecht finished their plans for 4th Army's revised version of 'Hagen' and for 18th Army's 'Elector' on 6 August. They were so confident that they would soon go on the attack that they had paid insufficient attention to improving their defences, an omission that was to prove costly.

On 3 August 2nd Army reported that there was indication that the enemy troops around Villers-Bretonneux were being relieved. They expected an attack south of the town. On 4 August the entire 2nd Army was placed on the alert but the attack never came. On 5 August von Kuhl reported to the OHL that 2nd and 18th Armies were in excellent form. Most units were near to full strength, morale was good, defensive positions were satisfactory and the Entente was remarkably inactive.

2nd Army launched a counter-attack on 6 August but it resulted in only modest gains. An outstanding division of Württembergers successfully disrupted III Corps' preparations for the offensive, reinforced their positions, and were ready for the attack on 8 August. As a result III Corps was unable to keep pace with the other corps in Fourth Army on 8 August, thus leaving the left of the Australian Corps open to enfilade fire from the north bank of the Somme which caused heavy casualties.

Sounds of motor vehicles opposite the left wing of the army indicated that the Entente was preparing to attack. German artillery barrages designed to disrupt these preparations resulted in the loss of twenty-five British tanks.[24] Air reconnaisance noted heavy traffic from Dunkirk to Amiens but there was still no definite sign that the Entente was preparing a major offensive, though they still expected an attack by General Sir Henry Rawlinson's Fourth Army at Villers-Bretonneux, due east of Amiens.

Ludendorff was convinced that the failure on 18 July could have been avoided if the infantry had been on its toes and the artillery had been placed in depth. He also put the blame on poor leadership at the top, and began a series of frantic changes. 9th Army had been led by General Eben as a replacement for von Below, who was sick. He was now to be replaced by General Eberhardt with Hasse as chief of staff. A new commander was also needed for 7th Army. General von Einem, who commanded 3rd Army, Lieutenant-Colonel Baron von Lenz, chief of staff to 6th Army, and Colonel von Tschischwitz, chief of staff to 2nd Army, were all to be replaced. Hergott was to take the place of Lenz, but it was difficult to see where suitable officers for the other vacant positions could be found.[25] Still, Ludendorff was confident that the army had learnt its lesson and was well prepared to counter the Entente's next move. He now welcomed an enemy offensive, announcing that it would merely lead to their exhaustion.

Foch had first suggested an offensive by I and III Armies against the southern flank of the Amiens pocket at the beginning of April. The idea had to be abandoned on 27 May when the Germans launched their 'Yorck' and 'Blücher' offensives on the Aisne. Encouraged by the success of the Mangin offensive he revived the plan in a modified form on 21 July. This time the weight of the offensive would be on the northern flank, and would thus be the responsibility of the British Army, but I Army was still to attack in the south around Noyon. Pétain then ordered X Army to draw up plans for an operation to force the Germans back from their positions on the Aisne and the Vesle.

At 0520hrs on 8 August the artillery of the British Fourth Army opened fire along the whole length of the German 2nd Army's front. The infantry and tanks began their attack almost as soon as the barrage began. Helped by misty weather and the effective use of smoke they made rapid progress across the dry ground, and Rawlinson's men quickly overran General von der Marwitz's forward positions. In some places the Germans were caught completely by surprise as the order to stand-to had not yet been given and the men were still in their dugouts. The tanks drove through the gaps in the forward positions and attacked from the rear. The German artillery was blinded by fog and smoke and thus rendered useless. When air cleared Allied air supremacy ensured that the British artillery had accurate spotters. Pockets of German resistance were also attacked from the air to considerable effect.

Within a few hours the British had penetrated the German lines on a twenty-kilometre front from the Avre to the Ancre, the Australian and Canadian divisions making the most progress. Three divisions of cavalry supported by light tanks moved ahead of the infantry, and finding little resistance reached some of the German divisional headquarters. They were well defended and the cavalry was obliged to retire and rejoin the infantry.

Rawlinson's attack was oblique, so that rearward positions were attacked on the flank and the lines of communication from the forward positions to the command posts and reserves to the rear were severed. The southern flank of the German pocket by the Avre was particularly vulnerable. This was attacked by General Debeney's I Army after a four-hour barrage. The artillery had done such an excellent job that the French infantry met with little resistance and soon linked up with the Canadians.

General von der Marwitz's headquarters in Péronne knew from the intensity of the barrage that a major offensive had been launched, but was completely in the dark as to what was happening at the front, the lines of communications having been severed. There were only two divisions in reserve, the 43rd Reserve Division and the 109th Infantry Division. Both were utterly exhausted and were waiting to be relieved. They had very few guns and were in no fit state to mount a counter-attack. Only where British and French units had pressed forward in isolated groups in front of the main body of attacking troops was it possible to drive them back.

The French breakthrough in the battle of Montdidier south of the Somme on a 27-kilometre front was of particular concern. New infantry divisions were rushed to the front in trucks, but they had virtually no artillery and the few guns they managed to bring back from the front were virtually without ammunition. Artillery was brought forward from the firing range at Lihons but this hastily improvised move brought little relief. Although the Germans managed to shoot down sixty-two enemy aircraft (eleven of them with anti-aircraft guns) the Entente still had an overwhelming superiority in the air on this section of the front. A number of anti-aircraft guns were lost as the French advanced, and many others had to be used as anti-tank guns. The German front was weakly held and was full of wide gaps. The divisions were tired and unable to put up much of a fight. There could be little doubt that the French would be able to make significant advances the following day.

By midday General von der Marwitz had a clear picture of the extent of the damage done to his army. He told the OHL that it seemed that he had lost the bulk of six divisions on his front along with most of their artillery. At first the OHL did not think the situation particularly serious. Ludendorff imagined that a counter-attack by three reserve divisions would be enough to drive the British back. When the Kaiser was put in the picture in the course of the afternoon he ordered Hindenburg to attack the flanks of the British bulge as they had done at Cambrai to such remarkable effect in 1917.

The OHL sent in all available reserves as quickly as possible to halt the advance but, as was the case at Montdidier, the infantry came by truck without artillery support. Army Group Crown Prince Rupprecht reported that von der Marwitz could have enough reserves by the morning of 9 August to stop the British, but that he would have to wait until at least the following day for the artillery to arrive before mounting a counter-attack. Since the army held fast between the Avre and the

Somme he hoped to be able to attack the southern flank of the British pocket at Amiens. On the other hand von Kuhl had to consider the eventuality of having to retire behind the Somme before stopping the Allied advance. He therefore ordered plans to be drawn up for a defensive line from Péronne, where the Somme and the Canal du Nord run due south, to Noyon.

Just as on 18 July the troops were caught by surprise on 8 August and Ludendorff panicked. The OHL had seriously underestimated the Entente, and had not realized how quickly they had been able to organize a counter-attack. The French response to 'Gneisenau' on 11 June, and the shocking setback on 18 July should have taught them to be on their guard. The rapid counter-attack was partly due to the use of large numbers of tanks, which rendered the time-consuming and technically challenging preparation by the artillery redundant. The Entente also had the advantage of better transportation to the rear, and their supremacy in the air made it difficult for German reconnaisance planes to get an accurate picture of what was afoot behind the enemy lines.

In his war memoirs Ludendorff said that 8 August showed that the German army had lost the will to fight and described it as the 'Black Day' of the German Army.[26] In October he told the Vice Chancellor Peyer that an elite bicycle brigade which was being brought up to the front was denounced as strike breakers. Elsewhere units cracked when the enemy was still 800 metres away.[27] Both the French and the British agreed that the German army was no longer the formidable fighting machine that it had been only a few weeks before, and they attacked on 18 July and 8 August confident in victory. It would, however, be a mistake to place the blame entirely on the failure of the German army's morale. The Entente had an overwhelming superiority in men and equipment and the tanks were at last used to considerable effect. North of the Somme where few tanks were employed the British made little progress. The Entente had four times the amount of artillery with ample supplies of ammunition. The skilful attack in the south on the flank and the rear placed the Germans in an impossible situation. It was thus not simply the exhausted divisions that fell apart. 117th Infantry division at Hangard Wood was fresh and in full strength, but completely collapsed in the face of a determined attack by the Canadians.

Colonel Bauer did not believe that the tanks were the secret of the Allies' success. Provided that the troops did not panic they could be relatively easily destroyed. Nor was it due to their offensive spirit, which if anything diminished in the course of the summer. The German army had adequate munitions, industrial production was satisfactory, but there had been a serious decline on morale on the Western Front. The greatest weakness, however, was the desperate shortage of manpower. The

Germans were critically short of new recruits at a time when hundreds of thousands of Americans were arriving in France.[28]

The OHL made the fatal mistake of ordering counter-attacks which were ill prepared and had totally inadequate support from the artillery. These proved to be a waste of manpower and caused further discontent among the troops. Men were lost in these hastily improvised actions who would have been better employed improving defences in preparation for a renewed attack. Even in 1917, counter-attacks had not brought any substantial gains. Lost ground was won back, holes in the defensive lines were plugged, but the cost was usually far too high. They did not result in many prisoners being taken, nor did the enemy lose much equipment. Ludendorff's frantic and ill-considered interference on 8 August, down to the corps level, led to further confusion and his calls for pointless counter-attacks was exasperating to commanders in the field.

The Entente had gained a significant tactical advantage on 8 August but for most senior commanders it was hardly a 'Black Day'. Crown Prince Rupprecht felt that the crisis could be overcome and that the situation would only be serious if the offensive against 2nd Army was followed by attacks on the left flank of 6th Army and the right flank of 17th Army.[29]

The Allies made further piecemeal advances on 9 August. Montdidier was surrounded and evacuated during the night. Once again the higher commanders did not realize what was happening until late in the day. In the morning the OHL ordered a counter-attack à la Cambrai, but at the same time they were concerned that the offensive would extend south and involve 18th Army. This raised the question of whether 18th Army should retire to the Gothic Line.

At 1720hrs 2nd Army reported to Army Group Crown Prince Rupprecht that the situation was extremely grave. At 1825hrs General von der Marwitz telephoned General von Kuhl and told him that his army would not be able to hold the line in the morning unless he got some fresh troops. His corps commanders all reported that the troops would not be able to hang on even for one more day. Crown Prince Rupprecht agreed that the troops were on the point of collapse, and therefore decided to retire behind the Somme the following night. General von Kuhl insisted that this would leave 18th Army dangerously exposed. If von der Marwitz were to pull his army back, von Hutier could easily be outflanked. Since he did not think that the situation was quite as critical, he suggested holding on until fresh troops could be brought forward. After all, the Entente had not been able to repeat the successes of 8 August and had made only modest gains the following day.

Ludendorff was highly alarmed at 2nd Army's predicament and sent one of his most trusted aides, Mertz von Quirnheim, to investigate the situation. Mertz reported back that von der Marwitz and his chief of staff Colonel von Tschischwitz had lost their nerve and were no longer on top of the situation. Ludendorff promptly replaced von Tschischwitz with Lieutenant-Colonel von Klewitz, who had previously served as chief of staff to von Einem's 3rd Army.[30]

General von Kuhl eventually managed to convince his very reluctant superior officer not to retire precipitously behind the Somme, but to retire gradually in carefully prepared stages. 2nd Army had to stand firm in order to let 18th Army retire in an orderly fashion. On 12 August Crown Prince Rupprecht generously confessed that von Kuhl had been absolutely correct and that it would have been a grave mistake to retire behind the Somme under duress. The Germans were now free to move behind the river should they wish to do so.[31]

All the while Ludendorff repeatedly telephoned von Kuhl issuing orders down to the battalion level. Crown Prince Rupprecht was full of admiration for his chief of staff's patient and diplomatic handling of Ludendorff's agitated outbursts. He would calmly reply with such phrases as 'it's too early to tell' or 'all depends on how things develop'.[32]

After much discussion it was decided that 18th Army should pull back to the Gothic Line. Ludendorff telephoned von Hutier at 10.30 that evening informing him that 2nd Army had been defeated and would have to be pulled back.[33] Only his left wing was to remain in position so as to maintain contact with 9th Army. At 2300hrs General von Hutier spoke on the phone to General von Kuhl and told him that III Corps was in serious difficulty. Since General von der Marwitz had said that his troops were cracking, and since the new group of three divisions under General von Endres which was designed to stiffen 2nd Army's resistance at Roye could not be formed until the afternoon of 10 August, 18th Army would have to retire beyond the Gothic Line to positions from Noyon to Roye.

The Army Group, prompted by the OHL, did not agree to this suggestion and inquired further into the situation of III Corps. Getting no clear answer von Kuhl agreed to a compromise. 18th Army was to retire beyond the Gothic Line, but not quite as far as von Hutier had suggested. Von Hutier had been initially extremely reluctant to leave the positions which he had so carefully prepared, but once he saw the necessity of such a move he argued that they should pull back far enough to take up strong defensive positions, and use this breathing space to bring all units up to strength. Ludendorff was strongly opposed to retiring even this far. He was constantly on the phone to all levels of command, issuing confusing and often contradictory orders, causing staff officers to despair and reducing commanding generals to desperation. Eventually the ever firm but tactful von Kuhl managed to persuade him that he would have to accept the fact that the forward positions were untenable. Meanwhile

Crown Prince Rupprecht remained cool and calm, in spite of the fact that he was clearly deeply worried about Germany's prospects. He left his staff to get on with the job, never interfering with their work, and arriving promptly for the conferences at midday and 7 p.m.[34]

General von Hutier was driven to distraction by confusing orders, frequent changes of plans, and dithering by the OHL. He blamed the whole unfortunate situation on the OHL for having starved the Amiens front of men, leaving his army overworked, exhausted and demoralized as a result. On 10 August he first heard that men moving up to the front were being denounced as 'strike breakers'.[35] He also felt bitter that 2nd Army had failed so badly.

By 10 August it was clear that the British offensive was losing steam and that the Germans were recovering from the initial shock. The Australians attacked hill 109 but the German 51 Corps put up a fierce fight. One German unit was encircled in a wood and fought to the last man.[36] It took until evening before the Australians took the hill. The Canadians attacked on a broad front towards Maucourt and made good progress in a very tough fight.

The German infantry had precious little artillery support and suffered heavy losses. 2nd Army's new chief of general staff, Lieutenant-Colonel von Klewitz, who arrived at headquarters in the morning of 10 August, ordered all divisions to stand firm and to deliver counter-attacks along the whole front. The artillery was ordered to fire at the tanks over open sights. General von Hofacker, commanding 51 Corps, told him that he could not hold the line against the Canadians unless he got two fresh divisions. Fearing that his rousing call to push the enemy back might be based largely on wishful thinking, von Klewitz made prudent provision for a retirement to the old German Somme positions of 1916.

The Allies thus made only modest gains on 10 August and the Germans felt that the immediate crisis was over. 2nd Army's left wing had made an orderly withdrawal and had suffered relatively light losses. Von Klewitz reported to General von Kuhl that there had been a marked improvement in 2nd Army's morale, and that the situation had significantly stabilized in the last 24 hours. He had also managed to stiffen von der Marwitz, who now agreed that the army should stand and fight.[37] Von Klewitz insisted that 2nd Army should remain in front of the Somme so as to be able to hit the enemy's flank should they attack 18th Army. This would also tempt the Allies to wear themselves out in a series of futile attacks. Retirement behind the Somme would also have a disastrous effect on the army's morale, which had only just been restored.

General von Kuhl agreed in principle with von Klewitz's arguments but felt that in the long run the Péronne bridgehead would need too many men for an effective defence. He was also very concerned about the danger posed by an attack at Albert which would serious endanger the army's rear echelons. In his report to the OHL von Kuhl described the situation as firm, adding that the present positions could be held for the time being, but eventually they would have to withdraw behind the Somme, even if the Allies no longer attacked. His main concern was still the possibility of an attack from Arras to Albert against 17th Army which might enable the Allies to outflank 2nd Army. He therefore suggested pulling 17th Army back from the Hébuterne salient. Von Klewitz remained adamant that the Germans should stand firm with their backs to the Somme. General von Kuhl continued to argue that this would be both costly and dangerous.

Ludendorff was still undecided how to proceed. He was worried that the British might attack at Kemmel, Béthune or Lens and that the army had to win time to recover from the setback on 8 August. Being reluctant to retire all the way behind the Somme he suggested that they should stand their ground and only move back to the battle zone at points which seemed particularly vulnerable.[38]

At a conference at Army Group Crown Prince Rupprecht's headquarters on 11 August, Lieutenant-Colonel Herrgott, who had replaced Lieutenant-Colonel Baron von Lenz as chief of staff to 6th Army, reported that the OHL was still undecided as to what to do next.[39] General von Kuhl had repeatedly pointed out to the OHL that he needed to know what to do with his reserves. Were they, he asked acidly, to be wasted away by being sent to the front, or were they to be held to the rear in preparation for a withdrawal behind the Somme? The OHL had full confidence that General Boehn would soon get the situation under control, and felt that von Kuhl was exaggerating the dangers.[40]

Although the 2nd Army lost Lihons on 11 August and on the extreme left wing was forced back to the Gothic Line, the situation was not one to cause alarm. 18th Army was able to ward off a series of fierce attacks, and inflicted severe damage on the French.[41] On the following day both 2nd and 18th Armies held their ground, and the Entente's offensive seemed to have lost momentum. 2nd Army's headquarters were moved back to Cambrai. Fourth Army's corps commanders told Rawlinson that the German defence had grown much stronger. Just as the Germans had discovered before them, the infantry was finding it hard to advance across the cratered landscape of the old Somme battlefields, and the ground was virtually impassible for the tanks. The troops were tired and the heavy artillery had not yet been brought forward. The situation in the French Army was similar, and Foch therefore decided to pause before striking again.

Although von Kuhl knew that for the moment the situation was relatively stable, and 2nd Army, which had seemed in danger of falling apart, was now holding its ground, he still believed that the German Army had to withdraw behind the Somme to improve its defensive posture and to ensure against a flank attack. General von Hutier also agonized as to whether to use this golden opportunity to retire in an orderly manner, or whether to stand and fight.[42] The OHL did not share their concerns. Their daily reports talked of great victories won, crippling casualties inflicted upon the enemy, and the operational freedom that was afforded by the tremendous gains won in the spring offensive. All these empty phrases did not conceal the fact that the German Army was in an exceedingly exposed position across the Somme. The right flank near Albert was especially vulnerable. Should the Entente attack at that point part of the Army would be stuck with their backs to the Somme. Now was the time to act. The enemy's offensive had been halted, and the Army had time to retire in an orderly fashion.[43]

The chief of staff to General von Boehn's new Army Group, the defensive specialist General von Lossberg, did not have quite such a gloomy view of the situation. He argued in favour of 2nd Army maintaining a bridgehead across the Somme near Péronne. General von Kuhl felt that this would be far too costly, and Crown Prince Rupprecht, who now appeared to be close to panic, insisted that the entire Army Group should retire as quickly as possible.[44]

The Entente had won a victory at Amiens and had shown that the German army was not invincible. But they had not made any great operational gain. Marshal Foch's objectives had been modest, and were only extended when he came up against surprisingly weak resistance from the enemy. The tactical success of 8 August was not exploited and the end results were not very impressive. Instead of driving the Germans back to the Somme the British and the French had merely nipped off the tip of the advance made during the 'Michael' offensive. They had not made any deep impression on the flanks.

The number of prisoners taken were indication that the German army was losing the will to fight. Of the 36,500 men lost by 2nd Army an amazing 27,500 were missing, most presumed to have been taken prisoner. In 18th Army, of 11,500 losses 5,500 were listed as missing. The German army could not afford such losses within a few days given the serious shortage of manpower. On the other hand, Allied losses were even higher. The British lost 51,000 men in August, the French I and III Armies 24,000. Most of these 75,000 men were lost between 8 and 10 August.

The Battle of Amiens was in no sense decisive, but it clearly increased the Entente's determination to press on. In Germany demands for an negotiated peace were getting louder. In that sense it was a turning point in the war, but the OHL remained optimistic. They noted that the British had used 'especially good Canadian and Australian troops' who were well rested and admirably trained. The French were also exceptionally well trained. Surprise attacks by tanks had caused widespread panic, and many tanks had been able to drive right through the artillery positions without a shot being fired against them. Proper training in anti-tank warfare would ensure that such mistakes were not repeated, and the OHL had full confidence that General Boehn would soon get the situation under control.[45]

On 14 August a meeting was held at GHQ in Spa chaired by the Kaiser. Admiral Hintze, the secretary of state for foreign affairs, informed the meeting that he had been told by Hindenburg that further offensives were not possible and that Germany would now try to wear down the Entente by adopting a defensive strategy. He had suggested that he should draw the political consequences from this assessment of the military situation. Hintze went on to paint a gloomy picture of Germany's predicament. Given their overwhelming superiority in men and matériel the Entente was bound to win the war. Germany's allies were all on the brink of collapse. Austria-Hungary was falling apart and would not be able to continue the war into the New Year; the Bulgarian army was no longer an effective fighting force and the country was financially ruined; Turkey was more of a hindrance than a help to Germany and was concentrating all its efforts on a 'war of plunder and murder' in the Caucasus.

The Kaiser said that the time had come to 'reach an understanding' with the enemy. Chancellor Hertling agreed and suggested that negotiations should begin when the army next had a success on the Western Front. Hindenburg ended the meeting by announcing that that he hoped that the army would remain on French soil and would thus be able 'to impose our will upon the enemy'. Ludendorff insisted that Hindenburg's cautious hope should be changed to read that the army would succeed in remaining in France. Hintze's lame response to this fatuity was to say: 'The political leadership would give way to the ideas of the greatest general that had emerged in the course of the war.'[46]

There were still considerable differences of opinion among Army Group commanders about the appropriate strategy to adopt after the setback on 8 August. General Gallwitz still insisted that a purely defensive strategy would be disastrous and that the army should respond to the enemy's offensives with determined counter-attacks. The German Crown Prince disagreed and argued in favour of a purely defensive strategy. The army should withdraw to the positions it held before the March offensive, with Army Groups Crown Prince Rupprecht and Boehn retiring to the Siegfried Line and Army Group German Crown Prince to the Hunding, Brunhild and Argonne Lines.

The final absurdity was that in March the OHL had announced that only if the German Army went on the offensive could the war be won. Now in August they were claiming that a defensive strategy would bring the final victory.

Conclusion

In spite of the astonishing successes scored by the German Army in 1918 their last great gamble failed. In the four months from March to July they advanced far further than any army had previously been able to on the Western Front. The British Fifth Army was destroyed, and the French suffered a humiliating defeat on the Chemin des Dames. At times it seemed that the Channel ports, vital to the supply of the British Army, might fall and that Paris might have to be abandoned. The British believed that their French allies were close to capitulation, the French that the British would pack their bags and go home. But at the end of the day the Allied Armies recovered their balance and in two counter-attacks in July and August seized the initiative. During the Hundred Days from August to November they delivered a series of tactical blows in quick succession that finally brought the war to an end on 11 November. The Allies managed to hang on in the face of a series of ferocious attacks and their grim determination brought them final victory.

From the very beginning of the war voices had been raised doubting that Germany could possibly win against such overwhelming odds. Field Marshal Gottlieb von Haeseler was convinced that with the failure of the Schlieffen Plan Germany should seek to end the war. Some dismissed such talk as the ramblings of a seventy-eight-year-old who should never have been taken out of retirement, but Moltke's successor Falkenhayn came to the conclusion after the dreadful butchery at Langemarck in November 1914 that Germany could not emerge from the war victorious. The Kaiser began to mutter about dying with honour, and Falkenhayn speculated about a third Punic War. By 1918 most responsible senior commanders saw no alternative to a negotiated peace.

Hindenburg and Ludendorff had won great victories in the East and when they were appointed to the High Command in August 1916 they were convinced that they could have similar successes on the Western Front. As Colonel von Thaer shrewdly observed, the 'Eastern Warriors' and 'Victors in Italy' were bubbling over with confidence. The hardened 'Westerners' were deeply sceptical.

Talk of a Punic War was hardly surprising from staff officers brought up worshipping at the shrine of Count Alfred von Schlieffen who took the Battle of Cannae as a model engagement. The comparison between Ludendorff and Hannibal is instructive. Both were soldiers of genius, iron-willed tactical masters who won brilliant battles but lost wars. Both claimed to have been stabbed in the back by niggardly politicians, Hannibal with justification, Ludendorff without. Ludendorff proved unable to translate his tactical successes into an operational breakthrough; Hannibal possessed to the full this essential prerequisite of great generalship.

Ludendorff was perfectly correct in insisting that in trench warfare tactics came first. Without a tactical breakthrough nothing could be achieved operationally. A breakthrough on the scale of the 'Michael' offensive had never been attempted before. He attacked on an eighty-kilometre front having made meticulous preparations, and the initial success was spectacular. His great mistake was to refuse to think beyond the tactical level. He weakened the main attack and carried out subsidiary attacks with excessive forces in order to exploit an immediate short-term advantage. This failing he repeated again and again. During 'Michael' 17th and 2nd Armies, which faced stiff opposition in the Cambrai salient, were weakened in order to lend weight to von Hutier's 18th Army which was advancing rapidly against light forces. The end result was that the Germans found themselves defending a greatly extended front with seriously weakened forces. Within two weeks the German Army lost 250,000 men. These were the highest losses ever, and they could barely be replaced. The initial success of the offensives on the Aisne in May and June led Ludendorff to lose sight of the offensive in Flanders for which these were designed as preliminaries in order to draw French troops away from the 'Hagen' front.

After the war Ludendorff blamed Colonel Wetzell, the chief of his operations staff, for the failure of the offensive. He had always argued in favour of a 'hammer blow' strategy in which the German Army would launch a series of powerful attacks in rapid succession until the enemy was exhausted. There was, however, a decisive difference of opinion between the two men as to what could be achieved by these means. In November 1917 Wetzell believed that it might be possible to achieve a 'decisive success' by a series of attacks. At the same meeting on 11 November at Mons where Wetzell put forward these ideas Ludendorff had insisted that the German Army would only be able to mount one offensive around Saint Quentin. As soon as it was obvious that 'Michael' would not lead to a decisive victory Wetzell felt that the most that could be hoped for was to wear the Allies down sufficiently until they were prepared to negotiate a compromise peace. Ludendorff by contrast clung to the fantastic illusion that Germany could win such a resounding victory by these means that extensive annexations would possible. As early as 19 August 1917 he had told von Kuhl on the telephone that if Germany were to give up claims to Belgium they could have peace at any time. Even this claim was highly dubious.

Ludendorff's tactical considerations were thus determined by a belief that it would be possible to achieve an overwhelming victory, a '*Siegfrieden*', even though there were no rational grounds for believing that it would be possible. A sober assessment of the military situation was impossible as long as Hindenburg and Ludendorff stuck to their fantastic political demands. Any efforts to make them see reason were dismissed out of hand. All that was needed, they argued, was to keep up the pressure and the enemy would collapse. They assured their bewildered and frustrated staff that that was precisely what had happened in Russia.

Although initially a tremendous success, 'Michael' failed to separate the British and French Armies. The British had lost their Fifth Army, but they were still in the war, fighting clumsily but with impressive determination. The Germans now found themselves defending a front that was sixty kilometres longer against superior artillery and air power. Supply problems across the old Somme battlefields were exceedingly difficult to overcome.

'Georgette' on the Lys delivered yet another severe blow against the British Army, but the Germans were unable to exploit it operationally and once again could not deliver a knockout punch. The German Army suffered heavy casualties that could not be replaced and its front was further extended. Much the same was true of the Chemin des Dames offensive which sent the French reeling but left the Germans dangerously exposed to flank attack in a deep salient. It failed in its main objective of drawing reserves away from Flanders and that meant that 'Hagen' had to be postponed. The attack either side of Reims also failed to attract significant numbers of Allied troops from Flanders and the prospects for 'Hagen' grew even dimmer. Ludendorff then began to pin his hopes on an offensive towards Paris, but he was now living in a fantasy world. By July the German Army on the Western Front had 883,000 less men than it had had in March, ten divisions had been dissolved, and the remainder were seriously under strength. With the Mangin offensive in July it was obvious to clear-sighted officers like Lossberg that the German Army would have to retire and adopt a defensive stance. Ludendorff, with his totally unrealistic political ambitions and his reluctance to lose the initiative, refused. He was not alone in his refusal to face the bitter truth that the war could not possibly be won, but the number of his supporters was rapidly dwindling. Crown Prince Rupprecht summed up the situation very well when he remarked that some officers simply refused to face the truth, while others were afraid to admit it.

The major problem facing commanders on the Western Front was to integrate firepower and movement. The Germans brought the rolling barrage close to perfection and thus enabled the infantry to move forward behind a protective screen of artillery. The infantry also brought their own firepower with them in the form of light machine-guns, mortars, grenades and flame-throwers. But this only partially solved the problem. Once the initial breakthrough was achieved it was a painfully slow business to bring the artillery and supplies forward and the attack necessarily lost momentum. The troops were left in pockets without artillery protection and vulnerable to counter-attack. Storm-troopers reached the limits of their endurance after about four days of intense fighting. It was not until September that the Allies were able partially to solve the problem by using tanks on a large scale. The 500-odd tanks used at Villers-Cotterêts and Amiens were enough to cause initial confusion, but losses were very heavy and they could not be effectively used in the days that followed. In both instances the Germans were in very weak temporary positions that were wholly inadequate for an effective defence. Only in late September when some 1,500 tanks were used was there sufficient weight to keep up the momentum, and they were used against an army that was demoralized by the failure of an offensive in which they had placed such high hopes. The Germans were eventually to solve the problem of keeping up the momentum of storm-trooper tactics by creating the Panzer Divisions, which could penetrate the enemy lines by as much as 60 kilometres in one day.

A further problem was one of command. In the German Army considerable discretion was left to commanders on the spot, down to NCO level. This emphasis on 'Mission Tactics' (*Auftragtaktik*) gave the German Army great flexibility and encouraged innovation and initiative. The rigidity of the top-down British system, by which orders were issued by senior commanders who had no idea of what was actually happening at the front, was avoided. But the German system created its own problems. Command from the front line all too often meant the pursuit of immediate tactical advantage at the expense of a clear operational concept. The sheer scale of operations on the Western Front coupled with miserably poor communications resulted in a further subordination of strategy to tactics. All too often the advantages of this delegation of authority were offset by Ludendorff's increasing tendency to meddle with tactical minutiae, even down to the battalion level.

In such circumstances it was folly to think in terms of a shattering victory which would make it possible to achieve wildly exotic war aims. Clemenceau got it just about right when he told the Chamber of Deputies two weeks before the Germans launched their March offensive that the secret of success was to maintain one's faith in victory a quarter of an hour longer than the adversary. Pétain felt that the Allies should wait for tanks and Americans. General Robertson was not simply an 'echo of 'aig' and no longer believed in the possibility of a major break-though on the Western Front which would lead to the destruction of the German Army in one fell swoop. As late as October 1918 even Haig felt that the Allies were running out of steam and might have to settle for a compromise peace.

The Allied victory in the Hundred Days was the result of setting limited objectives without losing sight of modest operational goals. This was in accordance with Pétain's '*stratégie des gages*' in which the French and British Armies moved forward step by step and abandoned the hope that they could cause a major rupture in the German front.

Germany failed in 1918 not simply because Ludendorff was incapable of thinking beyond the tactical level, and certainly not because the Allies had tanks and the Germans virtually none, but because of the chronic lack of manpower and a desperate shortage of horses and motor vehicles. They were unable to replace the heavy losses sustained in a series of costly offensives without enlisting men from the munitions industry which in turn would mean men without weapons. As it was they had the weapons, but not the men. The British and the French faced similar problems, but fresh American troops were pouring in to Europe at a time when both the size and the quality of the German Army was in serious decline. By the end of June there were about 1 million Americans in France, which about equalled German losses. There were more Americans to come, but virtually no more Germans.

Above all the OHL's war aims made a rational assessment of the mili-tary situation impossible. Until August they could only think in terms of the offensive and simply looked for any excuse, however shallow, to justify yet another offensive. It was always hoped, against all the evidence, that the next blow would be the knockout punch that would result in a 'Hindenburg Peace' which would leave Germany the undisputed master of Europe. Thus there was no military argument against Lossberg's plan in July to withdraw to strong defensive positions and let the Allies wear themselves out in a series of attacks. But even this strategy was only likely to postpone the date of Germany's defeat.

Along with the enormously complicated planning for a series of major offensives Ludendorff was fully engaged in political intrigues. He closely followed the negotiations at Brest-Litovsk and Bucharest. He was involved in detailed discussions over the future of the Ukraine, Poland, Finland and the Baltic States. He secured the dismissal of Valentini, the chief of the civil cabinet, and of Kühlmann, the secretary of state for foreign affairs. He was constantly interfering in the smallest details of domestic politics. It is thus small wonder that he appeared to many senior officers not to be on top of the situation, and the strain eventually proved to much for him. At the end of August he suffered a nervous breakdown. Two months later he resigned after a stormy interview with the Kaiser.

The German Army had a number of brilliant initial successes, but they were unable to maintain the momentum of their offensives for more than five to ten days. Allied resistance was strengthened and morale remained relatively firm in the face of great adversity. The appointment of Foch as generalissimo helped smooth over the tense relationship between the British GHQ and the French GQG, and led to a better deployment of reserves. Foch promptly saw to it that French reserves were sent to prop up a nervous British Army and to help defend the vital communications centre of Amiens. Problems for the Germans were compounded when Pétain's concept of a defence in depth, based on their own model, was finally put into effect in July. Overwhelming Allied superiority in the air was another major factor. German soldiers feared strafing from the air far more than they did tanks, and German airmen were denied Allied airspace that was vital for adequate reconnaisance.

Germany had no alternative but to go on the offensive on the Western Front early in 1918. A defensive strategy would have been tantamount to capitulation. The Allied blockade was beginning to really hurt, and after the gruelling defensive battles of 1917 morale would have cracked had the army taken more of the same for yet another year. The battle had to be fought before the Americans could be brought up to the front in large numbers. Furthermore, the presence of the American Army in France made the Allies far less likely to agree to peace talks. The offensive had to be on the Western Front because a success, however spectacular, in Salonika or in Italy would not have made a decisive difference, any more than had the victory over Russia.

Given the OHL's state of mind there could be no levelheaded discussion of whether or not victory was possible, and the notion of a compromise peace could not be entertained. They were blinded by their conviction that the alternatives facing Germany were *Weltmacht* (world power) or *Niedergang* (extinction), a belief that was shared later by Adolf Hitler. Admiral Tirpitz announced that if Germany did not emerge victorious the Germany people would be little more than 'racial manure' (*Volksdünger*). The politicians had no influence whatsoever over the OHL. The chancellor, Hertling, was a tired old man who was quite incapable of standing up to the demigods in the General Staff, and anyone who met with their displeasure was soon to lose his job.

It is difficult to imagine how a general who proudly announced that he refused to think beyond the tactical level could possibly imagine that he could achieve a decisive victory. With the failure of 'Michael' Ludendorff managed to convince himself that it would be possible to 'soften up' (*zermürben*) the Allies to the point that they would collapse, just as the Russian Empire had fallen apart. This was doubly absurd. The Germans had insufficient means, both in men and materials, to win a war of attrition, and neither Britain nor France was in an advanced state of disintegration as the Russian Empire had been in 1917. Clearer heads among the senior commanders were well of this and argued in favour of a compromise peace. But they were too late. Perhaps some political capital could have been made by a serious peace offer on the eve of 'Michael' as the well-known Swiss military historian Hermann Stegemann had proposed in February 1918, but by the summer it would have been unacceptable.

Germany was doomed to defeat, and the painful realization that this was so resulted in a frantic and highly successful attempt to blame Germany's desperate state on the home front, on the democratic parties and sundry groups from Jews to Jesuits. The 'stab in the back' myth was born of the overbearing hubris of a military elite that refused to abandon its fantastic ambitions and denied the bitter fact that for all their professional skill and tactical brilliance their ingenious plans had come to nothing. Having failed to achieve world power they were determined that the democratic forces which had now gained the upper hand should face extinction. The fearful consequences of this attitude are all too painfully familiar.

Notes

I: THE WESTERN FRONT: FEBRUARY 1917–FEBRUARY 1918

1   Andreas Michelson, *Der U-Bootkrieg 1914-1918*, Leipzig 1925; *Der Krieg zur See 1914-1918*, vol. 3, Berlin 1934; Hans-Jürgen Schwepke, *U-Bootkrieg und Friedenspolitik*, phil diss., Heidelberg, 1952; K.E.Birnbaum, *Peace Moves and U-Boat Warfare. A Study in Imperial Germany's Policy Towards the United States April 18, 1916 – January 9, 1917*, Stockholm 1958; Arno Spindler, *Wie es zu dem Entschluss zum uneingeschränkten U-Bootkrieg 1917 gekommen ist*, Göttingen 1961; Baldur Kaulisch, 'Die Auseinandersetzungen über den uneingeschränkten U-Bootkrieg innerhalb der herrschenden Klassen im zweiten Halbjahr 1916 und seine Eröffnung in Februar 1917', in: *Politik im Krieg 1914-1918*, Berlin 1964.

2   *Der Weltkrieg 1914 bis 1918*, vol. 14, *Die Kriegführung an der Westfront im Jahre 1918*, Berlin 1944, p. 2.

3   Martin Kitchen, *The Silent Dictatorship. The Politics of the German High Command under Hindenburg and Ludendorff, 1916-1918*, London 1976, pp. 59-62. Dirk Stegmann, *Die Erben Bismarcks*, Cologne 1970, p.497. Crown Prince Rupprecht of Bavaria was very concerned with the excessive war aims of the Vaterlandspartei, which he feared would cause the peace negotiations with Russia to drag on dangerously long. Kronprinz Rupprecht, *Mein Kriegstagebuch*, vol. 2, Berlin 1921, p. 310 (6.1.1918).

4   BHSA Kriegsarchiv I Armee Korps 1373.

5   Wilhelm Dittmann, *Erinnerungen*, Frankfurt 1995 pp. 525-534.

6   SKA (Potsdam) 20337: Oberost 30.1.18. Heeresgruppe Linsingen 31.1.18.

7   SKA (Potsdam) HGr. Linsingen 8.2.18.

8   For details of the January strikes in Austria-Hungry see: Richard G.Plaschka, Horst Haelsteiner, Arnold Suppan, *Innere Front. Militärassistenz, Widerstand und Umsturz in der Donaumonarchie 1918*, 2 vols., Vienna 1974 and Ernst Winkler, *Der Große Jänner-Streik*, Vienna 1968.

9   SKA (Potsdam) 12587 Karl Legien 13.3.18.

10   Niall Ferguson, *The Pity of War*, London 1999, p.275.

11   Crown Prince Rupprecht of Bavaria confided this concern to his
      diary on 11 December 1917. Rupprecht, *Kriegstagebuch*, vol. 2, Berlin
      1921, p.302. He was particularly concerned at Prussia's annexationist
      ambitions in the Baltic, which he felt would further diminish Bavaria's
      influence within the German Empire. He was also concerned about
      Ludendorff's insistence that most of Alsace-Lorraine should become
      Prussian.

12   *Weltkrieg*, 14, p.26.

13   SKA Potsdam 20337: Ludendorff 10.2.18. ordered that each infantry
      regiment should have six light mortars, with six one-horse carts
      with forty-four rounds, and six two-horse carts with eighty rounds
      and other equipment. Mortar companies were to have four medium
      mortars on two-horse gun carriages, eight one-horse carts with five
      rounds each, twelve field wagons with ten rounds apiece, two small
      field kitchens, two wagons with food and fodder and one wagon for
      luggage.

14   The Gruppe Dormoise reported to AOK 3rd Army on 20.3.18. that
      one infantry regiment, a mortar company and several transport units
      were unable to move for lack of horses. SKA (Potsdam) 20337.

15   Rupprecht, *Kriegstagebuch*, vol. 2., 31 December noted that the
      Germans were losing 20,000 horses per month and there were virtu-
      ally no replacements. Petroleum was in short supply in part because
      the Danube was frozen and it was thus difficult to transport oil from
      Romania.

16   *Das Werk des Untersuchungsausschusses der Verfassunggebenden Deutschen
      Nationalversammlung und des Deutschen Reichstages 1919-1928, Vierte
      Reihe, Die Ursachen des Deutschen Zusammenbruches im Jahre 1918, vol. 3,
      Gutachten der Sachverständigen General d. Inf.a.D. von Kuhl und Geheimrat
      Prof.Dr.Hans Delbrück, 'Entstehung, Durchführung und Zusammenbruch
      der Offensive von 1918'*, Berlin 1928, pp.80-81. Henceforth cited as von
      Kuhl.

17   Wolfgang Schneider and Rainer Strasheim, *German Tanks in World War
      I. The A7V and Early Tank Development*, West Chester Pennsylvania,
      1990.

18   *Der Weltkrieg*, vol. 14, p.37.

19   R.G.Binding, *A Fatalist at War*, London 1929, p.202.

20   *Weltkrieg*, 14, p.15.

21   Leo Haupts, *Deutsche Friedenspolitik 1918-19*, Düsseldorf, 1976, p.146.

22   Fritz Fischer, *Griff nach der Weltmacht*, Düsseldorf 1964, p.828.

23   For the situation in Romania see: *von Kuhl*, pp.10-16.

24   Winfried Baumgart, *Deutsche Ostpolitik 1918*, Munich 1966; John S.
      Reshetar, *The Ukrainian Revolution 1917-1920. A Study in Nationalism*,
      Princeton 1952, Peter Borowsky, *Deutsche Ukrainepolitik 1918*, Lübeck
      and Hamburg 1970; Orlando Figes, *A People's Tragedy. The Russian
      Revolution 1891-1924*, London 1996, pp.548/9.

25   *von Kuhl*, p.25.

26   This point is argued forcefully by Hans Delbrück in: *Die Ursachen des*

Deutschen Zusammenbruchs im Jahre 1918, vol. 3, Berlin 1928, p.252.

27 General Rüdiger von der Goltz, *Meine Sendung in Finnland und im Baltikum*, Leipzig 1920; J.O.Hannula, *Finland's War of Independence*, London 1929; G. Mannerheim, *Erinnerungen*, Zurich 1952; Erkki Räikkönen, *Svinhufvud baut Finnland*, Munich 1936; M.G. Schybergson, *Politische Geschichte Finnlands 1809-1919*, Gotha und Stuttgart 1925; C. Jay Smith Jr., *Finland and the Russian Revolution 1917-1922*, Athens, Georgia 1958; W. Hubatsch, 'Finnland in der deutschen Ostseepolitik 1917/18', *Ostdeutsche Wissenschaft*, Band 11, 1955.

28 Manfried Rauchensteiner, *Der Tod des Doppeladlers. Österreich-Ungarn und der Erste Weltkrieg*, Graz, Vienna, Cologne 1994.

29 August von Cramon, *Unserer Österreich-Ungarischer Bundesgenosse im Weltkriege*, Berlin 1920, p.148. In these memoirs Cramon insists that the OHL should have stood firm as Austria had ten divisions that could have been sent to the Western Front where they could have been used on quiet sections of the front.

30 *Weltkrieg*, vol. 14, p.41.

31 'Der Angriff im Stellungskriege und einige Verfügungen, die in den Erfahrungen über den Angriff ihren Niederschlag finden', in: Erich Ludendorff, *Urkunden der Obersten Heeresleitung über ihre Tätigkeit 1916/18,* Berlin 1920, pp. 641-686.

32 SKA (Potsdam) 20337: Ludendorff 9.2.18.

33 Binding, *Fatalist*, p.201.

34 SKA (Potsdam) 20337: 8.2.18 Headquarters 3rd Army designated 5th, 33rd and 52nd Jäger Divisions, 1st Bavarian Jäger Division and 51st Reserve Division. Only the commanders were informed of this decision and were ordered to keep the information secret.

35 SKA (Potsdam) 20337. HGr, German Crown Prince 27.2.18.

36 SKA (Potsdam) 20337: HGr. German Crown Prince 4.2.18.

37 SKA (Potsdam) 20337: report from Army Group German Crown Prince 7.2.18.

38 Ludendorff constantly emphasized this point. SKA (Potsdam) 20337 9.2.18.

39 Rupprecht, *Kriegstagebuch*, vol.2, p.307.

40 Ludendorff, *Urkunden der OHL*, p.648.

41 Max Hoffmann, *Die Aufzeichnungnen des Generalmajors Max Hoffmann*, vol. 2, Berlin 1929, p. 171ff. At another point Hoffmann states that Ludendorff did not talk of a decisive battle at this meeting, but merely intended to seek out the weak point on the enemy's front, p. 316.

42 *Weltkrieg*, vol. 14, p.51 The Americans had 254,378 troops in France by the end of February 1918.

43 Kuhl Diary 1.11.17. Kuhl accused Wetzell of engaging in 'Pointless attacks' (*nutzloses Bataillieren*).

44 Kuhl Diary 6.11.17.

45 *Weltkrieg*, vol. 14, p.52.

46 von Kuhl, p.100.

47 Details in Kuhl's diary entry 11 November 1917. See *Weltkrieg* , vol. 14, p.53. Rupprecht, *Kriegstagebuch*, vol. 2, pp. 284-287. von Kuhl, p.101 describes himself in the third person and provides few details of his

presentation.

48 Erich Ludendorff, *Die überstaatlichen Mächte im letzten Jahre des Weltkrieges*, p.14.

49 Rupprecht, vol. 2, p. 285-6.

50 *Weltkrieg*, vol. 14, p.55.

51 It would seem that the Crown Prince had little to do with the planning: Rupprecht, *Kriegstagebuch*, vol. 2, p. 290 where he mentions that the plans were forwarded to the OHL but makes no mention of their content.

52 *Der Weltkrieg* 14, p.56.

53 SKA (Potsdam) 20337: 2nd Inf. Div. Report 18.2.18. 52nd Reserve Division also seconded this suggestion.

54 Von Kuhl Diary 14.12.17.

55 *Weltkrieg* vol. 14, p. 59. Von Kuhl diary 19 December 1917, von Kuhl, pp. 113-114.

56 Both 'George' and 'Michael' appeared sometimes as saints and sometimes not in these early planning stages.

2: PLANS FOR THE SPRING OFFENSIVE: DECEMBER 1917–MARCH 1918

1 Brigadier-General Sir James E. Edmonds, *History of the Great War. Military Operations in France and Belgium, 1918*, London 1935, p.143.

2 von Hutier Diary 12.12.17.

3 von Hutier Diary 31.12.17.

4 Hindenburg, *Aus meinem Leben*, p.327.

5 von Kuhl Diary 3.2.18. Pulkowski insisted that lengthy preparatory barrages should be avoided.

6 *Weltkrieg* vol 14, p.63; von Krafft, diary 14.12.1917.

7 *Weltkrieg* 14, p.66.

8 von Kuhl Diary 31.12.17.

9 '*Das ist gut gesagt!*'

10 von Kuhl Diary 2.1.18.

11 von Hutier Diary 1.1.18.

12 von Hutier Diary 4.1.18.

13 General Buat criticized Ludendorff for not mounting diversionary attacks in 1918 in his *Ludendorff* p.282. Ludendorff replied in his *Kriegführung und Politik*, Berlin 1922, p.216 that the OHL would have liked nothing better but lacked the means for anything other than some deceptive moves along the length of the front. These, he claimed, were successful.

14 Kuhl Diary 22.1.1918.

15 Rupprecht, *Kriegstagebuch*, vol.2, p.312, 8.1.1918. The Germans noticed that some British batteries had been pulled back.

16 Rupprecht, *Kriegstagebuch*, vol.2, p.313, 10.1.1918.

17 von Kuhl Diary 6.1.18., 8.1.18 and 10.1.18.

18 Krafft von Dellmensingen, *Der Durchbruch*, Hamburg 1937 pp.163 ff. Crown Prince Rupprecht considered Krafft to be 'one of our best

generals with the most experience of offensive warfare'. *Kriegstagebuch*, vol.2. p.315 (15.1.1918).

19 Fritz von Loßberg, *Meine Tätigkeit im Weltkrieg 1914-18*, Berlin 1939, p.320.

20 Rupprecht, *Kriegstagebuch*, vol. 2., p. 317 (17.1.1918) von Kuhl Diary 22.1.18.

21 *ibid.*, p.319 (19.1.1918).

22 Kuhl diary 22.1.18. Ludendorff *Erinnerungen* pp. 473 ff.

23 Ludendorff, *Erinnerungen* p. 475. Kuhl's diary entry is followed by two exclamation marks which could be interpreted as a degree of amazement and frustration that 18th Army had been taken from his army group.

24 Ludendorff, *Kriegserinnerungen*, p 474.

25 Hindenburg used the word *'gelegentlich'*.

26 von Kuhl, pp.118-9.

27 Rupprecht, *Kriegstagebuch*, vol. 2., p.322 (21.1.1918).

28 *ibid.*, p.323.

29 von Kuhl Diary.

30 Rupprecht, *Kriegstagebuch*, vol. 2., p.326 (2.2.1918).

31 von Kuhl Diary 8.2.18.

32 von Kuhl, p.68.

33 Max Bauer, *Der große Krieg in Feld und Heimat*, Tübingen 1921; , G.D. Feldman, *Army, Industry and Labor in Germany, 1914-1918*, Princeton 1966.

34 von Kuhl Diary 9.2.18.

35 von Kuhl Diary 10.2.18.

36 von Kuhl Diary 9.2.18.

37 von Kuhl Diary 13.2.18.

38 *Weltkrieg* 14 p. 83.

39 Rupprecht, *Kriegstagebuch*, vol. 2., p.329-330.

40 Rupprecht noted in his diary on 1.1.18 that a number of Flemish soldiers had deserted complaining of being called *'Boches'* and *'sales Flamins'* by their officers. *ibid.*, p.309.

41 *ibid.*, pp.330-332 (19.2.1918).

42 *Ursachen*, vol. 2. pp.136-139.

43 Krafft, *Der Durchbruch*, p. 174.

44 Edmonds, p.146 argues that the experience on the Aisne in 1914 showed that an advance beyond the river and canal 'obviously was the better tactical choice'.

45 *Weltkrieg*, 14, pp.85-6.

46 Wetzell unconvincingly claims that this was the only time that he had a serious difference of opinion with Ludendorff. (Letter to von Seeckt 24 July 1919 quoted in *Weltkrieg*, 14 p.87).

47 von Kuhl Diary 23.3.18.

48 Position paper by Colonel Bernhard von Schwertfeger in: *Die Ursachen des Deutschen Zusammenbruches im Jahre 1918*, vol. 2., Berlin 1925, pp.96-99.

49 Rupprecht, *Kriegstagebuch*, vol.2, p.343 (20.3.1918).

50 Nothing had occurred to relieve Crown Prince Rupprecht's pessimism. On the eve of the attack his chief of general staff, General von

Kuhl, was extremely pessimistic about the outcome of the offensive. Colonel Schulenburg, chief of general staff to Army Group German Crown Prince, prophetically told Major (later General) Beck that at the end of battle they would be worse off than before, and then the Americans would arrive. *Weltkrieg* 14, pp. 92-93.

51   Bind, *Fatalist*, p. 204.

52   Hans Spiess to his sister 12.2.18 in: Bernd Ulrich and Benjamin Ziemann (eds), *Frontalltag im Ersten Weltkrieg. Quellen und Dokumente*, Frankfurt 1994, p.185. Hans Spiess survived 'Michael' but was killed by a shot through the heart on 22 October 1918.

53   Gerhard Ritter *Staatskunst und Kriegshandwerk*, vol. 4, Munich 1968, p. 283.

3: THE ALLIES: JANUARY–MARCH 1918

1   CAB 23/5 DMO 2.1.18. CIGS 7.1.18. CIGS 22.1.18. DMI 1.2.18.

2   CAB 23/5 CIGS 15.1.18.

3   CAB 23/13 War Cabinet 7.1.18

4   CAB 23/5 DMI 1.2.18. DMI 11.2.18.CIGS 21.1.18

5   Tim Travers, *How the War was Won. Command and Technology in the British Army on the Western Front 1917-1918*, London and New York 1992, p. 31.

6   SHAT 16N 3266 Pershing was also invited to the meeting.

7   Lord Hankey, *The Supreme Command 1914-1918*, vol.2, London 1961, p.801.

8   Travers, *How the War was Won*, p. 34.

9   SHAT 16N 1691.

10   Keith Graves, 'Total War? The Quest for a British Manpower Policy 1917-1919', *Journal of Strategic Studies*, 9,1,March 1986. David Woodward, 'Did Lloyd George Starve the British Army of Men Prior to the German Offensive of 21 March 1918?', *Historical Journal*, 27, 1, 1984 Travers, *How the War Was Won*, p.36.

11   Travers, *How the War was Won*, p. 44.

12   AFGG vol. 6. Part 1, pp. 90-91.

13   CAB 23/5 CIGS 7.2.18.

14   The decision to establish a Supreme War Council was made at a meeting in Rapallo in November 1917. The Allies were represented by Foch (France), Wilson (Britain), Cadorna (Italy) and Bliss (USA). Weygand replaced Foch at the end of the month. Wilson was appointed CIGS in February. *Les Armées Françaises dans la Grande Guerre*, vol.6 part 1, Paris 1931 pp. 14-25 (henceforth AFGG).

15   Sir James Edmonds, *Military Operations. France and Belgium*,1918, vol. 1, pp.72-73.

16   Jean-Baptiste Duroselle, *La Grande Guerre des Français 1914-1918*, Paris 1994.

17   Hankey, *Supreme Command*, p.830.

18   Robert Blake (ed.), *The Private Papers of Douglas Haig*, London 1952, 283.

19   AFGG vol. 6, part 1, pp.61-65.

20   Tim Travers, *How the War Was Won*. Robin Prior and Trevor Wilson,
        Passchendaele: The Untold Story, New Haven 1996.

21   Edmonds, pp. 77-78.

22   *ibid.*, p.81.

23   *ibid.*, pp.92-93.

24   *ibid.*, p.94.

25   Anthony Farrar-Hockley, *Goughie: The Life of General Sir Hubert Gough
        CGB, GCMG, KCVO*, London 1975 pp.255-257.

26   *ibid.*, p.259.

27   WO 256/28 Derby to Haig 5.3.18.

28   *ibid.*, p.263.

29   *ibid.*, p.265.

30   *ibid.*, p.270.

31   SHAT G.Q.G. 3e Bureau 3042. Pétain's staff had initially suggested
        thirty divisions, but this he corrected with the note: 'plus de 30, plutôt
        40'.

32   AFGG pp.70-71.

33   Guy Pedroncini, *Pétain général en chef (1917-1918)*, Paris 1997 pp.274-5.

34   AFGG Vol. 6 Annexe 202. 'G.Q.G. directive no 4 pour les groupes
        d'armées, 22759, 22 décembre 1917.

35   See the remarks by 3e Bureau on 21 January in SHAT GQG 3e
        Bureau 3042. The French liked to emphasize that they were defend-
        ing their homeland, and the British were not.

36   SHAT 16N 3266 Clemenceau to Pétain 8.2.18.

37   Farrar-Hockley, *Goughie*, p.272.

38   Pedroncini, *Pétain*, p.288. Edmonds, p.104.

39   CAB 23/5 DMI 26.2.18. DMO 28.2.18. CIGS 1.3.18. CIGS 4.3.18.
        and 5.3.18.

40   WO 256/28 Haig diary entry for 2.3.1918.

41   Edmonds pp.114-115.

42   AFGG vol. 6.1 pp.81-82.

43   PRO/CAB 24/39 Robertson 15.1.18.

44   General Sir Hubert Gough, *The Fifth Army*, London 1931, p.222.

45   Edmonds, p.99.

46   Travers, *How the War was Won*, p. 36.

47   Gough, *op. cit.*, pp.232-3.

48   Winter, *op. cit.*, p. 181.

49   WO 256/38 DMO report for CIGS 27.5.18.

50   See the report by the Staff College Tour examining the Western Front
        in March 1918 in WO 95/521. In one instance 21st. Division with-
        drew ninety minutes before 9th. Division so that 9th. Division was
        promptly turned.

51   The Cambrai Court of Enquiry report is in WO158/53. The report on
        Hutier's tactics a Riga on 3.9.1917 are in CAB 25/6. Haig's staff argued
        that such methods could not be used on the Western Front and would
        have to be drastically modified. The Court of Enquiry only examined
        the reasons for the British Army's failure. The 'lessons' were drawn later
        and emphasized that German success depended on an intense initial
        barrage, surprise, weight of attack and stormtroop tactics.

52   Travers, *How the War Was Won*, p.31.

53   Travers, *How the War Was Won*, p.53.

54   Edmonds, pp.122–123.

55   Edmonds, p.126.

56   Travers, *How the War Was Won* , p.40. Fuller as a tank man detested
        Butler who had little time for this newfangled weapon and believed
        in men not machines.

57   CAB 23/5 Director of Military Intelligence (DMI) report 21.3.18.

58   CAB 23/5 CIGS 6.3.18.

59   CAB 23/5 CIGS 12.3.18.

60   WO 256/28 Report on Doullens Conference 2.3.18.

61   Haig Diary 17.3.18

62   See the report of General Laguiche, head of the French Mission to
        GHQ, to Pétain 3.3.18 quoted in AFGG vol.6.1. pp.219–220.

63   WO 256/28 Haig 5.3.18.

64   WO 256/28 Haig 8.3.18.

65   WO 256/28 Report on Meeting 14.3.18.

66   WO 256/28 Haig 17.3.18.

67   CAB 23/5 CIGS 21.3.18.

68   WO 256/28 Haig 21.3.18.

69   CAB 23/5 CIGS 22.3.18.

4: 'MICHAEL': THE FIRST PHASE 21–23 MARCH

1   *Weltkrieg* 14, pp. 102–103.

2   Bibliothek für Zeitgeschichte, Stuttgart (BZS) Paul Knoch papers, let-
        ters home 29.3.18 and 7.4.18.

3   *Weltkrieg* 14, p.104.

4   David T. Zabecki, *Steel Wind: Colonel Georg Bruchmüller and the Birth of
        Modern Artillery*, Westport 1994.

5   Edmonds, pp. 159–160.

6   *Weltkrieg*, 14, appendix 39a.

7   Binding, *Fatalist*, p.205.

8   *Weltkrieg* , 14, p.126.

9   Farrar-Hockley, *Goughie*, p.278.

10   Edmonds, p.167.

11   Edmond, p.208; Pedroncini, p.295.

12   AFGG vol. 6, part 1, pp235–237.

13   Terence Denman, *Ireland's Unknown Soldiers: The 16th (Irish) Division in
        the Great War*, Dublin 1992, pp. 153–170. Denman defends the Division
        against attacks by Haig who wrote: 'Certain Irish units did very badly
        and gave way immediately the enemy showed.' Their corps com-
        mander Sir Walter Congreve said: 'The real truth is that their reserve
        brigade did not fight at all and their right brigade very indiffer-
        ently…' Some attributed their poor performance to their being politi-
        cally undermined. One battalion was greeted at the rear with cries of
        'There go the Sinn Feiners!'. An investigation of the performance of
        Irish troops by CIGS concluded that there was no evidence that they

had not fought well, but pointed out that only two-thirds of the men were of Irish birth. The performance of 16th Division had immediate bearing on the question of introducing conscription in Ireland.

14   WO 256/28 Haig 23.3.18.

15   Farrar-Hockley, *Goughie*, pp. 278, 291, 302.

16   Rupprecht, *Kriegstagebuch*, vol.2, p.345 (21.1918).

17   To add further confusion there were two von Belows as Army commanders in March 1918. Otto von Below commanded 17th Army, Fritz von Below 1st Army.

18   Rupprecht, *Kriegstagebuch*, vol.2, p.348 (22.3.18).

19   Walter Görlitz, *The Kaiser and his Court. The Diaries, Note books and Letters of Admiral Georg Alexander von Müller Chief of the Naval Cabinet 1914-1918*, New York 1964, p. 344.

20   *Weltkrieg* 14, pp. 142-143.

21   WO 256/28 Haig Diary 23.3.18.

22   Edmonds, p.265.

23   Travers, *How the War Was Won*, p.78.

24   *Weltkrieg* 14, p. 145.

25   AFGG vol. 6, part 1, pp. 245-248. According to an agreement in February the French agreed initially to send seven infantry and three cavalry divisions, along with twelve regiments of artillery to support the British. Five more infantry divisions were to follow as quickly as possible. SHAT 16N 3266 14.2.18.

26   Edmonds pp. 327-328; 371.

27   Jean-Baptiste Duroselle, *La Grande Guerre des Français*, p.356.

28   Hankey, *Supreme Command*, p.786.

29   SHAT Conseil Supérieur de Guerre (Etat-Major de l'armee; Groupe de l'Avant; 2e Bureau): 21.3.18.

30   Edmonds, p.368.

31   Edmonds, p.368. Travers, *How the War Was Won*, p.76.

32   Edmonds, p.420.

33   Army Group German Crown Prince to von Hutier on the evening of 22 March, quoted in *Weltkrieg* 14, p.157.

34   von Kuhl, p.133.

35   Görlitz, *The Kaiser and his Court*, p.344.

5: 'MICHAEL': THE SECOND PHASE 24-26 MARCH

1   *Weltkrieg* 14, pp.167-8.

2   Rupprecht's concerns to this effect in *Kriegstagebuch*, vol. 2, p 351 (23.3.18).

3   Hermann Josef von Kuhl, *Entstehung, Durchführung und Zusammenbruch der Offensive von 1918*, Berlin 1927.

4   BZS Paul Knoch papers, letters home 29.3.18 and 7.4.18.

5   *Weltkrieg* 14, p.175.

6   Edmonds, pp.404-409.

7   *Weltkrieg* 14, p.180.

8   Hankey, *Supreme Command* , p. 286.

9   Wetzell to Rupprecht on evening of 24 March. Rupprecht,
        Kriegstagebuch, vol. 2, p.354-355 (25-26.3.18).

10   Krafft Diary, 24.3.18.

11   *ibid.*, p. 355.

12   von Kuhl Diary 26.3.18.

13   SHAT 3e Bureau 3023 for orders alerting the various Divisions.

14   Edmonds, p.449.

15   CAB 23/5 DMO (Maurice) 25.3.18. and 26.5.18.

16   Pedroncini, pp.305-306.

17   AFGG vol. 6, part 1, pp.270-272.

18   Zeller, *Foch* p.56 quoted in Pedroncini, p.319.

19   Wilson, *op. cit.*, p.567 describes Haig as 'unshaken by misfortune' while
        'Pétain's resolution seemed to be crumbling' and suffered a 'failure
        of nerve'. Randolph York Holmes in: *The March Retreat of 1918: an
        Anatomy of a Battle*, Ph.D. University of Washington 1966, p.347 waxes
        even more eloquent: 'The same characteristics which kept Haig bat-
        tering away at Third Ypres and the Somme, courage, faith and desper-
        ate want of imagination' kept him going 'in a sea of troubles'.

20   Winter, *op.cit.*, p.185.

21   Edmonds, p.448.

22   WO 158.

23   CAB 45/192.

24   Travers, *How the War was Won*, p. 54.

25   Binding, *Fatalist*, p.215.

26   Edmonds, p.493 and pp.511-517.

27   WO 158/28 Haig to Weygand 25.3.18.

28   Rupprecht, *Kriegstagebuch*, vol.2, p. 357 (26.3.18).

29   Görlitz, *The Kaiser and his Court*, p.345 Contemplating this scene
        many years later Admiral Müller attributed this extraordinary outburst
        to the Kaiser having lost his mental balance as a result of a long and
        nervewracking war.

30   Rupprecht, *Kriegstagebuch*, vol.2, p. 359.

31   von Kuhl Diary 27.3.18.

32   Hermann von Kuhl, *Der Weltkrieg 1914-1918*, Berlin 1929, vol. 2, pp.
        340-1.

33   Binding, *Fatalist*, p. 207.

34   Hankey, *Supreme Command*, p. 787.

35   Binding, *Fatalist*, p.209, writing on 28.3.18.

36   See the history of 3 Garde-Regiment z. F. (Tagebuch Loebell) quoted
        in Wilhelm Deist, 'Verdeckter Militärstreik im Kriegsjahr 1918' in
        *Wolfram Wette (ed.) Der Krieg des kleinen Mannes. Eine Militärgeschichte
        von unten, Munich 1995*. See also from the same author: 'Auf dem Weg
        zur ideologisierten Kriegführung: Deutschland 1918-1945' in Wilhelm
        Deist, *Militär, Staat und Gesellschaft. Studien zur preußisch-deutschen
        Militärgeschichte*, Munich 1991; 'Der militärische Zusammenbruch
        des Kaiserreichs. Zur Realität der 'Dolchstoßlegende" in Ursula
        Bittner (ed.), *Das Unrechtsregime. Internationale Forschung über den
        Nationalsozialismus*, vol 1, *Ideologie, Herrschaftssystem, Wirkung in Europa*,
        Hamburg 1986. For an overview of the problem of morale in the

German Army during the war: Friedrich Altvater, *Die seelischen Kräfte des Deutschen Heeres im Frieden und im Weltkriege*, Berlin 1933.

37   Benjamin Ziemann, 'Enttäuschte Erwartung und kollektive Erschöpfung' in' Jörg Duppler and Gerhard P. Gross, *Kriegsende 1918. Ereignis, Wirkung, Nachwirkung*, Munich 1999, p.170.

38   Binding, *Fatalist*, p.209.

39   WO157/218 26.3.18.

40   Pedroncini, p.324.

41   Edmonds, p.76.

42   Loucheur, the French Minister for Munitions, agreed with Clemenceau. At the Doullens conference he said: 'Je vous ai toujours dit, monsieur le president, que c'etait un rude bougre.' *L'Illustration*, 24.3.28.

43   CAB 23/5 Milner to War Cabinet 26.3.18 reporting on the conference. The War Cabinet immediately approved the measure.

44   Edmonds, p.542.

45   CAB 45/177 A.A. Montgomery-Massiongbird 19.11.25.

46   CAB 45/177 Lawrence to Edmonds 21.5.18.

47   CAB 45/177 Milner in '*New Statesman*' 23.4.21 writing on the Doullens Conference.

48   CAB 45/177 GHQ's version of the Doullens Conference 26.3.18.

49   Farrar-Hockley, *Goughie*, p.305.

50   Edmonds II, p. 8.

51   Pedroncini, p.339 and Edmonds II, p.5.

52   AFGG vol. 6, part 1, pp.341-342.

6: 'GEORGETTE': THE FIRST PHASE 9–14 APRIL

1   Ulrich and Ziemann, *Frontalltag*, quoting a graphic letter home by Franz Xavier Bergler 12.4.18. He was killed later that day.

2   SKA (Potsdam) 20337: Report on visit by an officer from Army Group German Crown Prince to 18th Army 28-30.3.18.

3   *Weltkrieg*, 14, pp.260-1.

4   FO371/3213 6.4.18. George V made the suggestion on 14,4,18 to meet the eventuality of both Amiens and Le Havre falling into German hands.

5   SHAT 15N 10 GOGA Etat-Major Haig to Foch 6.4.18.

6   SHAT 15N 10 GOGA Etat-Major Wilson to Foch 7.4.18.

7   CAB 112/80 7.4.18.

8   Albrecht von Thaer, *Generalstabsdienst an der Front und in der OHL*, ed. Siegfried Kaehler, Göttingen 1958 p.181.

9   von Kuhl, pp.146-7.

10   von Kuhl diary, 4.4.18.

11   *Weltkrieg* 14, p.268.

12   The codename 'Blücher' was later used for the offensive on the Chemin des Dames.

13   Edmonds II, p.139.

14   WO 256/29 Haig Diary 5.4.18.

15   WO 256/29 Haig to Foch 6.4.18.

16   Edmonds II, p.142.

17   WO 256/29 Haig Diary 8.4.18.

18   WO 256/29 Haig Diary 9.4.18.

19   My father, who served on the Lys front, and was seriously wounded in the 'Georgette' offensive, told of a regimental order which read as follows: 'Gentlemen of the Regiment are reminded to refer to the Portuguese as "our gallant allies"; and not as "them fucking Pork and Beans"!'

20   Edmonds II, p.147.

21   *Weltkrieg* 14, p.304.

22   WO 158/75 Report 31.5.18. by XI Corps, First Army, on the conduct of the Portuguese during the battle.

23   Von Hutier Diary 9.4.18.

24   SKA (Dresden) 4212: XIX AK report on fighting on 9.4.18 written 29.4.18.

25   Binding, *Fatalist*, p.217.

26   Edmonds II, p.189.

27   CAB 23/6, 9.4.18.

28   CAB 23/6, 10.4.18.

29   SHAT 15N 10 GOGA Etat-Major Haig to Foch 10.4.18. WO 158/72 The French moved four divisions north-west of Amiens on 9.4.18. and on 12.4.18. agreed that they would be sent north-east if necessary.

30   AFGG vol. 6, part 1, p. 432.

31   Pedroncini, *Pétain*, p.349.

32   Edmonds II, p.78 persistently misrepresents Foch, and finds every possible excuse for Haig. For him this move to the north was an inconvenience to the British, because it weakened Fourth and Third Armies, and even goes as far as to suggest that: 'General Foch had given up on the British troops covering the Channel ports north of the river (Somme), and was preparing a new front behind them which should guard Paris.' Edmonds also accuses Foch of refusing to take over more of the front south of the Somme. He appears to be unaware of the contradiction.

33   SHAT 15N 10 GOGA Etat-Major: 11.4.18 Haig to Foch. Plumer 12.4.18.

34   WO 256/29 Haig Diary 11.4.18.

35   Trevor Wilson, *The Myriad Faces of War: Britain and the Great War 1914-1918*, London1986, pp. 570-571 quoting William Moore, *See How They Run*, London 1975 p. 218.

36   AFGG vol. 6, part 1, p. 439.

37   SHAT 15N 10 GOGA Etat-Major 11.4.18 Wilson to Foch, Foch to Wilson.

38   SHAT 15N 10 GOGA Etat-Major: Lawrence (signed Dawnay) for Foch 12.4.18.

39   SHAT 15N 10 GOGA Etat-Major Colonel Desticker to the Belgian Etat-Majeur 13.4.18. Foch's motto was: '*Si une voie d'eau se produit quelque part, l'aveugler le plus tôt possible*'.

40   WO 256/29 Haig Diary 12.4.18.

41   Edmonds II. p.276.

42   WO33/920 Grant to CIGS 15.4.18.

43   SHAT 15N 10 GOGA Etat-Major French Military Mission to
       GHQ to 3e Bureau 12.4.18. *'le commandement est inexistant'*. Desticker
       14.4.18.

44   Hankey Diary, 8.4.18.

45   von Hutier Diary 11.4.18.

46   *Weltkrieg* 14, p.280.

47   von Kuhl Diary 13.4.18.

48   Rupprecht, *Kriegstagebuch*, vol. 2, pp. 379-381 (12.4.18).

49   *Weltkrieg* 14, p.305.

50   SKA (Dresden) 4212: report by XIX AK 29.4.18.

51   SHAT 15N 10 GOGA Etat-Major: Colonel Desticker to 3e Bureau
       13.4.18. Edmonds II, p. 284 curiously enough describes the German
       attack on the three brigades covering Neuve Eglise as a success.

52   Edmonds II, p.297-8.

53   von Kuhl Diary 14.4.18.

7: 'GEORGETTE': THE SECOND PHASE 15 APRIL–15 MAY

1   SKA (Potsdam) 22914: The statistically diligent medical officer of XIX
       Army Corps, which was fighting the British in Flanders, reported that
       36.54% of the wounded could be classified as serious, 63.46% as light.
       60.18% was due to artillery fire, 37.40% due to infantry fire, 1.78% to
       gas. Mortars caused a mere 0.38% , and close combat 0.25%.

2   von Kuhl Diary 15.4.18.

3   SHAT 15N 10 GOGA Etat-Major: Haig to Foch 14.4.18.

4   SHAT 15N 10 GOGA Etat-Major: French Military Mission to GHQ
       to 3e Bureau 14.4.18. The phrase used was: '*Prendre la bataille à leur
       compte.*'

5   WO 256/29 Haig Diary 14.4.18.

6   SHAT 15N 10 GOGA Etat-Major: Haig to Foch 14.4.18.

7   SHAT 15N 10 GOGA Etat-Major: French Military Mission to GHQ
       to 3e Bureau: 16.4.18.

8   SHAT 15N 10 GOGA Etat-Major French Military Mission to 3e
       Bureau 16.4.18. A large exclamation mark is pencilled in the margin
       opposite the remark that the British would withdraw to the west of
       Ypres.

9   SHAT 15N 10 GOGA Etat-Major: Wilson to Foch 17.4.18.

10   SHAT 15N 10 GOGA Wilson to Foch 17.4.18. Plumer 17.4.18. Haig
       to Foch 18.4.18. French Military Mission to 3e Bureau 19.4.18.

11   Edmonds II, p.315. Even Edmonds is obliged to admit his admiration
       for Foch's resolution in this crisis situation, and his refusal to give way
       to Haig.

12   SHAT 15N 10 GOGA Etat-Major French Military Mission to 3e
       Bureau: Memorandum from the First Lord of the Admiralty, Wemyss,
       20.4.18.

13   FO 371/3441 Lloyd George to Reading 14.4.18.

14   Rupprecht, *Kriegstagebuch*, vol. 2, pp. 382-383 (14.4.1918).

15   SHAT 15N 10 GOGA Etat-Major French Military Mission to GHQ
      to 3e Bureau 12.4.18.

16   Rupprecht, *Kriegstagebuch*, vol. 2, p. 385 (16.4.1918).

17   SKA (Dresden) 4212: report of XIX (Saxon) AK 29.4.18.

18   von Kuhl Diary , 16.4.18. (see Avesnes remarks on 13 April).

19   Pedroncini, *Pétain*, p. 351.

20   Deuxieme Bureau estimated that the German Army had increased
      by five divisions between 9 and 17 April, and the reserves by thirteen
      divisions. It can be assumed that these came from the Eastern Front.
      No notice was taken of their very poor quality.

21   SHAT 4N16 Conseil Supérieur de Guerre (Etat-Major de l'armée;
      Groupe de l'Avant; 2e Bureau) 17.4.18.

22   SKA (Potsdam) 22914: GK XIX AK at Laventie 17.4.18.

23   *Weltkrieg* 14 p.287.

24   CAB 23/6 IIGS 19.4.18.

25   WO 158/28 Foch to Haig 18.4.18. Haig to Foch 19.4.18.

26   SHAT GQG 3e Bureau 3043, Pétain 23.4.18.

27   AFGG vol. 6, part 1, p. 462.

28   von Kuhl Diary 18.4.18.

29   Rupprecht, *Kriegstagebuch*, vol.2, p. 386 (18.4.18).

30   Kuhl p.348.

31   von Kuhl Diary 18.4.18.

32   von Kuhl Diary 19.4.18.

33   AFGG vol. 6, part 1, pp. 472-3.

34   von Kuhl Diary 19.4.18.

35   von Kuhl Diary 22.4.18.

36   Binding, *Fatalist*, p.220.

37   *Weltkrieg* 14, p.309.

38   SHAT 15N 10 GOGA Etat-Major 24.4.18.

39   Hankey, *Supreme Command*, p.794.

40   The times given in Edmonds are one hour earlier (British time).

41   CAB 23/6 Radcliffe 26.4.18.

42   Görlitz, *The Kaiser and his Court*, p.351.

43   Edmonds II, p.443.

44   Edmonds II, p.444.

45   WO 158/72 Report on Abbeville conference 27.4.18.

46   AFGG vol. 6 part 1, p. 520.

47   From 21 March to 30 April the British had lost about 250,000 men.
      Of a total of sixty divisions fifty-five had been involved in the fight-
      ing, twenty-nine of them twice, six of them three times. The French
      had lost 92,000 men, forty-one divisions went into battle, three of
      them twice, and their front had been extended ninety-seven kilome-
      tres. The Germans still had 206 divisions facing 171 Allied divisions.
      AFGG vol. 6 part 1, p. 522-3.

48   Kuhl p.155.

49   Rupprecht, *Kriegstagebuch*, vol.2., p.394 (4.5.18).

50   *ibid.*, p.396 (8.5.18).

51   '*glänzend, aber hoffnungslos*'. *ibid.*, p.399 (17.5.18).

52   *ibid.*, p.401 (20.5.18).

53   SKA (Potsdam) 12777: Report on Dresden Conference 17.5.18. See
      also: Walter Nicolai, *Nachrichtendienst, Presse und Volksstimmung im
      Weltkrieg*, Berlin 1920.

54   See Wilhelm Deist, *Militär und Innenpolitik*, vol. 1, p. lvi.

55   Delbrück, p.258.

56   Testimony of General von Haeften 3 March 1922 in: *Die Ursachen des
      Deutschen Zusammenbruchs im Jahre 1918*, vol. 3, pp. 266–271.

57   Ulrich and Ziemann, *Frontalltag*, p.193 from a letter to the Bavarian
      Christian Farmers' Association, Georg Heim, from his brother Otto
      21.4.18.

58   *ibid.*, p.192, 3.2.18.

59   *Weltkrieg* 14, p.302.

60   Rupprecht, *Kriegstagebuch*, vol. 2. p.392 (29.4.1918). von Kuhl Diary
      30.4.18.

61   von Kuhl Diary 1.5.18.

62   von Kuhl Diary 2.5.18.

63   von Kuhl Diary 3.5.18.

64   SHAT 15N 10 GOGA Etat-Major Haig to Foch 4.5.18.

65   SHAT 15N 10 GOGA Etat-Major Haig to Foch 5.5.18.

66   FO371/3441 Lloyd George to Reading 3.5.18. Reading to Foreign
      Office 9.5.18. Lloyd George to War Office 14.5.18. Reading to
      Foreign Office 17.5.18. Lloyd George to Clemenceau 2.18.18.

67   Hankey, *Supreme Command*, p.797.

68   von Kuhl, pp.160–1 von Kuhl Diary 4.5.18.

69   von Kuhl, *Weltkrieg*, vol 2, p.353.

70   *ibid.*, pp 162–4.

8: 'BLÜCHER': THE FIRST PHASE 27 MAY–30 MAY

1   von Kuhl, *Weltkrieg*, vol. 2, p.354.

2   *Weltkrieg* 14, p.312.

3   *Weltkrieg* 14, p.316.

4   von Thaer, *Generalstabsdienst*, p.192.

5   Ludendorff's remarks were recorded in Major Baron (*Ritter*) von
     Prager's diary. See: *Reichsarchiv* 14, p.314.

6   Conscription was never extended to Ireland for fear of the con-
     sequences. H.E. Duke, the chief secretary for Ireland, told the War
     Cabinet that it 'might as well recruit Germans'. CAB 23/5 25,27–
     28.3.18.

7   CAB 23/6 contains many details of the Maurice affair. See also:
     Nancy Maurice (ed.), *The Maurice Case*, London 1972.

8   Although the ration strength of the BEF had increased by about 20
     per cent from January 1917 to January 1918, the actually number of
     fighting men had declined by about 3 per cent.

9   SHAT 15N 10 GOGA Etat-Major Laguiche to 3e Bureau 9.5.18. and
     18.5.18.

10   See the official French History.

11   von Kuhl Diary 17.5.18.
12   *Weltkrieg* 14, p.322.
13   von Kuhl Diary 21.5.18.
14   Kronprinz Wilhelm, *Meine Erinnerungen aus Deutschlands Heldenkampf*, Berlin 1923, p. 315.
15   von Kuhl, pp.167-8.
16   Kronprinz Wilhelm, *Erinnerungen*, p.316.
17   *Weltkrieg* 14, pp.328-330.
18   Rupprecht, *Kriegstagebuch*, vol. 2, p.402 (26.5.1918).
19   *Weltkrieg* 14, p.335.
20   Pedroncini, *Pétain*, p. 366 '*produirait la plus fâcheuse impression sur l'opinion publique.*'
21   Edmonds, pp.40-41.
22   Edmonds, pp.48-49.
23   WO 256/38 From a report on operations in 1918 by General Staff at GHQ (Montreuil) written after the armistice and vetted by Haig.
24   General Mordacq, *Le Ministère Clemenceau*, vol. 2, pp. 42-43.
25   *Weltkrieg*, 14, p.349.
26   AFGG vol. 6, part 2, p139.
27   AFGG vol. 6, part 2, pp. 149-51.
28   von Kuhl Diary 29.5.18.
29   SKA (Potsdam) 22914: GK XIX AK 1.7.18.
30   SKA (Potsdam) 21174: Quartermaster General at OHL 12.5.18.
31   Edmonds, p.120.
32   AFGG vol. 6, part 2, pp. 177-9.
33   von Hutier Diary 29.5.18.
34   SHAT 16N/1696/99 GQG 3e Bureau: Pétain's orders 29.5.18.
35   SHAT 16N/1696/99 GQG 3e Bureau: Pétain 30.5.18.
36   Hankey, *Supreme Command* , p.813.
37   Edmonds, 1918, vol. 3. p.133.
38   von Kuhl, p.168.
39   von Kuhl Diary 31.5.18.
40   von Kuhl Diary 2.6.18.
41   Görlitz, *The Kaiser and his Court*, p.359.

9: 'BLÜCHER', 'YORCK' AND 'GNEISENAU': 31 MAY–14 JUNE

1   von Kuhl, p.170.
2.   General Gordon's four tired divisions had been sent to the Chemin des Dames in April, which Foch designated as '*un secteur calme*'. Edmonds vol. 6. Part 3. p. 12.
3   Reichsarchiv 14, p.368.
4   Reichsarchiv 14, p.373.
5   SHAT 16N/1696/99 GQG 3e Bureau: Pétain 31.5.18.
6   SHAT 16N/1696/99 GQG 3e Bureau: Dufieux to Weygand 31.5.18. Dufieux said: '*La bataille est dure et mange du monde.*'
7   Mordacq, vol. 2, pp.44-47.
8   Edmonds, 1918, vol. 3, p.147.

9   SHAT 16N/1696/99 GQG 3e Bureau: Pétain 1.6.18.

10   SHAT 16N/1696/99 GQG 3e Bureau: Pétain 1.6.18.

11   SHAT 16N/1696/99 GQG 3e Bureau: Telephone log of conversation between Dufieux and Desticker 1.6.18.

12   SHAT 16N/1696/99 GQG 3e Bureau: EM of VI army 1.6.18. Guy Pedroncini, *Pétain général en chef 1917-1918*, Paris 1974, p.376.

13   Alan Palmer, *The Gardeners of Salonika*, New York 1975, pp.225-226. The General was appointed without consulting the British which caused great exception.

14   SHAT 5N/256.

15   SHAT 16N/1696/99 GQG 3e Bureau: Pétain 2.6.18.

16   FO 371/3214 Derby to Foreign Office, June 1918.

17   von Kuhl, *Weltkrieg*, vol.2, p. 373.

18   Rupprecht, *Kriegstagebuch*, vol. 2., p.405 (1.6.18).

19   'Gneisenau' was the offensive further west in the direction of Compiègne.

20   SHAT 15N 10 GOGA Etat-Major Haig to Foch 2.6.18. and 4.6.18.

21   SHAT 5N 260 Cabinet du Ministre: Foch to Clemenceau 1.6.18.

22   AFGG vol. 6, part 2, pp. 237-239.

23   SHAT 15N 10 GOGA Etat-Major French mission to 3e bureau 6.6.18.

24   SHAT 16N/1696/99 GQG 3e Bureau: log of telephone conversation between Dufieux and Weygand 3.6.18.

25   SHAT 16N/1696/100 GQG 3e Bureau: Telephone log Dufieux to Desticker 4.6.18.

26   SHAT 16N/1696/100 GQG 3e Bureau: Lt-Gen. Telephone log Pagezy to Dufieux 4.6.18.

27   SHAT 16N/1696/100 GQG 3e Bureau: 5.6.18.

28   SHAT 16N/1696/101 GQG 3e Bureau: Dufieux to Desticker 7.6.18. The phrase he used was: '*cascade hierarchique*'.

29   Edmonds, 1918, vol. 3, p.164.

30   SHAT 5N 260 Cabinet du Ministre: Fayrolle to Foch 4.6.18.

31   SHAT 16N/1696/101 GQG 3e Bureau: Foch to Pétain 6.6.18. SHAT 5N 260 Cabinet du Ministre: Foch to Pétain 9.6.18. Paris had to be defended '*pied à pied*'.

32   Johnson, 1918, p.189.

33   SHAT 15N 10 GOGA Etat-Major Minutes of Paris conference 7.6.18.

34   von Hutier Diary 4.6.18.

35   SHAT 16N/1696/101 GQG 3e Bureau: Pétain 8.6.18.

36   SHAT 16N/1696/101 GQG 3e Bureau: Pétain to V Army 8.6.18. Pétain to IV Army 9.6.18. Debeney to Pétain 11.6.18.

37   SHAT 16N/1696/101 GQG 3e Bureau: Foch to Pétain 8.6.18. Pétain to Foch 12.6.18.

38   *ibid.*, p. 407 (7.6.1918).

39   SHAT 15N 10 GOGA Etat-Major : Report of General Laguiche 10.6.18.

40   SHAT 5N 260 Cabinet du Ministre: Foch to Pétain 9.6.18.

41   SHAT 5N 260 Cabinet du Ministre: Foch to Haig 11.6.18.

32   Görlitz, *The Kaiser and his Court*, p.361.

43   Actually the general was being uncharacteristically modest. In fact he had taken 65,000 prisoners, nearly 900 guns and more than 2000 machine-guns. Reichsarchiv 14, p. 392.

44   SKA (Potsdam) 20337. Ludendorff 9.6.18.

45   SKA (Potsdam) 20337: Ludendorff 25.6.18.

46   SKA (Dresden) 4214: Report of Saxon military plenipotentiary 8.8.18.

47   SKA (Dresden) 4214: Ludendorff 25.6.18.

48   SHAT 5N/256 for the commission's papers. The three-man commission comprised M. Boodenoot (President of the Senate Armed Forces Commission), M. René Renoult (President the Chamber of Deputies' Armed Forces Committee) and General Guillaumat(Military Governor of Paris). Guillaumat was replaced by General Moinier in October.

10: THE AISNE: 15 JUNE–14 JULY

1   There is some confusion about the number of deserters. The French official work (VI, 2, notes 1063, 1218,1243 and 1272) talks of 'some deserters' but only mentions 2 deserters on 6 June and 4 on 8 June. Reichsarchiv 14, p.408.

2   General Sir William Robertson, quoted in Christoph Jahr, *Gewöhnliche Soldaten: Desertion und Deserteure im deutschen und britischen Heer 1914-18*, Göttingen 1998, p.29.

3   Erich Ludendorff, *Meine Kriegserinnerungen 1914-18*, Berlin 1919, p.100.

4   Martin Middlebrook, *The Kaiser's Battle. 21 March 19189: The First Day of the German Spring Offensive*, London 1978, p.44.

5   Ernst Jünger, *Im Stahlgewitter*, Sämtliche Werke, vol. 1, Stuttgart 1978, p.204.

6   Jahr, *Gewöhnliche Soldaten*, p.150. There were 4,196 cases of desertion in 1917 and 3,591 the following year. The figures are somewhat dubious since a number of cases were not prosecuted at the very end of the war, but they are still remarkable.

7   *ibid.*, p. 238.

8   HSAS Militärarchiv M1/7 36 War Ministry, Berlin 7.6.18.

9   SKA (Potsdam) Reports from AOK 3rd Army.

10   Jahr, p.258.

11   *ibid.*, p. 282.

12   HSAS Militärarchiv M1/7 36 Minister of War, 14.9.18.

13   'Gneisenau' is known in English as the Battle of the Matz.

14   von Hutier Diary 5.6.18.

15   Edmonds, 1918, vol., 3, p. 174-178.

16   Reichsarchiv 14, p.410.

17   French Official Account VI, 2, p.347.

18   Ulrich and Ziemann, *Frontalltag*, p. 186. Hans Spiess to his parents and sisters 3.7.18.

19   SHAT 5N 260 Cabinet du Ministre: 2e Bureau 2.7.18.

20   Reichsarchiv 14, pp.412-413.

21   Reichsarchiv 14, p.414.

22   von Kuhl Diary 7.6.18.

23   Binding, *Fatalist*, p.230.

24   von Kuhl Diary 11.6.18. in a comment on the Avesnes meeting.

25   von Kuhl Diary 9.6.18.

26   von Hutier Diary 16.6.18.

27   Ludendorff, *Kriegserinnerungen*, p.516.

28   von Kuhl Diary 14.6.18.

29   von Kuhl Diary 19.6.18.

30   SKA (Potsdam) 22914: GK XIX AK 22.6.18.

31   Rupprecht, *Kriegstagebuch*, vol. 2, pp. 410-11 (17 and 18.6.18).

32   SHAT 5N 260 Cabinet du Ministre: protocol of meeting 15.6.18.

33   SHAT 5N 260 Cabinet du Ministre: Foch to Pétain 14.6.18 and
      16.6.18.

34   SHAT 16N1697/102: Pétain 16.6.18.

35   *ibid.*, Anthoine 16.6.18.

36   SHAT 16N1697/102: Anthoine to War Minister 19.6.18. Also SHAT
      16N 1694/92 Etat-Majeur 3e Bureau 7.4.18.

37   Pedroncini, p.384.

38   SHAT 5N 260 Cabinet du Ministre: Foch issued these orders on
      16.6.18. Pétain told Foch of his refusal the following day.

39   SHAT 5N 260 Cabinet du Ministre: Pétain to Foch 16.6.18 and
      17.6.18.

40   SHAT 16N1697/102: Pétain 16.6.18 and 17.6.18.

41   SHAT 15N 10 GOGA Etat-Major: Colonel Dufieux to Colonel
      Desticker 17.6.18. '*actuellement nous ne vivons pas, nous vivotons.*' also in:
      SHAT 16N1697/102.

42   SHAT 15N 10 GOGA Etat-Major: French military mission to GHQ
      to 3e Bureau 21.6.18. The proposal was first put forward by Foch in a
      letter to Haig on 19 June. See: SHAT 5N 260 Cabinet du Ministre.

43   SHAT 5N 260 Cabinet du Ministre: Foch to Haig and Haig to Foch
      in reply 23.6.18.

44   SHAT 15N 10 GOGA Etat-Major: Haig to Clemenceau 23.6.18.

45   SHAT 5N 260 Cabinet du Ministre: Foch memorandum 22.6.18.

46   SHAT 5N 260 Cabinet du Ministre: Foch to Pétain 27.6.18.

47   SHAT 15N 10 GOGA Etat-Major: Pétain to GAN 20.6.18.

48   SHAT 15N 10 GOGA Etat-Major: Fayolle 27.6.18.

49   SHAT 16N1697/103: Pétain 23.6.18. the phrase used was '*à peine
      dégrossi et débourré*'.

50   SHAT 16N1697/103: Pétain to GAE 23.6.18.

51   SHAT 16N1697/103: Pétain 24.6.18.

52   SHAT 16N1697/103: Pétain to Foch 27.6.18.

53   SKA (Potsdam) 22914: GK XIX AK 20.7.18.

54   SHAT 5N 260 Cabinet du Ministre: Foch Directive Number 4:
      1.7.18, this directive should not be confused with Pétain's Directive
      No. 4 of December 1917 on defence.

55   SHAT 15N 10 GOGA Etat-Major: Pétain 3.7.18.

56   SHAT 15N 10 GOGA Etat-Major: Pétain 7.7.18.

57   SHAT 15N 10 GOGA Etat-Major: 2e Bureau 1.7.18.

58   SHAT 15N 10 GOGA Etat-Major: Pétain 12.7.18.
59   SHAT 15N 10 GOGA Etat-Major: Pétain to Foch 13.7.18.
60   Edmonds 1918, vol. 3, pp. 221-26.
61   Rupprecht, *Kriegstagebuch*, vol. 2, p.418 (4.7.1918).
62   *ibid.*, 420 (11.7.1918).
63   Görlitz, *The Kaiser and his Court*, pp.344 -363.
64   von Kuhl Diary. Reichsarchiv 14, p.429.
65   von Kuhl Diary 23.6.18.
66   Wetzell memo 22.6.18. Reichsarchiv 14, pp.430-431.
67   von Kuhl Diary 12.7.18.
68   von Kuhl Diary 14.7.18.
69   von Hutier Diary 3.7.18.
70   von Hutier Diary 9.7.18.
71   Ludendorff, *Kriegführung und Politik*, p.221.
72   SHAT 15N 10 GOGA Etat-Major: Wilson to Foch 12.7.18.
73   SHAT 15N 10 GOGA Etat-Major: Lloyd George to Clemenceau
      13.7.18.
74   CAB 112/25 British Section, Supreme War Council 6.7.18.
75   Crown Prince Wilhelm, pp. 328-30.
76   von Kuhl, *Weltkrieg*, vol,2, p.386.
77   SHAT 15N 5G.Q.G.A. Etat Major 2e Bureau 2.7.18.

11: 'REIMS', 'MARNE' AND THE MANGIN OFFENSIVE: 15-31 JULY

1   SHAT 5N 260 Cabinet du Ministre: Foch 3.7.18. This is based on
      Pétain's memorandum on defensive warfare of 24.6.18 in the same file.
2   SHAT 5N 260 Cabinet du Ministre: Foch to Pétain 11.7.18.
3   SHAT 5N 260 Cabinet du Ministre: Foch to Pétain and Haig 12.7.18.
4   SHAT 5N 260 Cabinet du Ministre: Pétain to Fayolle 15.7.18.
5   SHAT 15N 10 GOGA Etat-Major: two notes from Haig to Foch
      dated 17.7.18.
6   SHAT 5N 260 Cabinet du Ministre: Foch to Pétain 15.7.18.
7   SHAT 5N 260 Cabinet du Ministre: Pétain 15.7.18.
8   SHAT 5N 260 Cabinet du Ministre: Foch to Pétain, Foch to Haig
      13.7.18.
9   SHAT 5N 260 Cabinet du Ministre: Haig to Foch 15.7.18.
10   AFGG vol. 6, part 2, p.508.
11   This was noted in 7th Army's war diary – Reichsarchiv 14, p.448.
12   AFGG vol. 6, part 2, p.468.
13   AFGG vol. 6, part 2, p.513.
14   SHAT 5N 260 Cabinet du Ministre: Pétain 15.6.18.
15   SHAT 15N 5G.Q.G.A. Etat Major 2e Bureau 16.7.18.
16   BZS Paul Knoch letters: letter home 18.7.18.
17   von Kuhl Diary 16.7.18.
18   Reichsarchiv 14, p. 451.
19   Binding, *Fatalist*, p.234.
20   SHAT 5N 260 Cabinet du Ministre: Pétain's orders to this effect

15.6.18.

21   Binding, *Fatalist*, p.239.

22   Ludendorff, *Kriegserinnerungen* p.536.

23   SHAT 5N 260 Cabinet du Ministre: Foch to Pétain 16.7.18.

24   SHAT 15N 10 GOGA Etat-Major: Haig to Foch 17.7.18.

25   SHAT 15N 10 GOGA Etat-Major: Haig to Foch 18.7.18.

26   SHAT 5N 260 Cabinet du Ministre: Pétain to Foch 16.7.18 and report by 3e Bureau 16.7.18.

27   SHAT 15N 5G.Q.G.A. Etat Major 2e Bureau 17.7.18.

28   SKA (Potsdam) 20337: AOK 3 Army 17.7.18.

29   As laid down in OHL 1a/II Nr 9135 op.V. 6.7.18.

30   SKA (Potsdam) 20337: AOK 3 Army 20.7.18.

31   SKA (Potsdam) Ludendorff 1.8.18.

32   Rupprecht, *Kriegstagebuch*, vol. 2, p.421 (17.7.18).

33   Reichsarchiv 14, p.474.

34   von Kuhl Diary 2.8.18. (a later addition of material from the diary of Lieutenant-Colonel Lindenborn who was present at the conference.)

35   Ludendorff, *Kriegserinnerungen*, p.537.

36   von Kuhl 18 July.

37   Görlitz, *The Kaiser and his Court*, p.372.

38   Pedroncini, p.411.

39   Heinz Hürten and Georg Meyer (eds.) *Adjutant im peußischen Kriegsministerium Juni 1918- Oktober 1919. Aufzeichnungen des Hauptmanns Gustav Böhm*, Stuttgart 1977, p.27.

40   Hindenburg, *Aus meinem Leben*, p.349.

41   Rupprecht, *Kriegstagebuch*, vol. 2, p.423 (19.7.18).

42   Fritz von Lossberg, *Meine Tätigkeit im Weltkriege*, p.344 sec. Lossberg incorrectly dates his arrival at Avesnes as 19 July (the book appeared in 1939 after Ludendorff's death and is based on his notes taken at the time.)

43   Rupprecht, *Kriegstagebuch*, vol.2, p.427 (26.7.18).

44   Hindenburg, *Aus meinem Leben*, p. 349.

45   Rupprecht, *Kriegstagebuch*, vol. 2, pp. 424-5 (20.7.18).

46   Rupprecht, *Kriegstagebuch*, vol.2, p.425 (21.7.18).

47   von Kuhl Diary 20.7.18.

48   *ibid.*

49   von Kuhl Diary 21.7.18.

50   von Hutier Diary 21.7.18.

51   Reichsarchiv 14, p.490.

52   von Hutier Diary 22.7.18.

53   Görlitz, *The Kaiser and his Court*, p.374.

54   BZS Paul Knoch letters 23.7.18.

55   Edmonds, 1918, vol. 3, pp. 267-8.

56   Reichsarchiv 14, p.493.

57   von Kuhl Diary 29.7.18.

58   Edmonds 1918, vol. 3, pp.286-7.

59   Reichsarchiv 14, p.503 sees Allied tanks as the main cause of weakness. Furthermore the Germans were not well dug in and the terrain did not have shell holes that could provide protection. The sugges-

tion that the Allies had tremendous advantage because they advanced through tall cornfields is altogether preposterous.

60 Rupprecht, *Kriegstagebuch*, vol.2, p.427 (25.7.18).

61 Kronprinz Wilhelm, p.372.

62 Duroselle, *La Grande Guerre*, p.388.

63 Oberst Bauer, *Konnten wir den Krieg vermeiden, gewinnen, abbrechen? Drei Fragen*, Berlin 1918, p.37.

64 Hindenburg, *Aus meinem Leben*, p.392.

65 Among these Cassandras were General Hermann von François, a forceful and outspoken officer, and Major Ludwig von Beck who was then serving on the headquarters staff at Army Group German Crown Prince and who later served as Hitler's highly critical Chief of the General Staff from 1935 to 1938. von Kuhl Diary 2.8.18.

66 Heinz Hürten and Georg Meyer (eds.) *Adjutant im preussischen Kriegsministerium Juni 1918-Oktober 1919. Aufzeichnungen des Hauptmanns Gustav Böhm*, Stuttgart 1977 p. 27.

67 von Kuhl, *Weltkrieg*, vol.2, p.400.

68 Böhm, p.93. The interview was given on 5.12.18 and published the *Frankfurter Zeitung* the following day.

69 Johnson, *1918*, p. 189.

12: GERMANY'S PROSPECTS: MAY–AUGUST

1 Ludendorff's 'Assessment of the Situation VIII' is dated 13 May. Reichsarchiv 14, p. 507.

2 See his son's 'Ein Jahr in der Reichskanzlei', p.103 sec.

3 Rupprecht, Kriegstagebuch, II, p.398.

4 Heinz Hürten and Georg Meyer (eds.) *Adjutant im preussischen Kriegsministerium Juni 1918-Oktober 1919. Aufzeichnungen des Hauptmanns Gustav Böhm*, Stuttgart 1977 p. 93. The interview was given on 5.12.1918. Schulenburg was to join the Nazi party in 1934.

5 von Kuhl Diary 9.5.18.

6 Untersuchungsausschuss, IV Reihe, Band 2, p.188. Hertling op. cit.

7 Urkunden der OHL, p.478.

8 There was in fact no sign of war-weariness in the BEF in 1918 and there was less labour unrest. The Labour Party also desisted from criticizing the government in this moment of crisis. J.G. Fuller, Troop Morale and Popular Culture in the British and Dominion Armies 1914-1918, Oxford 1990.

9 Untersuchungsausschuss IV Reihe, Band 2, p.191. Hertling, Ein Jahr p.139.

10 Untersuchungsausschuss IV Reihe, Band 2, p.199.

11 Kühlmann, *Erinnerungen*, p.575.

12 Stenographische Berichte Band 313, p.5635. Westarp, *Konservative Politik*, Band II, p.608.

13 von Kuhl, *Weltkrieg*, vol.2, pp. 374-5.

14 Deutschland im Ersten Weltkrieg, vol. 3, p.214 Kühlmann made this remark to a Saxon diplomat.

15   Kühlmann, Erinnerungen, p.564.

16   ibid., p.560.

17   DZA Potsdam Reichskanzlei Allgemeines 2398/11; DZA Hist. Abt.
      Merseburg Rep 89 H XXXVI Militaria. Bundesarchiv Koblenz,
      Nachlass Hertling, Band 41.

18   Potsdam ibid.

19   Matthias and Morsey, _Der Interfraktionelle Ausschuss_, p.415, footnote 8.

20   Stenographische Berichte, Band 313, p.5640. Matthias Morsey, _Der
      Interfraktionelle Ausschuss_, p.419, footnote 3. Helfferich, Der Weltkrieg,
      p.631.

21   Ludendorff, _Urkunden der OHL_, p.491. Bundesarchiv Koblenz
      Nachlass Hertling, Band 41. _Untersuchungsausschuss_ IV Reihe, Band 2,
      p.203. The version in Urkunden der OHL is incomplete and does not
      mention Hindenburg's refusal to work with Kühlmann.

22   Reichsarchiv 14, p.513. The Germans always referred to the British
      Army as the English Army. It is not clear from the minutes whether
      Hindenburg or Ludendorff spoke for the OHL.

23   PA Bonn AA Gr. HQ Kriegsziele 16a. Fritz Fischer, _Griff nach der
      Weltmacht_, p.842 gives a characteristically trenchant analysis of the Spa
      conference.

24   BA Koblenz, Nachlass Berg, Aufzeichnungen. Winfried Baumgart,
      Deutsche Ostpolitik, p.89, fn. 91 has managed to transcribe Berg's
      ghastly handwriting.

25   BA Militärarchiv Nachlass Haeften N35/4.

26   Hindenburg in a letter to his wife 13.7.1918, quoted in Hubatsch,
      p.26.

27   Hintze reported to this effect on 14 August 1922, but it is fully consis-
      tent with Ludendorff's wildly optimistic mood at the time.

28   Bundesarchiv Militärarchiv Freiburg, Nachlass Groener N46/63
      Tagebuch Generals von Mertz 31.7.18.

29   Müller diary 15.7.18.

30   Baumgart, _Deutsche Ostpolitik_ for a brilliant and detailed account.

31   There were 3.5 million Russian prisoners of war in Germany.

32   Feldman, Army, Industry and Labour. _Urkunden der OHL_ p.107.

33   Rupprecht, _Kriegstagebuch_, vol.2, p.430 (3.8.1918).

34   See the memorandum by GOC Luftwaffe 6 June 1918. Reichsarchiv
      14, p.525.

35   'Grundsätze für die Führung der Abwehrschlacht im Stellungskrieg'
      in: Ludendorff, _Urkunden der Obersten Heeresleitung_, pp.604-640.

36   Reichsarchiv 14, p.528.

13: AMIENS: 8–14 AUGUST

1   See the detailed and cogently argued report by a captain at the
      Württemberg divisional headquarters in Hauptstaatsarchiv Stuttgart
      M30/1 Bü 162a dated 1.8.18.

2   Hermann Kantorowicz, _Der Offiziershaß im deutschen Heer_, Freiburg
      1919.

3   von Kuhl Diary 22.5.18.

4   SKA (Potsdam) 20337: War Ministry, Berlin 6.2.18.

5   SKA (Potsdam) 200416: viz. the orders of General von Einem, AOK 3 Army 13.5.18.

6   SKA (Potsdam) 20337: Saxon War Ministry, Dresden, 7.3.18.

7   SKA (Potsdam) 20337: AOK 19 Army 25.4.18. The army was stationed in Alsace, and the behaviour of officers in Metz was considered particularly reprehensible.

8   SKA (Potsdam) 20337: AOK 19 Army 29.4.18.

9   *ibid.*, AOK 19 Army 11.5.18.

10   SKA (Potsdam) War Ministry, Berlin 22.7.18.

11   SKA (Potsdam) Deutscher Werkmeister-Verband, Düsseldorf 12.8.18.

12   The Siegfried Line ran approximately from Arras to Saint Quentin to the Aisne.

13   Reichsarchiv 14, p.532.

14   F. von Lossberg, *Meine Tätigkeit im Weltkriege 1914-1918*, Berlin 1939. When asked about this episode after the war the section chiefs at the OHL General Wetzell (Operations Section 1a), General von Mertz(Operations Section B), General von Tieschowitz (Personnel) and General von Oldershausen (Railways) could not confirm that Ludendorff had threatened to resign on this occasion. Hindenburg was asked in November 1933 but also could not recall the incident. Neither could General von Haeften.

15   Reichsarchiv 14, p.535.

16   von Hutier Diary 27.7 and 28.7.18.

17   Reichsarchiv 14, p.538.

18   von Hutier Diary 29.7.18.

19   von Hutier Diary 1.8.18. He ruled out the possibility of a '*Siegfrieden*' that would secure the OHL's exotic war aims.

20   von Kuhl, p.192.

21   von Kuhl pp.192-4.

22   von Hutier Diary 4.8.18.

23   von Kuhl Diary 4.8.18.

24   Major-General Archibald Montgomery, *The Story of the Fourth Army in the Battle of the Hundred Days, August 9th to November 11th 1918*, London 1942, p.28.

25   von Kuhl Diary 6.8.18.

26   Ludendorff, *Kriegserinnerungen*, p.551.

27   Hürten and Meyer, *Böhm Aufzeichnungen*. p.48. These remarks were made 26.10.18.

28   Bauer, *Konnten wir den Krieg vermeiden*, p.38.

29   Rupprecht, *Kriegstagebuch*, vol.2, p.432 (8.8.1918).

30   Von Kuhl Diary 10.8.18.

31   Rupprecht, *Kriegstagebuch*, vol.2, p.437 (12.8.1918).

32   Rupprecht, *Kriegstagebuch*, vol.2, p.435 (9.8.1918).

33   von Hutier Diary 9.8.18.

34   von Kuhl Diary 10.8.18.

35   von Hutier Diary 10.8.18.

36   Montgomery, p.59.

37   von Kuhl Diary 11.8.18.

38   von Kuhl Diary 11.8.18.

39   von Kuhl Diary 11.8.18.

40   SKA (Dresden) 4214: report of the Saxon Military Plenipotentiary to the OHL 11.8.18.

41   von Hutier Diary 12.8.18.

42   von Hutier Diary 15.8.18.

43   von Kuhl Diary 12.8.18.

44   von Kuhl Diary 15.8.18.

45   SKA (Dresden) 4214: report of the Saxon Military Plenipotentiary to the OHL 11.8.18.

46   *Amtliche Urkunden zur Vorgeschichte des Waffenstillstandes 1918*, 2 Auflage, Berlin 1924, p.3

Bibliography

UNPUBLISHED SOURCES

Hauptstaatsarchiv Stuttgart: Militärarchiv, Stuttgart
M1/736
M1/2 102; 113; 165; 167; 173; 223; 245
M1/3 819
M1/11 407; 439; 794; 795; 988;
M30/1 2; 5; 36; 37; 39; 74; 76; 77; 78; 83; 84; 85; 89; 111; 112; 162a; 225; 232; 323
M34/42; 43; 45; 46; 48; 55; 57; 241
M38 1; 5; 39
M77/1 453; 455; 456; 457; 475; 476; 495; 496; 950
M200/88
M660/038 (Soden papers)

Bibliothek für Zeitgeschichte, Stuttgart
Papers of Adolph Stack, Jacob Blecher and Paul Knoch

Bayerisches Hauptstaatsarchiv, Kriegsarchiv, Munich
HGr. Rupprecht 32/15; 49
HGr. Rupprecht 80/8
HGr. Rupprecht 81
HGr. Rupprecht 91/45; 46; 48; 49; 50; 51
HGr. Rupprecht 103/116; 117;
HGr. Rupprecht 104/119; 120; 244; 245
HGr. Rupprecht 105/121; 122
HGr. Rupprecht 106/123
HGr. Rupprecht 108/130
HGr. Rupprecht 110
HGr. Rupprecht 112/156; 158
HGr. Rupprecht 113
HGr. Rupprecht 117/173

HGr. Rupprecht 124/201
HGr. Rupprecht 126/211
St.Gen.Kdo.1.b.A.K. 1371; 1372; 1373; 1375; 1895; 1972; 1998
AOK 6/9
AOK 6/9a; 121
AOK 6/12
AOK 6/413/218; 219; 223
AOK 6/414/231

Sächsisches Hauptstaatsarchiv, Sächsisches Kriegsarchiv, Dresden
Akte Nr. 4211; 4212; 4214

Sächsisches Hauptstaatsarchiv, Sächsisches Kriegsarchiv (Potsdam), Dresden
Akte Nr. 11283; 12499; 12587; 12777; 12875; 20300; 20337; 20416; 20433; 21174;
   22914

Bundesarchiv (Militärarchiv), Freiburg
Msg.1/839
Msg.2/338; 433; 943; 997; 1307; 4769
N18/4 (Heye memoirs)
N35/4; 35/15; N35/20 (Haeften papers)
N87/2; 87/65 (Hans von Below papers)
N324/2 (von Einem papers)
W-10/50640 (von Hutier diary)
W-10/50652 (von Kuhl diary)

Service Historique de l'Armée de Terre, Vincennes
4N1 (Conseil Superieur de Guerre)
4N16 (Conseil Superieur de Guerre: Groupe de l'Avant; 2e Bureau)
5N 256 (Enquiry into Chemin des Dames offensive)
5N 260 (Cabinet du Ministre)
15N 5 (G.Q.G.A Etat Major 2e Bureau)
15N 10 (G.Q.G.A Etat Major)
16N 1691; (G.Q.G 3e Bureau)
16N 1692/83; 84; 85; (G.Q.G 3e Bureau)
16N 1694/90; 91; 92; 93 (G.Q.G 3e Bureau)
16N 1695/94; 95; 96 (G.Q.G 3e Bureau)
16N 1696/98; 99; 100; 101; (G.Q.G 3e Bureau)
16N 1697/102; 103; 104; 105 (G.Q.G 3e Bureau)
16N 3266 (G.Q.G 3e Bureau)

Public Record Office, Kew
CAB 23/5; 6
CAB 25/6
CAB 45/177; 192
CAB 112/25; 80; 111

FO 371/3212; 3213; 3214; 3441
WO 33/920
WO 95/16; 17; 18; 369; 521
WO 157/28; 29; 30; 218
WO 158/28; 72; 75
WO 256/28; 29; 38

OFFICIAL PUBLICATIONS

Der Weltkrieg 1914-1918, Reichsarchiv, Reichskriegsministerium und
    Oberkommando des Heeres, 14 vols, Berlin 1925-1944
Der Krieg zur See 1914-1918, Marinearchiv, 23 vols, Berlin 1920-1938 and 1964-
    1966
*History of the Great War, Based on Official Documents by Direction of the Historical
    Section of the Committee of Imperial Defence*, 33 vols, London 1920-1935
Les armées françaises dans la Grande Guerre, Ministère de la Guerre, 11 vols, Paris
    1922-1939
Oesterreich-Ungarns letzter Krieg, Österreichisches Bundesministerium für
    Heerwesen und Österreichisches Kriegsarchiv, 7 vols, Vienna 1929-1938
*Untersuchungsausschuß: Das Werk des Untersuchungsausschusses der Deutschen
    Verfassungsgebenden Nationalversammlung und des Deutschen Reichstages, 1919-
    1926*, IV Reihe, vols 1-3: Die Ursachen des deutschen Zusammenbruchs
    im Jahre 1918, Berlin 1925

PRINTED WORKS

'Agricola', *Als ich im Stabe Hindenburgs war*, Leipzig 1934
Altvater, Friedrich, *Die seelischen Kräfte des Deutschen Heeres im Frieden und im
    Weltkriege*, Berlin 1933.
'Arminius', *Feldherrenköpfe 1914/1918*, Leipzig 1932
Arz, Artur, *Zur Geschichte des Großen Krieges 1914-18*, Vienna 1924
Ashworth, Tony, *Trench Warfare 1914-1918: The Live and Let Live System*, London
    1980
Asprey, Robert B., *The German High Command at War. Hindenburg and
    Ludendorff Conduct World War I*, New York 1991
Baden, Prince Max von, *Erinnerungen und Dokumente*, Stuttgart 1927
Barnett, Correlli, *The Swordbearers: Studies in Supreme Command in the First
    World War*, London 1963
Bauer, Max, *Der große Krieg in Feld und Heimat*, Tübingen 1921
Bauer, Max, *Der Irrwahn des Verständigungsfriedens*, Berlin 1919/20
Bauer, Max, *Ludendorff oder Delbrück*, Tübingen 1922
Bauer, Max, *Konnten wir den Krieg vermeiden, gewinnen, abbrechen? Drei Fragen*,
    Berlin 1918
Baumgart, Winfried, *Deutsche Ostpolitik 1918*, Munich 1966
Becker, Jean-Jacques, *La France en Guerre 1914-1918: La grande mutation*, Paris
    1988
Bernhardi, Friedrich von, *Denkwürdigkeiten aus meinem Leben*, Berlin 1927

Bernhardi, Friedrich von, *Deutschlands Heldenkampf 1914-1918*, Munich 1922

Beyerhaus, Gisbert, *Einheitlicher Oberbefehl*, Munich 1938

Bidwell S. and D. Graham, *Firepower*, London 1982

Biese, Franz, *Ludendorff, wie er wirklich war*, Pähl 1969

Binding, R.G., A *Fatalist at War*, London 1929

Blake, Robert (ed), *The Private Papers of Douglas Haig*, London 1952

Blume, Hellmuth, *General Ludendorff im Urteil der öffentlichen Meinung*, Potsdam 1936

Breucker, W., *Der Tragik Ludendorffs*, Oldenburg 1953

Bruchmüller, Georg, *Die deutsche Artillerie in den Durchbruchsschlachten des Weltkrieges*, Berlin 1921

Buat, Edmond, *Die deutsche Armee im Weltkrieg* (translated by H. Krause), Munich 1921

Buat, Edmond, *Hindenburg*, Munich 1922

Buat, Edmond, *Ludendorff*, Lausanne 1920

Callwell, Charles E., *Field Marshal Sir Henry Wilson: His Life and Diaries* (2 vols.), London 1927

Campbell, P.J., *The Ebb and Flow of Battle*, Oxford 1979

Cecil, Hugh and Peter H. Liddle, *Facing Armageddon: The First World War Experienced*, London 1996

Churchill, Winston S., *The World Crisis 1911-1918*, London 1923-29

Clemenceau Georges, *Größe und Tragik eines Sieges*, Stuttgart 1930

Coffman, Edward M., *The War to End All Wars: The American Military Experience in World War I*, Madison 1986

Cohen, Eliot A. and John Gooch, *Military Misfortunes: The Anatomy of Failure in War*, New York 1986

Conrad von Hötzendorf, Franz, *Aus meiner Dienstzeit 1906-1918*, 5 vols, Vienna 1921-25

Creveld, Martin von, *Supplying War: Logistics from Wallenstein to Patton*, Cambridge 1977

Cron, H., *Die Organisation des deutschen Heeres im Weltkriege*, Berlin 1923

Crone, Wilhelm, *Achtung! Hier Großes Hauptquartier*, Lübeck 1934

Crone, Wilhelm, *Das ist Ludendorff*, Berlin 1937

Cruttwell, C.R.M.F., *A History of the Great War 1914-1918*, Oxford 1934

Daniel, Ute, *Arbeiterfrauen in der Kriegsgesellschaft. Beruf, Familie und Politik im Ersten Weltkrieg*, Göttingen 1989

De Groot, G.J., *Douglas Haig 1861-1928*, London 1938

Deist, Wilhelm, *Militär und Innenpolitik im Weltkrieg 1914-1918*, 2 vols., Düsseldorf, 1970

Deist, Wilhelm, 'Der militärische Zusammenbruch des Kaiserreichs. Zur Realität der 'Dolchstoßlegende', in Ursula Büttner (ed.), *Das Unrechtsregime. Internationale Forschung über den Nationalsozialismus*, 2 vols., Hamburg 1986

Deist, Wilhelm, 'Verdeckter Militärstreik im Kriegsjahr 1918?', in Wolfram Wette (ed.), *Der Krieg des kleinen Mannes: Ein Militärgeschichte von unten*, Munich 1995

Delbrück, Hans, *Die Ursachen des deutschen Zusammenbruchs 1918*, Berlin 1925

Delbrück, Hans, *Ludendorffs Selbstporträt*, Berlin 1922

Denman, Terence, *Ireland's Unknown Soldiers: The 16th (Irish) Division in the Great War*, Dublin 1992

Dieckmann, Wilhelm, *Die Behördenorganisation der deutsche Kriegswirtschaft 1914-1918*, Hamburg 1937

Duncan, G.S., *Douglas Haig as I Knew Him*, London 1966

Duppler, Jörg and Gerhard P. Gross, *Kriegsende 1918. Ereignis, Wirkung, Nachwirkung*, Munich 1999

Duroselle, Jean-Baptiste, *La Grande Guerre des Français 1914-1918*, Paris, 1994

Einem, Karl von, *Ein Armeeführer erlebt den Weltkrieg*, ed. J. Alter, Leipzig 1938

Eisenhardt-Rothe, Ernst von, '*Wege zum Siege*', *Wissen und Wehr*, 9, 1940

Eisenhardt-Rothe, Ernst von, *Im Banne der persönlichkeit Ludendorffs*, Berlin 1937

Elze, Walter, *Der strategische Aufbau des Weltkrieges*, Berlin 1933

Erfurth, Waldemar, 'Die Überraschung im Kriege', *Militärwissenschaftliche Rundschau*, 6, 1937, 1-3, 1938

Erfurth, Waldemar, 'Die Verteidigung im Landkriege', *Militärwissenschaftliche Rundschau*, 5, 1936

Erfurth, Waldemar, *Der Vernichtungssieg*, Berlin 1939

Erzberger, Matthias, *Erlebnisse im Weltkrieg*, Stuttgart 1920

Falls, Captain Cyril, *The First World War*, London 1972

Farrar-Hockley, A.H., *Goughie: The Life of General Sir Hubert Gough CGB, GCMG, KCVO*, London 1975

Feldman, G.D., *Army, Industry and Labor in Germany, 1914-1918*, Princeton 1966

Felger, Friedrich, *Was wir vom Weltkrieg nicht wissen*, Berlin 1930

Fischer, Fritz, *Griff nach der Weltmacht*, Düsseldorf 1961

Foch, *Memoirs*

Foerster, W., *Der deutsche Zusammenbruch 1918*, Berlin 1925

Foerster, W., *Der Feldherr Ludendorff im Unglück*, Wiesbaden 1952

Foerster, W., *Hindenburg als Feldherr*, Berlin 1934

Foerster, W., *Kämpfer an einsamen Fronten*, Berlin 1931

Foerster, W., *Wir Kämpfer im Weltkriege*, Berlin 1929

Frauenholz, Eugen von, 'Politik und Kriegführung 1918', *Berliner Monatshefte*, April 1937

French, David, *The Strategy of the Lloyd George Coalition 1916-1918*, Oxford 1995

Frentz, Hans, *Der unbekannte Ludendorff*, Wiesbaden 1972

Freytag-Loringhoven, Axel von, *Menschen und Dinge, wie ich sie in meinem Leben sah*, Berlin 1923

Gallwitz, Max von, *Meine Führertätigkeit im Weltkrieg*, Berlin 1929

Gallwitz, Max von, *Erleben im Westen 1916-18*, Berlin 1932

Gehre, Ludwig, *Die deutsche Kräfteverteilung während des Weltkrieges*, Berlin 1928

Goodspeed, Donald James, *Ludendorff: Soldier: Dictator: Revolutionary*, London 1966

Görlitz, Walter, *The Kaiser and his Court. The Diaries, Note books and Letters of Admiral Georg Alexander von Müller Chief of the Naval Cabinet 1914-1918*, New York 1964

Gough, General Sir Hubert, *The Fifth Army*, London 1931

Graves, Keith, 'Total War? The Quest for a British Manpower Policy 1917-1919', *Journal of Strategic Studies*, 9,1, March 1986

Griffith, Paddy, *Battle Tactics of the Western Front: The British Army's Art of Attack 1916-18*, London 1994

Groener, Wilhelm, *Der Feldherr wider Willen*, Berlin 1930

Groener, Wilhelm, *Der Weltkrieg und seine Probleme*, Berlin 1920

Groener, Wilhelm, *Lebenserinnerungen. Jugend, Generalstab, Weltkrieg*, ed.
    Friedrich Freiherr von Gaertringen, Göttingen 1957

Groener, Wilhelm, *Politik und Kriegführung*, Stuttgart 1920

Gudmunddsson, Bruce I., *Stormtroop Tactics: Innovation in the German Army,
    1914-1918*, New York 1989

Guinn, Paul, *British Strategy and Politics 1914 to 1918*, Oxford 1965

Haeften, Hans von, *Hindenburg und Ludendorff als Feldherren*, Berlin 1937

Hagenlücke, Heinz, *Deutsche Vaterlandspartei: Die nationale Rechte am Ende des
    Kaiserreiches*, Düsseldorf 1997

Hankey, Lord, *The Supreme Command 1914-1918*, London 1961

Haussmann, Conrad, *Schlaglichter. Reichstagbriefe und Aufzeichnungen*, ed. U.
    Zeller, Frankfurt 1924

Helfferich, Karl, *Der Weltkrieg*, 3 vols, Berlin 1919

Hentig, Hans, von, *Psychologische Strategie des großen Krieges*, Heidelberg 1927

Hertling, Carl Maria Graf von, *Ein Jahr in der Reichskanzlei. Erinnerungen an die
    Kanzlerschaft meines Vaters*, Freiburg im Breisgau 1919

Herwig, Holger H., *The First World War: Germany and Austria-Hungary 1914-
    1918*, London 1997

Hindenburg, Paul von, *Aus meinem Leben*, Leipzig 1920

Hirschfeld, Gerhard, Gerd Kumreich and Irina Renz (eds.), *Keiner fühlt sich
    hier mehr als Mensch... Erlebnis und Wirkung des Ersten Weltkriegs*, Essen 1993

Hoffmann, Max, *Der Krieg der versäumten Gelegenheiten*, Munich 1923

Hoffmann, Max, *Die Aufzeichnungen des Generalmajors Max Hoffmann*, ed. Karl
    Friedrich Nowak, 2 vols, Berlin 1929

Holmes, Randolph York, *The March Retreat of 1918: an Anatomy of a Battle*,
    Ph.D. University of Washington 1966

Holtmeier, Friedrich, *Der Entschluß der Obersten Heeresleitung zur Offensive 1918*,
    Munich 1937

Hubatsch, Walter, *Hindenburg und der Staat. Aus den Papieren des
    Generalfeldmarschalls und Reichspräsidenten von 1887 bis 1934*, Göttingen 1965

Hürten, Heinz and Georg Meyer, *Adjutant im preußischen Kriegsministerium Juni
    1918–Oktober 1918: Aufzeichnungen des Hauptmann Gustav Böhm*, Stuttgart
    1977

Hutchinsom, Lt. Col. G.S., *Warrior*, London 1932

Jahr, Christoph, *Gewöhnliche Soldaten: Desertion und Deserteure im deutschen und
    britischen Heer 1914-18*, Göttingen 1998

Johnson, J.H., *1918: The Unexpected Victory*, London 1997

Kabisch, Michael, 'Ludendorff als Soldat und Feldherr', *Deutsche Infanterie*, 1,
    1938

Kabisch, Michael, *Ergänzungen zu Streitfragen*, Stuttgart 1927

Kabisch, Michael, *Die große Schlacht in Frankreich im Lenz 1918*, Berlin 1935

Kabisch, Michael, *Streitfragen des Weltkrieges 1914-18*, Stuttgart 1924

Kabisch, Michael, *Um Lys und Kemmel*, Berlin 1936

Kantorowicz, Hermann, *Der Offiziershaß im deutschen Heer*, Freiburg 1919

Kielmansegg, Peter Graf, *Deutschland und der Erste Weltkrieg*, Frankfurt 1968

Kitchen, Martin, 'Ludendorff' in Hugh Cecil and Peter H. Liddle, *Facing
    Armageddon: The First World War Experienced*, London 1996

Kitchen, Martin, *The Silent Dictatorship: The Politics of the German High Command under Hindenburg and Ludendorff, 1916-1918*, London 1976

Kocka, Jürgen, *Facing Total War: German Society, 1914-1918*, Leamington Spa 1984

Krafft von Dellmensingen, Conrad, *Der Durchbruch*, Hamburg 1937

Kriegsbriefe gefallene Studenten, Munich 1929

Kuhl, Hermann Josef von, 'Der Krieg der versäumten Gelegenheiten', *Preußische Jahrbücher*, 195, 1924

Kuhl, Hermann Josef von, 'Ludendorffs Selbstporträt', *Preußische Jahrbücher*, 195, 1922

Kuhl, Hermann Josef von, *Der deutsche Generalstab in Vorbereitung und Durchführung des Weltkrieges*, Berlin 1920

Kuhl, Hermann Josef von, *Der Weltkrieg 1914-1918*, 2 vols, Berlin 1929

Kuhl, Hermann Josef von, *Der Weltkrieg in Urteil unserer Feinde*, Berlin 1922

Kuhl, Hermann Josef von, *Die Kriegslage im Herbst 1918*, Berlin 1922

Kuhl, Hermann Josef von, *Entstehung, Durchführung und Zusammenbruch der Offensive von 1918*, Berlin 1927

Kuhl, Hermann Josef von, *Französisch-englische Kritik des Weltkrieges*, Berlin 1921

Kuhl, Hermann Josef von, *Ursachen des Zusammenbruchs*, Berlin 1925

Kühlmann, Richard von, *Erinnerungen*, Heidelberg 1948

Kunowski, Felix von, *Der Durchbruch im Frühjahr 1918*, Berlin 1927

Lehmann, Carl, *Ludendorffs Schuld an der Militärischen Katastrophe*, Leipzig 1920

Liddell Hart, B.H., *A History of the World War 1914-1918*, London 1934

Lloyd George, D., *War Memoirs*, London 1938

Lossberg, F. von, *Meine Tätigkeit im Weltkrieg 1914-1918*, Berlin 1939

Ludendorff, Erich, *Der totale Krieg*, Munich 1935

Ludendorff, Erich, *Kriegführung und Politik*, Berlin 1923

Ludendorff, Erich, *Mein militärischer Werdegang*, Munich 1934

Ludendorff, Erich, *Meine Kriegserinnerungen 1914-18*, Berlin 1919

Ludendorff, Erich, *Urkunden der Obersten Heeresleitung über ihrer Tätigkeit 1916/18*, Berlin 1920

Ludendorff, Margarete, *Als ich Ludendorffs Frau war*, Munich 1929

Ludendorff, Mathilde, *Erich Ludendorff*, Munich 1940

Marcks, Erich and Ernst von Eisenhardt-Rothe, *Paul von Hindenburg als Mensch, Staatsmann, Feldherr*, Berlin 1932

Marcks, Erich, *Angriff und Verteidigung im Großen Kriege*, Berlin 1924

Matthias, E. and R. Morsey (eds), *Der Interfraktionelle Ausschuß 1917/18*, 2 vols, Düsseldorf 1959

Maurice, Major General Sir F., *The Life of General Lord Rawlinson of Trent*, London 1928

Maurice, Nancy (ed.), *The Maurice Case*, London 1972

Meier-Welcker, 'Italienische Anschauungen über die deutsche Märzoffensive 1918', *Militärwissenschaftliche Rundschau*, 43 and 44, 1939

Middlebrook, Martin, *The Kaiser's Battle: 21 March 1918: The First Day of the German Spring Offensive*, London 1978

Montgomery, Major-General Archibald, *The Story of the Fourth Army in the Battle of the Hundred Days, August 9th to November 11th 1918*, London 1942

Mordacq, Jean, *Le Ministère Clemenceau, Journal d'un témoin*, 4 vols, Paris 1930

Morrow, John H. Jr., *German Air Power in World War I*, Lincoln 1982

Müller, Georg Alexander von, *Regierte der Kaiser? Kriegstagebücher, Aufzeichnungen und Briefe des Chefs des Marine-Kabinetts Admiral Georg von Müller1914-1918*, ed.Walter Görlitz, Göttingen 1959

Müller-Brandenburg, Hermann, *Von der Marne zur Marne*, Berlin 1919

Müller-Brandenburg, Hermann, *Von Schlieffen bis Ludendorff*, Leipzig 1925

Müller-Eberhart,Waldemar, *Kopf und Herz des Weltkrieges - Ludendorff*, Leipzig 1935

Nicolai,Walter, *Geheime Mächte*, Leipzig 1924

Nicolai,Walter, *Nachrichtendienst, Presse und Volksstimmung im Weltkrieg*, Berlin 1920

Niemann, A., *Kaiser und Revolution. Die entscheidenden Ereiginisse im Grossen Hauptquartier im Herbst 1918*, Berlin 1922

Niemann, A., *Kaiser und Heer. Das Wesen der Kommandogewalt und ihre Ausübung durch Kaiser Wilhelm II*, Berlin 1929

Palmer, Alan, *The Gardeners of Salonika*, New York 1975

Paschall, Rod, *The Defeat of Imperial Germany 1917-1918*, Chapel Hill, 1989

Payer, Friedrich von, *Von Bethmann Hollweg bis Ebert. Erinnerungen und Bilder*, Frankfurt am Main 1923

Pedroncini, Guy, *Pétain général en chef (1917-1918)*, Paris 1997

Pierrefeu, Jean de, *Trois ans au Grand Quartier Générale*, 2 vols, Paris 1920

Pitt, Barrie, *1918: The Last Act*, London 1962

Powell, G., *Plumer: The Soldiers General*, London 1990

Prior, Robin and Trevor Wilson, *Command on the Western Front*, London 1992

Prior, Robin and Trevor Wilson, *Passchendaele: The Untold Story*, New Haven 1996

Rauscher,Walter, *Hindenburg: Feldmarschall und Reichspräsident*,Vienna 1997

Riebecke, Otto, *Was brauchte der Weltkrieg? Tatsachen und Zahlen aus dem deutschen Ringen 1914/18*, Berlin 1936

Ritter, Gerhard, *Staatskunst und Kriegshandwerk. Das Problem des 'Militarismus' in Deutschland*, 4 vols., Munich 1968

Robertson, Field Marshal Sir William, *Soldiers and Statesmen*, London 1928

Rupprecht von Bayern, Kronprinz, *Mein Kriegstagebuch*, ed.Eugen Frauenholz, 3 vols, Berlin 1929

Schäfer,Theobald von, *Ludendorff, der Feldherr der Deutschen im Weltkriege*, Berlin 1935

Scheck, Raffael, *Alfred von Tirpitz and German Right-Wing Politics, 1914-1930*, Atlantic Highlands New Jersey 1997.

Scheidemann, Philipp, *Der Über-Ludendorff*, Berlin 1921

Scheidemann, Philipp, *Der Zusammenbruch*, Berlin 1921

Scheidemann, Philipp, *Memoiren eines Sozialdemokraten*, 2 vols, Dresden 1928

Schwarte, Max, *Der Grosse Krieg 1914/1918*. Leipzig 1921

Schwertfeger, Bernhard, *Der Tiger*, Berlin 1921

Schwertfeger, Bernhard, *Die politischen und militärischen Verantwortlichkeiten im Verlaufe der Offensive von 1918*, Berlin 1927

Schwertfeger, Bernhard, *Ursachen des Zusammenbruchs der Offensive von 1918*, Berlin 1923

Schwertfeger, Bernhard, *Weltkriegsende*, Potsdam 1937

Seherr-Thoss, Hans C. von, *Die deutsche Automobilindustrie*, Stuttgart 1974

Siney, Marion C., *The Allied Blockade of Germany 1914-1918*, Ann Arbor 1957

Sixsmith, E.K.G., *Douglas Haig*, London 1976

Spickernagel, Wilhelm, *Ludendorff*, Berlin 1919

Stoß, Alfred, *Ludendorff – der ewige Recke*, Landsberg 1936

Stürgk, Josef Graf, *Im deutschen Grossen Hauptquartier*, Leipzig 1921

Sulzbach, Herbert, *Zwei lebende Mauern*, Berlin 1935

Terraine, John, *Douglas Haig: The Educated Soldier*, London 1963

Terraine, John, *Impacts of War: 1914 and 1918*, London 1970

Terraine, John, *The Great War 1914-1918*, London 1977

Terraine, John, *To Win a War, 1918 - The Year of Victory*, London 1978

Terraine, John, *White Heat: The New Warfare, 1914-1918*, London 1982

Thaer, Albrecht von, *Generalstabsdienst an der Front und in der OHL. Aus Briefen und Tagebuchaufzeichnungen 1915-1919*, ed. Siegfried A. Kaehler, Göttingen 1958

Toland, John, *No Man's Land – The Story of 1918*, New York 1980

Travers, Tim, *The Killing Ground*, London 1987

Travers, Tim., *How the War Was Won. Command and Technology in the British Army on the Western Front 1917-1918*, London 1992

Tschuppik, Carl, *Ludendorff. Die Tragödie des Fachmanns*, Vienna and Leipzig, 1931

Ulrich, Bernd and Benjamin Ziemann (eds), *Frontalltag im Ersten Weltkrieg. Quellen und Dokumente*, Frankfurt 1994

Vasold, Manfred, *Pest, Not und schwere Plagen. Seuchen und Epidemien vom Mittelalter bis heute*, Munich 1991

Venohr, Walter, *Ludendorff. Legende und Wirklichkeit*, Berlin 1993

Vincent, C.L.Paul, *The Politics of Hunger: The Allied Blockade of Germany 1915-1919*, Athens Ohio, 1985

Warner, Philip, *Field Marshal Earl Haig*, London 1991.

Wette, Wolfram (ed.), *Der Krieg des kleinen Mannes: Ein Militärgeschichte von unten*, Munich 1995

Wilhelm II, *Deutscher Kaiser, Ereignisse und Gestalten*, Leipzig and Berlin 1922

Wilhelm, Deutscher Kronprinz, *Meine Erinnerungen aus Deutschlands Heldenkampf*, Berlin 1923

Wilson, Trevor, *The Myriad Faces of War*, Oxford 1988

Winter, Denis, *Haig's Command: A Reassessment*, London 1991

Woodward, David, 'Did Lloyd George Starve the British Army of Men Prior to the German Offensive of 21 March 1918?', *Historical Journal*, 27, 1, 1984

Woodward, David, *Lloyd George and the Generals*, Delaware 1983

Wrisberg, Ernst von, *Erinnerungen an die Kriegsjahre im Königlich Preußischen Kriegsministerium*, vols 1-3, Leipzig 1921/22

Wrisberg, Ernst von, *Heer und Heimat 1914-1918*, Leipzig 1921

Zabecki, David T., *Steel Wind: Colonel Georg Bruchmüller and the Birth of Modern Artillery*, Westport 1994

Ziekursch, Johannes, 'Ludendorffs Kriegserinnerungen', *Historische Zeitschrift*, 121, 1920

Ziese-Beringer, Hermann, *Der einsame Feldherr*, Berlin 1934

Appendix I

GERMAN ORDER OF BATTLE, 21 MARCH 1918

Army Group Crown Prince Rupprecht (82 Infantry Divisions)

Field Marshal Crown Prince Rupprecht of Bavaria
Chief of Staff: General von Kuhl

4th Army (18 Divisions)
General Sixt von Arnim   Chief of Staff: General von Lossberg

6th Army (15 Divisions)
General von Quast   Chief of Staff: Lieutenant-Colonel Baron
                                         von Lenz

17th Army (28 Divisions)
General Otto von Below   Chief of Staff: General Krafft von
                                         Dellmensingen

2nd Army (21 Divisions)
General von der Marwitz   Chief of Staff: Colonel von Tschischwitz

Army Group German Crown Prince (61 Infantry Divisions)

General Wilhelm Crown Prince of the German Empire and of Prussia
Chief of Staff: Colonel Count von der Schulenburg

18th Army (27 Divisions)
General von Hutier   Chief of Staff: General von Sauberzweig

7th Army (11 Divisions)
General von Boehn   Chief of Staff: Lieutenant-Colonel Reinhardt

1st Army (12 Divisions)
General Fritz von Below   Chief of Staff: Lieutenant-Colonel von
Klüber

3rd Army (11 Divisions)
General von Einem   Chief of Staff: Lieutenant-Colonel von
Klewitz

Army Group Gallwitz (24 Divisions)

General von Gallwitz   Chief of Staff: Colonel von Pawelsz

5th Army (12 Divisions)
General von Gallwitz   Chief of Staff: Lieutenant-Colonel von
Pawelsz

Army Section B (12 Divisions)
General Fuchs   Chief of Staff: Colonel Baron von Ledebur

Army Group Duke Albrecht (24.5 Infantry and 2 Dismounted Cavalry Divisions)

Field Marshal Albrecht   Chief of Staff: Colonel Heye
Duke of Württemberg

19th Army (10.5 Divisions)
General Count von Bothmer   Chief of Staff: Colonel Baron on Hemmer

Army Section A (5 Infantry and I Dismounted Cavalry Divisions)
General von Mudra   Chief of Staff: Lieutenant-Colonel Baron
von Esebeck

Army Section C (9 Infantry and I Dismounted Cavalry Divisions)
General von Gündell   Chief of Staff: Lieutenant-Colonel Drechsel

Appendix II: Maps

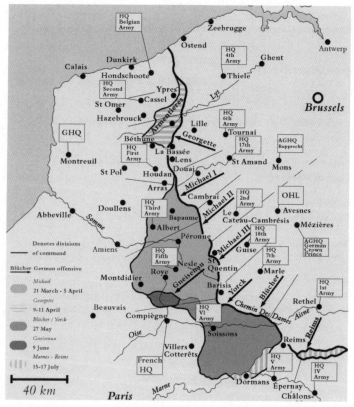

The German Offensives of 1918

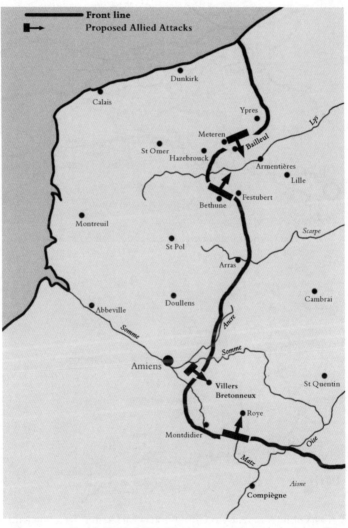

Foch's General Directive No. 3, 20 May 1918

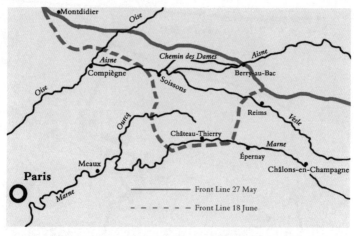

The German Offensive at Chemins des Dames, 27 May

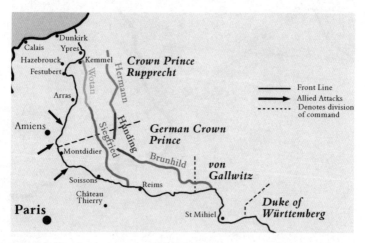

Foch's plan for the Amiens Offensive showing German Rear Positions

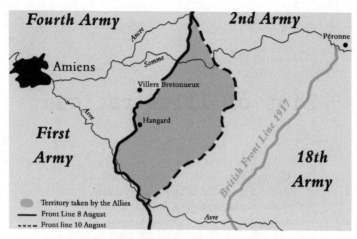

The Allied offensive at Amiens, 8 August

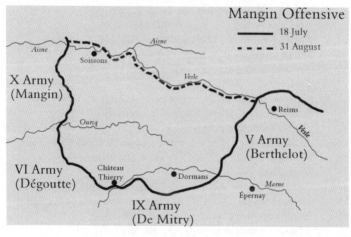

Mangin Offensive

List of Illustrations

Index

TEMPUS – REVEALING HISTORY

Private 12768
Memoir of a Tommy
JOHN JACKSON
'Unique... a beautifully written, strikingly honest account of a young man's experience of combat' **Saul David**
£9.99
0 7524 3531 0

D-Day: The First 72 Hours
WILLIAM F. BUCKINGHAM
'A compelling narrative'
The Observer
£9.99
0 7524 2842 X

English Battlefields
500 Battlefields that Shaped English History
MICHAEL RAYNER
'A painstaking survey of English battlefields... a first-rate book' **Richard Holmes**
£25
0 7524 2978 7

Trafalgar Captain Durham of the Defiance:
The Man Who Refused to Miss Trafalgar
HILARY RUBINSTEIN
'A sparkling biography of Nelson's luckiest captain' **Andrew Lambert**
£17.99
0 7524 3435 7

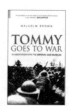

Battle of the Atlantic
MARC MILNER
'The most comprehensive short survey of the U-boat battles' **Sir John Keegan**
£12.99
0 7524 3332 6

Okinawa 1945 The Stalingrad of the Pacific
GEORGE FEIFER
'A great book... Feifer's account of the three sides and their experiences far surpasses most books about war' **Stephen Ambrose**
£17.99
0 7524 3324 5

Gallipoli 1915
TIM TRAVERS
'The most important new history of Gallipoli for forty years... groundbreaking' **Hew Strachan**
£13.99
0 7524 2972 8

Tommy Goes To War
MALCOLM BROWN
'A remarkably vivid and frank account of the British soldier in the trenches'
Max Arthur
£12.99
0 7524 2980 9